D1243835

THE SERPENT AND THE GODDESS

THE SERPENT AND THE GODDESS

Women, Religion, and Power in Celtic Ireland

MARY CONDREN

HarperSanFrancisco

A Division of HarperCollins*Publishers*

The author and publisher are grateful for permission to quote from the following: "Masculus Giganticus Hibernicus" is used with the permission of Nuala Ní Dhomhnaill, the translator, Michael Hartnett, Raven Arts Press, and the original Irish publisher, An Sagairt. "The Questions of Ethne Alba" are used with the permission of James Carney. Quotations from *the Táin* are used with permission of the translator, Thomas Kinsella. "Eve's Lamentation" and "Mother's Lament" are used with the permission of the publisher, SPCK.

THE SERPENT AND THE GODDESS: *Women, Religion, and Power in Celtic Ireland.* Copyright © 1989 by Mary Condren. All rights reserved. Printed in the United States of America. No part of this book may be used or reproduced in any manner whatsoever without written permission except in the case of brief quotations embodied in critical articles and reviews. For information address HarperCollins Publishers, 10 East 53rd Street, New York, NY 10022.

Library of Congress Cataloging-in-Publication Data

Condren, Mary.
  The serpent and the goddess.

  1. Women—Ireland—History. 2. Patriarchy—Ireland—
History. 3. Women—Ireland—Religious life—History.
4. Church and state—Ireland—History. 5. Ireland—
Church history. I. Title
HQ1600.3.C66 1989   305.4'09415   88-45990
ISBN 0-06-250156-9

95 96 RRD(H) 10 9 8 7

To the memory of my father, Daniel Condren,
and to my mother, Harriet Condren
with love and gratitude

Contents

Preface ix

Acknowledgments xv

Introduction: *The Problem of History* xvii

PART I. THE AGE OF EVE

1. Eve and the Serpent 3
   The Foundation Myth of Patriarchy

2. Crushing the Serpent 23
   *The End of Matricentered Ireland and the Curse of
   the Goddess Macha*

PART II. THE AGE OF BRIGIT

3. Brigit as Goddess 47
   Mother Goddess and Virgin Lawmaker

4. Brigit of Kildare 65
   From Goddess to Saint

5. The Sexual Politics of the Early Irish Church 79
   The Clerical Control of Reproduction

6. The Blasts of Temptation 95
   The Impact of Male Asceticism

7. From Kin to King 113
   The Blood Covenant Made among Men, Excluding Women

PART III. THE AGE OF MARY

8. The Anglo-Norman Invasion of Ireland 131
   Popes, Kings, and Bishops Reform the Old Laws of Ireland

9. Clerical Celibacy   144
   The Quest for Power in Church and State

10. The Politics of Virginity   154
    *The Cult of the Virgin Mary and the Consolidation of Patriarchal
    Theology*

11. Conclusions: The Age of the Fathers   183
    *Male Reproductive Consciousness: Its Contemporary Influence in
    Church and State*

Abbreviations   211
Notes   215
Index   261

Preface

Father Desmond Wilson, a Northern Irish Catholic priest, forced by the ecclesiastical politics of our time to take "early retirement," has recently written, "It must be difficult to solve problems humanely when so much of the resources of our political, cultural, and religious institutions are also occupied helping to create or prolong them."[1]

Almost two thousand years after the birth of the Fisherman of Nazareth, we find ourselves facing the most horrendous possibility in human history. There are enough nuclear weapons now that, whether by accident or design, any of the superpowers could render the earth permanently uninhabitable. And yet in Western culture little has changed in our way of thinking.

In the political and theological realms we are still stuck on the merry-go-round of church and state, capitalism and communism, Christian or Jew, Catholic or Protestant. We seem incapable of envisioning anything other than the dualistic and tired stalemate of contemporary patriarchal polity where, as René Girard claims, "groups agree never to be completely at peace, so that their members may find it easier to be at peace among themselves."[2]

Desmond Wilson wrote his comments after a veritable lifetime of trying to come to terms with the particular insanity that passes for normal life in Northern Ireland today. In the past twenty years, over two and a half thousand men, women, and children have died violent deaths, and countless numbers have been permanently maimed in the war between Republicans and Loyalists in Northern Ireland. Although not entirely religious in its origins, this conflict has been fought by professing Roman Catholics and Protestants. And although the religious leaders periodically exhort the people to "Christian unity," their liturgical, educational, and theological policies make such unity impossible. The problem is, as Desmond Wilson put it so bluntly, that, far from the religious and political leaders having failed in Northern Ireland, "they succeeded. There lies the tragedy of the place."[3] His insights throw the relationship between Christianity and power politics into sharp relief, forming a distinct contrast to the optimism and hope for the future of Christianity being expressed in the "liberation theology" movements in Latin America, southern Africa, and Asia. In Ireland some attempts have been made to develop a "liberation theology," but despite Ireland's fame for producing great writers, the "Northern struggle" has counseled the best of its writers to silence or exile. How does one begin to speak of the horror of two and a half thousand dead bodies, shattered bodies consigned to their graves with all the trappings of religion, Protestant or Catholic? How does one call for a "renewed Christianity" in Ireland when there is a sickening realization that the language of Christianity is itself a pawn of terrorist and state power?

The conflict in Northern Ireland has been a festering sore on the body politic of Irish life for some time now. But it would be a mistake to think that the violence there, while certainly graphic and lethal, is simply an unfortunate aberration of an otherwise healthy social order north or south of the Irish border. For Irishwomen, fear of wife-beating, rape, incest, the oppression of unmarried mothers, and lack of freedom with regard to reproduction are facts of ordinary life.

What is the connection between these public and domestic forms of violence? How have we arrived at this point in history where either form of violence passes for normality in political and religious life? And how do we even begin to frame these questions when we are bound up, apparently so totally, in the mind-set of what feminists have come to call patriarchy? These questions permeate the writing of this book, and in attempting to answer them we will be exploring the realms of myth, history, dogma, theology, and politics. The lines between these realms have been traditionally hard to draw. As one scholar remarked, "In medieval Ireland there were no categorical divisions between history and literature or between sacred and profane fictioneering. The same men wrote them all impartially."[4] Our intention, therefore, is not to dismember the "facts" in order to arrive at "truth." Rather, our focus will be to deconstruct the composite mythology presented by all these realms in order to begin to create those political and religious conditions whereby such violence against both women and men is exposed, highlighted, and eventually overthrown.

We take it for granted that the Fisherman of Nazareth has long since ceased to bear much relationship to historical Christianity. Can it be that we find ourselves in our current situation not because Christianity has failed, or has never been tried, but because as the historical carrier of patriarchy in the West it has succeeded?

Central to our approach will be a focus on the dialectical relationship between church and state. These two realms have been played off against one another in the establishment of women's rights or, indeed, "religious freedom." But within a feminist framework they will be seen to be simply two alternate realms whose lifeblood has traditionally depended on the subjugation of women.

Church and state have struggled for the control of women's bodies and for the control of life and death. At times they have cooperated and at other times been in opposition. Women have often been the scapegoats used to mark out the winners and losers in their discourses of power. For instance, while Hitler, who carried contempt for women to a fine art,[5] was sending millions of Jews and others to the gas chambers, German theologians, although themselves anti-Hitler, were proclaiming the news that "man had come of age" in their arguments for a "religionless Christianity." Similarly, as Western democracy continued its Cold War in the 1960s, "radical" theologians were proclaiming the "death of God." Significantly, they argued that "the mother must be destroyed, the mother who represents security, warmth, religion, authority, but who has become corrupt, an evil bearer of all she is supposed to represent."[6]

And there is a curious phenomenon that those involved in taking or threatening to take life through armaments maintain the ultimate respect for human life—in its fetal form. Hitler, for instance, was utterly opposed to abortion. An American president has, in the same breath, curtailed reproductive rights for women and fostered, encouraged, and even financed armaments shipments throughout the world in the interests of "safeguarding democracy."

For both church and state, women served as moral scapegoats, cloaking the evils of public policy with the veneer of private respectability. And whereas, historically, Christian theology fostered the scapegoating of women under the guise of preparing for the afterlife, now Christian democracy will happily scapegoat women for the sake of the present.

This book will trace the development of the patriarchal mind-set and the sexual political struggle in Irish cultural history. Although Ireland forms the scenic background, the themes have a wide relevance to women throughout the Western world.

The book is divided into three main sections: the Age of Eve, the Age of Brigit, and the Age of Mary. This division roughly corresponds to the pre-Christian, early Christian, and contemporary periods.[7] Our emphasis shall not be on wars and battles, kings and queens. Rather, we shall concentrate on the "discourses" of patriarchal power typical of the philosophical framework of each period.

Since the Jewish and Christian traditions, rather than the Celtic, are now the main Western sources of cultural authority, in the Age of Eve we shall begin by looking at ancient Israel, which provides ample material for documenting the rise of patriarchy. This is not to say that the "Jews invented patriarchy." If anything, Christianity was to go far beyond anything the early Hebrews could have imagined.

In the Age of Brigit we will look at the sexual politics of the early Irish church in the form of saint's lives, penitential practices and literature. We shall find that women helped and fostered Christianity in early Ireland as an alternative to the harsh male warrior ethos. But we shall see how, as Christianity took hold, and as male reproductive consciousness permeated the culture, the church essentially facilitated male control of women's reproductive powers and sexuality and the men of the early church eventually blamed women for their own inability to control their passions.

The figure of Brigit moves through these pages in her metamorphosis from Mother Goddess to Virgin Saint. And we will see that, whereas Brigit once may have been a Mother Goddess defending the rights of women, as the Irish political structure moved toward a hierarchical and military form of organization and as the Irish church, in line with Roman ambitions, developed a centralized hierarchy, Brigit would lose whatever little power she still had: a power that she had maintained so precariously, often at the expense of other women.

The Age of Mary, beginning in the twelfth century, deals with the struggle between church and state that resulted in enforced clerical celibacy and a new ideology of virginity. This fight originally took place in the context of the invasion of Ireland by Anglo-Norman forces, an invasion orchestrated by and benefiting the papacy in its struggle to centralize its power base. In this section we shall explore how the Virgin Mary was set up in opposition to the figure of Eve, and how the adoption of either role model was extremely problematic for women.

In our conclusion, the Age of the Fathers, we shall see how these struggles, which also resulted in the permanent exclusion of women from religious officiation, were intimately tied up with issues of sexual politics and were to have long-term implications for women's reproductive and political rights.

Throughout our discussion it will become apparent that, historically, women as the givers of life have become subservient to men, the takers of life. Women's ethics, based on nurturance, on care for the young, and on responsibility, have been made subservient to those based on transcending nature. Men as "takers of life" could sacrifice on the altar or on the battlefield, enabling them to enter the "higher" realms of culture, the realm of the Common Good. Women could only sacrifice themselves and plunge themselves into powerlessness and particularity.

Now the emerging consciousness of women represents a fundamental challenge to the gods of Western culture. Far from not wanting to have anything to do with religion, a position adopted by some feminists, the voices of women call for a renewed religious consciousness. We must undergo a profound conversion to a spirituality and worldview that honors womanhood and empowers our being; one that reveres the earth upon which all our foundations rest. Such a conversion will require a radical leap of faith into the unknown; we will often confront the ghosts and demons of the past, and all we will have to sustain us will be the barest hope and possibility that our efforts will succeed. Far from knocking at the door of patriarchy to get in, we need to overthrow the patriarchal "gods of displaced responsibility,"[8] together with their warriors and priests if our world is to survive.

TAMHLACHT
IMBOLC, 1989

TWILIGHT

Acknowledgments

Many people have contributed to this book in different ways. I wish to thank Roisín Conroy and Mary Paul Keane, who first suggested that I write it, and Caroline Smith, who persuaded me to agree. Carmel and Patricia Kelleher, Ann Hope, Rosemary Hale, Annick Mahieu, and Ted Fleming all gave me valuable encouragement at the early stages of the manuscript. Edith Bloch, Margaret Kelleher, Pat Scott, Anne Breslin, Sylvia Meehan, and Marie Redmond gave me invaluable technical and practical help and initial feedback and encouragement when it was sorely needed. My colleagues in the writing program at Harvard were a constant source of encouragement and good humor.

I wish to thank the Women's Division of the Board of Global Ministries of the Methodist Church in the United States for first enabling me to meet with the American feminist theological community at Grailville, Ohio. I also wish to thank the American Association of University Women for an International Fellowship, the Woodrow Wilson Foundation for a Charlotte Newcombe Fellowship, the P.E.O. for an International Peace Fellowship, as well as Boston College and Harvard Divinity School for their generous financial support. This book represents the first installment of the fruits of my doctoral research, and I owe a particular debt to Clarissa Atkinson, Sharon Welch, and Marilyn Massey, my academic advisors.

It was my privilege, as coordinator of the European Women's Project of the World Student Christian Federation, to come into contact with the Christian feminist community in Europe and to be challenged and stimulated by their insights. The members of the Women's Task Force of the Grail (Janet Kalven, Elizabeth McGee, and Mary Buckley) have been my "triple Godmothers" while in the United States. They, together with Tom Groome and Rosemary Radford Ruether, have sponsored my theological education at crucial moments, for which I will be forever grateful. I especially wish to thank Constance Buchanan and the Harvard Women's Studies in Religion Program, which first afforded me the opportunity to study and teach in the United States and to join the international community of scholars who make up that program. It was in

Mary Daly's classes at Boston College that I first came to grips with the evil of sexism and its contemporary political implications. To her, to Rosemary Radford Ruether, Elisabeth Schüssler Fiorenza, and the wide community of feminist scholars in Boston and beyond whose insights permeate this book, I owe a particular debt of thanks.

The staff of Widener Library at Harvard, the Royal Irish Academy, and Trinity College in Dublin have offered me invaluable help in finding the most obscure and diverse sources.

Elizabeth Gray of Harvard University first excited my interest in Celtic studies, and I have also benefited from conversations with Margaret MacCurtain, Kim McCone, Philip O'Leary, Charles Doherty, John de Paor, and Richard Kearney. Seán Ó Coileáin, while he was Professor of Irish Studies at Harvard, was extraordinarily generous with his time and resources. He read the manuscript several times, answered my many questions, saved me from embarrassing errors, and pointed me in very fruitful directions. Women's studies, in its interdisciplinary mode, will be well served in the future by friends such as him.

Susan Bruno read an early draft of this manuscript, and has generously shared her insights with me. Both she and Patty Gleason have been true friends, lightening the long hours of loneliness that go into the writing of any book. Patty, in addition, painstakingly read the manuscript in what I (mistakenly) hoped was its final form and offered many valuable suggestions and critical insights for which I am very grateful.

This book took final shape in Dublin, and I wish to express my thanks to the Gaia group, which met regularly to discuss various chapters. My thanks to Joni Crone, Aileen Ryan, Gráinne Healy, Marina Forrestal, and Vivian Moffett. Particular thanks must also go to Anne Louise Gilligan and Katharine Zappone, whose wellspring of love and integrity has often overflowed in my direction in the past several years. It would be no exaggeration to say that they have taught me the meaning of friendship. Nuala Ní Dhomhnaill's enthusiastic support for the project revitalized my flagging energies in the last year. Ger Moane's honesty and integrity in critiquing the manuscript has helped me enormously in the final stages, while her care and support has sustained me through many a difficult period.

As is true of a growing number of scholars in feminism and religion, I have been privileged to have as my friend and editor Marie Cantlon. Her encouragement has been invaluable to me over the years, and her gracious patience and insightful comments have added immeasurably to the final form of the book. I also wish to thank Jan Johnson and Yvonne Keller as well as Dorian Gossy and Philip Harnden at Harper & Row for their care and dedication in seeing the manuscript into print.

Finally, I wish to thank my large and extended family, inlaws and outlaws, for all the love they bring to my life. They will each have different and contradictory reasons for disagreeing with all or part of this book, but collectively they provide me with my greatest source of inspiration and happiness.

Introduction:
The Problem of History

The Irish male's obsession with history has given him a place to stand, a fortress of certainty: the stories of heroes, warriors, and saints have created a sacred space in the world where men could feel free of the humiliations and trivialities of daily life imposed by their own or a conquering race or by the weight of economic necessity. History has provided the forum wherein men have safeguarded their arena of political and religious power.

But the sacred space of male history has often been carved out, literally, over the bodies of women. Using the language of Tradition, Precedent, and even Divine Will, men in many cultures have appealed to, or established, a mythical or sacred past to justify social dominance in the present.

Furthermore, behind the creation of this history lies the problem recently formulated by the former midwife turned philosopher Mary O'Brien: "Underlying the doctrine that man makes history is the undiscussed reality of why he must."[1] Whereas men have felt at home in the world of history, where the stories of their great deeds, battles, and triumphs are constantly recalled, women have been relegated, over and over again, to the world of nature, a world that, historically, has been subordinate to the world of culture, or to the world of men.[2]

For countless millennia women have been urged to conform to the dictates of their "natures," by generations of philosophers, psychologists, theologians, and politicians: men for whom their own anatomy was anything but destiny, but rather pregnant with historical possibility. Consigned to the realm of nature, women have represented for men that triviality, that humiliation, and, in the realm of nature, that death that have provided the main obstacles to the achievement of their historic and heroic enterprises, the key to their sense of importance in the world.

Indeed, the struggle between the world of nature represented by women and the world of history or culture represented by men is the crucial battle in the war between the sexes in Ireland and in all patriarchal societies. Known as *sexual politics,* this battle is fought in the realms of law, mythology, religion, and literature.

Since "those who forget their history are doomed to repeat it," our first task is to understand how women have arrived at our present state of subjugation, and we will have to tread carefully through the Land of the Fathers. Insofar as this book is history, it is a history of sexual politics; an exploration into some selected events, literary sources, and theological documents that highlight the struggle for power between the sexes. By no means the final word on the topic, this is a view from one particular perspective that I hope will empower other women to begin similar explorations uncovering the past for the sake of the future.

Our study will begin with what is known as the *charter texts* of the Celtic, Jewish, and Christian traditions. Charter texts serve as the basis for a particular community's identity by elevating in importance the founding act of a nation, founders themselves, or a particular set of teachings or opinions the founder or founders held.

For the ancients, documents were of crucial importance. Those unaware of their history were "lost in the abyss of time," and those responsible for maintaining the charter documents were highly honored in ancient societies, often having the same legal status as the political, religious, or royal leadership. The professional historians and scribes in Ireland were treated with great respect because their preservation of the ancient histories gave their people a place to stand, an Archimedean point from which they could look out at the world and assert their identity, usually by maintaining some form of their own national or ethnic superiority. As the guardians of the spirit of the people, they were clearly aware of the vital importance these stories played in the formation of a people's consciousness. As a recent historian noted, "Ownership of the past was, in a sense, control of the future."[3]

The Celtic and Christian tradition was formative, not only for Ireland, but also for the growth of Christianity throughout Europe in the Middle Ages, as well as being a formidable influence in the religious lives of the new worlds, in the United States and Australia in particular, through the influence in recent centuries of Irish missionary activity. The analysis of this tradition is of prime importance to us as we seek now to analyze the origins of patriarchy and the predominance of male values and ethics in the West today.

The Hebrew Bible, the charter document of the Jews, also known as the Old Testament, had a tremendous influence on the early Celtic Christians. Unlike the stories from the New Testament, many of which took their final form in the city-states of ancient Greece and Rome, the Hebrew Bible documented the struggles of a tribal society, a form of social organization very similar to that of the early medieval Irish. Stories from the Hebrew Bible and from the synoptic Gospels (the Gospels of Matthew, Mark, and Luke) captured the imagination of ordinary tribal people to a greater extent than the abstract theologizing so much a feature of St. John's Gospel or the various Epistles or Acts of the Apostles.

The Irish incorporated these stories into their own oral history, telling them again and again around their hearths and, indeed, elaborating on them, often producing their own versions of the stories if they deemed the original to be too harsh, not harsh enough, or even improbable.[4]

But Ireland also had a set of charter documents. These were myths, sagas, genealogies, law codes, and pseudohistorical accounts of the origins of the Irish or Celtic race. The Irish charter texts are an extremely rich collection of material of crucial importance for anyone attempting to study the origins and premises upon which Western civilization was founded. The contribution of these documents was greatly undermined during the seven hundred years of the British occupation of Ireland. But over the last hundred years or so, a tremendous effort has gone into making these documents available again in translation.[5]

Within these documents, in an attempt to merge the Christian and Celtic traditions, it was not unusual for the Irish to trace their genealogies back to figures from the Bible. Noah was a favorite choice, as was his granddaughter Cessair, an enterprising woman who, it was claimed, led an expedition comprised of fifty women and three men to Ireland, following Yahweh's refusal to allow any more of Noah's relatives into the original Ark when the Flood was about to arrive.[6] In reverse, since the old Celtic heroes died before the advent of Christianity, it was not unusual for the storytellers to resurrect them on occasion so they could receive baptism and thus be incorporated into the Communion of Saints.[7]

As the rabbinical scribes underwent intense years of training before being allowed to practice their profession, the training for an Irish poet was extremely rigorous, reflecting the subsequent importance that person would play in the life of the people. Dire punishments, including loss of office, corporal correction, expulsion from the people, fines or imprisonment, awaited any poet who abused his office by fabricating the truth.[8]

The fact that the scribes underwent such rigorous training and were subject to internal discipline did not guarantee that what they ultimately produced would be the "truth." With the best of intentions, these scribes were subject to problems well known to contemporary historians: the problem of objectivity, the problem of selection whereby some events or texts are chosen and not others, and the problem of bias for one's own value system. Still other decisions as to which texts would survive were based on who was paying for the transcription. For instance, one Irish scribe wrote in his margins, "I send my little dripping pen unceasingly over an assemblage of books of great beauty, to enrich the possessions of men of art—whence my hand is weary with writing."[9]

In the Irish context, despite the great emphasis placed on the notion of truth, one finds increasingly that the Irish scribes were by no means passive recorders of history. Historical memory is highly selective, and as a prominent Irish historian has said, "We have seen reason to suspect that their traditional memory of earlier times was coloured by the limitation of their interest to the fortunes of those who had succeeded."[10]

In the Celtic sagas, the notion of "truth" was essentially a matter of public prestige rather than private integrity. The argument even can be made that the notion of truth is itself part of the mythology.[11] The "men of art" made crucial decisions as to what should be recorded. Their decision was influenced by the fact that a new form of social organization was in vogue, which the Christians themselves called patriarchal. Many stories survived because of the light they would throw on the Celtic heroic culture, which had been by no means entirely overthrown by the new religion. Indeed, if anything, the Christian scribes elaborated on these stories to suit their own purposes. Other editorial decisions must have been influenced by the hope that the stories would illustrate the superiority of the Christian beliefs that the church was trying to impose on the native traditions. To this day there is no agreement among scholars as to exactly what pre-Christian Irish beliefs were, given the paucity of the sources that were left.

In dealing with the pre-Christian sagas—the charter stories of ancient Ireland—the Christian scribes were in a bind. These stories were based on oral tradition and written down and preserved mostly by Christian monks and nuns whose theological worldview was radically opposed to the one being recorded.[12] On the one hand, the scribes knew that the charter documents were a vital part of Irish cultural history and had to be maintained; on the other hand, a competing worldview, that of the Judeo-Christian tradition, had taken hold. If Ireland was not to remain isolated from the mainstream of world history, this new worldview would have to be taken seriously. Nevertheless, the monks were no slaves to "objectivity." The "Four Masters," the famed Franciscan monks who collected and recorded much of Irish history,[13] simply omitted from their vast collection events that reflected badly on their predecessors.[14]

But the problem with which we will be most concerned in this present work will be that derived from the gender of the scribes themselves. Whereas in ancient Ireland women poets were well known and respected, with the advent of Christianity in the early Middle Ages they became a dying breed. So, in addition to the normal problems inherent in any historical enterprise, the exclusion of the perspectives of half the human race ensured that the charter documents were skewed in their very essence.

Up until recently, not only has history been written by men, usually about men, and for men, but men have also taken upon themselves the interpretation of the sources in ways that traditionally have guaranteed their own supremacy. Women have never been included or represented in the teaching authority of the major religious traditions. This is graphically illustrated by a story in the Gospels when Jesus first appeared to the women who went and told the male disciples about the Resurrection. The women were not believed, and the male disciples had to go and see for themselves. The word of women at the time of Jesus had no standing in Hebrew legal systems. Biblical texts have been used throughout Christian history to justify discrimination against women, and in the event of a challenge to the biblical authority for a particular text, the problem has been "resolved" by appealing to the competent theological authorities, all of whom have been male.

As if it were not enough that the texts themselves were so prejudicial to women's interests, the subsequent history of the formulation and dissemination of Christian theology ensured that little would change. Women would have some part to play in the church but would be banned from playing any role in commenting seriously on the charter texts or in deciding the question of which texts were to be included in what eventually became known as the *canon* of Christian teaching.

In light of the male monopoly of theology and written culture, fundamental questions are now being asked, not only about the interpretation of these charter documents, but also about the process by which certain texts and not others were chosen as having ultimate authority and, therefore, were included in the various sacred or literary canons.

The process of unmasking repressive ideologies in relation to women now represents a watershed in the history of thought. In the past twenty years, there has emerged an unprecedented movement in the history of Christianity, a movement destined to change fundamentally the conditions of the possibility of knowledge in Western society. Women have begun the academic study of theology, hitherto almost the exclusive prerogative of men. The work of these scholars has shattered the myth of the objectivity of theological scholarship and has revealed the extent to which this scholarship is in continuity with, and indeed maintains, patriarchal interests.[15] Women have, in the words of one of the foremothers of contemporary feminist theology, Nelle Morton, "heard each other into speech,"[16] and they have begun the process whereby patriarchal religion must become accountable to contemporary society and, in particular, accountable to women who have suffered historically under its development.

As one scholar asks, "What subject-effects were systematically effaced and trained to efface themselves so that a canonic norm might emerge?[17] Whose interests were being served? Which groups were in power when the documents took shape? Did the text selection serve the interests of the kings, nobles, or tribal leaders, or were the concerns of the poor or women given any consideration?[18]

This kind of critique, needless to say, challenges the ultimate status that has, until fairly recently, been given to the Bible and is a direct result of major changes that have taken place in world culture in the past several centuries. During the period when the Hebrew Bible and New Testament were written (approximately seven hundred years before the common era—B.C.E.—and the year 400 of the common era—C.E.)—people had little appreciation or awareness of other cultures; there were few books, and people relied for their information on wandering travelers between different cultures. They had very little opportunity to compare different forms of social development under varying conditions. Under these circumstances it was easy to consider one's own culture or charter documents as being the Ultimate Manifestation of the Word of God.

From the sixteenth century onward major technological and cultural changes took place: the invention of the printing press, which made texts widely available to people cross-culturally; improved methods of travel; and the discovery, and often conquest, of new continents. The widespread dissemination of information engendered the rise of historical consciousness and cross-cultural relativity that were to have strong repercussions in theology.[19]

Historical consciousness offers us the opportunity to reevaluate religious beliefs and to put them in the context of the needs and perspectives of those who created them. We may then decide to accept or reject them, but our decision will be based on the effects these beliefs might have had historically rather than on an abstract notion of their "truth" or "falsity," alienated from the social reality in which they are placed. As Elisabeth Schüssler Fiorenza recently maintained, "The task of liberation theologians is not to prove that the Bible or the church can be defended against feminist or socialist attacks, but rather to critically comprehend how the Bible functions in the oppression of women or the poor and thus to prevent its misuse for further oppression."[20] Under these circumstances one can still acknowledge the Bible, and indeed the Celtic texts, as part of our common cultural and religious heritage but not at the price of closing our ears to our grave human responsibilities today. As Fiorenza continues, "The litmus test for invoking Scripture as the Word of God must be whether or not biblical texts and traditions seek to end relations of domination and exploitation."[21]

The texts we will be dealing with here were designed to exalt the monastic, biblical, or warrior heroes, and the treatment and role of women are merely incidental details to the narrators. However, this "subtext" is crucial, as it provides one of the few sources for women's history. In looking at the texts, we will be looking at them directly for what they say about women, their attitudes to sexual politics, and their implications for a power structure based on male dominance. Needless to say, in most cases these issues were not at the forefront of the author's agenda; in many instances the consequences for women were an indirect result of religious or political policies. We will be looking, therefore, not at the author's "intentions" but at the "effects" of texts for women, not necessarily the same thing.[22] As Nelle Morton continues:

I have taken my stance among the masses and listened with the common woman's ear to that which patriarchal religious institutions must begin to accept responsibility for. No longer can they hide behind: "But the real intention is . . . "; "In the original language it says . . . "; "The real truth is . . . " when the world is hearing something else again as it continues to bow hopelessly under poverty, threat of nuclear war, and discrimination. Not accepting responsibility for how what one says is heard is only a step from the refusal to care about and accept responsibility for the world.[23]

THE MYTH OF OBJECTIVITY

One result of such a self-conscious feminist perspective is that, whereas most writers assume that they are "objective" and, therefore, can arrive at "truth," feminist scholars, among others, increasingly recognize the need to challenge this approach. History is not the objective science it was once thought to be but a particular form of power and knowledge, involving the manipulation of academic and political resources and serving to ensure the dominance of certain groups. Although in a class-ridden society it is obvious that not all men have benefited economically from male dominance, as some men are obviously at the bottom of the economic and social heap, all men, nevertheless, have in some ways benefited from the ideology of male supremacy.

The myth of "objectivity" serves to conceal the hidden agenda of those in power. In reality, the philosophy underlying this myth does not recognize a moral responsibility to anything other than the growth or independence of the human mind and is usually indifferent to the world of women and children. For this reason scientists in the 1940s could go ahead happily building atom bombs as "pure scientific projects" without taking moral responsibility for how they were going to be used. Once they were made, however, their "objective scientific" curiosity got the better of them, and the bombs were exploded on Hiroshima and Nagasaki.[24] Similarly, reproductive scientists have developed a technology for surrogate motherhood, cloning, and test-tube babies. The moral questions are usually only raised, if at all, after the fact.[25] The myth of objectivity serves to conceal the fact that the male mind has become sacred and is allowed to experiment regardless of the social, human or ecological consequences.

The sacredness of the male mind is allied to the struggle for power in that men, claiming objectivity, can also claim universal validity for their values. In this sense the word *man,* correctly in their view, can encompass women, although the converse is not true and the word *woman* can never stand for the general but only for the particular.[26]

Feminist scholars, on the contrary, insist that all knowledge is "context bound" and that the issues of gender and sex are crucial factors in locating context.[27] Rather than attempting to freeze history in a plethora of dates and battles, feminists are attempting to unmask the hidden agendas behind the power struggles and to deconstruct those ideologies that continue to oppress women today. History is used, not to justify the present by appealing to "Tradition," but to explore the premises upon which our civilization is founded and the continuing effects of these premises on contemporary thought.[28] Rather than pretend to a spurious "objectivity" feminists argue that we must find a way to read texts that will serve to illuminate the "masks of truth with which phallocentrism hides its fictions."[29] Feminist scholars, therefore, usually make a point of setting out their values, assumptions, and agendas and declaring their self-interest.[30] The moral or practical questions to be addressed are fundamental and are asked at the beginning, rather than at the end, of any enterprise.

Feminist scholars are called, not just to break our way into patriarchal society, but to challenge radically the nature of that society, the premises that govern its creation and continued existence, and the mythologies that sustain its being. Not only will we be looking at patriarchal stories, but, in the process, we will be creating new stories and new models, which will serve to liberate rather than to enslave.[31]

Many feminists, realizing the type of culture and history we have inherited, increasingly see it as a mixed blessing.[32] As the feminist historian Joan Kelly-Gadol argued, "We could probably maintain of any ideology that tolerates sexual parity that: 1) it can threaten no major institution of the patriarchal society from which it emerges; and 2) men, the rulers within the ruling order, must benefit by it."[33]

For every foot that women put forward, we may be taking two steps backward. As Mary O'Brien comments, "We are now emerging from a stage of feminist utopianism, which calls for the destruction of the world of male supremacy, and even sometimes expects the ruling sex to assist in its own funeral rites."[34] Historically, no oppressor has willingly relinquished power. As an exiled African nationalist once said to me in regard to his own struggle, "The British will only leave Africa when the Africans have learned how to oppress themselves."

Central to our understanding is the supposition that the dominant mythology governing our time is based on the *law of the phallus*. The law of the phallus refers to the whole constellation of patriarchal symbols, structures, modes of production and social reproduction. The concept of the law of the phallus was formulated in reaction to the accusation of "penis envy" of which those women were accused, who, from the nineteenth century onward, protested or reacted against the dominant social structures.

Contemporary psychoanalysts and philosophers are coming around to the view that it is not the male penis but what the penis "signifies" that is at issue. The penis signifies male power, and it is the political reality of male power rather than the mere assertion of the biological superiority of male anatomy that is problematic for women. Instead of "penis envy," people now talk about the "law of the phallus" to signify the structure males have established to confirm and promote their own dominance especially in the realm where male and female relationships are regulated.[35]

The law of the phallus operates throughout both church and state. In the church, as we will see, the symbolism is fairly blatant. But much more insidious, because it is masked, will be the form that the law of the phallus takes in contemporary secular society.

The task for feminist scholarship is, therefore, both prophetic and theological and will be undertaken by those who have the courage to break out of those worldviews within which their subordination is held to be divinely ordained and the rule of the Fathers divinely guaranteed. Although we should ensure that we are using our sources responsibly and that we are showing respect to our ancestors, ultimately our efforts should be directed toward creating the future in the light of our knowledge of the past. The cult of the dead martyrs and heroes often provides a justification for action when all rationality is otherwise lacking and is thus one of the primary mythmaking machineries of patriarchy. Within this mind-set, greater homage is paid to the dead heroes than to the living generations, the children of which are often sacrificed to whatever "holy cause" is being promoted.

In contrast, our primary responsibility as feminist thinkers and historians lies not with the dead but with the living. And if rationale be needed for such a stance, it can be found in the hope that the terminal disease of patriarchy, of which the threat of universal nuclear war is the most visible manifestation, can be arrested before the living generations are finally obliterated.

THE SERPENT AND THE GODDESS

PART I

THE AGE OF EVE

CHAPTER 1

Eve and the Serpent
The Foundation Myth of Patriarchy

EVE'S LAMENTATION

I am Eve, great Adam's wife,
'Twas my guilt took Jesus' life.
Since of Heaven I robbed my race,
On His Cross was my true place.

In His Paradise, God placed me,
Then a wicked choice disgraced me.
At the counsel of the Devil,
My pure hand I stained with evil:

For I put it forth and plucked,
Then the deadly apple sucked.
Long as woman looks on day,
Shall she walk in folly's way.

Winter's withering icy woe,
Whelming wave and smothering snow,
Hell to fright and death to grieve—
Had been never, but for Eve!

UNKNOWN AUTHOR

To this day probably no other name strikes so many chords in the hearts of religious men and women as that of Eve. Eve has been the symbol of women's licentiousness, pride, seduction, disobedience, temptation, and spiritual weakness. Eve is the woman we most fear: the symbol of our negative natures, the depths into which we can sink unless we are faithful to our religious heritage. Despite Christian teaching that Christ, by his death and Resurrection, has overcome sin, women can never be free of the "curse of Eve." Men, no matter how high the lofty spiritual heights they have climbed, can never be sure of their salvation so long as there are "Eve" figures around.

There are several different accounts in the Bible of the creation of the world, but the story of the creation of Adam and Eve and their disobedience is the one that has had most influence in Western thought. This, in itself, is remarkable because the story is a very strange one, full of apparent contradictions that, had women had access to formal education, would have been exposed long before now.

The general impression of these stories is that Adam and Eve, having taken the forbidden fruit at the suggestion of the Serpent, were punished simply for their disobedience. This account, however, contains many problems. In the first place the Serpent appears as "more subtle than any beast of the field which the Lord hath made." Now if this beast were evil, why was it beautiful and "subtle," and how did it get into Paradise in the first place? When the Serpent asked the woman if she and Adam were allowed to eat of every tree in the garden, Eve answered:

"We may eat the fruit of the trees in the garden. But of the fruit of the tree in the middle of the garden God said. 'You must not eat it, nor touch it, under pain of death.' " Then the serpent said to the woman. "No! You will not die! God knows in fact that on the day you eat it your eyes will be opened and you will be like gods, knowing good and evil."[1]

So Eve took the fruit and "gave some also to her husband." When God saw what they had done, he cast them out of the Garden of Paradise.

The logical problem is that if man and woman were made in the image of God, why is there a problem when "they become as gods"? Surely, if eating the fruit helped Adam and Eve to know the difference between good and evil, they would be in a better position to know the will of God in the future and to follow it, so it seems infinitely petty to throw them out of Paradise for that. If they have become as gods by eating the fruit, why then should they lose Paradise? Since we are told that our lives are merely preparations for the time when we can come to know God fully, why in the Bible, when it seemed possible to know God, do Adam and Eve lose Paradise rather than gain it? At face value the story does not make much sense unless we want to promote an image of God as a tyrant who, on mere whim, says, "You can eat from this tree and not from that one."

A popular psychological interpretation of the story is that the sin of Adam and Eve is not just one of disobedience but of sexual transgression and that the Serpent is really a phallic symbol. This is reinforced by the account that "suddenly they found themselves naked and were ashamed." But this makes no sense when we recall that at the beginning of Genesis, the first command given to all God has created is "Go forth and multiply." Why then, if Adam and Eve proceeded to do just that, should they be punished?

This interpretation is particularly convenient in the light of the punishment given to the woman:

"I will multiply your pains in childbearing,
you shall give birth to your children in pain.

Your yearning shall be for your husband,
yet he will lord it over you."[2]

The man, however, is not punished sexually. His punishment has to do with his working conditions. "With sweat on your brow shall you eat your bread." If the sin had been sexual, why were they not punished equally? Although God had only told Adam not to eat of the fruit of the tree, Eve was also punished.

When God confronted Adam in the garden, his excuse for eating the fruit was that "it was the woman you put with me: she gave me the fruit, and I ate it." Here Adam almost blames God for having given the woman to him. Note that in the text it simply says, "The woman saw that the tree was good to eat and pleasing to the eye, and that it was desirable for the knowledge that it could give. So she took some of its fruit and ate it. She gave some also to her husband who was with her, and he ate it."[3]

The woman sought knowledge and ate the fruit. Adam simply gratified his hunger and then tried to shift the responsibility onto his wife. Yet Adam has gone down in history as the poor, misguided unfortunate man, a warning to all men not to listen to women. And Eve has gone down in history as the greatest Temptress of all time, the model for the seductive nature of the whole female sex.

Despite its contradictions, this story has had widespread implications that powerfully affected the treatment of women in society. Women have been identified with Eve, the symbol of evil, and can only attain sanctity by identifying with the Virgin Mary, the opposite of Eve. But this is an impossible task since we are told that Mary herself "was conceived without sin" and when she gave birth to Jesus remained a virgin.[4] To reach full sanctity then, women have to renounce their sexuality, symbol of their role as Temptresses and the means by which they drag men down from their lofty heights. For this reason most of the women saints of the Catholic church have been either virgins, martyrs, widows, or married women who have taken a perpetual vow of continence. Sex and spirituality have become polar opposites in Christian teaching.

From the simple statement that "she gave some to her husband," ecclesiastical scholars have built the most incredible theories of women's power to promote evil. One after another, the church fathers proclaimed solemnly that Eve exercised "wicked persuasion" or "corrupted her husband."[5] In the *Malleus Maleficarum* (the *Hammer of Witches*), the fifteenth-century witch-hunter's manual, it was stated, "In the Old Testament, the Scriptures have much that is evil to say about women, and this because of the first temptress, Eve, and her imitators."[6]

A modern commentary on the Paradise story sums up this mentality:

Eve winds her way into the subject like a serpent. Yes, there we have struck on an ominous affinity. . . . The serpent is the universal casuist for crooked wiles, the end whereof is dust and ashes. It was never till Adam, amorously sighing for companionship, parted with one of his proper ribs, that the talking serpent dared on the idea of beguiling God's gentle gardener.[7]

Some of these commentators also suggest that Adam's eating the fruit was a matter of generosity and self-sacrifice. Since his wife was to be condemned, Adam did not want to be parted from her. Other eminent Fathers suggest that he simply ate the fruit so as not to anger her.[8]

The story also had very practical implications for women, enabling discrimination between the sexes. Adam, for all practical purposes, represents the world of production; Eve, the sphere of reproduction. There is no comparison between the treatment of these spheres in Christian moral theology. For instance, although Adam was punished by having to work by the sweat of his brow, this has never prevented men from developing the tools of agriculture and technology that make the production of food much easier by lessening the labor involved. However, when women have sought to alleviate the pains of childbearing, the whole weight of moral theology has fallen on their heads.[9]

One of the punishments given to woman is, "Your yearning shall be for your husband, yet he will lord it over you." Again, when women try to lessen the weight of patriarchal oppression, this has been resisted with the full weight of biblical authority. In the Christian tradition it is assumed that her oppression is due to her Original Sin, and little should be done to alleviate it. Clearly, the story has been interpreted in such a way as to foster the subjugation of women. Was this necessarily the conscious intention of the original storytellers, or was this a consequence of the major changes taking place in Hebrew society that the story reflected? A closer look at the story in its ancient Near Eastern context gives us vital clues as to the complexity of what was actually going on.

At the end of the creation story Yahweh says:

See this man has become like one of us, with his knowledge of good and evil. He must not be allowed to stretch his hand out next and pick from the Tree of Life also, and eat some and live for ever. So Yahweh God expelled him from the garden of Eden, to till the soil from which he had been taken. He banished the man, and in front of the garden of Eden he posted the cherubs, and the flame of a flashing sword, to guard the way to the Tree of Life.[10]

In these verses we have evidence that there were, in fact, two trees, the Tree of Knowledge and the Tree of Life. Why did God not want man to eat from the Tree of Life and live forever, or how was it even in man's power to do so? It seems obvious that what we have here are remnants of themes that were common in the creation stories of the ancient Near East and that the compilers of the Genesis stories (Scripture scholars recognize that there was not just one writer)[11] drew extensively on the ancient traditions to give us, what they considered to be, a composite version. Unfortunately, however, their version radically altered the themes of the more ancient stories.[12]

SERPENT IMAGERY

We have seen that some biblical commentators identified Eve with the Serpent and that this identification was not justified by her role in the Genesis story. However, there is weighty evidence that the figure of Eve is based on much older stories in Near Eastern mythology and that the original Eve did appear in the form of a Serpent. The name Eve, *hawwah*, means "mother of all the living" but *hawwah* also means "serpent" in many Semitic languages.[13] Some scholars suggest that originally there may have been only three characters in the Paradise stories: God, Adam, and a Serpent deity.[14] If this were the case then the Serpent deity would have been blamed for cheating Adam of the Garden of Paradise.

The identification of the Serpent with Eve, therefore, is based upon much older sources and is probably the reason why both Eve and the Serpent are treated so badly in the Genesis story. So who or what was the Serpent; why was the Serpent a threat to Yahwism, the emerging faith of the Hebrew people; and why was it so important to overthrow its influence in human history?[15] To understand this we have to go much farther back in time, at least as far back as the culture of the ancient Sumerians.

Sumer was one of the great cultural capitals of the ancient world, and many other cultures borrowed its system of writing (cuneiform) to inscribe their own records and writings. Most of the Sumerian literary documents were composed about 2000 B.C.E., whereas biblical documents were not written much earlier than 1000 B.C.E. The image of the serpent is found frequently on the artifacts of the ancient Near East. Serpent symbolism came from many sources, and the biblical writers probably got theirs indirectly from the Sumerian influence on Canaanite, Hurrian, Hittite, and Akkadian literature, especially the latter, "since the Akkadian language was used all over Palestine and its environs in the second millennium B.C.E. as the common language of the Fertile Crescent." In fact, the tribe of Abraham was probably responsible for bringing Sumerian influence into Palestine.[16]

Already in the Sumerian mythology and that of the surrounding regions there were stories of the Creation, Flood, Fall, the quest for immortality, and similar later biblical themes. For instance, the Babylonians had a myth of a serpent stealing a plant of rejuvenation.[17] In these myths, the themes of the Tree of Life, the Tree of the Knowledge of Good and Evil, the Serpent, disobedience, and immortality all play major roles but are put together in different cultures, almost like different variations of characters on a chess board, to come to some very different conclusions.

Scripture scholars are in no doubt that the Yahwist (the name commonly given to the final editor of the story in Genesis) drew on many sources when compiling the narrative for his own particular purposes. Here we will explore the image of the Serpent in these earlier creation stories, since this has had such crucial significance for women.

The symbol of the Serpent was the one most widely used to represent or adorn the Goddess of the ancient Near East or to depict, or mediate, the relationship between goddesses and human culture.[18] In Egypt and Mesopotamia, according to the evidence derived from scarabs, scaraboids, and seals, the Serpent was an emblem of life.[19] In Sumerian mythology, the Goddess Ninhursag was the goddess of creation. Known as Nintu, she was "the Lady who gave birth."[20] One of her common images was that of a Serpent.[21] As a symbol of life, the Serpent had connections with both the sun and the moon and was even said to cause the sun to rise. In the "Book of Gates" in the tomb of Rameses VI there is a figure of a winged Serpent named "The Leader." Over its head is written, "She Who Causes to Rise Before Re. It is She who Leads the Great God in the Gate of the Eastern Horizon."[22]

In its association with life, the Serpent represented much more than mere sexual fertility, although fertility was an important theme of the cultic occasions when serpentine imagery was used. Serpents hibernate in the winter and reemerge in the spring. For this reason they were ideal symbols of the rebirth of nature every year and represented a guarantee that even though all of life might seem to die off in the winter months, there was yet hope for the earth. In Egypt the Serpent was called "life of the earth," the "son of the earth," "full of years," the "life of the gods," and the "life of forms and of nutritious substances."[23]

The image of the Serpent, because of its association with life, rejuvenation, fertility, and regeneration, was a symbol of immortality. The coiled Serpent with its tail in its mouth was a circle of infinitude indicating omnipotence and omniscience.[24] The Serpent, depicted in several successive rings, represented cyclical evolution and reincarnation. In ancient philosophy or mythological systems, creation and wisdom were closely bound together, and the Serpent was a potent symbol of both.[25] It is in this capacity that the Serpent appears in the Babylonian and Sumerian mythologies, which contain elements akin to the Genesis story. The Serpent has the power to bestow immortality but also has the power to cheat humankind. In many of the ancient Near Eastern stories—for instance, the Gilgamesh Epic and the myth of Adapa—the Serpent holds out the promise of immortality but then cheats man at the last minute.[26]

Probably the most important characteristic of the Serpent, for our purposes, is its dual nature and simultaneous capacity for good and evil. In the Egyptian *Book of the Dead*, the Serpent is said to be "wavering by turns between loving and hating the gods."[27] The Babylonian deities, many of whom were portrayed in serpent imagery, were portrayed as being both good and bad. They had their good days and bad days. Just like humans, they fought, made love, hated, died, were injured, were jealous, and gave birth. The main difference between the gods and humankind was the ultimate power the deities had to carry out their wicked or generous desires.[28] The Serpent was, therefore, used to represent both beneficent and hostile sacred powers. The Serpent was pictured as erect when good, but the crawling Serpent was a symbol of evil.[29]

This dual character of the Serpent closely represents the joys and tragedies of human life itself. Life and death, in religions where Serpent symbolism is common, are seen as both beautiful and tragic. When life has run its course, or sometimes even before that in particularly sad situations, death will come inevitably. But the end of a particular human life need not be cause for grief because with the coming of spring everything is reborn. That which has died merely returns to the earth to reappear anew. It may take new shapes and forms, but this is a cause for joy. Nothing is static—all will be renewed. Death is not the end but simply a new beginning. The Serpent religions, representing life and death, male and female, good and evil, provided an integrated representation of human life.[30]

The second major set of symbols in the ancient myths common throughout the ancient world was the Tree of Life and the Tree of the Knowledge of Good and Evil, which were the residences of the gods. Immortality does not belong automatically to the gods: they must constantly eat the fruit of the sacred trees. To refuse someone admission to the Tree of Life means that he or she is, and will remain, mortal. That is why so many of the themes of ancient mortality are concerned with gaining access to the Tree of Life or with being denied access to the tree by a Serpent or a god.[31]

The Serpent often appears in mythology in conjunction with the Tree of Life or the Tree of the Knowledge of Good and Evil. Serpents are often seen guarding trees upon which berries grow that can give immortality or good health to those who partake of them.[32] In some of these myths the hero has to slay the Serpent before he can partake of the fruits of the tree or give them to his loved one.[33]

We must place the Genesis story against this background in order to realize how radically the narrative departs from any version of the myth that had hitherto existed. We can begin by looking at one version, the Sumerian "Garden of Paradise" story that parallels the story in Genesis.

In "The Land of Dilmun," Paradise is a clean and bright land of the living that knows neither sickness nor death. One of the great mother goddesses of the Sumerians, Ninhursag,[34] who is represented as a Serpent or fishtailed woman,[35] causes eight plants to sprout. This is a very complicated and strenuous process, accomplished only after she had brought three generations of goddesses into being, all conceived, as it is repeatedly stressed, "without the slightest pain or travail." But now,

Enki, the Sumerian water god, enters into the picture.

Enki decides to eat the plants, possibly to wrest the power of fertility from Ninhursag. The angry Ninhursag pronounces the curse of death upon him, and then, so that she will not change her mind, disappears from among the gods. Enki's health begins to fail rapidly, "since as a male god he was not meant to be pregnant."[36] This causes great worry to the other gods, whereupon a fox offers to go and get Ninhursag back, on condition that he be properly rewarded. Eventually the fox succeeds, and Ninhursag returns. She seats Enki beside her vulva and asks him in turn about the eight organs of his that have begun to fail. One by one she brings into existence eight healing gods to replace the diseased parts. She forgives Enki, and the natural order is restored.[37]

This Sumerian story was written at least a thousand years before the biblical one, and when we turn to the Book of Genesis, we can see that the characters in the story have changed dramatically. In the Genesis story, although the Yahwist was clearly aware that the Serpent was "more subtle than any other wild creature that the Lord had made," nevertheless, the Hebrew word used for the Serpent here is simply that of an animal rather than a mythological being, god or goddess.[38] But the true identity of the Serpent comes out in other ways. The woman shows no surprise at the Serpent's being able to talk and simply takes it for granted that the Serpent is an authority on the consequences of partaking of the fruit forbidden by Yahweh. In the Genesis story, Enki's attempt to wrest fertility from the woman appears to have succeeded: the mortal Adam is responsible for giving birth to Eve. Yahweh reverses the natural order of creation.[39]

There are other comparisons to the Genesis story. Whereas the Sumerian goddesses all "give birth without pain or travail," in Genesis pain is the punishment given to Eve, and all women, for their disobedience. Even more strikingly, whereas Ninhursag is prevailed upon to forgive Enki, Yahweh condemns Adam and Eve to punishment. Clearly, something serious is happening to the Serpent imagery in Genesis. The Serpent contradicts Yahweh's telling Eve that she may eat of the fruit of the tree in the midst of the garden. "No! You will not die. God knows in fact that on the day you eat it your eyes will be opened and you will be like gods, knowing good and evil."[40]

As it turned out, the Serpent was right. The first couple did not die when they ate the fruit, and they came to know good and evil. Apparently what eating the fruit accomplished was granting them insight into the location of the Tree of Life, and for this reason Yahweh threw them out of the Garden of Paradise.

Now, even though the Serpent was proved to be right and Yahweh was trying to prevent the couple from "knowing good and evil," the Serpent is punished: "Be accursed beyond all cattle, all wild beasts. You shall crawl on your belly and eat dust every day of your life."

Worse is to come:

"I will make you enemies of each other:
you and the woman,
Your offspring and her offspring.
It will crush your head
and you shall strike its heel."[41]

And so in the Genesis version of the Paradise story, the Serpent is relegated to being a mere animal; women, who previously could rely on the Goddess for strength in childbirth, would now give birth to their children in pain.[42] Women were made subordinate to men, and they themselves would be responsible for crushing the old source of their strength and comfort: the Goddess in the form of a Serpent. The first couple would henceforth wander the earth with little to comfort them in sickness and, in sorrow, utterly dependent on the mercy of Yahweh, who, unlike Ninhursag, could not be prevailed upon to forgive them.

Taken at face value, the story is one of the most tragic episodes in human history, and yet it has been formative in the religious faith of generations. Clearly the overthrow of the Serpent represented something fundamental and crucial to the foundation of patriarchal culture.

How did it come about that Yahweh was so opposed to the Serpent, and why did the Israelites carry this myth with them in their wandering? To answer this question we will have to look critically at the political changes taking place at the time the Genesis stories were being written.

To put it simply and briefly: the form of religion that the Serpent represented was a major threat to the new religion of Israel or, indeed, to the future of Western civilization.[43] If Israel was to grow as a nation-state, with all the entailed political and military trappings, goddess religions would have to be overthrown. Allegiance would have to be to one god, Yahweh, and the central symbolism of the new religion would be based on Promise and History rather than on the Life and Cyclical Regeneration represented by the Serpent.

POLITICAL BACKGROUND

The Genesis narrative is commonly considered to have been written, at the earliest, toward the end of David's reign, and probably during the time of King Solomon.[44] The Israelites had to have had a certain "political assurance" before writing an historical work of this nature.[45] The Yahwist probably wrote before the appearance of the prophets Amos and Hosea and certainly before the disaster to the Northern Kingdom in 721 B.C.E. The narrative was written sometime between the tenth and the eighth century B.C.E. and was by no means the first biblical book to be written, even though it appears first in order.

The reign of Solomon had brought about alliances with several other nations, particularly Egypt and Tyre. This introduced a situation of great cultural diversity and there was extensive building, trade, intellectual activity, and the growth of urban development.[46] The monarchy reigned over the conquered Canaanites, but not all were converts to Yahwism. Solomon's loyalty to Yahweh, in particular, was called into question. He had pagan wives and encouraged religious tolerance.[47] There is evidence that polytheistic worship with extensive Serpent symbolism was practised in or near the Temple.[48]

Yahwism was struggling to be the official cult of the kingdom, but this was meeting with some difficulty since the high priest, Zadok, may have originally been the high priest of Canaanite Jerusalem.[49] David may even have permitted Zadok's promotion of the Serpent symbolism in the Israelite religion.[50] In the Book of Kings it says that "until those days the people of Israel had burned incense to the serpent,"[51] The Yahwist was writing, then, in a context where Serpent symbolism abounded and where polytheistic gods and goddesses were still in vogue.

In the midst of this political turmoil the Serpent was crushed, not only mythologically, but also in reality. The bronze serpent Moses made in the desert,[52] and which may have actually been in the Ark of the Covenant,[53] symbolizing the power of Yahweh,[54] was taken out and smashed by the young king Hezekiah, who "put his trust in the God of Israel."[55]

Prior to the monarchic period, Israel had been organized largely along tribal lines. Although Yahweh appears early on in their history, in general the cult was that of the clan, and animal sacrifices were practiced by the clan fathers.[56] The Ark of the Covenant, the throne of the invisible Yahweh, was carried with the clans in their wanderings. There were some local shrines, but none had central significance.[57] What held the tribes together was their common allegiance to the terms of the Covenant, which, in particular, laid down clear laws for dealing with others under the rule of Yahweh, i.e., those tribes included in the Covenant who were, therefore, Covenant brothers.[58]

Under the tribal system, Israel had no statehood, capital city, central government, or bureaucratic machinery.[59] During this time Israel did not engage in wars of aggression as a nation. There were certainly local disputes, but none of these were responsible for gaining territory for Israel, with the exception of Deborah's victory.[60] Should a dispute arise, the argument would be decided by the clans fighting it out since there was no central mediator.[61]

All this changed drastically at the end of the eleventh century with the rise of Philistine aggression.[62] Israel's decentralized system was simply unable to respond militarily to this outside threat. Its priesthood was killed or dispersed.[63] A prophet, Samuel, was mainly responsible for keeping the old traditions alive as he traveled throughout the clans stirring up fervor on behalf of Yahweh and the "holy war."[64] In this situation the question first arose: Should Israel elect a king?

There were many arguments in the Hebrew Bible as to whether or not there should be an Israelite king. The prophets were usually against and the priests favored this idea.[65] The early Hebrews had fought bitterly against kingship. Their God was a God of history, who brought them out of the land of Egypt. When Moses killed the Egyptian, his act of rebellion should have brought the local gods out in force. But, in fact, the reverse happened, confirming the Israelites' belief in Yahweh, who freed and who ruled them. Their God was more powerful than the local gods, and his favor could be maintained by obedience to his rules and regulations. The idea of electing a king seemed to show a lack of trust on their part, but now, in the face of outside aggression, the question took on great urgency.[66]

The Israelites were faced with a major challenge to their traditional social structure. They needed to find a form of political organization that would allow them to mobilize quickly in the event of war. This force would have to be one that transcended tribal loyalties and territories and was not dependent on immediate kinship ties.

This new ruler could not simply be an earthly "father," since then kinship would still have been the basis for social organization. The notion of "king," however, allowed the people to enter into a covenantal agreement with the king and rely on him, together with his priests, to adjudicate disputes. Justice then took on an abstract quality in that people began to relate to each other through the king rather than through tribal assemblies coming to agreement in the case of wrongdoing. More importantly, the king had the power to call his people to war.

This change in political organization could be accomplished only by a correspondingly dramatic reform of the religious practices and social organization of the people. There was no point in having a king if his mandates could be contradicted by allegiance to a particular tribal god or by internal power structures within a particular clan. In the polytheistic religions, social order was best maintained, not by the rule of a single king, but by the relationships that existed between members of the extended family, however complex and embittered these became at times. Now if Israel was to expand and prosper (and especially if it was to go to war), the importance of family or tribal allegiances had to be radically challenged. Political allegiance could not be owed simply to one's clan; nor could the people as a whole take the risk that some clans might be fighting one another at various times and would, therefore, refuse to fight together against a common enemy. Political loyalties had to be extended to include the whole people as represented by their king.

The political changes demanded by military considerations, and the theologies that accompanied these changes, would prove to be extremely problematic for any continuance of Serpent religions that were polytheistic. Sumerian religion, for instance, which was highly polytheistic,

perfectly reflected the Sumerian social structures since Sumer was organized on the basis of small city-states and it was believed, at least in its
initial stages, that political unification or domination by one particular
king would be contrary to the wishes of the gods.[67]

In polytheism, there was great freedom and fluidity in the worship of
particular gods. As with the later Catholic saints, people knew to which
gods to appeal for particular purposes, and no one god had power over
everything. Since human society followed the lead of the gods, having
many different gods resulted in antiauthoritarian forms of government.[68] Now Israel could not tolerate the polytheistic practices of the
old religion. Their God had to be much more abstract and not tied down
to localities or particular tribes. If Israel was to become a mighty nation,
it needed to be united under the worship of one God.

The early Hebrews were one of the first people to make the break
away from the polytheistic religions based on the cycle of nature to a
more abstract form of religion based upon historical experience. This
historically based religion, especially its history of their escape from slavery in Egypt, gave hope to the Israelites, during their many captivities
and oppressions, that life would not always be this way and that the power struggles that took place among the gods, so accurately reflecting
their own lives, would ultimately be resolved by a God with a profound
sense of justice and ethics who could be propitiated, not by means of cultic offerings, but by means of righteous behavior, particularly by adherence to those rules he had set down for his people.

This God would make the Israelites his "Chosen People." He gave
them the Promised Land, which they were entitled to keep on condition
that they obeyed the new set of abstract rules and regulations—the Ten
Commandments. The first of these commandments is highly significant:

Yahweh said, "I am about to make a covenant with you. In the presence of all
your people I shall work such wonders as have never been worked in any land or
in any nation. All the people round you will see what Yahweh can do, for what I
shall do through you will be awe-inspiring. . . . Take care you make no pact with
the inhabitants of the land you are about to enter, or this will prove a pitfall at
your very feet. You are to tear down their altars, smash their standingstones, cut
down their sacred poles. . . . *You shall bow down to no other god, for Yahweh's name is
the Jealous One; he is a jealous God* (emphasis added)."[69]

The change from polytheism to monotheism was to have far-reaching
implications. Polytheism was a direct threat to the religious and social
organization of Israel, and the Serpent personified that threat in the
Genesis story. That Adam and Eve took the fruit, therefore, symbolized
not only a petty act of disobedience but a possible sign that they preferred or were going back to the religion of the Serpent.[70]

We have seen how, in the earlier stories, the Serpent was responsible
for keeping human beings away from the sacred trees, but in the Genesis

story the Serpent actually encouraged the humans to partake of the fruit and to gain wisdom.

Whereas in the earlier stories death took on a tragic aspect, it was, nevertheless, integrated into the natural cycle of things. Now, not only does death come as a punishment for sin, but it comes at the hands of a woman—the Serpent/Eve. The "Mother of All the Living" becomes the carrier of death. Death had come into the world through sin, and evil was the result of the failure to keep to the terms of the Covenant with Yahweh.

The relationship between Yahweh and humankind took on a more legal character than had been the case with the polytheistic gods, particularly since Yahweh interacted directly with the Israelites.[71] Under Yahwism humankind was now made responsible for almost all evil in the world, rather than its being the responsibility of a jealous or inferior god. The Serpent religions had portrayed their gods as both good and evil, symbolizing the essential ambiguity and tragedy of existence. But the God of the Israelites, to be effective, could not be both good and evil. To earn the unquestioning allegiance of his followers, he had to represent pure goodness. That is not to say that evil did not befall the Israelites—their history was full of disasters. But in general (the Book of Job is an exception), the prophets and priests taught that evil was the result of human sin rather than divine caprice.

Wisdom and immortality would now come, not from observing the rhythms of the seasons and the beauty of nature, but from Yahweh alone, providing one kept to the terms of his Covenant. The terms of the Covenant, and indeed the will of God, would be interpreted by an elite body of religious functionaries. This perfectly suited the centralization of power taking place in the political realm, since now the people would have to rely on a centralized and increasingly hierarchical religious authority, especially in view of the fact that the religious and political fortunes of Israel were integrally connected.

Those religions that honored the Serpent, representing cyclical regeneration and polytheistic philosophies, had to be overthrown. What better way to do it than by making the Serpent the symbol of evil and, thereby, responsible for those disasters for which humankind, even with the wildest imagination, could hardly be held liable?

The Genesis story, as we have seen, reached its present form when these social upheavals were at their height. It has continued to serve as a warning of the consequences of the failure to obey God, no matter how seemingly pointless his commands.

MONOTHEISM

The religious consciousness of monotheism introduced into human religious history a profound dualism between God and the world, between good and evil, reason and passion, heaven and hell, God and the Devil, spirit and nature. The form this dualism took was to have profound implications for women's ability to officiate in future religious rites.

A monotheistic God destroyed the bisexual character of the old gods. Unlike the polytheistic gods, who created by rearranging the order of the material things, by giving birth themselves or by means of sexual union between the male and female gods, and who did not recognize dualist distinctions between body and spirit, this monotheistic God had the power to create alone without a sexual partner. Creation was, therefore, an act of *will* rather than one of fertility. Whatever God *willed* to be, came into existence. He was not at the mercy of passion, the caprices of womanhood, or mere sexuality.

Now that God did not belong to any clan or tribe, it was important to stress that God was above material or family interest, passion, or libido. In the creation stories, for instance, God created the whole world simply out of his mind by means of his Word. Reason and the "will of God" (as interpreted by the priests and prophets) became the whole point of existence, a theme found in the mythologies of many cultures.

Already in the polytheistic religions this process had begun with the appearance of the male gods. In the Babylonian creation myth, Marduk, in his efforts for supremacy, first slaughters the Goddess Tiamat and cuts her in half to create heaven and earth. His real test for kingship, however, comes when he is required to create "by word alone," that is to say, out of his mind.[72] Similarly, in Greek mythology, Zeus gives birth to Athena from his head. In Egyptian mythology the creator god is Ptah, who simply pronounced the "name of all things."[73] The stoic philosophers later went on to call creative reason *lógos spermatikós*.[74]

These religions devised sophisticated doctrines of rebirth in which women's mere biological birthing was not only superseded but seen to be a positive hindrance. Women's blood, or that which flowed through the veins of their sons, had now lost its power: rebirth, not birth, was important and would be the means of entry into the new social and religious life.

The religion of the Goddess had enhanced nature and helped it to fruition. God the Father, although occasionally helping nature along, was more interested in the development of the "spirit." Anything that hindered this development—nature, women, or sexuality—would be kept firmly under wraps.

Under polytheism, because the social order depended so much on the natural cycle of fertility, a great deal of energy must have been expended in religious ceremonies that kept the people in tune with the rhythms of the universe. The gods could be approached by both women and men. Originally there was very little conflict between lay and official priesthood,[75] and even when there was a distinction made between "high" religion and "folk" or domestic religion, the gods could still be approached in the temples by both sexes.

Women were revered since they held the divine principle of creativity within their own bodies. Spirituality belonged to all members of the clan, not merely to those specially chosen to perform rituals. Rituals had previously been performed communally as the people drew on the vital energies of the universe to support their needs. Humans felt themselves to be part of the cosmos. Inevitably as new centralized social structures arose, religious power began to take on an elite quality. The Goddess was no longer to be found in the bushes, trees, and holy wells. The male God, who functioned very much like the patriarchal father demanding obedience, was only accessible to certain members of the right sex who would undertake to "intercede" for the people. In turn, the people would no longer "participate" in the cosmos but submit to their divine Father or his representatives, who could be counted on to know his will at all times. In the new social order in Israel, Yahweh might indeed be above sexuality, but his representatives on earth would be firmly male.

Given these suppositions, it followed logically that, in the Jewish and Christian traditions, every effort would have to be made to overcome one's passionate nature. "Nature" was passionate and unpredictable and could undermine the relationship between God and man, based as it was on obedience. Passionate man would not be in control of his own will, let alone be able to communicate the "will of God" to his people. In consequence, anything that represented mere instinctive sexuality would be abhorrent to Yahweh and could not be tolerated in his temple. For men this would be a matter of abstaining from sexual activity for a prescribed number of days before the religious services. But what about women? How were women, caught up in the cycle of reproduction, to overcome what had now become a physical handicap? Their sexuality and creativity, far from the asset it had been in previous religious rites, was now a problem. At any one time a woman might be menstruating, be pregnant, or otherwise be unfit to enter the temple. She certainly could not participate or officiate in the rites.

These theological changes, taken together with the move from a tribal to a centralized society under a king, were to have profound consequences for the position of women, eventually succeeding in entirely abolishing any routes for female autonomous religious power. Although technically neither male nor female, God became in essence a male deity supporting the concerns of men in the emerging patriarchal order.

In the Book of Leviticus, women engaging in their natural bodily functions such as menstruation or pregnancy, were put on the same par with men who had discharges from their bodies (commonly lepers), and suffered similar ostracism. Even after the male role in paternity had been discovered and recognized, it was only the woman who had to be ritually separated and remain in seclusion after childbirth.[76] Furthermore, the birth of a female child made the mother even more unclean than the birth of a boy. After bearing a male child she was unclean for seven days, but after bearing a female, fourteen days. Similarly, her period of purification after a male child would be thirty-three days and double that for a female.[77]

Although there had been female prophets,[78] these women were strongest in a premonarchic Israel when charismatic forms of leadership were the norm.[79] As the religion of Yahweh grew in confidence, all the most important laws and Covenants were given to men such as Abraham and Moses. In the Ten Commandments, a wife was described as part of the property of the husband. Even where strong women are depicted, as for instance in the stories of Judith and Esther, only their beauty and sexuality guaranteed success over their enemies.[80]

In the polytheistic religions the gods interacted among themselves, and humans sought to curry favor with them, but the gods did not speak directly to humans. Now Yahweh began to communicate his intentions to *men* in the literal sense of the word. When the Israelites were about to receive the Covenant, according to the Bible,

Moses came down from the mountain to the people and bade them prepare themselves; and they washed their clothing. Then he said to the people, "Be ready for the third day; *do not go near any woman*" (emphasis added).

The Jerusalem Bible comments on this: "It is assumed that sexual relations make men unfit for sacred duties."[81] But it was not simply when hearing the word of God that men had to separate from women. At a time when the Israelites were preparing for war, David needed bread to feed his soldiers. Ahimlech the priest told him that he only had five consecrated loaves and the soldiers could eat them only if they had "kept themselves from women." David replied,

"Certainly women are forbidden to us, as always when I set off on a campaign. The soldiers' things are pure. Though this is a profane journey, they are certainly pure today as far as their things are concerned."[82]

Contact with women would weaken men's potency when engaging in their two most powerful activities—hearing the word of God or going to war. In this we can see a very clear connection between the development of a militaristic culture and the development of a new male identity independent of women or the world that women had represented.

The changes that Israel was experiencing had far-reaching consequences in other realms as the centralized state with its military ethos inexorably led to the overthrow of the matricentered system.[83] For instance, under the tribal and matrilineal system, the obligation to one's kin, and particularly the relationship between mother and child and among children of the same mother, was sacred. When a young couple married, the husband, like Adam, "left his father and mother and cleaved to his wife." But under patriarchy this marriage arrangement was destined to change, as matrifocal societies gave way to patrifocal and the future brides were taken from their homeland to that of their husband, ensuring that their children bore his name and that his goods would be passed on through the male line. The conflict engendered by this new social arrangement permeates the narratives of the Hebrew Bible.

We can see this theme in the story of the Levite and his "concubine." This is a very early story, but nevertheless, since it has come into the canon of Hebrew literature, it must be taken as representative of later values. In this story the woman left the Levite to go back to her father's house. We are not told why, but as the story progresses it is obvious that the woman was very unhappy with her marriage situation.

When the Levite came to fetch her back, his father-in-law greeted him joyfully: the integrity of the new political system must be upheld. The feelings of the nameless woman are not recorded. The Levite forced her back home and, passing through Gibeah among the Benjaminites, wanted to stay overnight. The Benjaminites refused to take them in, whereupon an old man from the Levite's part of the country invited them to stay with him. Later on the "men of Gibeah" came, demanding that the old man give them the Levite. The master of the house went out and said to them:

"No, my brothers; I implore you, do not commit this crime. This man has become my guest; do not commit such an infamy. Here is my daughter; she is a virgin; I will give her to you. Possess her, do what you please with her, but do not commit such an infamy against this man." But the men would not listen to him. So the Levite took his concubine and brought her out to them. They had intercourse with her and outraged her all night till morning; when dawn was breaking they let her go.[84]

The man's daughter, a virgin, was also dispensable. The woman made her way back to where her husband was staying but barely reached as far as the door. Next morning her husband found her there with her hand lying across the threshold. He told her to stand up since they had to continue on their journey, but the woman lay still, making no response. She had died of the injuries received during the gang-rape, her hand firmly on the threshold of the men's house in a gesture of accusation.

When the Levite realized that she was dead, he threw her across the back of his donkey and traveled homeward. He cut her body into twelve pieces and sent it around to the twelve tribes of Israel looking for retribution. The rest of the Israelites met and offered holocausts and communion sacrifices before Yahweh who told them to exact vengeance on the Benjaminites. They went ahead and "put all the males in the town to the sword." Then realizing that they might totally wipe out one of the twelve tribes of Israel, and also having decided not to give any of their own women to any remaining Benjaminites, they hit on another plan: Asking themselves which of their people had not come to this battle, they attacked Jabeshgilead and killed all present except for four hundred virgins, whom they turned over to the Benjaminite rapists. But then, as further evidence of their "compassion" for the Benjaminites, and as a guarantee that their tribe would not be blotted out, they put the finishing touches to their intrigues:

"But yet," they said, "there is Yahweh's feast which is held every year at Shiloh. . . . Place yourselves in ambush in the vineyards. Keep watch there, and when the daughters of Shiloh come out to dance in groups together, you too come out of the vineyards: seize a wife, each one of you, from the daughters of Shiloh and make for the land of Benjamin. If their fathers or brothers come to complain to you, we shall say to them, 'Forgive them because each one of them has taken a wife for himself, as men do in war. For if you had given them brides, you would have broken your oath, and so would have sinned.' " The Benjaminites did this, and from the dancers they had captured, they chose as many wives as there were men; then they set off, returned to their inheritance, rebuilt their towns and settled in them.[85]

And so the former rapists were given further license to kidnap the women of Shiloh in order to preserve the integrity of the oath. The war was fought to avenge the destruction of the property of the Levite (he had only consented to her mere rape, perhaps in punishment for her obstinance). Compassion was for the men of the Benjaminites who would be left without issue, not for the unfortunate woman, the virgins of Jabeshgilead, or the women of Shiloh. And as contemporary biblical commentators note, "not the lust but the violation of the sacred duty of hospitality is considered the more serious."[86] Hospitality, in this instance, clearly refers to the social arrangements made between men to which women as a whole were subservient.

This attitude to women is clearly illustrated by two stories with similar themes and with very different outcomes, the story of Jephthah and his daughter, and the story of Abraham and Isaac.

Jephthah was engaged in a war with the Ammonites and was doing very badly until he made a vow to Yahweh:

"If you deliver the Ammonites into my hands, then the first person to meet me from the door of my house when I return in triumph from fighting the Ammonites shall belong to Yahweh, and I will offer him up as a holocaust."[87]

Jephthah marched against the Ammonites, and "Yahweh delivered them into his power." But now as Jephthah returned home "triumphant," who should come out to meet him but his beloved daughter, his only child, who was dancing to the sound of timbrels. When he saw her, he exclaimed:

"Oh my daughter, what sorrow you are bringing me! Must it be you, the cause of my ill-fortune! I have given a promise to Yahweh, and I cannot unsay what I have said."

Note here that his daughter is not dignified by being given a name, and

Jephthah actually blames *her* for bringing misfortune onto *him*. His daughter replied:

"My father, you have given a promise to Yahweh; treat me as the vow you took binds you to, since Yahweh has given you vengeance on your enemies the Ammonites." Then she said to her father. "Grant me one request. Let me be free for two months. I shall go and wander in the mountains, and with my companions bewail my virginity."[88]

With her companions she went off into the mountains for two months where she "mourned her virginity." In the meantime, it apparently did not occur to Jephthah to wrestle or bargain with Yahweh again, nor did Yahweh intervene, because when she returned Jephthah "treated her as the vow that he had uttered bound him." The narrative finishes:

She had never known a man. From this comes this custom in Israel for the daughters of Israel to leave home every year and to lament the daughter of Jephthah the Gileadite for four days every year.[89]

As an earthly father, he had sacrificed his daughter to God the Father, an act that brought him earthly success. The implication is that Yahweh must have been pleased, because after this sacrifice Jephthah went on to rule Israel for six years. There is no mention of any retribution for his act, and he is apparently rewarded for his contribution toward getting religious land from the Ammonites.

Abraham, too, was asked to make the ultimate sacrifice when commanded by Yahweh to sacrifice his son Isaac: "Take now your only son, your only one whom you love, Isaac, and walk yourself to the land of Moriah and offer him there as a burnt offering on one of the mountains which I shall tell you." Abraham went to great pains to build the altar where his son would be sacrificed, but at the point where Abraham took his knife and was about to sacrifice Isaac, the angel of Yahweh appeared and told him not to slay his son: "For now I know that you are an Elohim fearing man, and you have not withheld your only one from me."[90] Tradition has it that when Sarah heard the news of what Abraham had proposed to do, she fell dead.[91] Her death was the symbolic death of matricentered ethics where the ties to one's children were an extension of one's own lifeblood. In the new patriarchal faith being born, immortality would finally be located in the sacred sphere, in obedience to God the Father, rather than in the Chain of Being between parent and child.

The ultimate test of patriarchal ethics was obedience to the point of death, or the willingness to sacrifice even one's own son in response to the demands of Yahweh, no matter how arbitrary. Nevertheless, the prime symbol of the agreement between Yahweh and Abraham was the seed of Abraham, as Yahweh guaranteed him "seed forever" in return for keeping to the terms of the covenant.[92]

A clear theme emerging from all these stories is that obedience to the word of God, either directly expressed to humans or by means of his commandments, is more important than human life itself, especially the life of mere women. In fact, the word of God can really only be heard when men have separated themselves from women. Obedience to the terms of the Covenant, freedom from passion or instinctive sexuality, allegiance to one God, and the great march into linear rather than cyclical history are the most important elements of the new faith. Obedience to Yahweh would be rewarded with "seed forever," a vivid reassurance to men of their future immortality through their children, an assurance made conditional upon the fathers' willingness to sacrifice their offspring to the ultimate Father of all, whether on the battlefield or the altar.

Although this faith was born in the soil of the land of Israel, the main elements of its theology were shared by many of the surrounding peoples as they passed from a matricentered society based on the kinship system to a patriarchal social structure. Patriarchy was a product of the new cities and depended for its existence on abstract justice represented by the king and administered by his representatives. Worship of the monotheistic God, Yahweh, to whom the king was accountable, ensured that no minor deity could be called upon to challenge the king's authority. The sacred ties that bound the people together through their common mothers were now being superseded by a social organization based on the king with the power to summon the people to war.

The Hebrew Bible gave to this great social upheaval a prophetic, poetic, and written tradition whereby its central themes could be spread throughout the world. But there was one main problem: one could not become a Jew simply by conversion into the faith. To become a Jew one had to be born of a Jewish mother. This was clearly a remnant of the old matricentered culture from which Judaism originated and was to provide a fatal obstacle to Judaism becoming the dominant religion of the Western world. Judaism was still, therefore, to some extent, a tribal religion.

The sacrifice of women was now taken for granted, but Abraham had been spared the sacrifice of his son. It would remain for a new faith, one that completely abandoned biological ties, and one that committed the ultimate transgression, to take on the task of unifying the whole world under the worship of one God. This new faith, fostered in the land of Israel, would become known as Christianity. The sacredness of birth would be replaced by a form of power that took on meaning only after death. The proprietors of this power, the Christian priests, would be effective only insofar as they were not at the mercy of their biology and resisted the temptations of women. God the Father was quite distinct from the Mother Goddess.

The body of a woman, the spouse of the Levite, had been broken and distributed among the twelve tribes of Israel: the woman herself passed into oblivion. But the next time a body would be broken and passed out among the Twelve, the consequences would be radically different.

CHAPTER 2

Crushing the Serpent

The End of Matricentered Ireland and the Curse of the Goddess Macha

And when he asked the Chief Priest who should be the first to profane the altars and shrines of the idols, together with the enclosures that surrounded them, Coifi replied: "I will do this myself; for now that the true God has granted me knowledge, who more suitably than I can set a public example and destroy the idols that I worshipped in ignorance?" So he formally renounced his empty superstitions and asked the king to give him arms and a stallion—*for hitherto it had not been lawful for the Chief Priest to carry arms or to ride anything but a mare*—and, thus equipped, he set out to destroy the idols (emphasis added).

VENERABLE BEDE

Crushing the serpent in the Hebrew Bible was a mythological act of cosmic significance, an event destined to reverberate throughout the world. Immortality, the goal that had long eluded humankind, now became a possibility, but only for those who supported the emerging political and religious orders. Morality and mortality were now intimately connected. Centralized hierarchies would become the norm in the political and religious spheres, dictating the conditions for the achievement of immortality. The paradoxical and tragic view of human existence, where both life and death were intrinsic parts of the same process, lay shattered.

In pre-Christian Ireland the tragic, paradoxical, and ambivalent attitude toward life is symbolized by several kingship stories. In pre-Christian rites, of which we have little or no direct documentation, the king, as kings did throughout the ancient world, participated in an annual rite of sacred marriage. The king "mated" with the Goddess, ensuring fertility for the land and for its people in the year to come.

In the documents that have come down to us, written under the influence of early forms of patriarchal consciousness, this theme comes through clearly. But in patriarchal mythology, the future king had to find the Goddess, not in her form as the main source of creativity, but in the form of a hideous old hag, whom he would then have to embrace. The "old hag" then miraculously would turn into a young and beautiful woman, symbolizing the land of Ireland. Fertility would be restored, justice would reign, and the rightful king, having proved his wisdom, would be installed.[1]

In this version of the myth the king rather than the Goddess became the main agent of fertility. Nevertheless, there are remnants of the matricentered religious worldview. The future king was not the brash, brazen hero who obtained his power through conquest. Indeed, the king was expected not to seek for individual glory but to manifest all the qualities of wisdom necessary to take care of the welfare of his kingdom.[2] Many men shirked the ordeal, but the one who succeeded to the kingship was not the one who put his personal satisfaction or gratification first but the one who was wise enough to embrace symbolically the ambiguity and tragic consequences of the human condition. In an early story, even the Ulster hero, Cúchulainn, actually kissed a dragon who then turned into a beautiful maiden.[3]

As the patriarchal revolution progressed, however, even this form of sacred marriage would change. Ambiguity did not lend itself easily to the new patriarchal structures of power, particularly in those societies held together by the military might of the king's warriors. The natural tragedy of cyclical life and death, symbolized by the Goddess, would no longer be tolerated but would be eliminated forever by the hero's search for immortality.

Symbols of the Goddess would be systematically co-opted and later destroyed, to be replaced by symbols of her destruction. Cúchulainn is represented killing the Serpent in several myths and images.[4] St. George kills the dragon, and in Ireland St. Patrick is credited with banishing the reptiles.[5] The Goddess was one of the hardest images for Western culture to eradicate, and it can be said that only by killing the Serpent, severing the natural cycle of life and death, could dualistic patriarchal culture come into being.[6]

Killing the Goddess as such was not what was important. More critical was the destruction of those symbolic, political, familial, and religious sources of power traditionally associated with women. This would be the precondition for the new society to take root, a society where men would take it upon themselves to give birth; where women would be firmly under control; and where kings, warriors, and priests would develop elite forms of power, effectively abolishing or superseding the power structures of the clan systems.

Crushing the Serpent/Goddess, therefore, symbolized the overthrow of those societies, together with their religions, which were matricentered. In the Hebrew Bible we have seen that the overthrow of matricentered society came about in the move from a tribal to a centralized society when Israel mobilized its armies under a king. Similar forces were at work in Ireland, although the social and political conditions differed in many respects.[7]

In Irish mythology the salmon rather than the Serpent was the main symbol of immortality and wisdom, although the Serpent did appear in the sagas compiled during the Christian period.[8] With the introduction of Christianity, the Serpent, which still retained its multivalent symbolism, began to appear on Irish artwork, adorning such objects as bishop's croziers, Patrick's Bell, and Celtic manuscripts.[9]

Even before the serpent symbol arrived in Ireland, the essence of serpent or goddess religions was to be found. Just as in the Sumerian religion we saw that the idea of divinity could not be represented by any one divine image, so too in Ireland there were many gods and goddesses, all with their own particular functions to fulfill. The Irish, realizing that anything less failed to do justice to the complexity of divinity, gave their goddesses a triple form.[10] In some cases three wise women appeared at the birth of children.[11]

The tragic and cyclical view of life is expressed perfectly in the image of the Triple Spiral found on pre-Christian Irish monuments. At Newgrange, near Drogheda, in the ancient Boyne Valley, the Triple Spiral is carved on the most sacred stones of this ancient structure. The Triple Spiral represented the cycle of birth, life, and death; the Maiden, Mother, and Crone; the never-ending cycle of infinitude.[12] As the *Song of Amergin* expressed it:

> I am the womb: *of every holt,*
> I am the blaze: *on every hill,*
> I am the queen: *of every hive,*
> I am the shield: *for every head,*
> I am the tomb: *of every hope.*[13]

To understand the theology of the ancients, try to imagine for a moment the wonderful mystery of life confronting Ireland's earliest ancestors: the stars moved across the heavens, the moon waxed and waned, the sun rose across the sky; every so often violent thunderstorms would shake the earth or snowflakes cover the entire land. Rivers would overflow their banks or dry up in the warm seasons. In certain times, drought would fall and the parched earth would scream for rain. There was an essential wonder to life and an awareness that all things were connected. The earth might be dry, but soon falling rain would sprout seeds, bring the flowers to bud, and renew the soil. Fruit and vegetables would once again be plentiful and life could survive for one more year.

Within their very midst was another mystery. In the normal course of events someone who was seriously wounded, by a marauding animal for instance, was sure to die, but yet women periodically bled and did not die. Indeed women's bleeding in childbirth gave rise to the greatest enigma of all: that of life itself.

Since the source of life was so integrally associated with women, it would seem to follow that the origins of life were female. At times of joy or in moments of pain humans would turn to the Goddess, who was honored in her many guises.

Goddess images found throughout the ancient world and in many existing cultures represent her, not only by images of reproduction, but also with cultural creativity in all its aspects. The arts of smithwork, healing, poetry, writing, cooking, and teaching are among her talents, and in those societies that began to adopt patriarchal forms of organization, the Goddess eventually became associated with warfare and the martial arts.[14]

Goddesses permeated Ireland. Mountains, rivers, valleys, wells, all testified to her presence. Around the eleventh century, Ireland became known predominantly as Éire, a name derived from the Goddess Ériu, one of the Triple Goddesses: Ériu, Banba, and Fotla. In a famous story of one of the Celtic invasions, Ériu makes it clear that anyone wishing to enter Ireland would have to revere the goddesses if they wished to prosper and be fruitful.[15] Ireland was also often called "the island of Banba of the women."[16]

Some of the names for Ireland derive from an actual tradition of female ruling power. For instance, the Irish were also known as the Scots or Scoti. One tradition surrounding the origin of the name Scots is that it is derived from Scota, who, according to ancient sources, was the daughter of Pharaoh Nectonebus, king of Egypt. Her sons, the Milesian invaders, called the land after her, and for some time she is actually said to have ruled the land, together with her son Gadelas, "with great wisdom and unanimity."[17]

Rivers were a crucial source of life throughout the Celtic world. They were a source of food, of water, of transportation, and even provided the earliest forms of maps since they were constant points of reference for those who ventured beyond the clan boundaries. Rivers had an even more important function: they were the womb openings of the Great Mother, the symbol of life, and often bore her name in different forms.

Sacred temples were often situated near these sources of life, and this was certainly the case with *Brugh na Bóinne*, the present day Newgrange, in the Boyne Valley.[18] The river Boyne holds the secrets of early Irish life deep within her. The oldest form of this name is Bóand, and the river took its name from the Goddess Bóand,[19] who had many associations with cow symbolism.[20] The association of goddesses with cows is widespread; the Goddess is often imaged as the celestial cow who nourished the earth with her milk.[21]

Throughout Europe, rivers were called after the Goddess. For instance, the various Avons are called after Abnoba, goddess of the sources of the Danube. The Irish rivers, the Liffey and the Shannon, took their names from the goddesses Life and Sinnann.[22] The Goddess Brigit gave her name to the rivers Brigit, Braint, and Brent in Ireland, Wales, and England respectively.[23]

Given the symbolic and practical importance of women in early society it is not surprising to find that one's relationship to the mother was the crucial factor in determining one's status. Relationships between children of the same mother, or even children of the same sisters, were held to be sacred, and siblings were under sacred trust never to fight against one another.[24]

This relationship was not anything like the nuclear family we know today. All children born to a particular tribe were the responsibility of the whole tribe and not just that of the parent who had brought them into existence. This is not to say that men had no role to play in the upbringing of children, but the mother's brother, rather than her husband, was largely responsible for the children's well-being and for making sure that they received whatever tribal goods or positions were their due. In this way the men could be sure that the children they were taking care of were related to them by blood. This was a particularly ideal situation where property was minimally involved, since the woman would not be sleeping only with one man and any child born to her would automatically have a clan to which to relate. Illegitimacy was not a problem; in fact, the idea that a child might not be accepted socially would have been abhorrent to our earliest ancestors.[25]

Descent was sometimes traced through the mother. It would be impossible here to provide all the evidence of matrilineal descent in the Irish sources, but the following are representative samples. The Venerable Bede in the eighth century, when writing about the Picts of Scotland, maintained that they traced their descent through the female line and that was because, when they left Ireland, the Irish gave them wives on condition that lineage continue to be traced through the female line.[26]

Throughout Irish mythology, relationships to the mother are emphasized. The Tuatha Dé Danaan were "children of the Goddess Dana." Even famous heroes were called after their mothers; Buanann was "mother of heroes," while the Goddess Anu was known as "mother of the gods."[27] In some cases men were even called, not alone after their mothers, but after their wives.[28]

It is important to point out that, although women were held with great respect, matrifocal societies were not matriarchal, that is, societies where all power rested with the women. A matricentered society was not simply the reverse of patriarchy where public power does indeed rest with men.[29] In a matricentered society descent was sometimes traced through the female, and sometimes through the male, but under patriarchy most forms of descent through women were abolished.[30]

In early Irish Christian literature the relationship to one's mother is of crucial importance. In the Irish *Book of the Taking,* in describing how God made the earth, the author claims that God, "gave the bailiffry of Earth to Adam (and to Eve, with her progeny)."[31] The author of this text goes on to describe the disobedience of Adam and Eve and their expulsion from Paradise. Thereafter he refers to the "progeny of Adam" rather than that of Eve. The writer may have seen a connection between Original Sin and the breakup of respect for one's kin.[32]

Kin relationships also form one of the themes of the early Irish poems, *Poems of Blathmac,* which are addressed to the Virgin Mary. The writer, talking about the Crucifixion of Jesus, exclaims, "It was a hideous deed . . . that was done to him: that his very mother-kin should crucify the man who had come to save them."[33] Later, in the same poem the author cries, "Of shameless countenance and wolf-like were the men who perpetrated that kin-slaying; since his mother was of them it was treachery towards a true kinsman. . . . Jesus, darling son of the virgin, achieved a deed of pure victory; from him the salvation of the human race which great perversity encompassed."[34]

In this brief summary we can picture a society where women were highly honored, where female symbolism formed the most sacred images in the religious cosmos, and where the relationships with women through motherhood were the central elements of the social fabric.[35] It was a society where men, even where they might have known about their role in begetting children, were not their primary caretakers and had little power over their own children. The society was held together by common allegiance to the customs of the tribe loosely organized around the traditions of the Goddess.[36] When the men married, they moved out of their own family circles and into those of the women. Like the biblical Adam, "the man left his father and mother and cleaved to his wife."

DEVELOPMENT OF PATRIARCHY

Ireland had been invaded in pre-Christian times by successive generations of Celts from Northern Europe, a patriarchal people who traced their ancestry through their fathers. The Celts had exhausted their own territories and took to the seas seeking new land and resources in the centuries just before the introduction of Christianity to Ireland. A warrior people, they constantly risked violent death at the hands of those resisting invasion. Not surprisingly, the Celts thrived on heroic sagas where the violent death of the male in battle assured him of future immortality.

The Northern Celts, although they made great inroads into Irish culture, lacked any central political organization. Their warrior escapades were sporadic and undisciplined, and it was difficult for them to capitalize fully on their conquests. They had no recognizable religion or social structure and made little impression on the Irish, who also were not centrally organized.

All of this would change with the arrival of Christianity, which was destined to have a profound effect on the religious and social consciousness of the Irish. The Christian scribes played a major role in establishing the patriarchal revolution; their first task was to launch a major propaganda war against the symbols of the old religion.

We can see how the Irish viewed the Serpent/Goddess in one of their versions of the Adam and Eve story. The serpent is not really responsible for tempting Adam and Eve and cheating them of immortality. Instead, the *Devil* (an entirely separate creature) came to the serpent, crawled inside its belly, and went off to persuade the couple to eat the fruit. The serpent asked the Devil what reward it could expect for providing this service and the Devil replied: "Our union according to habit, to fury, let it be continuously mentioned."[37] In other words, the serpent became identical with the Devil as a result of temptation, rather than being the cause of temptation. The serpent, addressed as a "female feminine creature," suffered from the Fall as much as Adam and Eve.[38]

However, such benevolence toward the Serpent/Goddess was not destined to last much longer. As Christianity consolidated itself, in the great monastic houses the scribes busied themselves composing satires ridiculing the ancient goddesses, often using themes derived from Greek or Roman classical sources and in some cases elaborating upon existing folktales so that those tales, initially complimentary to women, eventually showed their downfall. We can see this process at work in the *Dindshenchas*, the stories of how places throughout Ireland got their names.

"Naming" itself would appear to have been a form of conquest. All the most important ancient festivals and market places (Oenach Tailten, Oenach Carmain, Oenach Macha, Oenach Culi, and Oenach Teite) derived their names from either the gang-rape, death, or overthrow of the goddesses. For instance, the Goddess Tlachtga was gang-raped by the three sons of Simon Magus, to whom she and her father had gone to "learn the world's magic." She bore three sons by the three different fathers at a single birth and died in the attempt. However, according to legend, "as long as the names of her sons shall be held in honour throughout Banba (this is a true saying to spread abroad) there comes no ruin to her men."[39]

Tlachtga's status as a goddess ended when men violated her control over her own fertility by means of a gang-rape. But even more significantly, her actual death took place in the act of giving birth to three famous warriors. Clearly the warrior culture had triumphed over her, and thereafter the warrior assemblies were held on the eve of *Samhain*, the November Celtic festival, at the fortress that bore her name.

Significantly, one of the features of the gathering would be the burning of the *torc-tened* (fire-boar) or *torc-caille* (forest-boar). The boar was one of the most sacred symbols of the Goddess, and a recent explanation as to why the fire was lit at *Samhain* is to "burn the witches."[40]

Likewise in the stories of how the rivers Liffey, Shannon, and Boyne got their names, the goddesses are undermined, being punished for their pride, haughtiness, or use of magic.[41] Traces of the goddesses are usually to be found only in stories describing their overthrow or subjecting them to ridicule. But there is one story where the true issues at stake come out very clearly: "The Curse of the Goddess Macha."

THE CURSE OF MACHA

The Goddess Macha was one of the most important goddesses in ancient Ireland. She gave her name to the present day Armagh, *Ard Macha*, and to the ancient forts of Ulster, *Emhain Mhacha*. An image of Macha is preserved in Armagh Cathedral to this day. At least four different accounts are given as to how the name Macha was bestowed upon these ancient sites. Studying these stories enables us to see the various transitions in status that the goddesses underwent in the course of time. The story of the overthrow of Macha could be described as *the* foundation myth of Irish patriarchal culture: the story of the Irish "Fall."

The first of these stories is that Macha was the wife of Nemed, son of Agnoman, one of the earliest Irish invaders. Macha was the name of the twelfth plain that Nemed cleared, and, according to the story, Nemed bestowed the plain upon his wife so that it might bear her name. Macha had died tragically, her heart "broke within her," when in a vision she had seen the forthcoming destruction caused by the *Táin Bó Cuailnge*, the "Cattle-Raid of Cooley," Ireland's equivalent to the Greek heroic warrior epics.[42] This story, although it links Macha with very ancient Irish history, is not the most revealing source of her early significance and is probably not the earliest story, since her importance is gained through her husband.[43]

The second, more colorful story indicates a more ancient source. There were three Ulster kings who agreed that they each should be seven years in the kingship. As guarantees of this agreement, they appointed seven Druids, seven poets, and seven captains. Three conditions were laid down as proof of the justice of each reign. Should any of these conditions fail to be met, the reigning king would be overthrown: the mast (crops) should appear faithfully every year; there should be no failure of dyestuff (dyeing was a woman's art); and no woman should die in childbirth. The proof of the justice of their reign would be that those traditional areas of women's creativity should prosper.

Things went well until one of them, Aed the Red, died. Aed left only one daughter, Macha of the Ruddy Hair, who demanded that she take her father's place in the succession. The other two kings refused to let this happen on the grounds that they would not surrender the kingship to a woman, so Macha fought and beat them. After seven years she then refused to give up the kingship because she had won the kingship in a battle rather than through the original agreement. Since they had broken the agreement, she argued, it no longer had validity. The sons of the second king, Dithorba, who had been killed in the first battle, fought with her again. Again she triumphed and banished them into the Connaught deserts. At this point she took the third king, Cimbaeth, to be her husband and to lead her armies.

Macha still was not satisfied. After her marriage she went off in search of Dithorba's sons in the form of a lepress, having rubbed rye dough and red bog-stuff all over herself. She found the men in the woods, whereupon one of them said: "Beautiful is the hag's eye! Let us lie with her." Macha let him carry her off to the woods. Once there she overcame him and bound him up. Then she went back to the men around the fire, who asked where their brother was. "He is ashamed to come to you after lying with a lepress," she told them. The men declared that this was no shame, and each in turn carried her off and was tied up by Macha. She then took them with her to Ulster.

Upon reaching Ulster, the Ulstermen wanted to kill the captives, but Macha had better ideas: " 'Nay,' she said, 'since it would be for me a violation of a prince's truth. But let them slave in slavery, and dig a *rath* [ring-fort] around me, so that it may be Ulster's chief city for ever.' Then she marked out the fortress with her brooch (*eó*) of gold that was at her neck (*muin*). Hence, Emuin . . . the *Eó* that was at Macha's *muin*."[44]

In this story we can see that not only would Macha not tolerate discrimination against women in the matter of political leadership, but also in choosing her husband Cimbaeth she was clearly taking the initiative in sexual relations. In addition, she rejected killing for its own sake and preferred nonviolent (and purposeful) forms of punishment.

The third account of how Armagh got its name brings us even closer to her true identity:

And men say that she was Grían Banchure, "the Sun of Womanfolk," daughter of Mider of Brí Léith. And after this she died, and her tomb was raised on Ard Macha, and her lamentation was made, and her gravestone was planted. Whence *Ard Machae*, "Macha's Height."[45]

Macha may originally have been a sun goddess, and one of the common images of the sun goddess was that of a horse.[46] The horse was a particularly fitting symbol for the sun, since the sun traveled the sky at great speed and the horse was the fastest animal then known. Macha was, therefore, the Ulster Epona, the horse goddess. It is in this context that we can begin to see the significance of the fourth story of how Macha stamped her name eternally on this Ulster city.

The story is usually called *The Debility of the Ulstermen* and is part of the preamble to Ireland's epic saga the *Táin*. The story begins with a rich man, Crunnchua mac Agnoman. His wife had died, and he was very lonely until one day a stately young woman came to him. She sat down by the hearth of the fire, stirring the embers without saying a word to anyone. Later she milked the cow and baked bread, still without speaking. In all her actions, however, she was careful to "turn right" following the direction of the sun; a clue as to her identity. When night fell, she crept into Crunnchu's bed and made love to him.

Everything went well for a time, and we are told that "his handsome appearance was delightful to her." His wealth increased, and he enjoyed prosperity in every respect, but trouble was soon to follow. The annual assembly of the Ulstermen was due to start in the near future and Crunnchu wanted to attend. Macha pleaded with him to stay at home, since his going to the assembly could only cause trouble for her. Crunnchu insisted, and finally Macha permitted him to go only after he had promised not to speak a word to anyone of their union, since only harm could come of that. Crunnchu duly promised and set off.

This annual assembly was a great occasion, and people came from all over Ireland. One of the main events was the horse racing competition. Although many competed, the horses belonging to the king and queen defeated all before them. At the end of the games everyone assembled to praise the monarchs. The people were heard to say, "Never before have two such horses been seen at the festival as these two horses of the king: in all Ireland there is not a swifter pair." Hearing this, Crunnchu could not resist. He cried out to the assembled people, "My wife runs quicker than these two horses." Furious, the king ordered him to be tied up until his wife could be brought to the contest to race against his horses.

Messengers were sent out to Macha, telling her to come urgently to the games. Macha was reluctant to go as she was pregnant and about to deliver. But upon being told that her husband would otherwise be killed, she agreed and set forth. When she arrived, they told her that she must race against two horses of the king. Hearing this she grew pale and turned to the assembled people with a wrenching plea that would echo in Ireland down the centuries: "Help me," she cried to the bystanders, "*for a mother bore each one of you*. Give me, O King, but a short delay, until I am delivered (emphasis added)."

Macha appealed to those assembled, not on the basis of an abstract system of ethics or for mercy: she appealed to them on the basis of their relationship to their mothers: "A mother bore each one of you." Childbirth was a supremely sacred activity, and the needs of a pregnant woman had hitherto overruled the demands of any egotistical king. But the king refused to delay the race, impatient as he was to demonstrate his own superiority. Finally, Macha threatened that a severe curse would fall upon Ulster. "What is your name?" asked the king, and Macha replied in ominous tones: "My name and the name of that which I shall bear will forever cleave to the place of this assembly. I am Macha, daughter of Sainreth mac in Botha (Strange son of Ocean)."

The horses were brought up and the race began. Macha won the race easily and before the king's horses had even reached the winning post, she gave birth to twins, a son and a daughter who gave their names to *Emhain Mhacha* (the Twins of Macha). Suddenly, all the men assembled were seized with weakness and "had no more strength than a woman in her pain," for at the moment of her tragic victory Macha pronounced a curse on the men of Ulster:

From this hour the ignominy that you have inflicted upon me will redound to the shame of each one of you. When a time of oppression falls upon you, each one of you who dwells in this province will be overcome with weakness, as the weakness of a woman in child-birth, and this will remain upon you for five days and four nights; to the ninth generation it shall be so.[47]

The "Pangs of the Men of Ulster," as Macha's curse was called, was said to affect all the men of Ulster but excluded women and children.

There are various interpretations as to what the curse of the Ulstermen actually meant. Some interpret it as a simple taboo against indulging in warfare at particular times, especially during the holiday period of the Ulster games.[48] There is a long tradition that interprets the "Pangs of the Men of Ulster" as a form of *couvade*, that is to say, a practice whereby men imitate the pains of childbirth during their period of initiation into warrior status.[49] A further interpretation is that in this initiatory period men, by imitating the pains of childbirth, hoped to draw on the help of the Mother Goddess as they went forth in their warrior bands. Apparently, they believed that if they imitated the movements of a woman in labor, the Goddess could be persuaded to give them the same help as she gave to women in childbirth.[50]

As we can see from these conflicting theories, there is no agreement among Celtic scholars as to what this story actually means. Like all great myths there is probably a wealth of meaning in the story, and any one interpretation does not exhaust its richness. In that spirit, we put forward another interpretation, one that draws on elements of all of the previous theories and helps to explain the radical change in status that the Goddess in Ireland went through with the rise of the patriarchal warrior cult.

In one of the stories about Macha, the kings had to provide three sureties as proof of the justice of their reign: that no woman should die in childbirth, that there should be no failure of dyestuff, and that mast should grow plentifully every year. *Mast* was a general term for food, but it could also mean the nuts and acorns that fed the animals sacred to the Goddess, the deer and the boar.[51] Dyeing was also a woman's art, and there are stories in which it was believed that if a man should come into the area where dyeing was taking place the dyes would not take effect.[52] The king's sureties in the early stages of kingship were intimately related to the needs and concerns of women, and unless the king could be seen to take care of the cultural and fertility needs of the clan, symbolized by these women's activities, he would be overthrown. However, when next we come across the "taboos of the kings of Ulster" there is no mention of childbirth, dyeing, or the fertility of the crops.[53]

When the king forced Macha to take part in a race just as she was about to deliver, it would seem that he violated the conditions of his kingship. It was an unjust request that would rebound back on his reputation for justice, and this unjust request was bound to be punished. He also forced Macha to give birth in a public place. The implication from the story would seem to be that Macha died in the act of giving birth, but this would be the least of the offenses: childbirth was a sacred occasion, and, indeed, some of the earliest religious centers were those in which women gave birth. For men to look upon the act of giving birth would be sacrilege of the highest order and in this case a sacrilege that also wrested power from the Goddess by exposing her ultimate act of creativity to the world.

Forcing Macha to give birth publicly was to force her to hand over her secrets to the watching bystanders. Thereafter, by imitating her movements in childbirth and by finding ways to give birth themselves, men could call upon the help of the Goddess in their warrior pursuits, thus bringing her sacred power to bear upon their enterprises. They would imitate the Goddess through the hysterical pregnancies, birth mimes, and physical mutilations that are performed in the initiation rites of young men.[54]

There are numerous parallels throughout the ancient world for this interpretation. Many patriarchal rites celebrate the drama of the mother's death and the seizing of her power.[55] Some scholars hold that the foundation of patriarchal culture itself is the killing of the mother (matricide) rather than the killing of the father as Freud argued.[56]

The Macha story had even more far-reaching implications. Not only would men imitate Macha in her act of giving birth: birth and fertility themselves were being redefined to suit the needs of the warrior society. The heads of those taken in battle by the Celtic warriors came to be known as the "masts of Macha," as though Macha delighted in making a head collection just as she had once delighted in providing fruits and grains for her hungry people. This view of Macha is in sharp contrast with her role in those stories where she appears as a character in her own right. For instance, as wife of Nemed, she died of heartbreak when she foresaw the destruction that would come in the *Táin Bó Cuailnge* (The Cattle Raid of Cooley).[57] In the second story, where she defeated the opposition in her insistence that women, too, could be political leaders, she had no interest in executing her captives but put them to work at the fruitful task of building her fort. In the third story, where she curses the men of Ulster and gives them her "pangs," once again, she had no wish to go into competition and, indeed, cursed the men for forcing her to do so since this was the only way she could save the life of her husband. In these actions she is clearly anxious to save life rather than take it need-lessly, and yet she has become known as one of the bloodiest women in Celtic mythology: a war goddess.

Thus we can see a steady and ominous change taking place in the im-age and activities of Macha. In the stories where Macha is most active in her own right as the Mother Goddess, she appears as Grían, the "Sun of Womanfolk,"[58] or "bright Grían and pure Macha."[59] When she next ap-pears as wife of Nemed, she stands by helplessly while he clears the plains and is powerless to prevent the carnage that she foresees in the coming *Táin*.[60] Finally, Macha has become part of the trio of "war goddesses": Macha, Badb, and Morrígan. In this capacity she is the daughter of Del-baeth, son of Neid.[61] Her status has declined from Mother Goddess to consort to daughter. It is tempting to speculate that she became a war goddess only when she had been displaced from her previous position of power and importance. The society in which Macha had flourished had been overthrown, and now her best efforts were directed toward under-mining the activities of the warriors.[62]

The idea of a "war goddess" is itself an interesting reflection of the distorted perspective of patriarchal scholarship.[63] Scholars are agreed that the so-called goddesses of war do not "themselves participate in bat-tle." Instead they usually try to undermine the male armies, to demoral-ize them or otherwise trick them into fulfilling their will. In some cases they will even confuse the armies into killing their own people rather than inflicting hurt on the opposition. Unlike the male gods who delight in the description of their weapons, the "war goddesses" use magical means to undermine the armies: weapons are not their province.[64]

The symbols of the Goddess were likewise opposed to battle. The blackbird of the "Nuns of Tuam" (probably priestesses of the Goddess) eased the pain of warrior wounds and those of pregnant women.[65] The milk from the sacred cow acted as an antidote to the poison of weapons. Rather than being called "war goddesses," they might more properly have been known as "those responsible for turning back the streams of war," a title given to the early Irish abbesses of Kildare.[66]

Macha's transition from Mother Goddess to war goddess reflects the new concerns of patriarchal consciousness. We saw how the Triple God-dess often appeared in abstract in the form of a Triple Spiral. The triple male gods, in contrast, are usually depicted as three-faced heads.[67] The head, rather than the body, was now the location of creativity. The "masts of Macha," the severed heads of warriors slain in battle, indicate the increased importance given to the "word" over against "fertility," a trend also in the Genesis stories. The warriors, who developed the head cult, took possession of the heads of those whom they conquered, believ-ing that they were, thereby, controlling the spirit of the person since the head symbolized the "very essence of being."[68] The "masts of Ma-cha," which previously meant the nuts fed to the sacred pigs, are now

"*Machae's* mast-feeding," i.e., the "heads of men that have been slaughtered."[69] The foods sacred to the Goddess would no longer be enough for the warrior: divine food would be the conquered heads he had taken in war.

At night, after a hard day's battle, the warriors would place the head of whomever they had slain in battle between their legs.[70] This was a very serious ritual and, in one incident, in order to show his respect for his defeated opponent, the warrior Fland kissed Cormac's head, rather than press it between his thighs.[71] One warrior was said never to have "slept without a Connaughtman's head under his knee."[72] Placing the head under the thigh was the ultimate symbol of conquest. The conquered head between the legs of the warrior dramatizes vividly the nature of the event. The warrior has given birth through killing his opponent; bloody skulls, rather than little infants, were the symbols of the new social life, where the warrior would be responsible for ensuring the "life" of the tribe and would reign supreme. "Life" now enters the world through death, a mentality that persists to this day and that is celebrated in military rituals throughout the world.[73]

Like the Goddess Tlachtga, who had been gang-raped, Macha was also effectively violated at the feasts of *Samhain* held in Ulster where she had reigned. *Samhain* had been primarily a harvest feast celebrating the successful growth and gathering of the fruits of the past year. Now the warriors came, conquered heads on their belts, and gave accounts of their deeds of valor, the new "fruits" and "harvest" of a warrior society.[74]

The cult of the warrior and hero would replace that of female creativity, with widescale repercussions for the future of humanity. For, whereas female creativity took place with regard to life, which included respect for death, male creativity had become inextricably bound up with the defiance of death. The reason for this was intimately related to another major change taking place in humanity: the development of male reproductive consciousness.[75]

MALE REPRODUCTIVE CONSCIOUSNESS

If human history has so far been delineated by the Stone Age, the Iron Age, or the Bronze Age, marking developments in productive culture, the male discovery of his role in procreation must surely also be an historical watershed. Men's subsequent determination to have that role honored and set up as the basis for political organization was to have widespread, and some would say now, devastating consequences for the future of the human race.

Male reproductive consciousness refers to a whole constellation of attitudes and strategies on the part of men. It is an historical development intimately tied up with the male child's experience of himself, his relationship to his primary parenting agent, his mother, and it refers to the consciousness men develop faced with their historical role in the whole process of reproduction, socialization, and nurturance. It is not an immutable category, one that is biologically determined and, therefore, not amenable to change. Indeed, such change is documented throughout this work.

Male reproductive consciousness is derived from several sources. At a purely psychological level, the act of procreation is a profoundly alienating experience for men. Whereas pregnant women live with their fetuses for nine months and feed their young from their own bodies for up to three years, men play their part in procreation in a momentary instance of passion when, by other human standards, they are totally out of control. They might never know whether or not their "seed" took the form of another human being, whether they were fathers of particular children, or whether they themselves would have continuity in the future.

Indeed, the philosopher Mary O'Brien argues that the foundation of patriarchy rests upon the insecurity involved in the "alienation of the male seed in the copulative act," an insecurity that has to be constantly placated by means of rituals, political structures, and control of the main forces of ideology. Whereas the relationship between a mother and her child is, in its initial stages, physiological, the establishment of paternity is essentially a social act. The development of the idea of paternity represents a "real triumph over the ambiguities of nature."[76] Firmly establishing paternity is a concern of Irish legal, mythological, and ecclesiastical literature.[77]

Paternity is essentially a cultural construct that, although making use of biological metaphors, is not primarily biological.[78] Rather, this is the way men have translated the uncertainty of their own fatherhood into the cultural structures of patriarchy and is a compensatory activity for the many inadequacies of physical paternity. Unlike maternity, biological paternity cannot finally be proven. Paternity is not constant but depends on tenuous factors. Impotence or uncontrollable women may all intervene to wipe out the male contribution to biological existence. Paternity itself is in a highly precarious position.

For, whereas women's role as mothers or potential mothers gives them a solid sense of "rootedness" and continuity in the world, men's strictly biological fatherhood gives them precisely the opposite. How, therefore, could men bridge the gap between their physiological act and their deeply psychological and social needs? This question became one of the first social problems for men to solve.

But there was a further problem. One of the components of patriarchal consciousness is that manhood is not a "given" for a male but something that has to be "achieved," first by relinquishing his original love-object, the mother, and then often by some extreme act of endurance or death defiance in which his biological ties become relativized. In his attempt to become masculine, the boy takes masculinity to be "that which is not female," or involved with women.

And just as manhood is not given automatically to men, neither is meaning. For men, meaning has had to be achieved or imposed upon reality. The natural cycle of birth and death simply condemns them to what they consider to be a "meaningless" existence. Unlike women, whose identity has been tied up with the visibility of childbearing, men have needed to externalize themselves by means of achievements, visible edifices, acting almost as a counterpart to women's natural functions. At the same time women's natural functions were denigrated by the extent to which men succeeded in carving out for themselves a sacred space not accessible to women. In the Irish source material we can see this theme clearly illustrated in another set of stories of the Ulster Cycle, the stories of the *Birth of Cúchulainn,* the famous Ulster warrior hero.

THE BIRTH OF THE HERO

The stories begin with the Ulster king Conchobor who had a sister named Deichtine. One day she and her fifty young maiden companions vanished from the Ulster fort, Emhain Mhacha, and were nowhere to be found. They left without permission from the king or the Ulstermen, an affront that the men found hard to suffer. For three years nothing was heard from them, until one day a flock of birds came to the Plain of Emania and devoured the grass, leaving not a blade. The Ulstermen jumped into their chariots and chased the birds until they came to the fairy dwelling of the Brugh on the Boyne, the present day Newgrange.

While the Ulstermen were there, Deichtine gave birth to a boy whom they named Setanta. (His name was changed to Cúchulainn in a later incident.) The next morning the house and the birds had disappeared and nothing was left except the baby boy and two foals that had been born at the same time. The Ulstermen gathered up their belongings, and Deichtine, her maidens, and the baby were brought back to Emhain Mhacha. But the baby was a weak little thing, and although Deichtine reared him until he was a boy, he caught a slight illness from which he died. Clearly, a baby born under such circumstances didn't stand much of a chance.

The second conception of Cúchulainn took place when Deichtine was beside herself with grief at the loss of her son. During her loud lamentations she asked for a drink of water. As she put the cup to her lips a tiny creature crept into it, which she swallowed. That night she had a dream in which a man appeared to her, telling her that she would bear a son to him. His name was Lug mac Ethnenn, and he told her to call the boy Setanta and that the boy should rear the foals. Deichtine was happy enough with this arrangement, but the people of Ulster complained that they did not know who the boy's father was. Some cast aspersions on

Deichtine's character and even suggested that Conchobor himself was the boy's father, as he had perhaps slept with her in his drunkenness.

Conchobor decided to put an end to all this upheaval when he gave his sister in marriage to Sualdam mac Róich. Deichtine was ashamed of the fact that she was not a virgin, so she vomited up the fetus and "the living thing spilled away in the sickness, and so she was made virgin and whole and went to her husband."[79] Now that she was safely in a legal marriage, she conceived again. This time when she grew pregnant she gave birth to Setanta, the future warrior-hero, Cúchulainn.[80]

These stories throw crucial light on the theme of male reproductive consciousness. In the first birth the origin of the child is completely mysterious: women are free to roam over the plains of Ireland, and the men have no control over them. The baby is born mysteriously and under these circumstances is a mere little weakling. The boy soon dies, leaving only his mother lamenting his departure. In the second instance, Deichtine's conception becomes a little clearer. We are still not sure exactly how she conceived. Her pregnancy could have been caused by the little creature she had drunk in the glass or by the God Lugh or from an incestuous relationship with her brother Conchobor. The Ulster people could not tolerate such uncertainty with regard to paternity, and Deichtine herself eventually became ashamed of the fact that she was not a virgin, something that apparently had not bothered her up until then. She vomited the fetus back again, or, according to one account, "crushed the child within her,"[81] and her virginity was restored. Clearly no future hero could have such an ignominious birth with his paternity so much in dispute.

When we come to the true birth of Cúchulainn, the patriarchy is very anxious to get things right this time. Conchobor *gave his sister in marriage to Sualdam mac Róich*. Now Sualdam was the brother of the male fertility god Fergus, and both Fergus and Sualdam were sons of the Great Goddess Macha.[82] We know very little about Sualdam, but we can be sure that the paternity of Cúchulainn was in good hands since his brother Fergus's fertility was so renowned that his name itself has been translated as "Male Ejaculation Son of Super Stallion."[83] His virility was such that seven fists fit in his penis and his scrotum was the size of a bushel bag. His sexual appetite was such that "it took seven women to curb him," unless he was sleeping with the Goddess Medb, or Flidais (the Deer goddess) who "used to change thirty men every day or go with Fergus once."[84] It was under these circumstances, with Fergus as the main principle of fertility and with the men firmly in control of the women, that Setanta was born.

Deichtine, by now, is no longer part of the decision-making process. Women running wild over the plains cannot be tolerated, and they should come to the beds of their husbands as virgins. In Deichtine's case her "virginity" was easily restored when she aborted the child of an uncertain father. Virginity in this context means that the fatherhood of her children can be clearly established, or that she is now under the control of one man.[85]

The lesson is clear: giving birth to a hero can only take place under conditions where the men are in control. Heroes can be born only when the fatherhood of the child has been clearly settled and where paternity is beyond dispute.[86] Women can take care of the child's elementary biological needs, but for anything else males would be much more suitable.

Although it would take generations to work it out and although it would pass through many different manifestations, the fundamental answer to the problem of male paternity was this: men could establish for themselves a rooted sense of their own importance in the world by means of the institution of the social, political, and religious culture known as patriarchy, a concept that is in turn based on the myth of male superiority. As Erik Erikson has maintained:

Behind man's insistence on male superiority there is an age old envy of women who are sure of their motherhood, while *man can be sure of his fatherhood only by restricting the female* (emphasis added).[87]

Inherent in patriarchal ideology is a commitment to the suppression and control of women in the religious, physiological, social, and political aspects of their existence. Most importantly, women's sexuality, containing as it did the potential for men's immortality through the children who would bear their names and inherit their property, would have to be controlled in the future by every force patriarchy could muster. Eventually the technicalities of this arrangement became known as monogamy, or the marriage between one man and one woman.

The needs of childbearing women would be made subservient to those of the society, but only after women's creativity had been colonized and their reproductive capacities were firmly under control. This process would take many different manifestations and would be reflected in different ways in the literature of many societies. Under these circumstances, where patriarchal consciousness dominated political, social, theological, and military practices, women's role in society was radically changed. Every effort would henceforth have to be made to denigrate all those things that had previously been held sacred. The names of the goddesses—Gráinne, Medb, Macha, Bóand—are now found only in sources where they were being satirized by the Christian monks. Female symbolism would be subject to many abuses: in some cases it would be eradicated entirely; in others, changed to suit male purposes; and in still others, taken over by the men, as they established superior forms of birthing and "rebirthing" to prove their superiority. Essentially, in this process the gods of the old religion would become the demons of the next, and a new system of values would come to the fore based on military might and upon male reproductive consciousness taken to its logical conclusion.

The development of patriarchy has, therefore, depended on several factors: the male discovery of his role in reproduction; the male realization of the insecurity of his position in the reproductive universe; his attempt to build a more secure basis for "fatherhood"; the creation of a specifically transcendent or "spiritual" culture achieved through death or death defiance.

Under the influence of this consciousness, a fierce warrior ethos prevailed. Societies would be constantly under attack, necessitating elaborate systems of defense and the centralization of power under the auspices of a king. All competing sources of power would be eradicated, and women, in particular, would be denied admission, symbolically and actually, wherever this power was religiously and bureaucratically maintained.

Nevertheless, while holding women in contempt, men imitated women's creativity in an attempt to draw upon its power. This attempt was never wholly successful: rebirth would eventually take place in more sophisticated ways, but for reasons intimately related to the development of patriarchal consciousness, the source of the energies and symbols drawn upon would not be those of life as they had been in matricentered religion but those of death.

It is in this light, therefore, that we can return to Macha's "curse" on the Ulstermen and begin to understand why they were not able to fight while they were "in their pangs." If there was indeed a period when men took it upon themselves to simulate birth and other forms of fertility in an effort to control the cultural and biological creativity of the tribe, then they could not simultaneously carry out acts of war. War belonged to "culture," fertility to "nature,"[88] and although men had redefined the meaning of fertility to suit their warrior needs, their definition was based on such an obvious lie, what some scholars call "patriarchal reversal," that the symbolic activities of war and fertility could not be confused without dire consequences to both.[89] War-making activities gave birth to "culture" and immortality, while contact with the traditional symbols of fertility immersed the actor in the eternal cycle of return. As the hero Cúchulainn put it so well, "Little care I, nor though I were but one day or one night in being, so long as after me the history of myself and doings may endure."[90]

The warriors would take it upon themselves to ensure the fertility of their endeavors by undertaking a period of hibernation when they would perform the birth mimes and other forms of *couvade* in imitation of those activities that had been so successful on behalf of the Goddess. Celebrating the overthrow of the Great Mother in childbirth, they could appropriate her power for their warrior enterprises. At the same time, they could initiate the young warriors into the full life of the tribe.

This is probably the meaning of the period of hibernation mentioned in the "curse," which has proved such an enigma to Celtic scholars.[91] Five days and four nights is roughly the length of time of an average

menstrual period. In societies throughout the world, women were se-
questered during their menstrual period not because of uncleanness but
because of the great miracle happening within their bodies.[92]

The warriors, in their menstrual "pangs," would prepare the cultural
life of the tribe for the coming year. But menstrual bleeding, symbolizing women's fertility, which for women had been a sign of their blessing
by the Goddess, would, under patriarchal culture, become a "curse," the
term popularly used for menstruation even today.[93]

Behind these stories in the Ulster Cycle there are several themes. Childbearing and -rearing were no longer honored activities but must become
subservient to the demands of the king (and eventually the state). Subsequently the relationship to the king rather than the relationship to one's
mother would become the new basis for patriarchal ethics.[94]

Fertility itself has been redefined: men would give birth to the cultural life of the people through death, either the death of the warrior slain
in battle or sacrificial death in a moment of glorious heroism. Carrying
the heads of the slain warriors on his belt, the hero would announce to
the world his triumphant cultural paternity. His form of birthing would
lead to immortality rather than to mortality, making it infinitely superi-
or to that of the mere childbearing woman.

In the course of overthrowing the matricentered religion, the widespread suspicion of women and their mysteries ensured that women
would never again hold positions of religious power and prestige. That
which had been sacred now became profane. Women would have no religious or sacramental power in those religions that sanctified the new
male reproductive consciousness, the cult of the hero, the politics of "fatherhood," or in those religions or philosophies that operated alongside
them by means of territorial or functional agreements.[95]

Even though men might have taken control of "culture," they by no
means lost their awareness of women's power. If men were to maintain
their tenuous hold on their newfound power, contact with women, at the
most crucial warrior moments of their lives, would have to be drastically
curtailed. Just as in the Genesis stories where those responsible for
preaching or hearing the "word," or undertaking a "holy war," had to
separate from women or any symbol of sexuality, likewise the Irish warrior heroes would have to limit their contact with women if they were to
retain their battle prowess and "reasoning" powers. This shunning of
women forms the theme of several "death" stories of Irish heroes, a literary form very popular in early Ireland. In the "Death Tales of the Ulster Heroes," one after the other, the brave warriors met their deaths
through the cunning or seductiveness of women.[96]

In a warrior society, motherhood was no longer a source of strength
but a handicap, preventing one sex from participation or representation
in the prestigious culture of the warriors. From now on whenever the
warriors wanted to ridicule a weakling or fallen warrior, they would say

with all the contempt of the triumphant philosophy, "He was as weak as a woman in childbirth."[97]

Death and birth are at polar opposites. Simone de Beauvoir has, in effect, accepted the premises upon which this philosophy is based, when she writes, "It is not in giving life but in taking life that mankind is raised above the animals. That is why superiority has been accorded in humanity, not to the sex which brings forth but to that which kills."[98]

Macha's cry, "a mother bore each one of you," was possibly the last symbolic attempt to appeal to motherhood as the basis for public social ethics. The Triple Goddess, whose spiral imagery represented life, death, and the cycle of eternal return, has been torn apart once and for all. The ambiguity and integration of the complex elements of matricentered religion, as represented by the Serpent/Goddess in the form of a Triple Spiral, would be overcome and replaced eventually by the Sign of the Cross. Cyclical regeneration would give way to linear history, and the cycle of eternal return would be replaced by the quest for personal immortality.

Men no longer need the Goddess in her life-giving form, yet the goddess of death is still active, seeking out their destruction. A major change has taken place: she has suffered a subtle transformation from the goddess of death into the goddess of war. In patriarchal culture, in fact, the only goddess who is tolerated is the goddess of war: she is the only one with any real part to play, whether her name be Mother Ireland, the motherland, or Brittania. She is the one against whom, or on whose behalf, men must constantly pit their wits and their strength, and if they fail in the attempt they can say (as was said in Ireland of the leaders of the failed "Easter Rising" of 1916) that they died for her sake.[99]

And yet in the Macha story, the Irish warriors saw their period of hibernation in their "pangs" as a curse, just as the fall from grace in the Garden of Eden was part of the curse of Yahweh. They were aware that the overthrow of the Great Mother meant the end of their idyllic existence in the clan. The life of the warrior, under the rule of the king rather than the clan collective, would be bloody and brutal. They were indeed cursed and cast out of the Garden of Paradise. But this time the curse came directly from the woman, the Great Mother Goddess Macha, who clearly recognized the downward spiral of destruction into which humanity would be plunged if its political and religious foundations rested on the suppression and control of women.

The Irish story has, therefore, preserved for us the true nature of the event: the matricide that lies at the heart of patriarchal culture and the Fall into patriarchal time and space that would have devastating consequences for the banished children of Eve.

PART II

THE AGE OF BRIGIT

CHAPTER 3

Brigit as Goddess
Mother Goddess and Virgin Lawmaker

MOTHER'S LAMENT AT THE
SLAUGHTER OF THE INNOCENTS

Then as the executioner plucked her son
from her breast, one of the women said:
"Why are you tearing
Away to his doom
The child of my caring,
The fruit of my womb.
Till nine months were o'er,
His burthen I bore,
Then his pretty lips pressed,
The glad milk from my breast,
And my whole heart he filled,
And my whole life he thrilled.
All my strength dies;
My tongue speechless lies;
Darkened are my eyes;
His breath was the breath of me;
His death is the death of me!"

Then another woman said:
"'Tis my own son that from me you wring,
I deceived not the King.
But slay me, even me,
And let my boy be.
A mother most hapless,
My bosom is sapless.
Mine eyes one tearful river,
My frame one fearful shiver,
My husband sonless ever.
And I a sonless wife,
To live a death in life.
O, my son! O, God of Truth!
O, my unrewarded youth!
O, my birthless sicknesses,
Until doom without redress!
O, my bosom's silent nest!
O, the heart broke in my breast!"

                                    UNKNOWN AUTHOR

The Great Mother Goddess Macha vanished from the stage of Irish history following her downfall at the hands of the king and his warriors. The disappearance of Macha symbolized the elimination of the possibility of any woman-centered social system, philosophy, or religion. The Male Word, rather than the Female Womb, would take responsibility for ensuring the continuation of the social order, albeit that this Word was reinforced and sustained by a discourse on, and the threat of, death rather than life.

With the arrival of Christianity in the fourth and fifth centuries, any remaining goddesses were destined to undergo a profound sex change. When Christianity first came to Ireland, it was, as a prominent historian put it, "at least in the early centuries of its mission . . . wholly revolutionary—a sort of seventh century Red China with all the fervour of the newest and rawest revolution of its time."[1]

Some hold that Christianity came in through the wine trade, others through various Roman missionaries, but the overwhelming consensus is that it came to Ireland through Patrick, who originally had been brought to Ireland as a slave. Having escaped to Wales, he heard the call of God while tending sheep on a mountain top. He returned in the early fifth century to become known to future generations as the great missionary apostle of Ireland. Whether historically true or not, and there is a great deal of myth and historical rewriting involved in this theory, the story of the returned slave-boy has captured the imagination of the Irish for generations.[2]

Since its foundation in the fifth century, the Irish church enjoyed a great deal of independence. The earliest form of church revolved around the bishops, but very quickly the major form of organization became that of the great monastic federations.[3] Originally, the abbots were mostly priests, not necessarily bishops. But eventually the custom of having lay abbots was established, and by the ninth century lay abbots working in cooperation with bishops were the norm.

Communication with Rome was sporadic and poor although a major ecclesiastical battle took place between the Roman and Celtic churches at Whitby in 664. This was organized by the Abbess Hilda of Whitby in England to settle the question of the date of Easter and the correct form of monastic tonsure.

The Roman party won the dispute on the grounds that they alone had access to the keys of heaven received directly from Peter and, therefore, had the power to admit people to everlasting life. This argument persuaded the English king Oswy, concerned as he was about the state of his soul, to come to the Roman side. Some Irish held out a little longer but eventually went over to the Roman observance. From then onward, although monasteries such as the one associated with Brigit of Kildare might hold onto ancient observances for as long as they could, there was a very strong *Romani* party in Ireland that worked to ensure the loyalty of the Irish to the universal church.[4] Following the initial fervor, many monasteries built on family land increasingly came under the control of the great families. Under these circumstances, many of the abbots diverged from Rome.[5]

Despite problems that may have existed between Rome and the Irish church, Ireland played a major role in European Christianity. The monasteries of Clonmacnoise, Durrow, and Kildare were great centers of culture and learning to which students came from all over Europe. During the Dark Ages, Irish missionaries, sent out from the great monastic federations, were largely responsible for the spread of Christianity and the preservation of classical culture in Europe.[6]

In the Ireland of those times, religious supremacy was intimately connected with political supremacy. The monasteries themselves were the most effective political centers in medieval Ireland.[7] Indeed the political and religious leadership worked hand in hand, and office in the Irish monastic federations was essentially hereditary, with that of abbot usually going to the "politically unsuccessful sub-segments of the ruling segments of the dynasty."[8]

In such a revolutionary situation there would be radical discontinuities with the society that had gone before. New thought patterns would emerge, new economic and religious systems would be formulated, and new political alliances would be made. But to think that such a revolution would affect all sections of society equally would be a mistake, for the revolution itself was the result of the widespread social tensions produced throughout the world in which the emerging patriarchal consciousness played a major part.

The Triple Goddess would be replaced by the Trinity of Father, Son, and Holy Spirit, a Trinity created by means of will and obedience no longer dependent upon the fertility of womanhood to fulfill its designs. As Christianity took hold in Ireland, it would make alliances and compromises with the warriors and provide alternative occupations for the old male religious leadership. But women and the energies they represented were a fundamental threat to the new religious consciousness.

In the new patriarchal order those who gave birth would be poorly equipped to function at all within the intellectual universe being established. The Christian church, which historically became the carrier of patriarchal values and symbols in the West, effectively declared that women would be equal to men only when they had renounced their femaleness and become "as men." In particular, they would have to renounce their powers of generativity and live as virgins or widows.

Not surprisingly, the ultimate qualification for becoming as men was martyrdom.[9] Several female martyrs are described as women "in sex but not in spirit" or as having "played the man." Women were women by nature, but they could become men by an act of the will. John Chrysostom put it well, speaking of a mother who baptized her daughters in the river in which they met their deaths. This woman, he claims, not only can baptize but "she becomes a priest. For she offers the spiritual sacrifice and the will takes the place for her of the imposition of hands."[10] The "blood of the martyrs was the seed of the church," and indeed, only before the lions would women's equality now be recognized.[11]

The contrast between the old religion of the Irish that honored women and that of Christianity is symbolized vividly by their respective artifacts. In the old stories of the heroes and heroines, especially those of Diarmuid and Gráinne, the eloping couple left traces of their journey all over the countryside in the form of the "beds" in which they had slept as Gráinne sought to escape from the demands of an arranged marriage.[12] But when the compilers of the "Lives of the Saints," the new heroes and heroines of a Christian society, wrote of their subjects, it was not their beds but their graves that were at issue. Indeed the cult of a saint was centered on the tomb rather than the womb and was celebrated on the anniversary of his or her *natalis* (birth), which for Christians in reality was the anniversary of the saint's death or burial.[13]

Despite all this, some women welcomed Christianity to Ireland. The Celtic invasions, which had brought hordes of warring tribesmen into Ireland from northern Europe, and the patriarchal consciousness they brought with them, had led to a warrior, elitist form of society.[14] Women especially must have thought they were bringing children into the world merely to be fed as fodder to the warring escapades of the political rulers. Women were forced to be warriors, and the rulers had reduced much of the population to slavery. A unit of currency at that time was estimated, not in coins, but in the number of slave women (*cumala*) needed for economic transactions.[15]

Jesus was known in Ireland either as the "son of the carpenter" or as "Mary's Son," and women, whose own children had been sacrificed to cruel political expeditions, would have had little difficulty identifying with the Virgin Mother taking her dead son from the Cross. Stories such as the "Slaughter of the Innocents" under Herod would also have directly resonated with their own experience. The new religion of the Cross, promising as it did freedom for captives, liberation for the poor, and justice for all in the sight of God, must have seemed a welcome alternative.

In particular, the new religion preached the Gospel of Peace, and among the warrior class the threat that Christianity posed to their way of life was taken very seriously. Some people were wary of having their children baptized since Christian baptism was thought to have an unwelcome "weakening" or "pacifying" effect on the recipient. In some cases parents kept the right arm of an infant out of the baptismal water that they might be strong enough to strike harsh blows against enemies.[16] The warrior's concern about the character of the new God being brought into Ireland by zealous missionaries ignited fierce debates about the nature of the new divinity and what the acceptance of this God might mean to Irish social and political life.[17] The old Irish scribes, the poet class, also had trouble accepting Christianity and composed satires against Patrick and his missionaries, calling him old "Adze-head."[18]

There may have been considerable debate among women about Christianity and about the implications of the new theology being imported to Ireland. One of these debates has come down to us in the form of a dialogue between Ethne Alba, a mythological figure, and Patrick. Patrick was attempting to preach the word of God, but Ethne had her own questions to put to him:

> Who is God
> and where is God,
> of whom is God
> and where His dwelling?
>
> Has he sons and daughters,
> gold and silver, this God of yours?
>
> Is he ever-living,
> Is he beautiful,
> was his son
> fostered by many?[19]
>
> Are His daughters
> dear and beautiful
> to the men of the world?
>
> Is He in heaven
> or on the earth?
> In the sea,
> In the rivers,
> in the mountains,
> in the valleys?
>
> Speak to us
> tidings of Him:
> How will he be seen,
> how is He loved.
> how is He found?
>
> Is it in youth
> or is it in old age
> He is found?[20]

The ancient Irish, represented by Ethne Alba, knew little of the fires of Hell and Everlasting Punishment being introduced by Christianity. For the ancients their future existence would be in a Land of Eternal Youth where sickness and death would be no more.[21] Tragic deaths such as that of a young woman in childbirth were often explained away as the dead ones having been spirited away by the fairies to a fairy bower behind the hills. It was believed that on the eve of Halloween the fairy bowers would open for a time and it would be possible to walk again with the loved ones and, in some cases, lead them to safety. Death in old age was not a problem: it was simply a natural phenomenon, part of the intrinsic tragedy of life itself.

The theology of the old religion had both benefits and drawbacks. On the one hand it accepted death as a natural phenomenon devoid of the threat of eternal punishment characteristic of Christian theology. But on the other it provided little by way of retribution for those who, in a patriarchal elitist and warrior society, carried out deeds of extreme violence and treachery against the weak. How could justice be done, and what possible social force would arise to curb the extremism of the warrior class? In this context a monastic writer wrote a brilliant piece of propaganda that would help to persuade women that Christianity was the answer.

The document is known as the *Cáin Adamnáin* (the *Law of Adamnán*), so-called after the seventh-century St. Adamnán (Adavnawn), who was famous for having "put a law on the tribes."[22] It begins by detailing the horrific conditions that prevailed for women living in a warrior society:

Cumalach was a name for women till Adamnán came to free them. And this was the *cumalach*, a woman for whom a hole was dug at the end of the door so that it came over her nakedness. The end of the meat spit was placed upon her till the cooking of the portion was ended. After she had come out of that earth-pit she had to dip a candle four men's hands in length in a plate of butter or lard; that candle to be on her palm until division of food and distribution of liquor and making of beds, in the houses of kings and chieftains, had ended. That woman had no share in bag nor in basket, nor in the company of the house-master; but she dwelt in a hut outside the enclosure, lest bane from sea or land should come to her chief.[23]

Vivid pictures are drawn in the document of women forced on by a husband "flogging her to battle," with a baby on one arm and her provisions on the other. On her back would be a thirty-foot pole with an iron hook at the end, her primitive "bayonet." The most prized trophies at the time are said to have been the heads or breasts of women. In many warrior societies, women were the first to be exchanged as hostages or taken as slaves. Men were usually killed on the spot, as too many warriors would be required to keep them in captivity.[24]

Adamnán one day invited his mother Ronnat to climb on his back so he could carry her around without getting dirty or wet. Ronnat refused, accusing Adamnán of not being a dutiful son.[25] Shocked, Adamnán listed his virtues asking his mother what possible duty remained to be fulfilled. Ronnat replied,

"Even so, your dutifulness were good; however, that is not the duty I desire, but that you should free women for me from encounter, from camping, from fighting, from hosting, from wounding, from slaying, from the bondage of the cauldron."

Adamnán was very reluctant to get involved, but Ronnat persisted, climbing onto her son's back and setting off for a battlefield. A stark scene met their eyes:

Such was the thickness of the slaughter into which they came that the soles of one woman would touch the neck of another. Though they beheld the battlefield, they saw nothing more touching or more pitiful than the head of a woman in one place and the body in another, and her little babe upon the breasts of the corpse, a stream of milk upon one of its cheeks, and a stream of blood upon the other.[26]

Ronnat commanded her son to use the power of his priesthood by raising one of the women from the dead. He raised Smirgat, wife of the king of the Luaigni of Tara, who repaid him by immediately putting him under a tabοo: "Well now, Adamnán, to thee henceforward it is given to free the women of the Western world. Neither drink nor food shall go into thy mouth until women have been freed by thee."[27] Adamnán protested, saying that if he saw food he would surely stretch out his hand and take it. But his mother was determined to have her way, so she put a chain around his neck and a flintstone in his mouth, giving him little choice but to obey.

Eight months later his mother came back to find him in a sorry state. He was scorched by salt water, and seagulls' droppings covered him from head to toe, but his prayers had not yet been heard. Ronnat decided that women were enduring much greater suffering than her son and resolved to continue her treatment. He pleaded with her to change his torture, which she did. This time she buried him in a stone chest, with worms devouring his tongue and the slime of his head bursting out of his ears. This went on for several more years until finally an angel appeared to Adamnán, telling him to leave his hiding place. Manfully, Adamnán refused, saying, "I will not arise until women are freed for me," at which the angel replied that his prayers would be answered.

Adamnán's troubles were not over, however, because when he went to negotiate the freeing of women from slavery and war, he was told by the kings, "It shall not be in my time if it is done. . . . An evil time when a man's sleep shall be murdered for women, that women should live, men should be slain. Put the deaf and dumb one to the sword, who asserts anything but that women shall be in everlasting bondage to the brink of Doom."[28]

All the kings "of the Western world" assembled to kill Adamnán, who went forth with his little altar bell as his only weapon, the "Bell of Adamnán's Wrath." Ringing his bell fiercely, Adamnán threatened the kings with dire consequences should they not heed his words. He threatened some that they would not succeed to the kingship of their fathers, others that they would leave no "seed nor issue" or that their present sons would die of plague or accident. The power of the altar bell, signifying the sacrifice of the Mass or the power of excommunication, was so feared that the kings immediately recanted and gave Adamnán "securities and bonds." They further threatened that dire punishments would befall anyone who would henceforth injure, kill, or otherwise interfere with the emancipation of women.

The story reflects a time when Irish women were greatly oppressed by the warrior elitist society. Christianity had come, yet obviously the priests, like Adamnán, needed drastic measures of persuasion before being prevailed upon to confront the ruling classes. The women had lost their own power during the Celtic invasions and desperately needed not only the mediation of the church but also the recourse to a higher power, one which men would be forced to respect. Under extreme pressure Adamnán was "persuaded" to take on the task.

On his own he could not do very much, but with his little altar bell Adamnán could threaten and curse the kings into obedience. The most effective threat was that the kings would not receive immortality through their sons or that their name would not be carried on, reflecting the importance attached, by that time, to their role in paternity.

The document illustrates also the serious alliances being made between the clergy and women. The *Law of Adamnán* maintains that "the enactment of this law of Adamnán is a perpetual law on behalf of clerics and women and innocent children until they are *capable of slaying a man,* and until they take their place in the tribe, and their (first) expedition is known" (emphasis added).[29] Women, clerics, and children (until the young male joins the tribe after a successful warrior initiation) are put on the same footing. The same securities and compensation would be required in the future from anyone injuring them. Neither women, clerics, nor children would have to go to war, and their social alliance was the only real alternative there was to the all-pervasive warrior ethic.

Significantly, in an alternative version of the story an angel who appeared to Adamnán at first, detailing the oppression of women, told Adamnán,

Thou shalt establish a law in Ireland and Britain for the *sake of the mother of each one, because a mother has borne each one,* and for the sake of Mary Mother of Jesus Christ, through whom all are. Mary besought her Son on behalf of Adamnán about this Law . . . for the sin is great when any one slays the mother and sister of Christ's mother and the mother of Christ, and her who carries the spindle and who clothes every one (emphasis added).[30]

Remember in the Macha story we heard her final cry, "A mother bore each one of you." To a matricentered society this would have been the ultimate plea, equivalent to our saying today, "For the love of God" or "For the sake of God."[31] This plea recalled people to their responsibilities toward their creator and their common origins through the Great Mother.

Ronnat's desperate actions symbolize the tacit agreement that has been entered into: women would support the Christian church in its attempts to "put a law onto the tribes" only if their own liberation could be guaranteed in advance. But their liberation would not be without cost. In this case, the *Law of Adamnán* goes on to list the immediate consequences of Adamnán's act. Women would be required to contribute whatever they could in the future to Adamnán's community, or his "reliquaries," which literally means those who would hold his relics. Horses would be expected from queens every three months, but other women should contribute whatever they were able: tunics, gold, cakes, pigs, lambs, or linen were just some of the suggestions. Should they fail to comply, the saint threatened that the "offspring ye bear shall decay, or they shall die full of crimes."[32] For their obedience, Adamnán promised to take "two women to Heaven every Monday, three women every Tuesday, four women every Wednesday, five women every Thursday, seven women every Friday, twelve women every Saturday, fifty women on Sunday."[33] Women could enjoy the "protection" of the church through Adamnán, but their "liberation" would make them permanently indebted to his successors.

THE GODDESS BRIGIT

Upon its arrival in Ireland, Christianity had to reckon, not only with the warriors, but also with the most powerful female religious figure in all of Irish history: Brigit, a figure who achieved the distinction of becoming a Triple Goddess, a Virgin Mother, a Lawmaker, a Virgin Saint, and finally, a folk image whose shadows still move over Ireland.

Brigit's role in Irish history is a complex one, the many strands of which few have attempted to untangle. Layers of separate traditions have intersected, making Brigit out to be one of the most contradictory figures in Irish history, but it could be argued that precisely this complexity has enabled the figure of Brigit to move, seemingly so effortlessly, through thousands of years. Brigit has traveled the generations, apparently intact, but, as we will discover, fulfilling very different roles in different time periods. In the transitions between these various roles we can seek the clues we need to uncover the process that ensured women's eventual subordination.

The Irish are generally accustomed to thinking of Brigit as one of three national patron saints. Brigit was said to have founded a famous convent in Kildare in the south of Ireland, from which her main claim to fame is derived. While there is certainly some truth in this image of Brigit, this does not account for the cult of Brigit that spread not only over the whole of Ireland but also throughout western Europe.[34]

We will be using the term *Brigit*, therefore, to speak of a fifth-century historical saint and also of a series of diverse religious traditions that grew up around the name *Brigit*. In Irish literature, Brigit is almost the "good female" principle personified. To distinguish "myth" from historical "fact" will be difficult. The figure of Brigit moves imperceptibly from the theater of myth to that of history. Some traditions of scholarship see this distinction as crucial, but for our purposes we are interested primarily in "discourse," that is to say, in the stories about the "event," as much as in the actual historical happenings. At the same time we cannot lose sight of the fact that, even though separating history from folklore is difficult, there must have been some basis for the claims made about Brigit in the historical fifth-century period in Ireland.[35]

Using a "Life" of a saint to get information about a goddess might seem like a roundabout way of doing things. In Brigit's case, this is the only way of so doing, since we have little information about her role as a goddess but even less about her role as an historical fifth-century Irish saint. Many scholars have exhausted their energies trying to distinguish between Brigit as a goddess, saint, or folklore figure, only to realize that the distinction is a fruitless one to begin with. The "Lives of the Saints" is a collection of folklore, myth, piety, and propaganda. Saint's "Lives," while often useful guides to the spread of their cults, tell us little about the saint's origins.[36] Even the list of the saint's relatives given in the "Life" was given simply to "conceal the fact that some of the notable clerics had been unpalatably plebeian."[37]

Many saint's "Lives" were compiled in an attempt to collect revenues in the forms of taxes to attract pilgrims to the monasteries where their relics were housed.[38] The "Lives" are full of themes drawn from the old Irish sagas. Some stories even list the eternal benefits to be derived from reciting saints' lives, as the church desperately attempted to replace respect for the old heroes with respect for the saints.[39] In addition, some stories were satires, told perhaps in order to discredit the monastic system itself.[40] The "Lives of Saints" are often, as the "Life of Patrick" has recently been described, works of "propaganda with a strong political bias."[41] As one scholar put it at the end of a lifetime of research, when all was said and done "the biographers of the Irish saints, with a few notable exceptions, knew scarcely anything about the persons whose lives they had set out to portray."[42]

What this amounts to with regard to Brigit was recently summarized by a Brigittine scholar who claimed that "if there was an historical Brigit we have absolutely no reliable information about her, and the pagan Goddess Brigit, known to have been worshipped in early Ireland, may well be all we need to explain the origins of her cult and legend as a saint."[43]

What can we reasonably know about Brigit and, in the process, about the images that have shaped Irish religious identity?

One scholar has suggested that *Brigit* was not simply the name given to one figure but rather the name *Brigit* was possibly the one given to all Irish goddesses and, in the European context, the name of the collective

"Goddess."[44] Brigit clearly had an international ancestry, and the Irish form of her name simply means "high" or "exalted." *Brigantia*, her Latinized form, is a name found throughout Europe.[45] The stories and images connected with Brigit contain remnants associated with several goddesses in Ireland and in other parts of the ancient world, among them, Belisama, Juno, Isis, Vesta, and Sul. Indeed the rites practised at the convent in Kildare in the south of Ireland were said to resemble those of the Roman goddess Minerva. Three of Brigit's most common symbols, the vulture, serpent, and cow, were all symbols of the goddess Isis. According to legend, her embroidery tools, Minerva's symbols, were preserved at a chapel near Glastonbury, at Beckery in England. Glastonbury also held objects of healing associated with Brigit, such as her bag and her bell. Her imagery was associated with the sun, moon, cows, sheep, vultures, baths, sacred fires, and milk.[46]

Her British equivalent is the Goddess Sul, associated with the hot springs at Bath and in whose temple perpetual fires were tended.[47] An ancient travel guide to Britain spoke of the

hot baths, finely kept to the use of men, the sovereign of which baths is that of the Goddess Minerva [Sul], in whose chapel the fire burneth continually, and the coals do never turn into ashes, but as soon as the members are dead, it is turned into balls of stone.[48]

Brigit was the patroness of poets, and in her honor the chief poet always carried a golden branch with tinkling bells.[49] Brigit was also known as a midwife,[50] and her feast day, February 1, or in some parts of the Celtic world, February 13, was also that of the Roman goddess Juno, the goddess of love and the "aid-woman" (midwife) of ancient Rome.[51] For this reason Brigit is known as the "Mary and the Juno of the Gael."[52]

We first encounter Brigit in Ireland in her role as Mother Goddess associated with the *Tuatha Dé Danaan*, the People of the Goddess Danu. In an ancient Irish dictionary called *Cormac's Glossary*, Brigit was known as

a female poet, daughter of the Dagda. This Brigit is a poetess, or a woman of poetry, i.e. Brigit a Goddess whom poets worshipped, for very great and very noble was her superintendence. Therefore, they call her Goddess of poets by this name. Whose sisters were Brigit, woman of healing, Brigit, woman of smithwork, i.e. Goddesses, from whose names with all Irishmen Brigit was called a Goddess. Brigit then, i.e. *breo-saigit*, a fiery arrow.[53]

In this description, Brigit, the Triple Goddess, is known as the "daughter of the Dagda" (the Good God),[54] but there are other instances where she is his mother or his wife.[55]

Like the Serpent, the Triple Goddess defied the categories of analysis, and, not surprisingly, one of Brigit's main symbols was that of a Serpent, and her sanctuary at Kildare may have been a cult center for the Serpent.[56]

Her feast day on February 1, *Imbolc*, is a major feast of the Celtic year, the others being *Beltaine, Lughnasa,* and *Samhain. Imbolc* has been translated variously to mean "ewe-milk,"[57] "parturition,"[58] "lustration," or "purification."[59] Dividing the Celtic year in two, *Imbolc* is associated with breastfeeding. It is possible that the pilgrimages that took place on the feast of *Imbolc* were remnants of a Druidic ritual celebrating the fluids of the womb, amniotic fluids, waters sacred to the old religion.[60]

January was considered to be a "dead month," and so on *Imbolc,* the first day of the Celtic spring, Brigit was said to "breathe life into the mouth of the dead winter."[61] According to one poem, Brigit was clearly a serpent and symbol of regeneration.

> Today is the Day of Bride,
> The serpent shall come from the hole,
> I will not molest the serpent,
> Nor will the serpent molest me.[62]

As the Serpent, she was also referred to as the "noble queen."[63] As part of the festival, an effigy of the Serpent was pounded.[64]

In the Christian "Lives of Brigit" there are several stories linking Brigit to some of the early Irish sagas that feature themes of immortality and resurrection with serpent and salmon imagery.[65] In Brigit's role as Mother Goddess, one of her symbols is that of a cow. Numerous legends exist throughout Ireland about this cow, and it is possible that Dumha na Bó (the Mound of the Cow) at Tara, a circular mound about six feet high and forty feet in diameter at the base, was associated with her Sacred Cow.[66]

The milk of the Sacred Cow (now a term of derision) was one of the earliest sacred foods throughout the world, equivalent to our present day communion. Milk represented the ideal form of food for its purity and nourishment.[67] Milk from the Sacred Cow was believed to provide an antidote to the poison of weapons.[68] Mother's milk was especially valuable and was believed to have curative powers.[69]

The Sacred Cow symbolized the sacredness of motherhood: through her milk the life-force itself was sustained and nourished. By no means a passive giver of milk, she was an active mother fighting for the health, safety, and well-being of her offspring; Brigit as Mother Goddess at all times appears as the woman who mourns for the fate of her children and who is particularly outraged by plunder and rape.[70]

Indeed, in a culture picturing a mother as its highest deity, rape, which potentially forced a woman to become a mother, was a dreadful crime. Men were subject to severe punishments,[71] and one incensed king removed rape from the list of pardonable crimes lest he ever be tempted to show leniency.[72] Should a woman become pregnant following a rape, this was taken to be a sign of her compliance: it was vital, therefore, that some means of resistance be put forth.[73] Brigit is said to have invented the first whistle for signaling at night, the equivalent of our contemporary "shriek alarms," to lessen the possibility that a woman putting up resistance would not be heard.[74]

In the stories that have come down to us in the historical tradition, there are few remnants of the figure of Brigit as the Mother Goddess. The figure we know as "Brigit" is a composite goddess who took over many positive aspects of the old Irish goddesses Tephi, Danu, Macha, and the Morrígan.[75] What came to be considered these goddesses' negative aspects became the subjects of derision and contempt, both in the secular and religious literature.

What was different about Brigit, and how did her image serve the new social structure that was threatened by other aspects of female imagery? We can begin to answer this question by locating the issue within the context of the Celtic invasions of Ireland that, as we have seen, took place in the centuries before the introduction of Christianity to Ireland.

In this context the word *Celt* is used very loosely to describe the hordes of warring tribesmen who came to Ireland from northern Europe, partly in response to the economic and social pressures encountered in their own territories. As a tribal people they would have had diverse religious traditions and, indeed, although there are many studies of the Celtic people, the task of deciphering their religion has eluded most scholars. The Celts would encounter the same problem as the Israelites as they struggled toward becoming a nation or even a fighting force to be reckoned with. In the Hebrew Bible we saw how the Israelites, when building national defenses in the face of hostile intruders, made strenuous efforts to eliminate polytheism. Like the Israelites, the Celts were faced with the problem of having too many gods, often tied down to local places or specific to a particular tribe, which prevented their political unification and, thereby, minimized the effectiveness of their martial invasions.

Similarly, in the centuries before the arrival of Christianity in Ireland, the religion honoring the Mother in her various forms would have lost power. The old Irish goddesses were tied to particular places and were intimately identified with the land itself. Thus, they were fairly static and did not lend themselves easily to being transported by warriors or to giving credence to a king who wanted to expand his territory beyond that sanctioned by his association with a particular goddess.

As in the case of Israel, patriarchal organization is based on territory rather than on relationship, on hierarchy rather than on consensus, on contract (or law) rather than on kinship. Military might rather than the rule of custom is respected, leaving the whole social fabric open to constant chaos as each new warrior tries out his strength or searches for new territory.[76] The Irish heroic sagas are full of such legends: bloody, gory, and arbitrary.

In early Irish society the heroes, when calling upon their gods, cried out, "I swear by the gods by whom my people swear," which is to say that each hero swore by the gods of his own tribe. This notion did not lend

itself to national unity or even to national defense in the face of the marauding warriors coming from the northern European kingdoms.

The patriarchal Celts themselves had not succeeded in replacing the
religion of the Mother with a systematic form of religion that would endure.[77] Unlike the Jews, they had not managed to develop a form of
monotheism under which a society could be united. Each warrior or warrior group would have their own gods to whom they paid homage, effectively leaving the way open for political chaos.

Like the Israelites, therefore, both the Irish and the Celts needed a
portable god, independent of territorial considerations, who could be
taken with them. Under these circumstances the first moves toward
monotheism were made in Ireland. However, they were made, not by
recognizing the One True Male God, but by the promotion of the Triple
Goddess Brigit, the earliest form of the Trinity, to the status of the central divinity in Irish cosmology. Indeed, it is possible that the imagery of
the Goddess Brigit was brought to Ireland by the various Celtic invasions
taking place in Ireland in the centuries prior to Christianity, a possibility
borne out by the fact that her main image, a Brigit's cross, does not appear on any Bronze Age pottery, rock surfaces, or on any of the ancient
megalithic monuments associated with other Irish goddesses such as
Bóand or Macha.[78]

Unlike these Irish goddesses, who were tied to particular areas or
tribes, Brigit and her traditions transcended territorial considerations.
The name of Brigit and Brigit symbolism provided some sense of unity
among the otherwise warring tribes of Europe, possibly enabling them
to unite. Her three sons gave their names to the soldiers of Gaul, otherwise known as the Brigantes, who were famous for having fought in wars
against Rome and Delphi.[79] For this reason she was known as the "Gaul-
ish Minerva" by Caesar.[80] Images of the *Dea Brigantia* are to be found on
inscriptions in northeast England.[81] No doubt the activities of her
"sons," as much as her "saintly" qualities, spread the name of Brigit and
the cult of the future saint throughout Europe.[82] The name *Brigit* provided a language whereby warring tribes could communicate with each
other through symbols and common allegiances to her memory.[83]

The Celtic invaders from northern Europe were coming into a matrifocal land where the relationship to the mother formed one of the central principles of social organization. Matrifocal societies can be pictured
as a series of intersecting rings, with the rings overlapping at various
points, having little sense of hierarchical organization. The primary focus of cultural unity is the Goddess, she who sustains and nurtures the
family group in its own territory. The particular image of the Goddess
would not always be shared by other groups, but this would not be a
problem since her responsibilities would extend only to those who were
her immediate worshipers. And so the local group could happily recognize the existence of other goddesses without feeling threatened.

Periodically, the intersecting rings of the society would come together on occasions of celebration and renewal. The ancient pre-Celtic ceremonial sites of Newgrange, Dún Ailinne, Emhain Mhacha, and Tara all bear traces of such ceremonial activity. While in Celtic history and mythology these places were associated with the heroic warrior age, there is little evidence on the sites themselves that they were anything other than places of ritual. Thus religion, rather than military might, seems to have held the society together.[84] Indeed, one of the most sacred places in Ireland, the Hill of Uisneech, in County Meath, was the place where "the five provinces meet."[85]

All this was to change with the advent of patriarchal forms of organization, and not surprisingly, in the narratives telling of the various invasions of Ireland, the clash between matrifocal and patrifocal cultures plays a significant part. We can see this conflict in the classic Irish tale, *The Battle of Moytura*. In this saga Brigit takes over the role of Danu, the mythical ancestress of the "People of the Goddess Danu," one of the earliest names given to the Irish.[86] Marriage is often a means by which mythological figures make new alliances, and in *The Battle of Moytura* Brigit appears as the wife of Bres of the Fomorians, the mythical Irish invaders, the bitter enemies of the People of the Goddess Danu. Brigit, through her marriage to Bres, acts as the intermediary between two opposing people both vying for power in Ireland. Her son Ruadán, in this battle, was given help by the People of the Goddess Danu, his maternal kin, who taught him how to make weapons. Ruadán profited by this help but, having perfected his art, went back to the camp and on behalf of his paternal kin, the Fomorians, wounded the sacred smith of the People of the Goddess Danu, Goibniu, who, nevertheless, had enough strength to kill Ruadán. Brigit came and cried bitter tears for her son, "the first time crying and shrieking were heard in Ireland."[87]

This story is a classic tale of conflicting loyalty between one's maternal and paternal kin. Brigit's crying can be seen as her lamentation for the loss of the loyalty that previously prevailed in respect to one's maternal kin as much as weeping for the death of her son. With the advent of the warring Fomorians (possibly representing the patriarchal warring Celts), her role as the cultural Mother Goddess was seriously in jeopardy. Her son Ruadán had made use of his maternal kin, but only to help foster the establishment of patriarchal forms of organization in Ireland. Brigit's crying could have been a lament for the old times when relationships with the mother were respected and valued. She grieved at Ruadán's Original Sin that cast the People of the Goddess Danu out of power.

In this story Brigit played a major part in the transition to the new form of social organization, and, to a large extent, her ability to move between categories and places was the secret of her success. Her role in this saga provides us with vital clues as to the changes about to take place in Irish culture with the advent of patriarchal forms of organization.

BRIGIT AS LAWMAKER

The warrior Celts needed a god who would be recognized in territories other than their own and who could become a focal point of national unity—a god who could be counted on, like Yahweh, to provide the common rules and regulations by which the people might live in peace and harmony rather than in perpetual warfare, or by the rule of "revenge."[88]

As we saw with the Israelites, codified law provided a central language through which they could communicate with each other, pass through each other's territory with definite rules of behavior and guarantees of safety, and a definite identity, based on legal prescriptions and ritual forms of purity that distinguished them from their neighbors and fostered their own sense of uniqueness. Brigit reappears, therefore, in a new role, that of the Supreme Lawmaker behind the creation of what was effectively the Irish parallel to the legal tracts of the Hebrew Bible, the *Senchus Mór* or Brehon Laws.

This collection of Irish laws provides a social commentary on issues of sexual politics whose detail and intricacy is unparalleled in ancient Europe. These laws remained in force in Ireland up until the seventeenth century, when the British occupation of Ireland finally succeeded in abolishing the native legal system.[89] As the Supreme Lawmaker, Brigit could, like Yahweh for the Israelites, provide the rules and regulations which those interested in "the Peace of the Realm" could enforce.

Before the laws were written down by the Christian monks in the seventh and eighth centuries, they had been committed to memory by generations of *brehons* who were obliged to memorize the traditions of their people. These brehons were both male and female, a factor that might explain the remarkable rights accorded to women in these laws as we have received them, even though on the admission of the texts themselves, the laws were "purified" by Patrick, who is said to have removed from them anything he found "offensive" to Christian doctrine or moral teaching. The ancient traditions of the brehons were eventually subjected to "Christianization" to such an extent that the introduction to the laws claims that "since Patrick's arrival, each utterance of these professions is subject to the man of the white language, i.e. of the Gospel."[90]

This statement may have been partly wishful thinking on the part of the clerical scribe, but nevertheless, as far as women were concerned, the influence of the Christian church was unmistakable when the laws assumed their written form. The church was involved in all aspects of committing the oral tradition to writing, ensuring that they would enshrine in the laws an "honoured place for themselves."[91] Indeed the opening salvo against women is fired in the introductory commentary to the *Senchus Mór* itself:

What [the text asks] is the reason that it is called the Senchus [wisdom] of the men of Erin as it does not treat more of the law of the men of Erin than of the law of the women? It is proper, indeed, that it should be so called, that superiority should first be given to the noble sex, i.e. to the male, for . . . "Christ is the head of the man, and the man is the head of the woman; and the man is more noble than the woman, and it was on account of man's dignity that it was ascribed to him."[92]

Although Brigit was clearly one of the major powers behind the early Irish laws, the laws eventually were said to have been called after Sencha, the supreme wise old man in Irish tradition. Later writers have not managed to eliminate Brigit, who constantly appears behind Sencha as his mother or daughter or even as his wife.[93]

Given such an unpromising beginning, we are fortunate that any vestiges of women's rights remain; once again, according to the texts, it is to Brigit that we can be thankful.[94] We have no way of knowing the extent to which the laws were "purified" by Christianity to eliminate the presence, power, and importance of women in early Irish society, but time after time Brigit emerges from her obscure role in the written laws as a way of explaining the extraordinary aspects of Irish law in relation to women.

The Irish laws provided in intimate detail for the sexual needs of women. For instance, it was a crime for men to refuse to give their pregnant wives the "longed for morsel" or for men to impregnate a woman against medical advice or the restrictions of her tribe, or even to neglect to cohabit with her so that "the narrow passage for childbearing results," making childbirth more difficult.[95] Irish law also provided extensively for the rights of women in marriage, for pregnancy out of wedlock, and for divorce.[96]

Brigit is said to have "pronounced judgments on female covenants" and to have established the regulations governing twins (usually an extreme anomaly in early societies).[97] In one famous incident she was instrumental in establishing the law that forced two warring sides to delay for five days before engaging in combat, a role similar to that of the Irish goddess Macha, or her European counterpart, the Roman goddess Minerva.[98]

In early Irish society, women's power rested on social networking and ties to their children. The power of men, on the other hand, came to rest eventually on their accumulation of material possessions, an issue with which the Brehon Laws are preoccupied. It could even be argued that the emphasis on material wealth became the crucial leverage point for wresting power from women. If material wealth was not the basis for female power, wealth was not unimportant, and at that moment in history when men tried to impoverish women altogether, Brigit once again came to the rescue.

Sencha had pronounced judgment in the case of a woman who wanted to take possession of her tribe's land following the death of her parents. Sencha told her that it was not right for women to demand land, whereupon blotches were raised on his cheek. This was the traditional sign that false judgment had been given and was an ominous sign for a judge, especially one of Sencha's stature. The following day the woman came again, and she had either forgotten or had never known the appropriate ritual for "possession-taking." Sencha deliberately misled her, whereupon "blotches" were raised upon his other cheek. At this point his mother, Brigit, could take no more and came to the rescue of the woman, establishing the correct means whereby she could take possession of the lands of her family.[99] Sencha emerged unscathed from the incident because his daughter (also called Brigit) came and composed a eulogy to him that was effective in removing the blotches from his cheek.[100]

According to the storyteller, the main point of the previous incident is to tell us how effective eulogies by relatives can be in countering the effects of false judgments. But from our point of view we can see that women are in a very precarious position. If their right to hold land is challenged even when all the rest of their family have died, they could literally be cast out on the roads. To counter this, Brigit was insistent on maintaining women's property rights. However, in a warrior society, such as early Ireland, the right to hold land was intimately associated with the ability both to attack or defend this land. So Brigit, it is said, made a further provision: should a woman not wish to hold this dubious "right," she could surrender half of her land to the tribe. But should she assume these responsibilities onto herself, she could hold the land in entirety.[101] Significantly, Brigit, as Lawmaker, is here seen bowing to the dictates of a warrior society, a society that would eventually be responsible even for her own overthrow.

CHAPTER 4

Brigit of Kildare

From Goddess to Saint

"Wherefore have the nuns come hither"? said bishop Mel. "To have the order of penitence conferred," said Mac Caille. "I will confer it," said bishop Mel. So thereafter the orders were read out over her, and it came to pass that bishop Mel conferred on Brigit the episcopal order, though it was only the order of penitence that she herself desired. And it was then that Mac Caille held a veil over Brigit's head, *ut ferunt periti* [as the learned say]. And hence Brigit's successor is always entitled to have episcopal orders and the honour due to a bishop.

COMMENTARY ON BROCCÁN'S HYMN

If Brigit made several transitions in her route through Irish history, this is not to say that her role as Mother Goddess was ever completely eradicated. Indeed, her maternal imagery reappears throughout her career as a saint: Brigit is the mother of particular saints, and in the medieval church at Killinaboy her image, a sheela-na-gig (a figure holding the entrance to her womb wide open) is carved on the top of the arch to the door, effectively allowing the congregation to enter the church through her "womb."[1]

Not surprisingly her *Lives* link her clearly with the early Irish Goddess. As one scholar summarized it,

Brigit was born at sunrise neither within nor without a house, was bathed in milk, her breath revives the dead, a house in which she is staying flames up to heaven, cow-dung blazes before her, oil is poured on her head; she is fed from the milk of a white red-eared cow; a fiery pillar rises over her head; sun rays support her wet cloak; she remains a virgin; and she was one of the two mothers of Christ the Anointed.[2]

The symbols associated with Brigit's function as a goddess recur in the stories told of her as a Christian saint. In images of the Saint Brigit, we find flames coming from her head just as they had from the Goddess.[3] The images of milk, fire, sun, serpents are common in stories of St. Brigit, while the themes of compassion, generosity, hospitality, spinning, weaving, smithwork, healing, and agriculture run throughout her various "Lives." Her sacred objects, her mantle, hair, and holy wells were taken over into her Christian devotional forms.[4]

Brigit was a form of the sun Goddess, and her symbolism remains attached to the sun in the form of Brigit's crosses. These swastikas are found throughout the world as sun symbols and probably reached Ireland originally sometime between the second century B.C.E. and the second century C.E.[5] Brigit's crosses are still used in parts of Ireland today to protect the harvest and the farm animals. In the Christian "Lives" of Brigit there are numerous references to her association with the sun. Her mother, a slave,

went at sunrise with a vessel full of milk in her hand, and when she put one of her two footsteps over the threshold of the house, the other foot being inside, then she brought forth her daughter, even Saint Brigit.[6]

As an infant, her mother left her in the house on her own. While she was away, the neighbors saw flames rising from the house and rushed to it, thinking it was on fire. Instead, the baby slept peacefully in her crib, and they came to the conclusion that she was full of the "grace of the holy Spirit."[7] She is said to have hung her cloak on the rays of the sun.[8] One of the earliest Irish hymns to St. Brigit begins with these words:

> Brigit, ever excellent woman, golden sparkling flame,
> lead us to the eternal Kingdom, the dazzling
> resplendent sun.[9]

As a saint, Brigit was historically associated with the foundation of a convent of nuns in Kildare. Most of the written information about Brigit is deposited in the several "Lives of Saint Brigit" scattered throughout Europe where her cult was widespread in the early Middle Ages.

It is said that Brigit chose for her monastery an elevated spot over the plain of the Liffey that was called in ancient times *Druim Criad,* or "ridge of clay."[10] Brigit's main symbol was that of the sacred oak from which the present day Kildare (Cill Dara), "Church of the Oak," takes its name.

But the area surrounding Kildare, about thirty miles from Dublin, had a long history predating Christianity and possibly even Brigit herself. Only six miles from the present-day Kildare town was a religious site, Dún Ailinne, a site of major importance in the Iron Age and the largest "royal fort" in Ireland after Emhain Mhacha in the north.[11] Like Emhain Mhacha and other sites that took the name of a goddess who had been raped, killed, or otherwise defiled, Dún Ailinne was called after Ailinn, who died of shame after having been abducted. "Aillenn's Appletree" grew up on the site of her grave, while the "Yewtree of Baile," a famous tree in ancient Ireland, grew over the grave of her beloved lapdog.[12]

A central feature of the monastery of Kildare was the preservation of the sacred fire, but there is evidence that a similar fire was already at Dún Ailinne. In the Iron Age both Emhain Mhacha and Dún Ailinne were major religious sites, and there is archaeological evidence of feasting and periodic burning. In later times, Dún Ailinne became known as a royal cemetery with a nearby wealthy residential site for kings.[13] It is possible that the traditions surrounding the fire at Dún Ailinne were transported to Kildare when Dún Ailinne lost its importance.

Dún Ailinne was abandoned as a royal residence sometime between 695 C.E. and the end of the eighth century,[14] dates that coincide with the rise of the importance of Kildare as a major site for the Leinster kings. The structure at Dún Ailinne, like that of Emhain Mhacha, was dismantled rather than just left to rot away, suggesting that its continued existence might still have presented a threat to the importance of nearby Kildare. Indeed, it is given to Brigit to proclaim victory over the ancient mound. In a poem celebrating the demise of several ancient sites, we read the following: "Aillenn's proud citadel has perished with its warlike host: great is victorious Brigit: fair is her multitudinous cemetery."[15] It could be the case that the Christian Brigit set up Kildare as a direct religious rival to Dún Ailinne, an act that led eventually to its overthrow. But more probably, in the opinion of several scholars, the monastery of Kildare itself was originally a pagan sanctuary.[16]

Like the goddesses Macha and Tephi, who drew the boundaries of their forts with a pin taken from their brooches, so too Brigit is said to have drawn the boundaries of her monastery at Kildare by spreading her cloak as far as it would reach.[17] In pre-Christian times the whole area surrounding the present-day Kildare was known as *Civitas Brigitae* (the City of Brigit).[18] There are records of there having been a famous school at Kildare.[19] One scholar maintained that the head of the college of Kildare was regarded as the incarnation of the Goddess and automatically, when elected, took the name *Brigit.* He maintained that it is possible that one of her successors in Christian times was converted to Christianity and managed to turn the college at Kildare over to Christian purposes, a feat that was "far more wonderful than the miracles with which her biographers credit her."[20]

The area surrounding such sites took on religious significance. For instance, the land surrounding Brugh na Bóinne, or Newgrange, was sacred until Christian times when it was first penetrated to build a Christian church—an act so outrageous that the storyteller says that "this was the first time that the green of the Brugh was *injured*" (emphasis added).[21] The Curragh at Kildare, an area of lush green meadows, was also a sacred place. From there the legendary Merlin was said to have transported the religious site of Stonehenge to Salisbury Plain in England.[22] As at Newgrange, no one was allowed to put a plough near the land known as "Brigit's Pastures."[23] Brigit's oak tree was so sacred that no one was allowed to place a weapon near it, and, indeed, fines were often imposed for cutting the sacred trees found at religious sites.[24] Even if we have overwhelming evidence about the pre-Christian origins of Kildare, we still have to rely on the slightest clues to find out exactly what was going on in this ancient institution.

Possibly we will never find the full answer to that question. We know, however, that the rites practised at Kildare were clearly problematic for the early church—so problematic that several stories are told about Brigit's persistent but unsuccessful attempts to get a Roman "Ordo" (the official prayer book) that ensured orthodox worship throughout the Christian church. Brigit sent out several expeditions to obtain the "Ordo," but each time her messengers came back, having promptly "forgotten" what they had been told. Eventually she found a blind boy who could memorize perfectly. Even he had to spend several years at the bottom of the sea in a "Submarine City" before returning to Brigit.[25] Another life of Brigit tells us that one of her messengers deliberately falsified the copy of the "Ordo," which explained why the rites at Kildare were different from those practised elsewhere.[26] In any case, the storytellers were anxious to tell us that Brigit made every effort to get the Roman liturgy—which indicates to us at least that what she did use was far from being acceptable and orthodox.[27]

In one version of the story of Brigit's attempts to get the "Ordo," we obtain valuable clues as to the origins of the Kildare rites. Following one attempt, the blind youth finally brought one from Placentia in Italy, or Placentia in the Isle of Wight.[28] "Placentia" is the modern-day town of Piacenza in northern Italy that had been so strategic militarily for the Roman army in its conquest of Britain, while the Isle of Wight was an important supply center for the Roman army.[29] In any military conquest in ancient times it was of crucial importance that the conquering forces insert their own gods and destroy those of the vanquished. That the rites used by Brigit's monastery were imported into Ireland by one or another of the Celtic invaders (possibly by members of the Brigantes who were refugees from the Romans), in their attempts to establish cultural credibility in Ireland, is extremely possible.

Several "Lives" of Brigit say that the monastery of Kildare actually used the "Ordo Placentinus."[30] We have no way of knowing what the "Ordo Placentinus" might have been, but we do know that one of the earliest types of religious foundation in Roman times was that of convents of vestal virgins. We have seen also that Brigit's symbolism overlaps with that of several continental goddesses, including Minerva and Vesta. In the rites associated with these goddesses, and particularly those of the vestal virgins, we most likely can find clues regarding the original purpose of the college of Brigit.

VESTAL VIRGINS

As with every other facet of women's history, the sources for reconstructing the history of these women at Kildare is fragmentary, and the "vestal virgin" theory has received little attention in recent years despite major advances in other aspects of Irish history. However, we do have enough information to make this a worthwhile issue of investigation. We can begin this process by looking at their role in Roman culture, where the records have not been erased to the same extent as they have been in Ireland by the zealous Christian monks.

The vestal virgins played a vital symbolic part in Roman culture: at their ceremony of dedication they were clasped by the chief priest, the Pontifex Maximus, who said to them, "My Beloved, I take possession of thee!"[31] One of the women's main responsibilities was to preserve the blood of the horse shed during the sacrifice at the October festival, as this blood symbolized the life of the state.[32] They tended the sacred fire, another symbol of the unity of the Roman state, and on this account the vestal virgins were held in such high esteem that not even Juvenal, the great Roman satirist, dared to criticize them. In return for their great prestige, a major price had to be paid: should the sacred fire ever be extinguished through carelessness, they were scourged mercilessly by the chief pontiff, who then took on the responsibility of relighting the sacred fire.[33]

In return for dedication to the cause of the state, and as symbolic wives of the chief priest, the vestal virgins enjoyed great legal and social privileges not accorded to any other women.[34] They were the only women exempt from the authority of the *pater familias.* They could give evidence in court and bequeath property; they had an officer of the Roman army as their personal attendant, and, although virginal, they had all the rights and privileges of mothers. In this respect the vestals enjoyed many rights usually accorded only to virgins, mothers, and men, symbolizing their unique ability to represent all segments of the population in their intercessions with the gods.[35]

More important than any symbolic items they looked after was the virginity of the vestal virgins themselves. Their virginity was paradoxically a source of the fruitfulness of the institution of the state itself. The virgins symbolized the collective, they were not at the behest of any one man, and their willingness to deny their bodies imparted to the women a powerful aura that reflected on the state officiaries and provided them with the symbolic authority to rule. The chastity of the women was so important that should any one of them defile her virginity she would be buried alive and her lover scourged to death.[36] In addition, should any serious political crisis arise in Rome, the vestal virgins would immediately be suspected of having indulged in sexual activity.[37]

In the stories that have come down to us, the vestal virgins' role concerning the sacred fire and the cultivation of their virginity are emphasized. But we also know that the women had to commit themselves to spending thirty years in service, after which they were free to marry. Ten of these years were spent in training, ten in practising their duties, and ten more in teaching them to others. Their duties must have extended beyond tending a sacred fire, and it is possible that their functions also included the preservation of the traditions, sciences, healing remedies, and possibly even the laws of the state.[38] The role of the virgins appears extremely reduced upon the foundation of the centralized mechanisms of the ancient state; eventually they performed an important, but merely symbolic, role.

We know that in early Ireland there were several orders of priestesses, since references to them crop up periodically in the literature, usually to describe their overthrow. The story of how Loch Erne got its name is one example. The lake took its name from the chief priestess Erne, who "knew no art of wounding" and who

> was chief among the maidens in Rath Cruachan, home of
> lightsome sports: women not a few obeyed her will.
> To her belonged, to judge of them,
> the trinkets of Medb, famed for combat
> her comb, her casket unsurpassed,
> with her fillet of red gold.

Erne was a priestess of the Goddess Medb, charged with preserving her memory and her religion. One day, however,

> there came to thick-wooded Cruachu
> Olcai with grim and dreadful fame,
> and he shook his beard at the host,
> the swift and fiery savage.

The women fled "at the apparition of his grisly shape and the roughness of his brawling voice." They fled toward the loch, which poured its flood over them and drowned them.[39] The story seems to indicate the dispersion of the priesthood of Medb with the advent of the Celtic warrior culture. We have no way of knowing what rites the "priesthood of Medb" had practised, but we do know that Medb was the tutelary goddess of Tara and that kings had to symbolically "mate" with her as part of the "Feast of Tara" to confirm them in their reigns.[40] It would not be surprising, therefore, to find a priesthood dedicated to her cult of which the Loch Erne story is a fragmentary survival.

In another famous incident, three hundred women were murdered at Tara by a rival aspirant to the Tara kingship. The place where they were killed was, thereafter, known as the "Mound Where the Women Were Betrayed."[41] Possibly the story is telling us that originally Tara had a college equivalent to that of the vestal virgins, "royal daughters" dedicated to the service of the king. Their presence may have fulfilled functions similar to those of the vestal virgins, maintaining the peace from Tara, which was the "quintessence of the State."[42] Although scholars are still in dispute as to what the "Feast of Tara" was, we do know that the confirmation of kingship took place then.[43]

One of the last pagan high kings of Tara, Diarmait, went to great lengths to defend the old religion. There are several stories where he defended women who wished to hold onto their (possibly sacred) cows. In one incident, he went so far as to kill his own son who had stolen one of these cows from a "nun."[44] The son was subsequently raised back to life by a "saint."

The records surrounding Tara are extremely scanty and sometimes suspect.[45] We know that following the slaughter of the women at Tara, perhaps symbolizing their inability to protect the "state" in a warrior society, the high king from then on exacted revenge on the men of Leinster, where Tara was located, in atonement for the death of the women: not that the rights of women themselves were at stake, since one of the "tributes" that the king demanded was the right to sleep with the wives of every local king in whose house he stayed, while going on his rounds exacting his tribute.[46] In other words, a new form of political power was being exerted. Whatever power the high king would command in the future would come, not from the veneration, or the work, of women in the sanctuary at Tara, but from his own military might.[47]

While we cannot assume that the monastery of Kildare fulfilled the same functions as the sacred colleges of priestesses in other parts of the ancient world, the fact that so much of the symbolism and so many of the themes overlap with those related to the vestal virgins helps to throw light on the role of Brigit in Irish culture.

There are several elements in the "Lives" of Brigit that link her to pre-Christian institutions. Some of the mythic figures of Leinster, such as Darlughdacha (the Daughter of Lugh) and Blathnait, associated with Dún Ailinne and Tara, appear in the "Lives" of Brigit converted to Christian nuns.

Brigit's successor at Kildare, Darlughdacha, was probably originally the Goddess Tea, after whom Tara is said to have been named.[48] The stories surrounding Tea, or later Tephi, are similar to those in other Indo-European myths concerning the rape or abduction of the corn spirit in the form of a woman, which caused the coming of winter and the death of all vegetation.[49]

In Brigit's "Lives" Darlughdacha was said to be "Brigit's pupil, who used to sleep with her" and who committed the great sin of looking at a soldier. As penance she filled her shoes with hot coals and put her feet into them, extinguishing the flames. "So the fire extinguished the fire of her ardour, and the pain conquered her pain; and she returned to her couch." Upon confessing her sin, Brigit healed her, promising her succession at Kildare.[50] What originated probably as an act of ritual purification connected with ensuring the fertility of the crops,[51] is turned into one of sexual morality under the influence of the Christian scribes. The "daughter of Lugh" in the original story was raped by the storm god Géide. In the "Lives" of Brigit, she no longer even merits a name of her own and is now, herself, unable to control her passionate nature and, thus, to blame. The Christian version serves the purpose of sexual repression rather than cyclical regeneration.

In several old Irish myths Brigit is mentioned as one of a company of nine women, "Women of the Judgments," who appear to act as advisors to the wife of the king.[52] There is a great deal of evidence in the ancient world that such companies of women played a vital role in political life. In the Roman and Greek world there were several groups of such women, whose role was to advise on the right time for battle, the best time for setting sail, and who, in general, seem to have acted as advisors to the rulers in the major acts of state. These women were sometimes classed as virgins; others lived with their husbands on the mainland for most of the time but retired to an island to practise their mysteries.[53]

Behind the stories surrounding Kildare, and Brigit's association with "Women of the Judgments," therefore, may lie remnants of a college of vestal virgins. For instance, we know that as late as the twelfth century, when a travel writer, Gerald of Wales, visited Kildare, the monastery had a perpetual fire that each of the "nuns" tended on a twenty-day cycle. The nuns were not allowed to blow on the fire, only to fan it with branches of trees. In this respect their traditions were similar to those of the Persian Magi who could not breathe upon the fire that was their sacred duty to keep alight.[54] On the twentieth day, the nuns left the fire, telling Brigit to tend to it herself, and Brigit duly obliged.

The fire was behind a circular hedge of shrubs or thorns, and no male was allowed to enter the enclosure. One young man who made the attempt was rewarded for his arrogance by having the one leg that made it over the hedge wither instantly. For the rest of his life he was lame and, according to the story, "an idiot." Another man apparently blew on Brigit's fire and then went stark raving mad. He ran around to his friends repeating the words, "See! That is how I blew on Brigit's fire." Eventually his friends caught up with him, and he asked to be brought to the nearest water. Apparently he was so thirsty by the time he got there he drank so much that "he burst in the middle and died."[55] Behind these stories there may be remnants of purification practices associated with the sacred fire. Both men and beasts were said to leap over the fire, thereby gaining new strength and countering the evil influence that might otherwise affect them.[56]

Apart from the evidence of the preservation of the sacred fire there are other motifs and symbols that link Brigit and the vestal virgins. The vestal virgins had to raise and rebuild their centers every year as part of their purification practices, and if a center fell they were severely punished. Likewise, Brigit was able to move a large tree "when the men of Offaly were unable to raise it."[57] In the *Martyrology of Oengus*, there are several references to sanctuaries of virgins.[58] One of the duties of the vestal virgins was to make cakes from the first ears of the last year's corn harvest. These cakes were distributed on the feast of Lupercalia, which corresponded with *Imbolc* and is now, following the decree of Pope Gelasius I[59] celebrated as the feast of Candlemas at the beginning of February. Distributing cakes forms an important part of the rites of February 1 to this day.[60]

The vestal virgins symbolized the unity of culture, and in the "Lives" of Brigit there are several stories concerning broken vessels. In the most important one, two men brought a vessel to Brigit, who blessed it and then let it fall accidentally. Remarkably the vessel did not break, nor did a drop of water fall from it. When Patrick, the chief missionary apostle to Ireland, heard what had happened, he ordered that the water in the vessel be divided among the principal churches in Ireland to be used when celebrating the Eucharist and that the remainder be sprinkled on the fields to ensure their fertility.[61]

Not only did Brigit maintain vessels whole, but she herself was the Unbroken Vessel symbolizing the unity of Irish culture, a unity that would endure despite the wars and petty struggles of minor kings and tribes. In fact, the Irish word for virgin, *óg*, means "whole, untouched, intact, inviolate." Her virginity was highly symbolic: she could not be compromised by allegiance to one lover; she belonged to no man and could thus mediate to ensure the good of all. In this sense we can understand why Patrick would want the water from the unbroken vessel blessed by Brigit to be used in all the churches and in celebrating the Eucharist. Symbolically, Brigit's virginity would give additional strength to the power of the Eucharist to foster unity among the peoples. But her virginity by no means meant a lack of fertility: on the contrary, Patrick ordered that the water also be used to ensure the regeneration of the soil and abundant harvest. Brigit was the Virgin Mother, or one of the last representatives of "She Who Created Without Spouse."

In her role as Unbroken Vessel, Brigit could represent the unity of culture. Certainly in the stories of the saint Brigit there are many instances of her attempts to be a mediator in disputes and prevent war from taking place: she was positively opposed to war and its trappings. As we have seen, the tree under which she built her first oratory was held with such sacredness that it was never once profaned by contact with a weapon of war. In another story, two opposing brothers asked Brigit for help in battle between them. Brigit put a film on their eyes so they could not recognize each other and thereby prevented the bloodshed. She was unable to prevent war from happening but, like the so-called war goddesses before her, she caused enough confusion that she fooled each side into thinking it had won, thereby ending the battle without bloodshed. In return for renouncing the weapons of war, Brigit promised each warrior her protection.[62]

SPIRITUALITY OF BRIGIT

Although the image of Brigit the saint may have come down to us as one of an obedient, if spirited, woman, in the "Lives" of Brigit there is evidence, even apart from the possible "vestal virgin" origins of Kildare, that made Brigit's spirituality problematic for the early Irish church.

Some of Brigit's biographers did their best to assure that Brigit would appear for posterity as a good woman saint in the Roman tradition and went out of their way to deny any association with the ancient Goddess. In one poem, worried about her pedigree, they listed all the things that Brigit was *not,* claiming, for instance, that she certainly "loved not the world" and that she was not a "stinging speckled snake."[63] In another incident Brigit is said to have "refused to wash her hands, feet or head before men,"[64] an inexplicable reference unless one is aware that this is precisely what was done in the pagan ceremonies of purification, a practice later condemned by the Christian church.[65]

Indeed, Irish folklore is full of stories of how Brigit eventually gave way to Mary, performing heroic deeds on her behalf, in return for which Mary granted Brigit a special feast day of her own, February 1, which was to take place the day before her own feast day of the Purification. When Mary had to bring the Babe to the Temple, the wind was blowing very hard, but Brigit walked in front of her with a lighted candle in each hand. During the long walk the flame never wavered, with the result that Candlemas Day is sometimes called the Feast Day of Bride of the Candles.[66] On another occasion Brigit is said to have helped Mary in her flight from Herod. Behind these stories is probably the Christian takeover of the ancient feast of Lupercalia for which Pope Gelasius substituted the Christian Candlemas. A clear policy of the early church was to take over the symbols and feast days of the old religion and to convert them to Christian uses. The only purification ceremonies that the church would sanction were those associated with the Purification of the Blessed Virgin Mary on February 2.[67]

Goats were said not to have been allowed in or near the church at Kildare because "of the curse of the virgin,[68] and yet the sacrifice of a goat formed a crucial part of the original ceremonies of Lupercalia with which *Imbolc* is intimately associated.[69] Following the sacrifice, two young men took strips of goatskin, called *februa,* and went around beating women with them, possibly symbolizing a purification or a transference of fertility ritual.

Brigit's biographers also maintained that she had made strenuous attempts to get the "Ordo" from Rome, but there is other evidence to suggest that her relationship with Rome was far from harmonious. For instance, her bishop Conlaed was particularly fond of fine vestments, while Brigit gave these vestments away to lepers, beggars, or to whomsoever she felt needed them most. Several times she had to make the clothing "reappear" to appease Conlaed's wrath. A crisis arose when he appeared one day in search of them, and all she had to offer was a "garment like to the skin of a seal's head." The garment was possibly like that worn in other Indo-European rituals, where the sacrificer had to simulate the condition of a fetus by wearing a tight-fitting animal skin, before being fit to sacrifice and be reborn.[70] In exasperation Conlaed set out for Rome for the third time, presumably to get more vestments, but Brigit said to him, " 'You will not get there and you will not come back.' And so it was fulfilled, for wolves devoured him."[71]

Possibly it was in relation to this and other incidents that a famous refrain of the early Celtic church was composed:

To go to Rome, much labour, little profit: the King whom thou seekest here, unless thou bring him with thee, thou findest him not. Much folly, much frenzy, much loss of sense, much madness (is it), since going to death is certain, to be under the displeasure of Mary's Son.[72]

St. Brigit may well have made a transition from Mother Goddess to Virgin Saint, nevertheless, Brigit would not give in to the norms of a patriarchal spirituality without a fight. Issues of sexual politics raised their head several times in Brigit's relationship with the male saints Patrick and Brendan. That these saints were contemporaries of each other, or that they even met, is extremely unlikely; the stories reflect struggles between the followers of their various traditions but are valuable accounts of the sexual dynamics at the time.[73]

Brendan, for instance, on one of his voyages encountered ferocious sea monsters who were attacking the boat and Brendan himself. The monsters refused to respond to the pleas of the crew when they drew on the names of Patrick and Brendan. But when the name *Brigit* was mentioned, they were instantly subdued. Brendan, fascinated by this, resolved to seek out the woman who exerted this power. Waltzing into Brigit's monastery one day he told her to make her confession. Brigit responded by saying, "Make thou, O cleric, thy confession first, and I will make mine thereafter." Each confessed to the other and Brendan concluded, "By God, Nun, it is right for the monsters that they honor thee rather than us."[74]

This version of the story is the one found in most of the texts, but the editor in one version has inserted a comment into the mouth of Brigit when Brendan asked her to confess: "You speak first, a man has the right to speak first." This, despite the fact that in the same version Brigit hangs her wet cloak on a sunbeam and when Brendan tries to do the same it falls immediately to the ground—a story clearly designed to make Brendan look ridiculous and to indicate Brigit's superiority.[75]

Despite being a virgin, Brigit kept her ancient role as goddess of fertility. On one occasion a man came to her complaining that his wife was frigid. Her cure was so successful that "the wife gave exceeding love to him, so that she could not keep apart from him, even on one side of the house; but she was always at one of his hands."[76] This is not to say that Brigit believed that women were simply to be at the mercy of their biology. For instance, there is a story of when Brigit made the fetus of a pregnant nun "disappear." This story is successively toned down in the various editions of the "Lives" until in the nineteenth century it vanishes altogether from the "official" version of her "Life" at the hands of a most prestigious Latin ecclesiastical scholar.[77]

Brigit and her successors enjoyed enormous power in the early Irish church, a power derived perhaps from the memories of her sacred past and from the reluctance on the part of the Irish to relinquish such an important part of their heritage. There is no question but that Brigit considered herself to be part of, and was treated as an equal in, the hierarchy in the Irish church. She regularly entertained bishops and clerics at her monastery. In describing her hospitality, we are told that "seven bishops came to her." The author plainly saw nothing unusual in this, and all that worried Brigit was whether or not she had enough food to give them.[78] As St. Cuimmin's poem says of her, in the context of a long list of penances that the other saints "loved to do," "Blessed Brigit loved lasting devotion which was not prescribed, shepherding and early rising, hospitality to wonder-working men."[79]

In the "virgin" stories we saw that St. Brigit was even credited with celebrating what amounts to an early Irish Eucharist.[80] Even though it is difficult to separate legend from folklore, there must have been some historical basis for the claims that were made for Brigit. Even if there is not, the fact that these claims surrounded Brigit is itself a highly significant indication of early Irish religiosity. The political significance of some of these stories has been apparent to the church for some time, and for this reason attempts have been made to suppress the most controversial elements. This can be seen in the story of Brigit's ordination as a bishop.[81]

Some "Lives of Brigit" are clearly embarrassed by the story. Interestingly, however, they do not attempt to deny it. Rather they claim that the bishop was "intoxicated with the grace of God" when he ordained her and could not have known what he was doing.

The bishop being intoxicated with the grace of God there did not recognise what he was reciting from his book, for he consecrated Brigit with the orders of a bishop. "This virgin alone in Ireland," said Mel, "will hold the episcopal ordination." While she was being consecrated a fiery column ascended from her head.[82]

Whether or not the bishop intended to consecrate her, Brigit and her successors clearly enjoyed privileges in the early Irish church that defied the usual explanations.

Brigit's fame as a peacemaker was such that the future abbess of Kildare would be known as a woman who turns "back the streams of war," or *An Chailleach Libhti*, the "Nun of *Life*."[83] These abbesses would often be asked to mediate in disputes between rival factions, and, like the vestal virgins who had the power to pardon a criminal if they met him by accident on his way to execution,[84] they would be entrusted with the "safe-passage" of certain prisoners.[85]

Still, in talking about the abbess who turns "back the streams of war" we have come a long way from Brigit as the Mother Goddess. On the surface they may both be fulfilling similar functions, i.e., providing a symbol of the unity of culture. But the first image achieved this through the exaltation of motherhood, while the abbess is essentially a Virgin Mother. A subtle shift of emphasis has taken place, but it is an emphasis of critical importance.

In the "Lives" of Brigit there is a story illustrating this difference. Brigit apparently contracted an eye disease, and Bishop Mel urged her to go to a physician. Brigit replied,

If thou hadst not been disobedient, I should not have desired any bodily physician; howbeit we will do what thou shalt say.[86]

As they were going along the road, Brigit fell out of her chariot, injuring her head very badly. She was deeply wounded, but the blood from her head healed two dumb women who happened to be lying on the road.

The story is very similar to that of *Deirdre and the Sons of Uisliu*. Deirdre had made desperate attempts to marry a man of her own choosing but was betrayed by King Conchobor, who wanted her for himself. She escaped with her lover, but at the end of the saga she was finally captured and was being carried along by Conchobor and Eogan (her husband's killer) to be ridiculed at the Great Assembly of Macha. Conchobor turned to her tauntingly, saying, "This is good Deirdre, between me and Eogan you are a sheep eyeing two rams." Upon hearing this, Deirdre, having "sworn that two men alive in the world together would never have her," got into their carriage, and as it moved away she dashed her head against a passing rock, committing suicide.[87]

The reference to Deirdre as a "ewe" possibly means that she was associated with the festival *Imbolc*. Like Brigit, therefore, she would have "breathed life into the mouth of the dead winter,"[88] symbolizing her powers of regeneration. Conchobor's taunt to Deirdre could imply that the power of fertility has passed from the female to the male.[89] In a patriarchal society women no longer have the freedom to choose whom they will marry, and the two rams will make the decision for her. Several other Irish women in the sagas die of shame, or commit suicide, rather than consent to the loss of their sexual integrity.[90]

The Christian version preserves some of the spirit of the story, but despite the similarities, the solution sought by Deirdre and Brigit would be radically different. Deirdre was intent on retaining her autonomy.

When this had been wrested from her, suicide was her only alternative. Brigit as a Christian nun would have to find other solutions if she wished to survive in a patriarchal society.

Whereas mothers derive status from their relationships with their children down through the kinship structure, virgins, as we have seen in the case of the vestal virgins, derive their status by stepping outside the bounds of the family and into the life of public culture. While they may not be dependent upon their fathers, or available for marriage, their power now rests, within a patriarchal society, directly on the extent to which they serve either the church hierarchy or the state (the alternative Fathers). In addition, their power is good only to the extent to which they can deny their womanhood and "become as men." In other words, whatever power they have, at times considerable, is gained at the expense of other women.[91]

The option of virginity was a limited one. Rather than fundamentally challenging the political order that made conditions for women so intolerable, virgins, as we have seen in the case of the vestal virgins, essentially served to secure the status quo. Unlike other women, now confined to the domestic sphere, virgins had the potential for status mobility, but they used this status to prop up symbolically what had increasingly become a hierarchical, centralized power structure where women in general were left at the bottom of the ladder.

As Virgin Mother, Brigit would serve the new society well, and for this reason her memory would be not only tolerated but also promoted by the patriarchal order, at least for the time being.

CHAPTER 5

The Sexual Politics of the Early Irish Church

The Clerical Control of Reproduction

Now two maidens with pointed breasts used to lie with him every night that the battle with the Devil might be the greater for him. And it was proposed to accuse him on that account. So Brénainn came to test him, and Scoíthin said, "Let the cleric lie in my bed tonight." So when he reached the hour of resting the girls came into the house wherein was Brénainn, with their lapfuls of glowing embers in their chasubles; and the fire burnt them not, and they spill (the embers) in front of Brénainn and go into the bed to him. "What is this?" asks Brénainn. "Thus it is that we do every night," say the girls. They lie down with Brénainn, and nowise could he sleep with longing. "That is imperfect, O cleric," say the girls: "he who is here every night feels nothing at all. Why goest thou not, O cleric, into the tub (of cold water) if it be easier for thee? 'Tis often that the cleric, even Scoíthin, visits it." "Well," says Brénainn, "it is wrong for us to make this test, for he is better than we are." Thereafter they make their union and their covenant, and they part *feliciter* [happily].

MARTYROLOGY OF OENGUS

Just as secular patriarchal ideology in the classical tradition promoted a profound dualism between culture and nature, so too the new theology brought to Ireland by Christianity promoted a profound dualism between the spirit and the flesh. For all practical purposes men inhabited the world of the spirit and culture, while women (except those virgins who became "like men") inhabited the world of the flesh and nature.[1]

Under the influence of a theology that relied on the power of the "will" or the "word," the success of the Christian priests would rest on the extent to which they could overcome "nature" by developing their "will." In the Christian church in order to participate fully in the new spiritual life of the "will," men had to separate themselves from anything representing mere instinctive sexuality. Rather than Christian priests enhancing nature and perfecting it, they could not be at the mercy of their sensual urges. Theirs was a "supernature," formed by "will" rather than "passion." Close proximity to women or nature fundamentally threatened the precarious universe they were establishing for themselves. This would have far-reaching ramifications for Christian theology and Christian practice. In particular, although the virginal Brigit would be adapted in the early stages of the Christian church, this would not be the case for those women who clung to the ancient traditions of the matricentered culture: women known to us as "witches."

WITCHES

The word *witch* comes from *wit*, "to know," and means "wise woman." The witches claimed to be in direct communion with the divine. Their gods and goddesses lived in bushes, holy wells, and in sacred groves and were to be found in all aspects of nature. Whereas the witches could consult their oracles, the Sun, Moon, or wind or observe the movement of the stars or have recourse to the body of knowledge that witches had accumulated over centuries, once a "witch" was established, she worked essentially on her own. She was not accountable to a hierarchy, and she was "charismatic," that is, her success was judged directly by the people whom she was serving. Should she continue to give wrong judgments or fail in her arts, such as those of healing and midwifery, people would just refuse her services.

One of the main problems that the Christian church had with these religious women was that the god of the Christians was very different from their god. Just as the Israelites overthrew the gods of the Canaanites when they developed their patriarchal forms of social organization, so too the Christian priests would formulate a concept of god that would reinforce and encourage their new patriarchal consciousness. In its initial stages, the church may well have counteracted the power of the warriors, but in many respects its priestly practitioners were blessed with an equally virulent form of male reproductive consciousness. Although the Christian god would have control over nature, this was not his primary concern. He was much more concerned with abstract rules and concepts like justice, law, and righteousness.

The Christian priests were, therefore, diametrically opposed to what the old religion represented. Developing powers of the "will" was not a concern for the witches. Their success depended on something different: how closely they could be in tune with natural processes and listen to their wisdom.

Women, according to the fully fledged theology of the church, were by nature incapable of mediating with the divine and should not be so arrogant as to assume these functions.[2] Thus a steady regression took place: at first Christianity merely claimed that its power was superior to that of the old religion; then it asserted that women only used these powers for evil ends; lastly, it denied that they possessed any sacred powers in the first place.

None of these things happened overnight. We can trace a gradual change of emphasis whereby what formerly was held sacred now became profane and the new expression of sacredness took on an increasingly male character.

In the various "Lives of the Saints" we can see how these women presented a serious threat to the new religious order, although we have to remind ourselves that the "Lives" were written to exalt the saints rather than to give us information about witches. As such, we have to read the "subtexts," as well as the main narrative, to gain a true picture.

The "Life of Saint Coemgen" presents a particularly interesting case of the tension between the symbolism of the old and new religions. After Coemgen's painless birth it is said that "women take him without question or vexation, to Crónán to have him baptized."[3] The fact that women "take him without vexation" to be baptized possibly means that on occasion there was considerable vexation about this issue. In addition, Coemgen was born in a fort, and "never did frost nor snow conceal the sod on which he was brought forth."[4] The "women of fair attendance" (probably sacred midwives) are mentioned several times. The story maintains that the fort in which Coemgen was born was sacred, but "tis the grace of the infant which causes it."[5]

The Druids had their own form of baptism that some of the early Fathers regarded as "heathen rites invented by the devil, with the deliberate intention of bringing discredit upon Christianity."[6] The passage here might imply that women would normally have baptized the child themselves, and the fact that they took it "without vexation" to Crónán was the first extraordinary sign of the future saint. In the early church, even when women consented to being "churched" after childbearing, they first made circles of fire around themselves before submitting to the Christian ceremony. In addition, they made fiery circles around their infants before they were baptized.[7]

We are also told that "at the time of Coemgen's birth no pains of labour nor pangs of childbearing came to his mother, as to other women, for innocent, faithful, righteous was the offspring that she bore."[8] This detail must be related to the fact that in the old religions women had the power to alleviate the pain of childbirth by means of herbal medicine and rituals. It may be that the narrator is trying to imply a direct connection between the woman's lack of pain and the future holiness of Coemgen. The implication might be that Christianity, in the form of a holy child, had similar power to prevent pain in childbirth for women, making a persuasive argument for the elimination of women's rites altogether.

Significantly, we also are told that a "pure white cow" was sent for his nourishment and that he was fed with the milk of a deer that would drop its milk into the "Doe's Milking Stead."[9] We know that the goddesses Flidais and the Caillech Bérri were associated with deer.[10] The Caillech Bérri is said to have created Newgrange by dropping stones from her apron down from the heavens.[11] Hollow stones, or stone basins, are to be found in several of the ancient forts such as Newgrange. In some stories the hollows in these stones are caused by a woman trying to delay the birth of a child because of a promise that special greatness will result.[12] Just as the fort became sacred because of Coemgen's birth within it, this particular story may also describe the way the old religion's sacred stone was converted for use by the Christian monks.

Coemgen clearly had connections with the old religion through his mother, a factor that throws light on another story. On one occasion, in the "Life of St. Berach," Berach came into conflict with Cainech and her band of witches who were plying magic in Glendalough. There was a foster child in Coemgen's monastery, which Berach was visiting, whose name was Faelen, apparently greatly favored by the monks:

But when Cainech, the step-mother of Faelen, heard that Faelen was a child of special promise, she was seized with envy and jealousy of him; for she feared— what afterwards came about—that the kingdom would be conferred on Faelen to the exclusion of her own children. She came therefore with her band of witches to Glendalough to ply druidism and magic craft, and paganism, and diabolic science upon the boy to destroy him.[13]

Berach, when told what was going on, went into deep prayer and then said to Cainech and her band of witches:

"Get you under the earth." The earth forthwith swallowed up Cainech and her band of women; and therefore the place is called Cainech's Swamp in Glendalough. And on her head the dogs of the monastery void their excrement from that time forth till doom.[14]

This same story is told in the "Life of Coemgen," but here we are told that the child had been given to Coemgen for fosterage because "a fairy witch, named Caineog, with her attendant women followed the infant, bent on destroying it, as they had destroyed every other son which the king of Uí Fáeláin had had previously."[15]

That the women, whose power rested on ensuring regeneration, would want to destroy the infant would be highly unlikely. The earlier version of the story where possession of land was in question is much more likely to have been the case. As late as the fifteenth century, all over Europe, women still were accused of being evil witches. Their land was confiscated by both church and state, and their children were often left penniless.[16]

Conflicts over land are evident elsewhere in stories where the male saints have first to deal with symbols of badgers, boars, salmon, or other animals sacred to the Goddess, before establishing their religious foundations.[17]

We have seen how important the cow was in ancient religious rites, and many conflicts occur between male saints and "old women" with cows who, in reality, were probably priestesses or midwives. In one of these incidents there was an old woman named Mona who had an extraordinary calf called Mona-an-laoigh. Although people often tried to persuade her to part with it, she held onto the calf for many years. Finally, the lord of the place where she lived went to her and killed her and her calf. He was followed by a "saint" who ordered the house where she kept the calf to be pulled down. The saint, furthermore, "left his curse on any one who would ever mention Mona's name, to prevent which he moreover changed the name of the hill from Cnoc-Mona-an-laoigh to Cnoc-man-a-lay."[18]

On another occasion when women "of the trumpet song" came to wash their "foul clothes" in a spring on their own land,[19] the future Saint Máedóc came and told them, "Do not wash here for this is the monk's domestic spring and it is not fitting for women to consort with them." "We will," said they. "To us belongs this side of the stream which skirts our land."[20] Soon after, a king's daughter came to wash at the stream. Máedóc was furious and angrily "made her feet clave to the clothes, and the clothes to the stones, and the stones to the earth: and thus she stood there like a statue or any human image, without movement or motion and did not dare to stir to one side or the other."[21] When the woman's father heard what had happened, he rushed to Máedóc asking him to release his daughter. Máedóc finally agreed, and the man "gave himself, and the place, and his family in perpetuity to God and to Máedóc."[22]

Interestingly, the stream had been created when Máedóc pulled down a great tree in the place where he was building his monastery. Trees were focal points of worship for the old religions, and the women may well have been making a protest at Máedóc for what he had done to their religious site. It would be fascinating to know more about the "women of the trumpet song."[23] Providing us with such information was not the intention of the saint's biographer.

Máedóc seems to have had particular problems in dealing with the old religion. One of his first miracles was to turn the "webstress's slay which Eithne [his mother] held at the child's birth made of hard dry hazelwood" into a hazel tree. It was said that when "earth from it over which nine Masses have been said is inserted between prisoners and their chains [lit., irons], they thereupon escape forthwith."[24] The webstress's slay would have been a sacred object in the old religion, as the hazel was sacred to the Goddess, and any instrument used in childbirth would have taken on sacred characteristics. The fact that Máedóc converted this symbol to the use of Christianity gives us an indication as to how important this object was; at the same time it illustrates how the new religion abolished its importance forever.

The power of the "wise women" was intimately related to sexuality, and if the priests were to move in on their territory, control of fertility would have to be wrested from them or, at least, the priests would have to display comparable or superior powers in order to make the women redundant. We saw an example of this in the lives of Coemgen and Declan, where religious objects and places sacred to the old religion were "Christianized." There are many other examples.

Molasius of Devenish made a barren woman pregnant.[25] Abban changed the sex of a female infant to male because the king wanted an heir.[26] St. Declan blessed a childless couple, and "she conceived and brought forth twin sons, Fiacha and Aodh who, together with their children and descendants were under tribute and service to God and Declan."[27] In Declan's case there were distinct financial as well as theological matters at stake since the fertility of the couple made the family permanently indebted to Declan's monastery. The saints are said to have taken it upon themselves to perform supernatural abortions,[28] possibly to counteract the power of those who performed them by "magic."[29] The male concern for paternity also gave men new inroads into sexual politics that did not always work to their advantage. For instance, as Columcille lay in his bier a woman came along asking if he had perchance left anything behind for the child he had fathered. Dead and all as he was, Columcille raised himself up protesting his innocence and went on to compose a poem that could be recited to a woman making a similar claim. Should she be lying, she would die within a year.[30]

> I am being accused of a son that is not mine,
> O God act as my protector,
> let there not be a legal contention about me
> because of the bright outburst of vehemence.
> There is no laypower in his abode
> West, East, or South, what a vigorous report.
> I say in front of the Son of God the Father
> that I am not father to anybody.
> Creator God, protector of us poor,
> a mysterious over-king has reared me,
> learning has to be attended to
> even though this son has been made.[31]

St. Moling was also accused of fathering a child. A woman had tried to seduce him, and he had resisted, prophesying that she would be raped. She was raped, and she bore a child, upon which her husband insisted that she take it to Moling. In the meantime her husband was killed by Moling's people in revenge for the slight, and when the woman came to Moling with her child in her arms, Moling's response to her was as follows:

I do not see anybody here who would have care
For the cry of the calf that is on your back.
Take your son away. The clerics have no care for your son.[32]

In yet another incident, Columcille came to Colmán Ela with a problem. Columcille's sister, who was Colmán Ela's aunt, had borne two sons, which Columcille had baptized. But now, upon finding out that they were born of an incestuous relationship, he wanted to "compass their destruction without shame to myself."[33] St. Colmán Ela solved the problem by asking that the children be brought to him, offering to feed them from his "two paps," one of honey and one of milk.[34] For good measure he compares the "evil of women" with the "sands of the sea."[35]

A further theme of this story is that the saint has saved the lives of the children by taking them for fosterage. There are several other instances where saints protect children whose parents wanted to kill them.[36] Perhaps the most vivid example of the practice was when Ultán adopted the "babes of the women whom the Yellow Plague slew." To feed these infants, Ultán used to "cut off the cows' teats and to pour milk into them, and to put them into the children's mouths, so that the infants were playing around him." From these fosterlings Ultán got a rich crop of future church workers: one hundred laborers, one hundred religious devoted to prayer, a hundred scholars, and fifty nuns mentioned only for their "fair colored form."[37]

Christianity was helping to solve a problem that arose with the new emphasis on men's role in reproduction. The saints, by taking in or otherwise caring for unwanted children, were alleviating the worst excesses of patriarchy, just as Adamnán had alleviated the exploitation of women warriors. But, as we saw with Adamnán, there was no question that a price had to be paid: such children effectively became "slaves of the church."[38] In a society that depended so heavily on labor power, these children must have been an invaluable economic asset to the monasteries, which could then use their services for farming, building, and taking care of the needs of the monks.[39]

While it might seem laudable that the monasteries would take in unwanted children, in many ways they were simply taking care of a problem arising from the patrilineal system they had helped to create. For good measure they were building up their own temporal empires by means of slave labor.

Under the matrilineal system, all children born to a woman would automatically become members of the clan. The notion of an "illegitimate" birth was unknown. The laws of the Christian church, in sharp contrast to those of early Irish society, effectively helped to create the status of illegitimacy.[40] Under the patrilineal system "illegitimacy" became a reality. Should a woman conceive a child outside wedlock, through concubinage, rape, or an extramarital affair, its status was extremely suspect. The child had no inheritance rights from the father, would not automatically belong to any lineage, and mothers would often abandon or abort such infants rather than subject them to such a fate or risk becoming social outcasts themselves.

Once patriarchal forms of organization became established, sexuality became problematic. If a father was to take responsibility for raising a child and the child would in turn inherit the father's property, the father would make every effort to ensure that he was, in fact, the biological father. The only way he could do this was to control the sexual behavior of his wife.

Since even limited sexual freedom on the part of women would obscure the lines of inheritance from men, the church's rules on sexuality helped to keep women under control. A woman who gave birth outside the accepted rules of church and society eventually would become an outcast, a status that did not apply to the father who could usually remain anonymous if he so chose. Should it be necessary to decide who the father of a particular child might be, the saints were not above performing miracles.

In one case, for instance, when a woman accused a bishop of fathering her child, Brigit miraculously made the three-year-old child identify its true father as a "low and ill-shaped man," the child adding on for good measure, "My mother is a liar."[41] In another case when a woman refused to identify the father of her child, Ailbe called out all the men of the village in an effort to discover who he could be. Again the infant named his father, and all present glorified God at such a great miracle. In both cases, needless to remark, the word of the child had greater standing than the word of the woman.[42]

The church fathers had every reason to maintain the new patriarchal relationships, exercising as they did such an important point of control over women. With the firm establishment of Christianity, the control of sexuality took on new dimensions as the Fathers took the problem of sexuality several steps further as a way of exerting control over men.

THE SCIENCE OF SEXUALITY

In the earliest form of society, sexuality was nonproblematic, that is to say, it was a form of behavior occurring between two people that may or may not lead to the conception of a child. Control over sexuality ultimately went far beyond what was necessary merely to ensure moral sexual relations. "Sexuality" became an entity that took on a life, language, and discipline of its own. The control of sexuality became a science. The male clerics, by proving their immunity to women's power, were uniquely qualified to become the new scientists.

The different aspects of sex were split apart into thought, word, intention, involuntary urges, and actual deeds of sex to form a science of sexuality or what a contemporary philosopher has called a "discourse on sexuality."[43] Sexuality was greatly elevated in importance and made the subject of serious study by the early church for the purpose of better controlling the people subject to its urges. This development, for which the early Celtic monks can take particular credit, put men and women into a serious double bind from which Christianity has never recovered. On the one hand, the early church taught that virginity and continence were infinitely superior to marriage and that anyone who could do so should live in a state of continence.[44] On the other hand, the natural urges became supremely elevated in importance.

Although in theory the purpose of sex was restricted to reproduction, in reality sexuality was "invested" with a new significance. Sexuality became a subject for confession, where the minutest details of one's most intimate bodily functions became a topic for discussion. In the same breath that the monks used to condemn sex, they were also elevating its importance. Desire and prohibition of sex went hand in hand, leading some contemporary thinkers to credit the monks with developing eroticism itself.

This emphasis involved the early Christians in a serious dilemma. Growth in "spirituality" was directly related to control over one's body, but the body was supremely unimportant and merely a vehicle for the "spirit" contained within it from the moment of the rebirth through baptism. The body was at once elevated in importance, only to be cast down by the weight of sinfulness. The body itself became extremely problematic for anyone who wanted to live a Christian life. The earliest saints were either martyrs, severe ascetics, or virgins; proof of their sublime indifference to their earthly fate.

We have seen in the Adamnán story that the church did not have, or could not use, physical force to restrain the kings. Adamnán's little bell, symbolizing the power to excommunicate from the church, was its only weapon. Likewise the church had no firm economic power in society, being dependent on the beneficence of the faithful. The church had to rely on other sanctions in order to gain a foothold in men's minds.

The power to grant men admission to eternal life was one such sanction. This was a very long-term proposition that worked well only when people lived in daily expectation of the world's end. The first Christians thought the apocalypse was imminent and formulated their teaching around this expectation. Once people had been baptized, if they fell into serious sin again, they had no hope of salvation. When people were in imminent hope of the Second Coming, this level of morality might have been possible, but in a situation where there must have been many lapses, this teaching must have led to incredible despair on the part of unfortunate sinners who could live for another fifty years in the certain knowledge that they were going to hell.

Gradually the awareness grew that the Second Coming was a spiritual as much as a historical event. The church settled down to live in and with ordinary human society. For the day-to-day control of men in this situation, other more short-term measures would be required.

Sexuality took on new dimensions from the simple question of who would take care of any child born of a sexual union. This was still an important issue, but far more important than the mere physical birth of the child was the rebirth offered by Christianity by means of baptism. If the male priests were to maintain control over "spiritual paternity," what better way than by making sexuality itself problematic. Just as men controlled the sexuality of women, now the priests, by making sexuality in almost all its forms intimately related to sin, controlled sexuality and, thereby, the minds of all the faithful. Historically, this would prove to be just as powerful a means of control as the weapons of the warriors. Sexuality was something like electrical energy. Left to its own devices it could wreak what the clergy considered to be inestimable harm. But by buying what amounted to the total "rights" to the use and control of this energy, the monks could direct its power for their own purposes.

The main sources for studying the attitudes of the early church toward sexuality are the *Penitentials*. The *Penitentials* estimated the relative seriousness of each sin committed, enabling the monks to devise penances that could be undertaken by a sinner enabling him or her to return to the ranks of the Christian community. The *Penitentials* also solved the problem caused by those who imposed too harsh or too lenient conditions for forgiveness. By devising standard penances for each offense, the confessor would not have to rely on his own judgment in each case. These confession manuals, regularly updated and used extensively by confessors until fairly recent times, provide invaluable evidence of the church's attitudes toward sexuality at different periods in history.[45]

The *Penitentials* go into every possible variation on the theme of sex. Oral sex, sex with animals, varieties of masturbation, homosexuality, rape, incest, fornication, and abortion are but some of the topics covered. As yet there has not been a study of the sexual politics of the *Penitentials*, but a cursory overview reveals some interesting patterns that support the developing relationship between control of sexuality and the rise of patriarchal power in the church.[46]

The highest penalty for fornication is given to bishops. The *Penitentials* made intricate calculations as to the number of years fasting or loss of rank required in each case of clerical sexual transgression, depending on the status of the cleric concerned.[47] An "inferior monk" simply got three years penance.[48] Obviously, the higher one went in the spiritual hierarchy, the more important it was to separate from women and the greater the consequence if one proved to be vulnerable to their wiles.

Certain parts of the *Penitentials* go into express details as to the penance due to priests who "cause their sperm to flow." Depending on whether this happened on contact with a woman, sleeping in church, through masturbation, sinful thoughts, shameful words, or involuntarily during sleep, the penance is different.[49] Just for loving a woman and talking with her the penance is forty days. But should the priest give her a hug, his penance is increased to one year.[50]

In the case of laymen, the crucial issue in fornication was not only the act itself but the extent to which intercourse with a woman had damaged another man's property. The penance for intercourse with a married woman in one *Penitential* is given as seven years, but for intercourse with a "neighbor woman" the penance is fourteen years.[51] Intercourse with a widow carried the penalty of one year,[52] whereas with a virgin the penalty was two years plus the dowry that she could normally have commanded upon marriage. This should be paid by the man to her relatives rather than to the woman injured, or else, "if her relatives agree, let her be his wife."[53] Should a man have intercourse with his female slave, he should sell her and not have intercourse with his own wife for a year. But if the man begets a child of the slave woman, he has to set her free and not sleep with his wife for a year.[54]

This new attitude toward sexuality also affected men very severely. For the pre-Christian Celts, homosexuality was a revered and honored institution, especially for the warriors, and there is evidence that in pagan Celtic rituals male homosexuality was practised.[55] The early Christian storytellers are quite open in discussing homosexual urges. St. Moling, for instance, had performed a particularly difficult feat, sucking the mucus from the nose of a leper. When the leper disappeared Moling threatened to "fast" against God until God appeared to him "clearly and evidently." An angel then appeared, asking Moling in which form he would like the Lord to appear. Moling replied:

"In the shape of a boy of seven years, so that I may make fits of fondness around Him." He noticed nothing at the end of a time afterwards, till Christ sat on his lap in the shape of a boy of seven years, and he was fondling Him till the hour of rising on the morrow. "If thou deemest that enough," says the angel, "get thee to thy monastery."[56]

In the early Irish church there is evidence that intense relationships between men were still treated with some respect.[57] By the time the *Penitentials* were formulated, homosexuality was treated extremely harshly, in one case listed with murder and given the same punishment of ten years.[58] In another, it was listed with bestiality (intercourse with animals) and also given ten years' penance. For men to adopt the "feminine" position in sexual behavior was seen as the ultimate degradation of their masculinity, one that symbolically threatened the masculinity of every other male. Clearly, if one man could "become like a woman" there was no telling what might happen to the rest. Therefore, male homosexuality was treated even more harshly than natural fornication.

John Chrysostom was outraged by homosexuality:

If those who suffer it really perceived what was being done to them, they would rather die a thousand deaths than undergo this. . . . For I maintain that not only are you made (by it) into a woman, but you also cease to be a man; yet neither are you changed into that nature, nor do you regain the one you had.[59]

The real crime of homosexuality was that men assumed the "feminine" position in sexual intercourse. Lesbianism, on the other hand, was not taken at all seriously by the early church.[60]

The *Penitentials* were extremely interested in the question of defilement and listed the penances to be performed by anyone who had eaten or drunk items contaminated by mice, worms, cats, dogs, and lay people. They were particularly concerned with punishing anyone who had eaten food contaminated by a pregnant slave woman, the lowest possible person on the social ladder.[61]

Female children in general were not worthy of much consideration. When sacred taxes (tithes) were being levied on all the first fruits of the field and the womb, female children did not count.[62] A woman would be unclean for thirty-three days after the birth of a son, but for a daughter her period of uncleanness lasted sixty-six days, according to the *Penitential of Cummaen.*[63] A later *Penitential* changed this penance to seven days of uncleanness for the birth of a male child. On the eighth day

he who is a male and acts as a man is cleansed immediately on the coming of that future world. And immediately the mother who bore him is made clean; for he shall receive in the Resurrection his flesh purified from its vices.

But if the unfortunate child

had nothing manly with which to resist sin, if he was remiss and effeminate in his actions, whose sin is such that it is not forgiven either in the present world or in that which is to come, he passes through both the first and the second week of his uncleanness, and finally, with the beginning of the third week, he is cleaned from the uncleanness which the woman incurred by child-bearing.[64]

One of the most interesting aspects of the *Penitentials* is their attitudes toward abortion. In one of the earliest *Penitentials,* that of St. Finnian, he maintains the following:

If a woman by her magic destroys the child she has conceived of somebody, she shall do penance for half a year with an allowance of bread and water, and abstain for two years from wine and meat and fast for the six forty-day periods with bread and water. But if, as we have said, she bears a child and her sin is manifest, (she shall do penance) for six years (with bread and water) as is the judgment in the case of a cleric, and in the seventh year she shall be joined to the altar, and then we say her crown can be restored and she may don a white robe and be pronounced a virgin. So a cleric who has fallen ought likewise to receive the clerical office in the seventh year after the labour of penance.[65]

This view of abortion is interesting for several reasons. An abortion is apparently less serious than the sin of bringing a child into the world "so that the sin become manifest." Whether a "sin had become manifest" could also determine the amount of penance given in other cases. As one *Penitential* decrees, "However if anyone has committed fornication with women, but has not begotten a child, and it has not become known among people: if he is cleric, three years, if a monk or deacon, five years, if a priest seven, if a bishop, twelve years."[66]

The *Penitentials* are clearly concerned not just with the legal technicalities of the sexual act but also with social consequences. Bringing a child into the world was something that should not be taken lightly. Only when a child has been born is virginity considered lost, and in the case of an abortion loss of virginity does not even arise. This view of abortion occurs in the *Penitentials of Finnian and Columbanus,* which probably originated in the sixth century.[67]

A different attitude toward abortion is taken by the later seventh- and eighth-century documents. Abortion of an "embryo" in the rules of the *Irish Canons,* the *Bigotian Penitentials,* and the *Old Irish Penitentials* carries the penalty of three years. However, the documents took it for granted that there was a big difference between an "embryo" and a "fetus" with flesh and spirit. In the *Irish Canons,* the penalty for the destruction of a fetus is seven and a half years of fasting with continence and in the *Bigotian Penitentials,* fourteen years on bread and water.[68] The *Old Irish Penitentials* makes an even further distinction:

A woman who causes miscarriage of that which she has conceived after it has become established in the womb, three years and a half of penance. If the flesh has formed, it is seven years. If the soul has entered it, fourteen years' penance. If the woman dies of the miscarriage, that is, the death of body and soul, fourteen cumals [slave women] (are offered) to God as the price of her soul or fourteen years' penance.[69]

This author sees three stages in the development of the infant. First the embryo is established, which presumably is composed of mere fertilized seed; then enfleshment of the seed; and finally ensoulment of the fetus, the stage at which abortion carried the highest penalty. The *Penitentials'* view of abortion stands in great contrast to the view of the Catholic church at present, which prohibits abortion even one hour (with certain forms of contraceptives) after intercourse has taken place. The early church considered the development of "personhood" to be a gradual process and not only the result of a biological transaction.

The early Irish church was likely influenced by theological speculation taking place in Rome and elsewhere on these matters. In the earliest treatment of abortion, the rules were not made in a vacuum but took into account the current social conditions. Abortion may well have been treated harshly, but so too was irresponsible sex, especially when it resulted in the unplanned birth of a child. Sex "with issue" was far more serious than sex without.[70] Seven years of penance were prescribed for those "who are given to lust, and that frequent various mates and have children born to them." Likewise, "those that shed blood and commit homicide, seven year's strict penance for them."[71] The giving or taking of life was treated with equal seriousness, and the social context in which the act took place and that received its effects was of paramount importance in determining the seriousness of an offense.

In all these rules and regulations we can see that there was no necessary agreement on moral matters, even if there was fierce debate. The early moral theologians pored eagerly over their subject matter with all the enthusiasm of modern-day lawyers. The main issue at stake was that of keeping the delicate balance between ensuring one's future salvation and maintaining control over one's present flock. This dilemma is well illustrated in documents that have come down to us from a movement known as the Céli-Dé.

The Céli-Dé movement in the eighth and ninth centuries was largely responsible for recording the *Penitentials*. The Céli-Dé was an ascetic movement that arose partly in response to the laxity of the earlier monasteries, many of which were now taken over by family groups with lay abbots at their head.[72] In some cases the Céli-Dé had their own foundations; in others they lived alongside the existing institutions almost like resident ascetics.

The Céli-Dé had a firm social consciousness and admitted people from all strata of society to their order, in sharp contrast with other monasteries, which by now had become elitist, with many of the most prestigious offices becoming hereditary. Their attitude toward the poor is particularly striking, as we can see in one example.

One time, as he was praying in his church, (Moling) saw the youth *coming* to him into the house. A purple garment *was* about him, and he had a distinguished countenance. "That is good, O cleric" said he. "Amen," said Moling. "Why dost thou not salute me?" said the youth. "Who art thou," said Moling. "I," said he, "am Christ the Son of God." "That is not possible," said Moling to him: "when Christ approaches to converse with the Céli-Dé *it is* not in purple . . . he comes, but in forms of the miserable, i.e. of the sick, and lepers."[73]

The Céli-Dé in general adopt a realistic attitude to human nature. For instance, carnal thoughts are not considered to be very serious, and the monks, according to one document, "do not find it easy to fix any penance for such straying of the thoughts."[74] If the natural impulses are stirred, this is of no great consequence, providing the man is keeping to the regular diet and not overindulging.

While every effort must be made through diet and fasting to control one's sexual impulses, the possibility of sex rearing its head in the most unlikely places is treated seriously. Maelruain, the abbot of the monastery at Tallaght, counsels that persons whose desires are excited, it may be through hearing confessions, or merely with meditating, or through youth, need strict abstinence to subdue them because it is excess of blood in their body, that is the cause.[75]

Although male sexuality seems to have been dealt with humanely by the Céli-Dé, the same cannot be said for their attitudes toward women. For instance, a layman came for counsel, and the monk asked him how long it had been since he had had sexual intercourse. The man replied that it was three years, whereupon the monk asked him if he had taken a vow. When the man said that he had not, the monk replied, "That is too long a time to part from the Devil without coming to God."[76] A man under spiritual direction should keep from his wife on Wednesday, Friday, and Saturday nights. But as for Sunday, "he should do so if he can."[77]

Maelruain, the abbot of Tallaght, seems to have shared the views of the early church, which held that, since menstruating women were unclean, they should not enter a church during their period nor should intercourse take place. Maelruain ordered, in addition, that women should not go to confession while menstruating and that the "virgins of the church" were free to miss the morning and evening prayers. At the same time he was solicitous for their welfare, ordering that soup be made for them at midday.[78] Men ought not have sexual intercourse with women during their menstruation period.[79]

Menstruating women were considered particularly potent and maybe even passionate creatures. For instance, in one case a monk was advising a friend, whose problem was that "desire lay heavy upon the girl, for it is a third part as strong again in women as in men." The monk dealt with her problem by reducing her diet until at her annual testing he pricked her fingers with a needle. When no more blood came out of her hand he told her to "keep on this pittance until thy death."[80]

The Céli-Dé believed that "excess of blood in the body" was the cause of passion. Since women menstruated and didn't die, they obviously had a lot of blood to spare. According to the definitions laid down by the Céli-Dé, reducing the women's diets until they suffered amenorrhea (absence of menstruation) was the treatment prescribed for those who wished to become holy. Such women would be so severely malnourished they would be incapable of exerting any leadership roles. This form of spirituality, therefore, further contributed to the diminished role they would play in the church of the future, giving even more encouragement to the development of male power.

And it was indeed power that was at stake. This comes out clearly in a story in one of the documents associated with the Céli-Dé. A monk went off on a journey when a woman happened to meet him: "She laid hands on him at last and there befell intercourse by tryst between them."[81] The horrified monk immediately raced off to see his confessor who said,

That shall not matter. A demon has contrived it to carry thee from us and set thee among the laity and bring thee into a penitentiary that thou mayst be publicly put to shame. . . . Thou shall go the sacrament, and shalt continue the same rule through each fast.[82]

Nevertheless, the monk "tempted by Satan" continued to be worried by the issue. He went to two other confessors in a row but was not satisfied with their advice. Finally he went to Columba, who said to him,

Thou hast crucified Christ once because of thyself by sin; secondly in the person of Findio, because thou didst not believe what he said by the Holy Spirit; thirdly in the person of Comgall; fourthly in mine. I pronounce upon thee fifteen years of penance because of the contempt thou hast shown for a true limb of Christ, namely, Findio.[83]

Although sexual transgression was important, of much greater importance was obedience to one's directors. Chastity was a symbol of the control of the "will," but obedience to one's superior was the ultimate test.

CHAPTER 6

The Blasts of Temptation
The Impact of Male Asceticism

Through a report made by the venerable Sparatus, we have learned that
you continually carry around from one of your fellow-countrymen's huts
to another, certain tables upon which you celebrate the divine sacrifice
of the Mass, assisted by women whom you call *conhospitae;* while you dis-
tribute the eucharist, they take the chalice and administer the blood of
Christ to the people. This is an innovation, an unheard-of superstition
. . . for the love of Christ, and in the name of the Church United and of
our common faith [we beg you] to renounce immediately upon receipt of
this letter, these abuses of the table in question, which we do not doubt
on your word, have been consecrated by the priests, and these women
that you call *conhospitae,* a name which I cannot hear or pronounce without a certain trembling, a name to defame the clergy and to throw shame
and discredit upon our holy religion. This is why, according to the rule
of the Fathers, we appeal to your charity, not only to restrain these *little
women* from staining the holy sacraments by administering them illicitly,
but also not to admit to live under your roof any woman who is not your
grandmother, your mother, your sister or your niece.

LETTER WRITTEN BY THE GALLICAN BISHOPS LICINIUS, MELANIUS,
AND EUSTOCHIUS, TO MEMBERS OF THE MISSION TO GAUL

In an ancient Irish document, the *Catalogue of Saints,* three distinct orders of saints are enumerated. The First Order was

in the time of Patrick; and they were all bishops, famous and holy . . . and full of
the Holy Ghost; three hundred and fifty in number, founders of churches. They
had one head (*caput*) Christ, and one Christ, and one chief (*ducem*), Patrick; they
observed (*sufferabant*) one mass, one celebration, one tonsure from ear to ear.
They celebrated one Easter, on the fourteenth moon after the vernal equinox,
and what was excommunicated by one church, all excommunicated. *They rejected
not the services and society of women . . . because founded on the rock Christ, they feared
not the blast of Temptation.*[1] (emphasis added)

The Second Order "refused the services of women, separating them
from the monasteries." In the Third Order, women receive no mention

at all. In the opinion of the writer of the document, said to be Tírechán in the eighth century, the First Order was "most holy." The Second Order was "very holy," while the Third was merely "holy."

> The first glows like the sun in the heat of brilliancy . . . the second is pale as the moon . . . the third shines like Aurora. . . . These three orders St. Patrick understood, taught by an oracle from above, when in that prophetic vision he saw all Ireland filled with a flame of fire; then he saw the mountains only burning and afterwards lights (*lucernas*) burning in the valleys.[2]

There are several ways of interpreting this document. Is it maintaining that the First Order was holy *because* it included women and fostered equality between the sexes? Alternatively, was it holy because, *in spite of the presence of women*, the First Order maintained its missionary zeal? Or finally, was it holy because, as Christian spirituality developed a life-denying and heroic spirituality, men realized that they actually needed "the blasts of temptation," represented by women, to spur them on to greater excesses and to set their spirituality in sharp relief?

The latter possibility seems to have been the most likely. The preoccupation of the early church with sexuality not only had implications for witches or sinners but was to reverberate throughout the whole society. Sexuality was such an effective means of plunging men back into nature and passion that they had best avoid it altogether. In addition, those responsible for the control of sexuality in society had better show evidence that they could control themselves. Indeed the holiness of men has become inextricable from the sensuality of women. As was said of Magnenn of Kilmainham, "He never looked a woman in the face (for fear that he should see the guardian devil of her)."[3] Maintaining women in their roles as "guardian devils" became a vital part of male spirituality.

Holiness in some male saints' lives is almost synonymous with the avoidance of women. For instance, we are told of St. Ciaran that "the holy Ciarán of Cluain, loves humility, from which he did not rashly swerve. He never uttered a word that was false, nor looked upon woman from his birth."[4] In the same *Martyrology*, the king of Munster, Cormac mac Cuileannáin, was said to have always been a virgin even though married. On the one occasion he gave his unfortunate wife a kiss after matins, he sang as a penance one hundred and fifty psalms while immersed in the icy fountain of Loch Tarbh.[5]

Sexual intercourse was highly suspect in the minds of the monks and many of the saints were said to have had miraculous births without their parents having had to resort to such low means of bringing them into the world. One occasion where this did not happen was in the birth of St. Bairre, a bishop of Munster. In order to atone for this oversight, Bairre spoke from his mother's womb and also "immediately after his birth in order to justify his father and mother."[6] St. Coemgen only sucked the breasts of his mother once on Fridays and on fast days, and from then on angels came to supply his needs.[7]

Men seemed very anxious to keep their territories separated from women. St. Cranatan's well at Killuragh supposedly dried up each summer because a woman had once washed her dirty linen there.[8] There are several stories where saints hid upon hearing the sounds of approaching sheep or cattle, on the grounds that "where there are sheep there are women, where there are women there is sin, where there is sin there is the devil, and where there is the devil there is hell-fire."[9]

In the "Life of St. Ciaran" (of Clonmacnois) we are told that for a time the daughter of the king of Temoria lived with him, studying theology until such time as a cell should be built for her. The fact that they maintained their chastity throughout this period was, according to the storyteller, the cause of "many being confirmed in the true faith."[10] One school counseled "complete avoidance of women," and in some cases the exclusion of women extended to the exclusion of female animals.[11]

Although monks and nuns may have chosen to live celibate lives, there is no attempt to deny the pain and loss of companionship felt. One of the most famous love poems of the early Irish church is that of Liadain and Curithir. This was written in the ninth century and concerns two young poets fiercely in love with each other. Curithir asked Liadain to marry him, but she was in the middle of her professional bardic circuit around Ireland and told him to wait until she returned. Curithir was anxious for them to have a son "who would be famous." Liadain, possibly realizing that in those times this would be the end of her career as a poet, decided to take a vow of chastity. When Curithir heard what she had done, he was distraught but took a vow of chastity also, and they both put themselves under the direction of the severe St. Cummine.

Cummine gave them the choice of either seeing each other or talking with each other, but not both. They chose to talk with each other behind gravestones. However, the pressure became too much. Eventually Cummine allowed them to sleep in the same bed for one night providing they had a "little scholar" between them to prevent any unseemly conduct. Nature must have taken its course, because Curithir, thereafter, was banished from the monastic settlement. Liadain daily went to the flagstone where Curithir used to pray, crying bitter tears, and eventually died of heartbreak. She was constantly tormented by the decision she had made, and her poignant struggle became a classic of Irish poetry.[12]

Liadain's story highlights the fierce dualism now being established between spirituality and human relationships. Sexuality was no longer a way to the Divine but a positive obstacle.[13]

The attitude toward sexuality was to have long-term implications for women's ability to participate meaningfully in the Christian church. As in many other revolutionary movements, women had formed the essential backbone for the church in the initial stages.[14] Pope Boniface, for instance, wrote to the English Queen Ethelberga in the seventh century, sending her a silver mirror and a gold and ivory comb and urging her to assist in the conversion of her husband, King Edwin. Quoting scripture, he argued that "the unbelieving husband shall be saved through the believing wife."[15]

The new Christian revolution had offered opportunities to women not to be found within the native social structure. One such option was spiritual marriage, in which women lived together with their "consortia" or "spiritual husbands" and undertook liturgical functions. The Celtic saints Scoíthín, Mel, Kentigern, and the Anglo-Saxons Aldhelm and Robert of Abrissel all lived *in consortio mulierum* and were nevertheless recognized as saints.[16] An old Irish poem, *The Crínóg*, refers to one of these relationships:

> In sinless sisterhood with men,
> Four times since then, has thou been bound,
> Yet not one rumour of ill-fame,
> Against thy name has travelled round.
> At last, their weary wanderings o'er,
> To me once more thy footsteps tend;
> The gloom of age makes dark thy face,
> Thy life of grace draws near its end.[17]

The custom was not peculiar to Ireland. There is evidence that it existed throughout the early church. A bishop of Antioch had several such "wives." According to St. Irenaeus in the second century, several heads of the Valentinian sect lived together with "sisters." At the time of Cyprian, bishop of Carthage in the third century, virgins who were dedicated to God "lived in the most intimate relationship with confessors, priest and laymen," and the rigorous Tertullian advised well-to-do Christians to take into their houses one or more widows as "spiritual spouses" who were "beautiful by their faith, endowed with their poverty, sealed by their age. . . . It is well pleasing to God to have several such wives." Sometimes a monk and a nun would retire together into the desert, seeking to unify their souls in a way that would bring them closer to God. The later church, seeking to suppress this custom, met with a lot of opposition. One poor bishop, Leontius of Antioch, castrated himself in order to be permitted to retain his beloved companion.[18]

In Ireland, St. Patrick did not approve of these relationships. At one time Patrick is said to have investigated the case of Bishop Mel and his "sister" and ordered the parties to separate. The "sister" appeared before Patrick holding burning embers in her apron (a proof of her virginity). Patrick was singularly unimpressed and upheld his decision.[19]

A more serious incident occurred when Patrick was enraged with a woman, Lupait, a "sister" who lived at the Fort of Macha and of whom he had heard rumors. He was away from his mission at the time. When he came back the woman went out to meet him and cast herself down before his chariot. Patrick said, "Drive the chariot over her." The charioteer did as he was told and the chariot went over her three times. The document concludes, "She went to heaven at the Ferta." Patrick also is said to have cut the hand off MacNisse, Bishop of Connor, who had such a sister and who had previously been baptized and ordained by Patrick. Patrick thereafter issued a decree: "Let men and women be apart so that we may not be found to give opportunity to the weak, and so that by us the Lord's name be not blasphemed, which be far from us."[20]

St. Patrick, however, was not very successful, and the custom appears to have continued. As late as the ninth century a Saxon saint named Bercert lived in County Cork with a "sister." Local tradition has it that each evening she returned home with burning embers in her apron. One evening, however, the embers burned a hole in her garments. Bercert questioned her, and she admitted that her foot had been admired by a shoemaker who was measuring her for a pair of shoes. Bercert thereupon sent her away, as the "brightness of her holiness was thus dimmed."[21]

The old Irish church, according to one historian, made these relationships a "foundation pillar of its organisation."[22] In these relationships, at least in Ireland, no difference was then made between man and woman, and both were allowed to take part in church functions. When the Celtic mission moved to Brittany, the Gallican bishops were scandalized at the fact that the men were accompanied by women who, like the men, assumed to themselves sacramental functions.[23]

We have no clear dates for the ending of spiritual marriage in Ireland, and the Irish apparently persisted in these relationships. Marriage, spiritual or otherwise, among the clergy proper (as distinct from monks and nuns) survived at least up to the twelfth century and in many cases up to the time of the Protestant Reformation.[24]

Convent life was also an attractive option for women, and "double monasteries" were formed where women often held enormous power. These were institutions where both men and women lived together to their mutual advantage. In many of these monasteries, the abbess presided over both men and women, and although only men seem to have had the official power of orders, there are numerous references in the canons and councils of the church complaining that abbesses were indeed performing functions that are now the prerogative of the male clergy. There is evidence that abbesses heard confessions, decided on the fitness of both monks and nuns to enter the order, selected confessors, and veiled their own nuns.[25] Several male saints were associated with double monasteries, but as male forms of asceticism took hold, the practice was discouraged when "women became objects of suspicion."[26]

For many women the convent provided the only alternative to a life of drudgery or slavery. Their value to their families often lay in the dowry they could extract from a prospective husband, and women's wishes were seldom taken into consideration. The literature also records the burning of adulteresses.[27] In one case, a father wanted to burn his pregnant daughter (since her pregnancy effectively destroyed her cash value to him). She was saved only when the profusion of her tears put out the flames.[28]

In early Irish law, women were allowed to have a "lifetime" interest in the property or land passed down from their fathers but not to own land outright. Therefore, no matter how sturdy the institutions they might found, the property itself would revert to their kin upon the death of the founder. In addition, in the seventh and eighth centuries, many monasteries effectively became "family" institutions where religious roles, even that of the *erenagh* or abbot, would be passed down from father to son, the abbots not necessarily being celibate. Given that the structure of Irish life was by this time firmly patriarchal, this would mean that any female religious institutions would come under the control of their family patrons.[29] As an early Irish law tract put it clearly:

Her father watches over her when she is a girl; her *cétmuinter* watches over her when she is the wife of a *cétmuinter;* her sons watch over her when she is a woman with children; her kin watch over her when she is a woman of the kin (i.e., with no other natural guardian, father, husband, or son); the Church watches over her when she is a woman of the Church. She is not capable of sale or purchase or contract or transaction without one of her (aforementioned) heads [superiors] save a proper gift to one of her heads, with agreement and without neglect.[30]

Throughout early Irish literature there are indications of the rough treatment women could expect if they went against their family's wishes. Many of the early women saints fled from marriage. Fainche the Rough fled from a forced marriage.[31] Samthann's father forced her to marry against her will, but the marriage was never consummated.[32] Brigit was perhaps the most dramatic example: Brigit's father and her brothers wanted her to get married to a man who had asked for her hand. Brigit told her suitor that there was a young girl nearby who would be more than happy to marry him and that she would bless his face and his mouth to make him more appealing. Her tactic succeeded, but her brothers were furious since they wanted to get her *tinscrae* or dowry. One of them taunted her saying, "That beautiful eye which is in your head will be betrothed to a man though you like it or not." In response, Brigit pulled out her eye and gave it to one of her brothers, taunting him that no man would want a blind girl. Having persuaded her brothers that she was not at their disposal, she cured her eye by holding her staff against it, cursing her brother and his descendants.[33]

Yet even though the convent offered opportunities to women, it would not be long before the patriarchal values from which the women were trying to escape would find themselves in new form in the religious realm fostered by the warriors for Christ.

One of the most famous stories concerning the exclusion of women from the monasteries is told in the "Life of St. Senán." One day a female hermit was praying when a tower of fire rose up before her from Inis Cathaig where Senán lived. This indicated to her that this should be the place of her resurrection, and so she set off. Upon reaching the island, Senán met her and told her that she should go and stay with her sister at another island. Canair insisted that this was the island where she was destined to be, but Senán insisted "women do not enter this island." Canair replied in terms worthy of any feminist theologian:

How canst thou say that? Christ is no worse than thou. Christ came to redeem women no less than to redeem men. No less did He suffer for the sake of women than for the sake of men. Women have given service and tendance unto Christ and His Apostles. No less than men do women enter the heavenly kingdom. Why, then, shouldst thou not take women to thee in thine island?

"Thou art stubborn" was Senán's comment before finally admitting her.[34]

In the "Lives" of the women saints there is a great deal of evidence of the important role women played in the early church and of the difficulties that would await them dealing with the maleness of Christian spirituality. Very few such "Lives" of women saints are still in existence, despite the fact that in the *Martyrologies* (calendars of saints) there are numerous references to women. The "Lives" that survived are a highly select example of what was available: there must have been many more such "Lives" that have not managed to survive to the present day.

St. Monenna was a fifth-century saint, and her "Life" puts her in contact with both St. Patrick and St. Brigit. She studied theology under the guidance of a priest, and during her lifetime she established foundations in St. Andrews in Scotland, Burton-on-Trent, Dundevenal, Dumbarton, Stirling, Edinburgh, Dunpeleder, Alyth, Swords, Armagh, Faughart, Killevy, and Cheneglas, among others.[35] In addition, she is said to have traveled to Rome several times and was paid the dubious compliment of having "a man's spirit in a woman's body."[36]

The "Life of Monenna" is an invaluable source of evidence for the struggle women would have in their encounters both with warriors and priests. Monenna dealt with the power struggles between saints, bishops, warriors, and kings throughout her life, and her foundations were successively undermined and impoverished in the process. At one point, a bishop, threatened by her nearby foundation, instituted cloister on the nuns, leaving them with very little water during a severe drought. Monenna had to pray to St. Elias, who duly obliged her with a spring of her own in the middle of the monastery.

But at the end of her life, Monenna was thoroughly disillusioned, and it is said that "she never looked upon the male sex" again. If her duties took her away from the convent, she would go out at night, and if the sun rose before she had time to return to her convent, she would sit under a tent to protect her from heat and rain rather than go out in the daytime. If absolutely necessary, she would "face or address men with her face covered by a veil, ever wishing to leave an example to the younger so as not to allow death to enter the soul in any way through the windows."[37] Nevertheless, she continued her work, which included redeeming captives. But as far as possible she "hid everything from men's notice except what clear necessity forced her to display to them."[38] Obviously, these were vital survival tactics in the hostile environment in which she found herself.

Samthann was also one of the great women saints of early Ireland. She was an abbess, a spiritual director, an educator, and a church dignitary who attended the church synods in Ireland. She was also associated with the Céli-Dé movement and was on close terms with Maelruain, one of the main leaders.[39] At one time she sent a messenger to him asking if he "received womankind to his confession, and will he accept my soul-friendship?"[40] The messenger set off and conveyed the request to Maelruain, telling him that he was Samthann's favorite among the "clerics of the desert." When Maelruain heard this, "He blushed down to his breast, and made three genuflections, and fell silent for a long time. Then he said: 'Tell her that I will seek counsel from her.' " When the messenger came back to Samthann and told her all that had transpired, she said angrily, "I swear that something will come of that youth." She drew out her brooch, and as a proof of the purity of her request, she pricked her cheek until only milk came out (blood being a symbol of passion). She held up the drops on her nail and then declared solemnly, "So long as there is this much juice in his body, let him bestow no friendship nor confidence upon womankind."[41] Samthann's action indicates her clear awareness of the complexity of male spirituality and of the dangers for women to be found therein. However, her only way of dealing with Maelruain's displaced lust was to eradicate her own source of passion.

But all women did not automatically accept the tenets of male spirituality. For instance, Brigit had trouble with Coemgen of Glendalough and his particular brand of asceticism, which included holding his hands up to heaven for seven years so that birds nested in his palms. Brigit predicted that a good snowstorm would soon drive him inside.[42]

Unlike the stories extolling the virtues of separatism told of the male saints, Brigit obviously believed that contact between the sexes was to be desired. On one occasion, an anchorite who had resolved to have nothing more to do with women was passing by Kildare on his way to an island, intending never to leave this island again. His disciples begged him to let them visit Brigit for the last time, but he refused. All of a sudden, their luggage was "lost" only to be found in Brigit's monastery. The monks concluded that they had sinned in not having visited Brigit and asking her blessing. As an act of penance they fasted, and then spent several days in Brigit's monastery, "where they all offered joint prayers to heaven.[43]

Brigit also does not seem to have thought much of Patrick's version of asceticism. Patrick was much given to spending his nights in icy pools of water. When Brigit went to do this herself the pools dried up miraculously every night. According to the stories, her friends "persuaded" her that this was against God's will—a clear indication that this form of male spirituality was not to be hers.[44]

Given the difficulties of finding the sources of "women's history," we will never know to what extent the new religion was successful in diminishing the power of women. We cannot assume that women automatically took the word of the priests in every matter. For instance, there is a story of the time when a woman of "bad character" died in the area near the church of Columcille. Columcille directed that she be buried in the "Women's Graveyard," a spot so far from the church that when the bells rang they could not be heard among the tombstones. He also left an injunction that the cemetery should never be entered by a living woman or a dead man. However, the story goes, "devout women in olden times used to request burial there, in the belief that *no one interred there would be damned*" (emphasis added).[45]

DEMISE OF BRIGIT

In the Age of Brigit, we have documented the several stages through which the early Irish church would pass in its search for consolidation, and we have seen that the attitude toward women was the palimpsest upon which progress in male spirituality was engraved. Logically, for full progress in Christian spirituality, women with their sensual natures should have been eliminated altogether. Instead, other more subtle measures would be employed to ensure that women would never again arise to challenge the power and spirituality upon which patriarchal society was now founded.

Possibly there were counterstrands in the Christian tradition fighting against this development and still working on behalf of women. In view of the problems we have already discussed with regard to the nature of our sources, we will never really know. However, should we wish to read between the lines once more, it is, not surprisingly, to the documents surrounding Brigit that we should turn.

Her metamorphosis from Mother Goddess to Virgin Mother and eventually to Virgin Saint has been difficult for many reasons. While the change would ensure her survival within a Christian framework, the emphasis on virginity is itself derived from a patriarchal mentality. St. Brigit has derived her power at the expense of other women, displacing motherhood from the revered position it enjoyed under a matrifocal society. Brigit's status and her survival would now depend on how well she would adapt herself to the new patriarchal order.

The city of Kildare in the southeast, with which Brigit was associated, was a very important city in ancient Ireland. Kildare is said to have held the "treasures of kings," offering sanctuary to those criminals escaping from any possible rough and ready treatment at the hands of their victims, and, obviously, had a firm religious foundation absolutely necessary in those times to "ensure the stability of the market-place." Kildare, in other words, was an important trading center and seat of the Leinster (the eastern provincial) kings: the power base from which they could exercise their ambitions in the future.[46] No doubt also Brigit's "virgins" helped to secure the "peace" of the city.

The first biographers of Brigit, said to be Ultán and Ailerán, showed little interest in Kildare. As far as they were concerned Kildare was in "enemy territory" to the south, and they were interested simply to glorify their saint who appeared in many places all over Ireland. They paid particular attention to her connecting with several old Irish sites of major religious importance, such as Uisnech and Teltown.[47] In other words, for them she was the saintly incarnation of the "Goddess" and her appearance at the old religious sites effectively "Christianized" these places, relegating their original pagan patrons to a position of unimportance.

If the first biographies of Brigit paid little attention to Kildare, the next major biography of Brigit made up for this lack. Written by Cogitosus, an ecclesiastical scholar in the seventh century,[48] Kildare here first comes into prominence for Brigit. Cogitosus was a member of the *Romani* party in Ireland, those who were trying to eradicate any vestige of the old religion in order to establish Christianity and bring Ireland into conformity with Rome on matters of faith and liturgical practice.

Cogitosus did his best to eliminate any references to Brigit as the "fire-goddess." As one scholar put it, "a strict censorship was clearly in operation among the *fratres* of Kildare in the matter of the ex-fire goddess's career."[49] Cogitosus edited out anything that might offend the "feelings" of the readers, but he also did his best to exalt the importance of Kildare over against Armagh in the north, going so far as to eliminate anything that gave the impression that Brigit was subordinate to Patrick.[50] Cogitosus's main intention was to extol Kildare and the greatness of Brigit, its founder. He refers to the place as *civitas Brigitae*, the "city of Brigit," but even he makes no attempt to attribute the foundation of Kildare to her.[51] The name *Kildare*, "Church of the Oak," seems to have been a later development.[52]

The efforts of Cogitosus and those of his contemporaries seem to have worked in part, because even though we know so little about the "historical Brigit" or her relationship to Kildare, nevertheless, in the seventh and eighth centuries there is no doubt that the abbess of Kildare enjoyed extensive rights. She appointed not only her own bishop but also those of neighboring territories, often extending very close to what was to become the primatial sea of Ireland, Armagh. Some of her nuns were in the *Regles Brighde,* the "Temple of Brigit," in the sanctuary of Armagh itself. But we have little information about this foundation as, according to one author, its endowments "would seem to have been absorbed in some more powerful interest even before the suppression of religious houses."[53] Indeed, Brigit's successor was said to have had special privileges recognized by the clergy and people of Ireland, that whomever she might recommend would be ordained.[54]

Historically, the abbess of Kildare was seen to have "special honour" among the women religious of both Ireland and Scotland.[55] The saint Lassar (Fire) transferred her church to Brigit in Patrick's presence. In addition, if any Irish nun were injured, compensation for her injuries was to be paid directly to Brigit's successor rather than to her own family or convent.[56] There seems to be no dispute that future abbesses of Kildare exercised the functions that would be appropriate to a bishop in his or her capacity as diocesan administrator. As one scholar of Irish monasticism claimed of the bishop whom Brigit engaged,

But it is equally clear that she had her bishop under her own jurisdiction. "She engaged him to govern the church *with her.*" If he was anointed head of all bishops, she was most blessed chief of all virgins; if he had an episcopal chair, *cathedra episcopalis,* she had a virginal chair, *cathedra puellaris,* of equal rank and dignity; if he was always "archbishop" of the Irish, she was always the abbess whom all other abbesses of the Scots venerated; for as he was pre-eminent among the bishops of Ireland, so she was pre-eminent among the abbesses of the Scots "in happy succession and in perpetual order."[57]

The bishop of Kildare was recognized as *ard* (chief) bishop. Kildare was the metropolitan see of Leinster in at least two different periods.[58] After the ninth century, wars, fire, and violence were known at Kildare, but the school continued until the Anglo-Norman invasion of the twelfth century.[59]

Already in the ninth century serious inroads had been made into the position of religious women. In 888 C.E., virgins, apparently for the first time, "cut their hair," an event so significant that it was recorded in one of the Irish annals amidst the accounts of wars and deaths of chieftains that normally constituted its "history."[60] Hair in the old religions of Europe had been a potent sign of women's power, so much so that one of the first things that the witch-hunters did was to shave the hair of those whom they accused.[61] Cutting the hair, therefore, must have constituted a symbolic break with the past so important that it found its way into recorded history.

Kildare had a network of subordinate churches and in the seventh century was "as serious an aspirant to the ecclesiastical primacy of Ireland as Armagh."[62] The successors of Brigit, and her political supporters, whoever they might be, in other words, were ideally placed for exerting religious and political supremacy in Ireland.

The possible aspirations of Kildare were never to come to fruition, for reasons both political and ecclesiastical. A full discussion of these reasons would take us far beyond the present narrative but we will summarize them here briefly.

The church of Armagh had made a powerful alliance with the Uí Néill, a dynasty that had seized control of a great deal of the north of Ireland and substantial parts of the midlands, including the ancient religious site at Tara from which the Leinster kings had traditionally received their religious authority. Kildare, on the other hand, became associated with the Leinster kings, who now, in turn, looked to Kildare to provide them with religious authority. We have already noted that some of the "fights" between Brigit and Patrick reflected the political struggles then taking place. Patrick eventually became patron saint of Armagh in the north and Brigit patron saint of Kildare in the south. But in the context of the wider issues we can see that their patronage was as much political as it was religious. In the political fight between the north and south of Ireland, of which the fight between Armagh and Kildare for control of the Irish church played a major part, the odds of Brigit's survival in any recognizable shape or form were heavily weighted against her. In this struggle Brigit, by becoming totally identified with specific political interests, lost her status as Mother Goddess and in her new guise as Virgin Saint would effectively be reduced to becoming a Virgin Warrior fighting on behalf of local political interests. In this role Brigit is seen, totally uncharacteristically, defending the rights of the Leinstermen, whose power was now seriously overshadowed by the ambitious Uí Néill. In one colorful incident she was even pictured in conjunction with the body of the dead Leinster king Illand, exhorting the Leinstermen to victory over the Uí Néill.[63]

Eventually a compromise seems to have been worked out between Kildare and Armagh in which Patrick told Brigit, "O my Brigit, your *paruchia* will be reckoned to your rule in your province, but in the eastern and western part it will be in my control."[64] Patrick would recognize the importance of Kildare in central Leinster, and the claims of Armagh would not be extended into her territory.[65] An equally important compromise was worked out in the area of sexual politics when Brigit and Patrick are said to have "divided Ireland between them, so that she is head to the women of Ireland, Patrick, however, is head to the men."[66]

The interplay of political and religious power continued in Ireland. The ninth and tenth centuries would see Ireland invaded by Viking forces from northern Europe who plundered the monasteries and centers of learning, raiding them for raw materials, food, and monastic treasures. Their raids left the country in constant turmoil, but this turmoil was nothing new to Ireland for in the ninth and tenth centuries intermonastic wars had themselves wreaked havoc on Irish church and society.[67] One famous Irish ecclesiastic, Feidlimid Mac Crimthann, described as "the best of the Scoti, a scribe and an anchorite," and who was king of Cashel in 819 C.E.,[68] is said to have been "responsible for more violence to the church than any other Irishman," having burned several churches, killing their occupants, and "greatly insulting" the religious incumbents.[69]

Ireland in the next several centuries was entering the world stage in an unprecedented way, and if the patriarchal Celts had radically affected the Irish social structure, the influence of the euphemistically called "Mother Church" would be even more devastating. We saw in the early laws that the king was so incensed by the crime of rape that he ensured that it was not in his power to forgive this crime or to mitigate the punishment due. By the twelfth century the rape of women in battle by those trying to gain power, especially that of the kingship, was commonplace. Brigit's metamorphosis had taken her from vestal virgin to becoming a political pawn, and now in 1132 the Abbess of Kildare was raped by the troops of King Dermot Mac Murrough, a Leinster king, in a battle in which many were slain and a large part of the monastery destroyed.[70] Dermot wanted to impose a kinswoman of his own on Kildare, and the rape of the abbess of Kildare was intended to render her unfit for office.[71]

The political machinery had moved, and the ecclesiastical machinery would follow. In 1152 the newly created diocese of Dublin won jurisdiction over Kildare when the metropolitan archdioceses were set up.[72] The death of the abbess of Kildare was always recorded in the Irish annals, symbolizing her power and prestige. The last mention of the abbess occurs in 1171, when Sadhbh, the daughter of "Gluniarainn (Iron-knee) Mac Murrough," died. The monastery at Kildare continued to exist but probably lost its independence when it was taken over by the regular canons of St. Augustine and presumably placed under the protection of the bishop, who happened to be Laurence O'Toole, the brother-in-law of the king of Leinster, Dermot Mac Murrough.[73]

By 1220 the papal legate, Henry of London, felt confident enough of the demise of Kildare to order that the sacred fire, which had burned since the beginning of the monastery, be extinguished. However, the outraged local people rose up against his decision, and the bishop of Kildare ordered that the fire be relit—a symbolic act that would not prevent the monastery from falling into relative insignificance until its final disbanding during the suppression of the monasteries in 1540–41.[74] Scholars have traditionally denied the claim that Henry of London extinguished the fire of Brigit in Kildare. This denial is in itself symptomatic of how far the erasure of women from Irish history has progressed.[75] These incidents have a symbolic significance that goes beyond mere historical facts: they strike at the heart of female religious power in Ireland.

The twelfth century would be known as the century of great reform throughout the church both in Ireland and abroad; however, the treatment of the abbess of Kildare would presage the treatment that women as a whole might expect. Mother Goddess, Virgin Mother, and Virgin Saint, Brigit was raped in her last incarnation as the abbess of Kildare: her successors disappeared from the Irish annals and her fire was extinguished on the orders of a Norman bishop. In other words, like the great Irish goddesses before her, she was raped, overthrown, made to disappear, and her fiery power extinguished. Finally, in the twentieth century, what little records we still have regarding her eventual overthrow and the role of the church in dousing her fiery power are dismissed.[76]

There has been a steady progression in the treatment and attitudes toward women in the Irish church. Women who clung to their ancient traditions were seen as dangerous—their ancient powers threatened those of the early church, and the men had no difficulty in taking violent measures against them. Those women who joined in the efforts to Christianize the country were initially welcomed when the monks "feared not the blast of temptation." As the power of the church took hold, however, based as it was on male asceticism, these women were increasingly marginalized and made subservient to the male hierarchy.

Brigit's successors alone survived the onslaught for two reason. First, the monastery of Kildare, as the site of the Leinster kings and possibly even as the last vanguard of the ancient Celtic church in Ireland, provided a clear check on the rising power of Armagh, with its increasing Roman influence, in the north. Second, Kildare was a renowned site of the old religion and, it could be argued, had successfully adapted itself to the early patriarchal form of church and state.

When women in general were denigrated by Christianity and female religious had little independent power, Brigit alone survived. Now with the centralization of power in church and state, women and their symbolism could no longer be tolerated. The "Nun of Life," the abbess of Kildare, symbol of the ancient unity of Ireland, would be overthrown and replaced with the military and ecclesiastical machinery of church and state.

In the new diocesan organization, Brigit's monastery, together with many other foundations at the time, was placed under the "protection" of the local bishop. From now on Brigit's successors would lose many of the privileges that she as abbess had held. Placing the monastery under the "protection" of the bishop effectively removed the abbess from her own independent source of power. In the twelfth century whatever remained of the early power and rites of Kildare would now be subject to close scrutiny and, with the new emphasis on orthodoxy, brought firmly into line. Apostolic succession would ensure that women were cut off from the last vestige of sacramental power, and any reverence that remained for Brigit would be relegated to the status of "folk belief."

In truth, however, the demise of Brigit had taken place much earlier and was reflected in some of her exchanges with Patrick. While these stories may reflect the struggles between their religious foundations for supremacy of the church in Ireland, this should not blind us to the fact that issues of sexual politics are brought to the forefront to justify Patrick's eventual supremacy. Ultimately, in the struggle between Patrick and Brigit, with the whole weight of patriarchal theology behind him, Patrick would get the upper hand.

On one occasion Brigit was asked to perform a miracle concerning a woman who had accused a priest "of Patrick's household" of fathering her child. Brigit caused the woman's lie to be discovered, at which time everyone present insisted that the woman be burned. Brigit refused and said that the woman should do penance instead.[77]

The story is interesting for several reasons. First, although Patrick was present, he clearly did not have the power on this occasion to determine the paternity of the child. Second, even though she absolved Patrick's cleric from guilt, she refused to let the woman become the scapegoat of the sexual politics of the time. In those days if a woman could not support a child, her alternative might be to donate it to a monastery to be clothed, fed, educated, and become a slave to the church.[78] Persuading a cleric to take responsibility for a child, by whatever means possible, would, therefore, be an alternative to child exposure or abortion. In refusing to let the woman be burned, Brigit recognized the desperation of the woman's act. Third, Brigit refused to perform her miracle in Patrick's presence. Only after she had left the assembly, would she agree to do it.

We are not given any explanation as to why she refused to perform miracles in Patrick's presence. A clue to the matter may be found in another story told of a man who had heard what happened in the assembly place and who sent for Brigit to consecrate his house. Up to that time the man had resolutely declared, "Patrick and his household would not baptize me." He had no problem accepting baptism from Brigit, but Brigit had to send out for a priest, saying, "Let someone go from us to Patrick that a bishop or priest may come to baptize this man." The priest duly came and performed the baptism, but Patrick then said to Brigit, "You should not go about without a priest. Your charioteer should always be a priest."[79]

With those few lines Brigit's religious power was doomed to extinction since ultimately the power of orders could not be conferred on a woman, a deprivation that would eventually greatly restrict her role and that of her successors.[80] Although Brigit might be more popular than Patrick (there are many more places in Ireland called after Brigit than after Patrick), might be better able to take care of the needs of women, might be able to perform more miracles than he, nevertheless, she would always be dependent on him or his representatives for the sacraments. One way of curbing her power would be to ensure that a priest would always be in tow, keeping an eye on her activities. Whatever powers Brigit or her successors might have from their gifts, talent, and wisdom would always be eclipsed and superseded by the power of orders conferred upon the priest by virtue of his manhood. As Patrick put it so well when looking for a bishop, "Seek for me a man of rank, of good family and of good character, with only one wife and child." "Why seekest thou that?" (to wit, a man of that kind) said Dubthach. "That he may be ordained," said Patrick, as though these requirements were nothing if not self-evident.[81]

Although there are several stories of interaction between Brigit and Patrick, we know that it is highly unlikely that they were both ministering at the same time. The stories were told about them, partly for political reasons in the disputes between the north and south for religious and political supremacy, but also to make clear to women that they should not take upon themselves sacramental functions that should more properly be undertaken by men in Holy Orders.

The power of orders was probably the crucial factor in the establishment of male religious power and in the demise of women. The fact that women could not celebrate Mass or administer the sacraments made them permanently dependent on men for those services. In addition, sacramental fees formed a very important source of revenue for the men of the early church. Cutting women off from this source of income would have far-reaching consequences beyond the matter of cultic purity. Needless to say, a great deal of energy was spent justifying this tremendous shift of power.

Behind the myriad of theological justifications given for excluding women from ordination were some very simple factors. The men of the early church became preoccupied with controlling their "passions" in favor of their "wills." This preoccupation was intimately tied to the new forms of power men were developing, and in this situation women became the scapegoats for men's inability to control their sexuality.

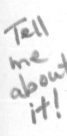

Not only would religious men ultimately abandon sexual relations with women, but, like the warriors, the priests could not tolerate the presence of women in the confines of their most holy ceremonies. Somehow the "energies" of women would pollute their most sacred ceremonies, weakening their power and destroying their efficacy.

And so it transpired that, just as the secular laws were instituting forms of power that would ensure male dominance, so too the church developed corresponding forms of power that would ensure the subordination of women. Just as women would only inherit property when no man was available, so too canon law would eventually prescribe that women could administer baptism only when no man was present. Just as women could not inherit property in their own right, so too they were now cut off from the "spiritual inheritance" of Holy Orders.

Excluded from Holy Orders, whatever power the women might retain in the future would be "charismatic," that is to say, it would be based on the recognition of their importance in the local community. By definition, charismatic power could not be transmitted. Each woman would have to earn for herself the respect and recognition of the local population.

In our journey through the development of the early Irish church we have come a long way from the story of Adamnán and his mother, Ronnat. In that story we saw that Ronnat considered her son unworthy to carry her across the field, given the position of women in society. But with the rise of male asceticism, and with the diminished role and status of the mother in the breakdown of the respect accorded to relations between kin, the situation is now reversed.

We saw then that women would have a high economic price to pay for their "liberation" by Adamnán and his successors; now we are coming to grips with the spiritual repercussions. Not only would women be permanently economically indebted to Adamnán and his monasteries, but they would also be permanently dependent upon the male members of the Christian church for any spiritual services they needed. The ascetic abbot Maelruain, for instance, was asked by a bishop whether or not he should take care of his mother, and Maelruain replied;

Though thou bring her not to thee to life, let her not carry thee to death: but if she be converted, thou art bound to take care of her.[82]

Maelruain, in common with the male functionaries of the early church, considered the "life" brought about by those powers vested in him as a priest to be far superior to anything of which mere women were capable.

Needless to say, women could not be bearers of the new "life" brought in by Christianity, for whereas in the old religion, the Goddess could be found in the trees, bushes, and holy wells, now access to God the Father took place through the mediation of the male priests. Certainly, one could pray to God the Father, but nothing that he replied would count— unless it met the approval of the male clergy.

The First Order of Saints admitted women to their ranks because "they feared not the blast of temptation"; by now, blasts of temptation were running riot. Like the Celtic warriors who, it was claimed, had met their deaths through the seductiveness and cunning of women, the "spiritual warriors," unable to take responsibility for their own passions, projected their anger onto women, casting them as "unclean," "seductive," and "weak willed." Like the warriors, the Christian priests had to be constantly on their guard.

As the "guardian devils" of men, women occupy the negative side of the dualism men have established in the theological world between good and evil, heaven and hell, spirituality and sex, God and the Devil. The tragedy, ambiguity, and cyclical regeneration of early Irish religion have been replaced by a harsh code of ethics and one in which women are the constant reminders to men of the depths to which their precariously established "souls" can fall.

The rape of the abbess of Kildare, begun by one of Dermot Mac Murrough's soldiers, was effectively completed by the ecclesiastical machinery of the twelfth-century reform movement. Her rape symbolized the end of an era for women and religion in Ireland. From now on, any power they had would be derivative; that is to say, it would be given or sanctioned by the local male ecclesiastics. No matter how brilliant, holy, or otherwise gifted any woman might be, her religious authority could be overruled by any male cleric, no matter how inept, power hungry, or degenerate.

Women in early Ireland have traveled an ominous path: once revered symbols of creativity, they have become signs of danger and pollution; transformed into virgins, they now need to be "protected." The church may well have begun by protecting women from the power of the male warriors, but who would now protect women from the power of the male church?

CHAPTER 7

From Kin to King

The Blood Covenant Made among Men, Excluding Women

When the whole people of that land has been gathered together in one place, a white mare is brought forward into the middle of the assembly. He who is to be inaugurated, not as a chief, but as a beast, not as king, but as an outlaw, has bestial intercourse with her before all, professing himself to be a beast also. The mare is then killed immediately, cut up in pieces, and boiled in water. A bath is prepared for the man afterwards in the same water. He sits in the bath surrounded by all his people, and all, he and they, eat of the meat of the mare which is brought to them. He quaffs and drinks of the broth in which he is bathed, not in any cup, or using his hand, but just dipping his mouth into it round about him. When this unrighteous rite has been carried out, his kingship and dominion have been conferred.

GERALD OF WALES

The rape of the Abbess of Kildare in the twelfth century was the final symbolic blow to independent female power in the Irish church. Just as the overthrow of the Serpent had occurred in Israel with the rise of new forms of political power, so too the demise of Brigit symbolized and was caused by major power shifts taking place in Irish society, fostered and encouraged by the Christian church. The rape took place in the context of the latest onslaught against women, itself the result of the Gregorian reform movement of the eleventh and twelfth centuries where an entirely new consolidation of power in Western Christendom was being effected.

In the next seven hundred years in Ireland several great women would appear on the historical stage as founders of orphanages, hospitals, schools, and as social reformers. The history of most of these women is as yet unwritten, and it would be premature to comment decisively on historical findings yet to come. We know, however, that these women experienced tremendous obstacles from the male clerics in their attempts to establish their religious foundations or to seek any kind of independence for their work. Several of these women died outside their orders or indeed outside the Catholic church.[1]

The power that men had attained by virtue of Holy Orders had enabled them to establish firm control over any independent forms of religion. But the power of orders was itself based upon male reproductive consciousness taken to its logical conclusion. For it was not enough that men should seize control of cultural and reproductive creativity at a personal level, now they would go on to consolidate this power throughout the political and religious consciousness of Europe.

In what is called the Gregorian reform movement of the eleventh and twelfth centuries the political and religious events taking place would permanently alter the character of the world-historical stage. New alliances would be made between kings and popes, new territories would be sought by means of the Crusades, new lands would be acquired on the part of the church, giving it an independent economic basis from which to operate. Corresponding with those changes, great theological and philosophical debates would take place about issues such as free will and grace, the sacrifice of the Mass, the nature of God, and the status of the Virgin Mary. This reform resulted in a new emphasis on sacramental theology, strict enforcement of the rules of clerical celibacy, an increasingly hierarchical understanding of church authority, and newly developed understanding and cooperation between church and state for the protection of their mutual interests.[2]

On the European continent these issues would be treated in highly philosophical and scholastic treatises by people such as Bernard of Clairvaux, Anselm of Canterbury, Peter Abelard, and Thomas Aquinas. To twentieth-century readers they may seem extremely esoteric, but as we discuss the underlying issues involved, the social and religious tensions being addressed, we will begin to see how the resolution of some of these issues was crucial to the survival of the new social and religious establishments.

The twelfth century also saw a great literary flowering in Ireland where the same topics were dealt with in the form of stories, myths, satires, and sagas. As one scholar has asserted, the Irish literature of the period appealed to imagination as much as to reason.[3] In contrast to the learned tomes that one would have to plough through to delve into the scholarly mind of the time, the Irish gift for story-telling has, therefore, preserved for us a fairly transparent and unique account of the issues at stake, for which we can be grateful.

Several documents give us valuable insights into the ways this power would be established. Female symbolism would be firmly rejected in all its facets. Forms of male bonding and exclusivity would be established that ultimately would find expression within the sacramental realm itself. In looking at these documents we will be moving back and forth between centuries as the Irish often used sixth- or seventh-century fig-

How many angels can dance on the head of a pin?

ures or events to illustrate the problems of later centuries. We will be moving in and out of history, myth, and poetry; the categories overlapped remarkably.[4] Bear in mind once again that we are not necessarily dealing with actual events but with the stories about the events that, nonetheless, became events in themselves. The reader should enter into the imaginative spirit in which these stories were written.

The cult of the warrior, itself based on male reproductive consciousness, had run into serious problems. Under the matricentered system, sacred bonds existed between the children of one mother, bonds that provided some alleviation of the impetus toward war. In a warrior society the importance of the mother was undergoing a radical change. Admission to the tribe necessitated a death-defying act by a young warrior, according to some accounts. At one time in Ulster "every young son of theirs who first took arms used to enter the province of Connaught on a foray or to seek to slay a human being."[5] Entry into manhood itself was dependent on someone being "capable of slaying a man."[6] Under these conditions each new generation of warriors, as they attempted to enter manhood, would destabilize whatever tentative "peace" had been arrived at.[7]

There were several solutions to this problem. The young warriors could conduct their warring escapades elsewhere, thereby diffusing the social tensions that the warrior cult would generate. Probably for this reason the Irish made many raids on foreign lands during their early history. Hostages could also be taken, rather than killing one's opponents. Still, these solutions were too short-term to be viable. Ultimately the problem could only be addressed by an entirely new form of social organization and religious consciousness.

The early Irish church was crucially concerned with these issues. In historical practice, it vacillated between providing sanctuary for criminals and persuading the political rulers to use capital punishment.[8] Alternatively, the church took homicides onto its own lands where they provided slave labor.[9] Presumably, the clerics thought, such measures would cut down on the blood feud. As the social structure changed from being tribally or territorially based to new forms of centralization under high kings or regional bishops, both the church and the emerging state would reach the same conclusion: what was required was a centralized agency, system, or philosophy of revenge or retribution. The ruler or the church, rather than the kinship or territorial structure, should take responsibility for establishing justice when someone had been wronged, thus introducing a measure of stability into the society at large.[10]

The way in which the church and state would go about establishing these agencies would be very different. To be simplistic, in theory (if not in actual practice) the church would largely postpone revenge or justice to an afterlife, while the secular powers would exact justice in this one. However, the underlying mentality of church and state, and the ways in which they would institute their systems, were remarkably similar in other respects.

Under these circumstances the basic notion of the Blood Covenant was first developed: an agreement made between men, the logic and mentality of which would eventually become the basis for the foundation of the centralized political system.

The first document we will look at that provides an introduction to the themes of the Blood Covenant is the story of the *Bóroma* (tribute). This story is overtly about the lifting of a tribute laid by an Irish high-king on the people of the eastern province of Leinster. But there are underlying religious issues that form a "subtext" and that provide us with crucial illumination on our themes here. The subtext describes the inadequacies of the traditional forms and mechanisms of social unity and the events that led to the creation of the Blood Covenant among men, with the aid of the Christian priests. In this story the legends of the warriors and those of the saints merge, reflecting the ties being cemented between the political and religious powers.

"The Bóroma" is a medieval historical text contained in a manuscript of the twelfth century, but the themes of the story clearly go back to an underlying social conflict that existed in Ireland long before that time and that the storyteller has used to illustrate the logic and necessity of the Blood Covenants themselves. Briefly, the story concerns a tribute that an Irish high king imposed on the people of the province of Leinster.[11] Initially this tribute was said to have been imposed in revenge for the death of his two daughters. This was later lifted following a battle but was reimposed after the slaughter of thirty princesses together with their retinues of handmaidens in Tara, one of the main centers.[12] Various kings "swore on the elements," the Sun, Moon, and Wind, that they would not impose the tribute. But once having gained the kingship, they quickly forgot their promise and sought payments, often by means of bloody conflict.[13]

One feature of the tribute was that when the king was making his circuit of Ireland he had the right to sleep with the wives of all the underkings. This was a token of the king's supremacy and must have given rise to great resentment.[14]

We take up the story where Cummascach, the son of the high king, decided to levy the tribute and called upon the king of Leinster, demanding to sleep with his wife. The king's wife managed to trick herself out of the situation, and the Leinster king forced Cummascach to flee in shame, whereupon Cummascach was killed by an abbot. In return, the Leinster king made the abbot's church tax-free forevermore.[15]

But now the high king's brother, Bishop Aedán, the bishop of Glendalough, heard what happened. He was incensed: not at his nephew's death, but at the deeds his nephew had tried to undertake in Leinster. When the king of Leinster asked how revenge could be taken on the high king for his oppression, the cleric answered, "I am willing though it be on *my mother's son* (emphasis added)."[16] Bishop Aedán no longer considered himself bound by the sacred bonds that existed between sons of the same mother and was willing to take revenge on his own brother. Messengers were sent to the high king telling him all that had transpired. He promptly rounded up his forces to attack Leinster in revenge for the death of his son.

The Leinster king became frightened at the size of the forces the high king had mustered and sent Bishop Aedán to him, asking for a truce:

"Thou gettest not that truce," said the high king, "till thou puttest thy hand to the three members which thou hast when thou makest thy children." The cleric is then enraged. And he said: "As God knoweth me," saith he, "may a she-wolf take those three members which *thou* hast as far as that hill yonder!"[17]

The battle between the kings continued until finally the high king was killed. The reason given as to why he was killed gives us further insight into the underlying themes.

It was believed that should someone wear a monk's cowl in battle they would not be killed.[18] In this part of the story the high king had come to the saint Columcille, asking if he would ultimately obtain the mercy of the Lord. Columcille told him that there was no chance of his obtaining clemency and going to heaven, and so the high king asked him at least to ensure that "the Leinstermen may not triumph over me."[19] Columcille considered the question for some time and said, finally,

That is difficult for me *for my mother was from Leinster* and the Leinstermen came to me to Durrow, and they began to fast against me that I might grant them the *gift of a sister's son*. And what they asked of me was that no foreign king should triumph over them. And I promised them this. However, here is my cowl for thee, and thou wilt not be slain so long as it is on thee (emphasis added).[20]

In his last battle the high king asked his servant to get the cowl for him, but it had been left behind at the palace: the king knew then that he would die.

Now an interesting diversion occurs in the text. The Ulstermen from the north arrive on the scene to ask the king of Leinster why he had captured (in a separate incident) many of their trainee warriors, including the Ulster king's son. The king of Leinster replied, "To take away from me your need (?) of battle." "It shall be taken away from thee for ever," said the king of Ulster, "and a covenant and union shall be made between us with our blood."[21] We will return to this covenant presently once we have reflected upon the vast changes taking place in religious consciousness that the "Bóroma" revealed and to which the Blood Covenant would be some kind of solution.

The fundamental issues were that men needed to find an alternative to battle. At first kings swore upon the elements, the Sun, Moon, and Wind, but rarely kept their promises. The sacredness of the elements, and the religion that had honored them, had been called into question, and a new symbol had to be found. In addition, bonds between children of the same mother were proving increasingly ineffective in preventing people from going to war against each other. In the new religion, kinship alliances would be superseded by religious considerations, and so, for both Aedán and Columcille, their duties as religious conflicted with their loyalty to their own kin.

With these symbols of unity gone, the high king taunted bishop Aedán to swear upon his testicles, the new symbol of patriarchal power, but Aedán is enraged at this reference to his genitals. Swearing on one's testicles is too blatant a symbol of the patriarchy whose power rests primarily on denying its dependence upon the body, mere biology, or its fruits.[22] Clearly whatever new form of political organization would be invoked would have to be a great deal more subtle. Taking captives as hostages and as an alternative to killing them is an improvement but is not enough: there needs to be a new basis for sacred relationships between men that would eliminate the need for war.

The Blood Covenant was a perfect solution. No longer would men be dependent merely on the sacred bonds existing between them because of their mother's blood flowing in their veins. The Blood Covenant was a voluntary act, one which they could control, and on the basis of which they could decide to whom they would be affiliated. Political, religious, and military considerations would all play a part in this decision.

By forging covenants of blood, men were no longer at the mercy of biological accident or change. Mothers could give birth biologically; only the voluntary union of men in some form of covenant could bring about rebirth into culture, a birth infinitely superior to the birthing by ordinary mothers. Indeed in some cultures blood brothers were known as "blood-lickers," as distinct from "milk-lickers," and the distinction signified a much greater degree of unity between them.[23]

The Blood Covenant mentioned here was not a new invention; indeed the first Blood Covenant had been instituted, according to the heroic cycle, by Scáthach, a woman who had taught many of the future famous heroes the martial arts.[24]

The Blood Covenant was an agreement made between men to treat each other as brothers, with the same respect as though they were sons of the same mother. The rules of the covenant were that blood brothers should not go to war against each other, marry or rape each other's wives or sisters, and that they should avenge each other's death in battle.[25]

But Scáthach's covenant was not always successful in preventing bloodshed; in some cases conflicting claims of "honor," or kin, took precedence, causing blood brothers to fight.[26] Also, since each warrior's death called forth vengeance, the continuous cycle of revenge was not stemmed. And so the question arose; where would the violence end?

How could the cycle of revenge be stopped? It eventually became clear that a higher form of covenant would be necessary and a superior power would have to be called into play. In the covenant described in the "Bóroma," a new element is being added: the decisive contribution of Christianity.[27]

The form of the covenant is described vividly in the manuscript. There should be a vat of crystal "with splendour of gold." One third of the vat should be filled with the blood of men; the second third should be filled with new-milk (signifying rebirth); the last third should be wine.[28] The meaning of the covenant is told to the king of Ulster in a vision:

This is the blood that was seen in the vat—the blood of the two provinces in meeting. This is the new-milk—the canon of the Lord which the clerics of the two provinces recite. This is the wine, Christ's Body and His Blood, which the clerics offer up.[29]

The men of Ulster and Leinster supped the covenant drink together, thus swearing not to go to war against each other.

Christianity was able to make a significant difference to the terms of the covenant because through Christianity one had access to an entirely superior form of power, one that would eventually surpass the Blood Covenant itself. This is brought out in an incident in the document when St. Adamnán calls upon another high king, Finnachta, to come to him. Finnachta refuses to go because he is playing chess. Adamnán threatens him with various consequences if he does not come immediately. First he threatens to deny the kingship to Finnachta's future sons. Then he threatens to cut short his life, and finally he threatens to deny him the mercy of the Lord. At this last threat Finnachta rose immediately and went to him. Adamnán asked him why he had not come to begin with, and Finnachta replied,

What thou didst threaten me with, namely, that none of my children, and that no man of my name, should take the kingship of Ireland, that seems good to me. What thou then didst promise me, namely shortness of life, seems to me of little weight, for Molling [a Leinster saint] promised me heaven. But the third thing which thou didst promise me, namely, that I should not find the mercy of the Lord, I could not endure to hear that without coming at thy call.[30]

Finnachta's future progeny were of no account to him: immortality was no longer to be sought in this way. Yet the warriors, uprooted from the cycle of eternal return in the Great Mother, could not reconcile themselves to mere death. Immortality through warrior fame was a shaky foundation on which to build one's hopes, and heaven was a much more simple, if demanding, proposition. Shortness of life was not a problem since life was a mere preparation for heaven. But to be threatened with being cut off from the mercy of God was a threat that he could not ignore.

The Christian church, symbolized by Adamnán, was the bearer of a lasting covenant, not only between *men*, but more importantly, between *God and men*. Future high kings, or indeed anyone else, would do well to jump up immediately the first time they were called by the clerics, God's representatives on earth.

The clerics had at their disposal, therefore, the power to grant entrance into the future life (as we have seen, Columcille told the high king that he hadn't a chance of getting there). This power ultimately was used to lift the tribute, the cause of so much bloodshed among men. The fact that the clerics involved were themselves fairly violent in their approach was a problem that would only be addressed later. For now it is enough to point out that the covenant, in whose name they spoke, and upon whose power their own power rested, to all intents and purposes replaced the earlier forms of covenant existing between men. In particular, the "Bóroma" tells us clearly that the bonds between the sons of the same mother were no longer sacred and that a new basis for religious power and social organization was being established. Not this life, but the next, was where their sights rested, and the rebirth in baptism, rather than mere birthing through their mothers, would provide them with access to eternal life.

The logic of the Blood Covenant survived well into the twelfth century, for when Gerald of Wales visited Ireland during this time, the Irish were still making treaties among each other sanctified by drinking each other's blood.[31] By then, Mass was often celebrated at the time of the Blood Covenant and, in some cases, the clerics presided over the covenants being made, providing evidence of pagan-Christian syncretism.[32]

In other respects, Christianity had had a limited impact on the sociopolitical symbolism since, according to Gerald of Wales, the Irish were still practicing essentially "pagan" ceremonies, which he found extremely offensive. The most repulsive of these was the confirmation of a king in Ulster. As Gerald reported, a white mare was slaughtered and the future king had to bathe in and drink of her broth before being confirmed in his reign.[33]

In this description we have a remnant of the kingship rites associated with the Goddess Macha. The rite is a form of communion where the horse, symbolizing the Goddess, is sacrificed and her body is then shared out among the participants in a gesture of solidarity with each other and in continuity with her power to bestow kingship upon the ruler. The Goddess would sanction the reigning monarch by ensuring the fertility of the soil and providing the fruits of the earth. This was essentially a late form of the sacred marriage of king and goddess, where the kings effectively had to bathe in broth before their authority would be recognized by the people.[34]

But in a society where male bonding and male reproductive consciousness were the operative political philosophies, such rituals were not destined to survive much longer. Female symbolism would have to be eradicated entirely from such crucial arenas of power. Christianity would have to have a much firmer grip on the central symbolism of the social structure and, more importantly, whatever ritual the king would undergo in the future would be formed by the logic of the Father God, rather than the Mother Goddess—an entirely different form of logic, as we shall see.

The final transition from the Mother Goddess to God the Father was not merely one changing the gender of the deity but one that expressed and supported the new political changes being made. The Mother Goddess in cultures throughout the world had fought desperately for the safety and well-being of her children. In the new power structures being established, such maternal ties were to be relinquished. Not the ties of particularity, but those of universality or the Common Good were those that mattered. Only those who acted on behalf of the Common Good, and not just on behalf of their own families, could be trusted to exert forms of power that transcended family interests.

The crucial question that both church and state addressed as they moved to centralized forms of government was as follows: Why should the people put their trust in these rulers, spiritual or temporal? How would they prove their impartiality, and how would the people know that they were not going to exercise their rule unfairly, in favor of particular personal interests or family connections?

These questions confronted almost every known Western culture in the move from decentralized forms of organization based on family or territorial ties, into centralized forms of politics and state. The questions raised took many forms but essentially boiled down to a question of conflicting loyalties. To whom was one ultimately responsible: to biological family, tribe, country, religion, political leader, or to one's God?

In the Age of Eve, we have already seen that this same problem confronted the early Hebrews when they established their covenant with God. How could their leaders prove that their loyalty would be to God? Let us look again at the story of Abraham and Isaac from another perspective.

Before cementing the Covenant with the Hebrews, Yahweh put Abraham's obedience to the test by asking him to sacrifice his only son. We saw that when Abraham was going to sacrifice Isaac an angel interfered at the last moment, saving Isaac's life. Nevertheless, Abraham had proved his loyalty to Yahweh by being willing to break his kinship relations, transcending his biological ties, in an act of obedience to his God, Yahweh. In return for this he was granted "seed forever," which is to say, Yahweh promised that the Covenant would pass on down through Abraham's descendants.[35]

Abraham had been willing to transcend his biological ties for the sake of Yahweh, but Yahweh's angel stayed his hand at the last moment. As we enter the world historical stage, where the claims of kinship would be superseded by the ambitions of successive popes and emperors, restraints on sacrifice would be lifted. Indeed sacrifice would become the means by which patriarchal forms of religion and social organization would become established.

In Irish mythology and in early ecclesiastical literature there are many stories dealing with sacrifice and the question, "To whom do we owe loyalty?"[36] Perhaps the one that stands out is one first committed to written record in the eighth century concerning Cúchulainn, the Ulster hero, and his dealings with his son, Connla, otherwise known as "Aife's One Son." This story explains in poetic detail the logic behind the institution of patriarchal sacrifice as a means of transcending biological ties, proving the integrity of the warrior, and establishing the "justice" of the king.

Connla had been conceived during a visit to the Otherworld when Cúchulainn, despite his promises of faithfulness to his wife Emer, had slept with Aife, a mythical Amazonian warrior. Aife conceived, and Cúchulainn left instructions with her that, should the child be a daughter, Aife could keep her, but should he be a son, he should be sent to him when he was big enough to fit a ring that he left with her.[37] Cúchulainn instructed her to tell Connla to "reveal his name to no one man, that he must make way for no one man, and refuse no one man combat."[38] It was this situation that found Connla on the seashore in Ulster seven years later.

Various Ulster heroes went out singly to Connla asking him to identify himself. Connla refused and defeated the warriors in turn, putting the army of Ulster to shame. Then Cúchulainn came down to the strand to confront the young lad.

Despite the fact that Cúchulainn's wife, Emer, was not the child's mother, she pleaded with Cúchulainn not to confront the boy:

> Don't go down!
> It is your own son there
> don't murder your son
> the wild and well born
> son let him be.[39]

On a point of honor (the rule laid down by his father), he had refused to give his name to the Ulster warriors. But Emer pleaded with Cúchulainn, "We know his name, if he is really Connla, the boy is Aife's one son." But Cúchulainn angrily replied,

> Be quiet, wife.
> It isn't a woman
> that I need now
> to hold me back
> in the face of these feats
> and shining triumph

> I want no woman's
> help with my work
> victorious deeds
> are what we need
> *to fill the eyes*
> *of a great king*
> the blood of Connla's
> body will flush
> my skin with power
> little spear so fine
> to be finely sucked
> by my own spears!

"No matter who he is, wife," Cúchulainn said, "I must kill him *for the honour of Ulster*" (emphasis added).[40] Cúchulainn and Connla engaged in combat; they were equally matched and fought viciously until Cúchulainn used the *gae bolga*, a weapon probably designed to disembowel the opponent. Mortally wounding his son, he went over and lifted him up, taking him in his arms to present him to the men of Ulster saying, "My son, men of Ulster. Here you are." Connla, bearing no grudge against his father, put his arms around each "man of Ulster" in turn, saluted his father, and breathed his last.

Connla's last words are highly significant: in his dying breath he moans that the trick of the *gae bolga* was something that Scathach, his martial arts teacher, had not taught him, but his dying words have also been rendered as, "Dearer to the womb is that which quickens than that which it bears."[41] Connla here asserts that he had been betrayed by a weapon made by his mother, a woman whose "longing was for her husband" rather than for her son, and any betrayal he felt was directed at her. Her loyalty was not to her son but to the man with whom she had slept. Cúchulainn emerges blameless and, indeed, triumphant.[42]

The story of Connla has many layers of interpretation.[43] For our purposes we can see that, whereas in a matricentered society one's place in the tribe was assured by relationship to one's mother, in this story Connla is forbidden to give his name. Throughout the story he is called "Aife's One Son," rather than the "Son of Cúchulainn." The narrators are making the point that before he can adopt this title he must be "named" or accepted into the tribe by his father, an acceptance he must earn by means of a test of his loyalty and strength. On his death the "men of Ulster" embraced Connla, accepting him now as one of their own.

But Connla's very existence in this story seems designed merely to provide an occasion for Cúchulainn to prove his superhuman impartiality and to illustrate, as Connla does in his dying breath, that social ties to women are no longer a reliable means of safeguarding one's life. The honor of Ulster, symbolized by the honor of the king, was the only sure guarantee of social stability, an honor that must be guarded even at the cost of killing one's only son. With the young lad dead, having been killed unfairly in an act of treachery by his father, Cúchulainn, as the Father of the Victim, presented his Only Son to the men of Ulster, proof of his loyalty to the warrior class and to the king.

In killing his son, Cúchulainn had committed the ultimate political act, the one from which Abraham had been spared. Cúchulainn's willingness to sacrifice his son confirmed his role as the king's superior warrior. From now on his loyalty to the king would be beyond dispute. The act of killing, in particular, the act of killing one's only son for the sake of the honor of the king, was the ultimate act of political creativity. Death, not birth, would now bring political life into the world.

Stories such as that of "Aife's One Son" were gradually shaping the religious consciousness of the Irish, forming a bridge between the old culture and that of Christianity, even though it was an uphill battle, as many of the old pre-Christian symbols and practices remained well into the twelfth century. Essentially the story was making the point that biological ties would have to be disregarded or transcended for full entry into the culture now being formulated throughout Europe.

The theme of transcending one's biological ties was by no means a new one and is to be found throughout the Christian Gospels as well as other writing from the very beginnings of Christianity. In the Gospels, Jesus makes several revealing statements, epithets that are regularly used in preaching. In the story of the "finding in the Temple," Jesus has been missing for several days, listening to and speaking with the Temple teachers. In response to his frantic mother who had gone in search of him, he replies curtly, "Did you not know that I must be busy with my Father's affairs?"[44] On another occasion when Jesus is healing, his mother and other relatives come looking for him, but Jesus replies, "My mother and my brothers are those who hear the word of God and put it into practice."[45] Once a woman from the crowd shouted out to Jesus, "Happy is the womb that bore you and the breasts that you sucked!" But Jesus replied, "Still happier those who hear the word of God and keep it!"[46] There are several other incidents in the Gospels where Jesus' words to his mother seem extremely harsh. Spiritual writers, who are also anxious to exalt the role of Mary, have tried to explain them away. When one realizes that the loyalty of Jesus lay only with his Father in heaven they become understandable. Mere biological ties, even to his Virgin Mother, Mary, were not to be taken seriously.

For those around the fireside listening to this saga, therefore, the theological imagery of "Aife's One Son" would not have been lost. They may already have encountered this theme through the theology of the Christian Atonement and the sacrifice of the Mass.

In the European church, perhaps the person whose writings would most influence Christian teaching on the Atonement was Anselm of

Canterbury, a man who, as we will see, had a very important role to play in the politics of the twelfth-century reform movement in Ireland. Anselm's views on Christian Atonement, which are intimately related to the doctrine of sacrifice, would well repay close study in the light of the issues raised here. Briefly, they are as follows.

Anselm assumes that the world is in a state of sin caused by the "Fall" and, therefore, in need of redemption. God could have chosen not to demand punishment for sin, but his "justice" would not then have been appeased. But how can the Father be appeased? How can God, the essence of justice, righteousness, order, and authority, be placated, especially looking down upon a world where sin is being daily committed, not to say, invented?

Anselm examines various possibilities. Could someone else have substituted for Jesus? But he answers negatively. Should anyone else have redeemed the world, man would then have been indebted to him, and it is not fitting that man should be indebted to anyone other than God. Could God the Father have simply forgiven the world? Anselm concludes negatively. Since the intrinsic honor of the Father is at stake, by definition, this honor must be maintained. In the end, Anselm's logic would conclude that nothing less than the sacrifice of God's Only Son was adequate.[47]

Restoring the honor of the Father, which had been compromised by sin, was a central theme in Anselm's theology, just as the honor of the king had been crucial for Cúchulainn. Anselm's theology by no means gained universal acceptance.[48] Despite opposition, Anselm's teaching was the one most influential in subsequent Catholic teaching on the matter.

Essentially, what the Christian doctrine of Atonement meant, in effect, was that the power of the church would be based upon a higher form of Covenant, that between God the Father and Son, made possible by the blood sacrifice of God's Only Son to the Father. The world would be redeemed through the blood of the Son, and participation in the Covenant could be gained by allegiance to the Son through his representatives on earth. No longer would men be merely sons of the same earthly mother: now they could be brothers of Jesus and sons of the same heavenly Father.

The formulation of the Christian doctrine of Atonement effectively enabled new forms of political and religious power structures to be established. All men now could be brothers of Jesus and sons of their heavenly Father. The Covenant would be celebrated at Mass, and the power of the Mass would also be essential in bestowing kingly power upon earthly emperors and local kings. In theory at least, this renewed understanding of the meaning of Christianity could put an end to the blood feud among those who recognized themselves as brothers. Christ as the "Lamb of God" had taken the "sins of the world" upon himself, making it unnecessary for people to carry out further acts of revenge. Either they could wait until the next life for social equilibrium to be restored or, more likely under the circumstances, wait for the mechanisms of either church or state to punish the offender. In any case the wronged should not attempt to exact justice themselves. "Vengeance is mine," says the Lord, a cry that helped to stabilize the societies who recognized the Lord, even if as a consequence those brothers previously at war with each other would later go out "converting" the heathen who did not recognize the Lord—a major motivating force in the Christian Crusades.[49]

The old rites of kingship would have to go. Essentially kings would receive their divine commission directly from God the Father, through the mediation of his representatives on earth. In the future, kings were to derive their religious power only from the moral authority of the church, particularly that derived from the sacrifice of the Mass, the new Covenant between God and men. As the Irish seventh-century *Penitential of Cummean* stated, "We ought offer the sacrifice on behalf of good kings, never on behalf of evil kings,"[50] an arrangement which, at least theoretically, left it up to the priests to decide who the good ones were on the basis of what the fruit of their reigns might have been.

The renewed awareness of the Fatherhood of God was a major cultural and political achievement, the implications of which were destined to reverberate down through the succeeding centuries. It would confer upon popes, emperors, and kings grave responsibilities or great opportunities. Armed with the authority of God the Father they could now feel free to take upon themselves the conversion of dissenters, heathen, and the unorthodox. The popes used the secular arm when their own authority was insufficient, while the kings and emperors relied upon the popes to confer kingly power.

Centralization of power had begun to take place, made possible by the new Covenant, the sacrifice of the Mass, to which all could adhere in the interest of maintaining the peace. Under these circumstances any other sources of authority, whether derived from hereditary succession, charismatic leadership, generations of religious tradition, or especially from symbols associated with women, were to be superseded and, if necessary, destroyed.[51]

The Christian doctrine of the Atonement, carried out to its logical political conclusions, goes way beyond the Blood Covenant that held particular warring tribes together, or the saintly covenants whereby particular monasteries guaranteed not to ransack each other. Both the church and state now existed in people's minds as distinct entities to be reckoned with. Whereas previously the king had been made legitimate through his sacred marriage with the Goddess, the Christian Covenant, celebrated by the priests and bishops, would be the first sign of a new sacred marriage, the marriage of church and state.

This new Covenant could be celebrated anywhere and at any time and had the supreme advantage of using identical words, language, chants, and rituals to foster a sense of the universal brotherhood. The church could not now be limited to any place or time; its power did not derive from family or geographical connections but directly from God the Father through the sacrifice of his Son. The brotherhood of men that this sacrifice established gave to the church and its representatives potentially universal jurisdiction.

Although women had been at the forefront of the early Christian church—they had been equal partners at the Agapés that announced the Christian revolution—with the male monopoly of theology this was destined to change.

The exclusion of women from religious officiation and even presence on the altar of sacrifice meant that the blood of women had become part of the language of defilement,[52] a cause of sin that only the sacrificial blood of men, and eventually one Man in particular, could cleanse. And if the blood of women defiled, the blood of men took on new dimensions. Once shed in warfare, now it could prevent war; once a cause of sin, now it could cleanse from sin; once a cause of division, now it could form covenants. Male birthing was infinitely superior to anything mere women could hope to achieve. This new prestige accorded to male blood had been made possible by the sacrifice of Christ in the Mass. But, in effect, a quite different sacrifice had also taken place; the sacrifice of the rights, blood, and power of women to the new patriarchal order.

In the Age of Eve, the needs of the childbearing woman were made subservient to the needs of the king. But in the Age of Brigit we have gone one step further. With the new patriarchal consciousness, the child has been claimed by the father, only to be sacrificed to the honor of the gods. The eradication of female symbols could be documented and even celebrated. More importantly, the eradication of female values, based on women's experience of care, nurturance, the ethics of responsibility, and the preservation of life above all else, proceeded simultaneously, although this elimination would be successfully disguised for centuries to come.[53]

This new consciousness would have vital implications for Irish social life, nowhere better expressed than in the strangely prophetic words of the Archbishop of Cashel in the twelfth century, speaking to Gerald of Wales, an experienced medieval traveler:

. . . a cleric of the church of Rome, criticized the church in Ireland for the enormity of its vice, arguing as proof that no one had ever won the crown of martyrdom. The archbishop of Cashel, Tatheus, replied: "It is true that although our people are very barbarous, uncivilized, and savage, nevertheless they have always paid great honour and reverence to churchmen, and they have never put out their hands against the saints of God. But now a people has come to the kingdom which knows how, and is accustomed, to make martyrs. *From now on Ireland will have its martyrs, just as other countries*" (emphasis added).[54]

PART III

THE AGE OF MARY

CHAPTER 8

The Anglo-Norman Invasion
of Ireland

Popes, Kings, and Bishops Reform the Old Laws of Ireland

On one occasion he [Aedh Allan] came, when a royal prince, to Othain-Mura; he washed his hands in the river which is in the middle of the town. . . . He took of the water to put it on his face, but one of his people checked him:

"O King," said he, "do not put that water on thy face."

"Why so?" said the King.

"I am ashamed to tell it," replied he.

"What shame is it for thee to tell the truth?" said the King.

"This is it," said he: "It is upon this water the jakes of the clergy is situated."

"Is it into it," said the King, "the (chief) cleric himself goes to stool?"

"It is verily," replied the young man.

"Not only then," said the King, "will I put it (the water) upon my face, but I will put it into my mouth, and I will drink it (drinking three sups of it), for to me the water into which his faeces drop is a communion."

. . . When Mura (the chief cleric heard about this) . . . he said to the prince: "Beloved son," said he, "I promise to thee, in the presence of God, the reward of that veneration which thou hast shown to the church: (viz.) that thou shalt obtain the sovereignty of Erin soon, and that thou shalt gain victory, and triumph over thy enemies; and thou shalt not be taken off by a sudden death, but thou shalt take the body of the Lord from my hand; and I will pray to the Lord that thou mayest depart old from this world."

It was not long after this until Aedh Allan assumed the kingdom of Erin; and he granted fertile lands to Mura-Othna.

FRAGMENTARY ANNALS OF IRELAND DUBHALTACH MAC FIRBISIGH

In our journey so far through the Age of Eve and the Age of Brigit, we have documented the changing social conditions of women as reflected in the religious imagery of their respective ages. History formed the scenic background against which our themes were discussed, but as we enter the Age of Mary we are entering more clearly into historical time. In this time the achievements of male reproductive consciousness would be consolidated to form the dominant theology in the Western world for centuries to come.

The Age of Mary signals the end of tragic vision, the essential unity of opposites hitherto symbolized for us by the image of the Serpent. In the Age of Eve, for instance, we saw that the Serpent was both good and evil. In the Age of Brigit this ideology changed. There were both good serpents and bad serpents. As was said to Mary in an eighth-century poem, "Your Son is the good shepherd . . . the gleaming white lamb . . . the blessed serpent by whom the perverse old serpent was smitten. . . ."[1] As the Age of Mary enters into its fullness, any possibility of ambiguity with regard to the Serpent would be finished. The Serpent certainly reappears: this time under the heel of Mary's foot.

The Fathers of the church never tired of repeating the fact that the Serpent had been crushed by Mary. Although the Serpent originally symbolized the mysterious and ambivalent secrets of the Goddess, Christianity identified the Serpent with the Devil, the enemy of Good. This enabled the Fathers to project all the evil in the world upon the Devil while holding God the Father responsible for all possible good. For Christendom, the Serpent/Goddess, with its multivalent symbolism, represented the enemy *par excellence*. Rather than eliminating the symbol altogether, Christianity promoted the image, but always as the subjugated, shadow side of the spiritual or military hero.

Standing triumphantly over the Serpent/Goddess, the Virgin Mary embodies the double jeopardy into which Christianity had plunged women. By accepting Mary as model, women would become complicit in their own oppression, helping to eradicate the essential mystery at the heart of life and positing a stark dualistic theological system in which good resided in the realm of the spirit and evil in the realm of their own uncontrolled sexuality. If they refused to accept the model of Mary, women would find themselves permanently consigned to the netherworld, the dark subterranean continent shortly to be inhabited by the primordial scapegoats, the witches, the embodiment of evil itself. All these theological changes took place in the context of the church-state battles for power being fought in Europe. Let us briefly place these battles in perspective.

Following an initial period of persecution, the early Christian church had settled down to a period of relative peace and expansion under the protection of the fourth-century emperor Constantine the Great (d. 337). The fortunes of the papacy during the next several centuries were mixed, and by the Middle Ages several popes had, in effect, become pawns in the hands of certain political powers. Not surprisingly, this left succession to the papacy open to wide abuse.[2] In 882, John VIII died at the hands of rival assassins; Stephen VI in 897 was strangled in prison;

Benedict VI was smothered in 984; while John XII, who was effectively a political appointee and a mere eighteen years of age when he became pope, is said to have died of "amorous excess while making love."[3]

Following the Dark Ages, both the bishops and the European rulers wanted to strengthen papal power, which in turn would confer upon them the authority to rule over their huge and often troublesome territories. Various reform movements sprang up in Burgundy and Lorraine in the eleventh century, supported by the kings. The power shifts that ensued, particularly those between the German and the rising Norman powers, eventually resulted in a schism, with two popes reigning at the same time.

The Germans had temporarily lost control of the papacy by the time the young emperor Henry IV came of age. Henry was determined to restore the power of the German emperor with regard to the papacy. Things came to a head when Pope Gregory excommunicated the emperor after Henry had called upon him to leave the throne of Peter. Henry underestimated the level of support that this move would have among the German bishops and princes. Following his excommunication the German princes issued an ultimatum: Henry was either to seek absolution or to lose his own crown.[4] This dilemma forced Henry to appear in the town of Canossa, near Reggio, in northern Italy in the bitter winter of 1077. It is said that he stood for three days, barefoot in the snow, outside the pope's lodging, begging for forgiveness. The pope finally granted him absolution, and Henry, for the time being, regained his political power in Germany.

The conflict between Henry IV and Gregory VII has become a vivid image as well as a classic case study for church historians of the relationship between church and state, and of the interdependence of religious and political power. In this period of tremendous cultural upheaval, church and state realized their interdependence, and made new arrangements for their mutual interests to be protected. These arrangements were to have far-reaching consequences for Ireland and for women in particular.

No longer could it be left to a decentralized or charismatic religion to provide the central cohesive philosophy underlying the social structure. It was, therefore, in the interests of both church and state to delineate clearly their spheres of operation. New understandings would have to be worked out between the religious and the political powers if their mutual interests were to be served. In this sense Ireland would not be left untouched by the great controversies happening in Europe. In fact, the Irish had been working on these issues for some time, and unlike the European solution where the pope effectively asserted his jurisdiction over church and state as both spiritual and temporal ruler, the Irish had long since argued for separate jurisdictions for these two realms.[5] From early times Ireland had been ruled by triarchies composed of abbots, kings, and brehons (judges), all of whom maintained a delicate balance of power.[6] In the twelfth century the Irish were not about to collapse these distinctions unilaterally to any new system, preferring to develop a working relationship between the different spheres.

The document that captures the spirit of the Irish debate over church and state is a story that, although transmitted to writing in the fifteenth century, was actually set in a much earlier period and features King Dermot of Tara and the saints, Ciarán, Ruadán, and Brendan of Birr. The story opens with excellent working relationships between Dermot and Ciarán. Dermot gives Ciarán land for his church, while Ciarán assures him of political success in his fight with the reigning monarch: church and state are happily coexisting. Things change, however, when Dermot's spear-keeper is killed by Aedh Guaire, a rich man, who immediately fled to the protection of Bishop Senach, the son of his mother's sister and, therefore, his own cousin. Senach took him for safekeeping to Ruadán, whose two sisters had reared Senach. In other words, the king was seeking to hang Aedh Guaire for the murder, while the bishop and Ruadán were making use of the maternal network to ensure his safety.

Eventually Ruadán hid Aedh Guaire in a hole within the sanctuary of his church. Dermot, finding out where he was, sent two of his aides to drag him out, but one was instantly blinded and the other's arms became paralyzed once they had breached the sanctuary of the church. Finally, Dermot himself came, pulled Aedh Guaire from the hole and brought him back to Tara to execute him according to royal law. At this, Ruadán called upon Brendan of Birr, and together the saints "fasted" against Dermot for a full year. "Fasting" against someone who had wronged you was a time-honored way of achieving justice in ancient Ireland. Standing outside Tara in wet and wind (like Henry IV before Gregory VII, only in reverse) they demanded the return of Aedh Guaire. Dermot replied that the church had no right to extend immunity to someone who infringed the royal law.[7]

Eventually the clerics tricked Dermot into believing that they had broken their fast by promising eternal life to his house-steward if he should lie to Dermot. Thinking he had won the fasting contest, Dermot broke his fast, effectively losing the struggle.

That night Dermot had a dream where he saw the clergy chopping down his tree, a symbol of Tara and, therefore, an omen of the destruction of his reign. Dermot and Ruadán then engaged in a fierce cursing match, each prophesying the ruination of the other, but eventually Dermot had to hand back Aedh Guaire since his own power to exact revenge as king of Tara was now shattered. Significantly, Dermot prophesied that the clergy would not benefit by the ruin of Tara or by destroying the kingship because doing so would leave the church open to the predations of the warrior class who would quarter their soldiers on the monks.[8]

The solution to the dilemma came to Dermot in a dream. One night he saw two people draw near to him, a cleric and a layman. Coming close, they took off his king's diadem, broke it apart, and divided it between them. Dermot woke up startled and asked his poet to interpret the dream. The poet replied,

"Thy dream's interpretation we have for thee: Thy kingdom is determined, of thy reign there is an end, and for the future thy princely grasp of Ireland is cast off: division between Church and Lay namely, that is what shall subsist now; and that which thy royal diadem's partition forbodes is even such another apportioning of Ireland's sovereignty betwixt Church and State." He proceeded: "A time will come when Church shall be enslaved by State, and when privilege of church-lands shall not exist; but they shall be obnoxious to free quartering at the hands of all. In lieu of this, however, evil shall overtake the State: so that the son, the father, the kinsman (of what degree soever) shall kill each other, and every man's weapon be red with another's blood. By perfidy of all men (fruits) of the earth shall perish, and mast of trees, and produce of the waters."[9]

The destruction of the power of Tara would not work ultimately in the interest of the clergy since, as they would soon find out, the church really needed the secular powers for their own protection. They were far better off in the idyllic times when Dermot and Ciarán had each assured the other's well-being.

As an interesting sidelight, the churchmen had first appealed to the maternal ties to save their captor. Originally the maternal network offered in their minds the only possible balancing weight against the power of the king. Ruadán at first refused sanctuary to Aedh Guaire and sent him to England. But when Dermot sought him out even there, he returned home, and Ruadán placed him in the sanctuary of the church, the new alternative to the maternal network. The king's aides had no right to violate the sanctuary and were severely injured when they attempted to do so. Only the king himself would not be harmed by this violation, signifying his supremacy over the church at that time.

Church and state plainly needed each other and would be well advised to take care of each other's interests in cooperation and in mutual harmony. The church should respect the state and call in its power to enforce discipline within the church's own ranks when necessary. The state should protect the church because otherwise the powers of revenge within the state would run riot. Kings would be ruthless in exacting justice from their subjects, who would be involved in a perpetual cycle of revenge themselves, with fathers and sons killing each other without any regard for kinship. The church would confer upon the rulers the religious authority they needed to carry out their reigns.

ANGLO-NORMAN INVASION

In Ireland the politics of the reform movement would become inextricable from yet another political agenda: the ambitions of British kings and bishops for the domination and control of Ireland. It is one of the profound tragedies and travesties of Irish history that, in the continuing interests of contemporary power structures, the Irish people as a whole have been largely unaware of the details and significance of these events: the invasion of Ireland by Anglo-Norman forces, an invasion orchestrated by successive archbishops of Canterbury, several popes, high-ranking Irish prelates, and an Irish king, Dermot Mac Murrough, renowned for his generosity to the church.[10] In the course of this reform movement, a pope effectively handed Ireland over to an English king, Henry II, an action that initiated the British occupation of Ireland. This occupation was to reach its full fruition in the sixteenth and seventeenth centuries and is still in place in the north of Ireland to this day.

When the church was being established during the first five or six centuries of Irish Christianity, the monastic federations may have been the best or only possible form of organization, given the tremendous power of the hereditary families. For the political ambitions of Rome or Canterbury, however, the Irish system of hereditary succession, even to church offices, left far too much control with the local people. If a person in the collateral line could be guaranteed succession to an abbacy, power was essentially derived, not from higher clerics, but from family connections. If Rome or Canterbury wanted to establish control over the church universal, control over church offices became essential. The real source of religious authority would have to be Rome. Anyone wishing to remain in the priesthood would have to become more closely subject to the dictates handed down by the reigning pope.

The first serious inroads into the Irish church were made by Lanfranc, who was consecrated Archbishop of Canterbury in 1070. Lanfranc was a "political appointee" of the Norman invader of England, William the Conqueror, who led what effectively was a holy crusade for the reform of the English church.

Lanfranc was destined to have a profound effect on the Irish church.[11] Several times Lanfranc tried to gain primacy over the Irish church but failed. Nevertheless, in the course of his reign he required several Irish bishops to submit to his authority, thereby setting dangerous precedents, and he inaugurated a propaganda war against the Irish that can only be described as "racial."[12] He complained about the form of infant baptism, the ordination of bishops, the Irish divorce laws, simony, and the Irish laws with regard to marrying within certain degrees of kinship.[13] Lanfranc died in 1089. In 1093 Anselm of Aosta, one of his former pupils, was named Archbishop of Canterbury.[14]

Anselm, too, complained about the Irish marriage laws, especially the rules pertaining to divorce, with a tone that implied claims to metropolitan jurisdiction in Ireland.[15] In the course of his reign, in 1095, Anselm extracted a vow of obedience from the bishop of Dublin.[16] Dublin at this time was controlled by Viking settlers and their descendants, and there was considerable tension between Dublin and the rest of the country.[17] The first reforming synod took place in Dublin in 1084, a synod that "met, organized, and assumed executive power in disregard or defiance of the *comarbai*" (the local hereditary abbots),[18] a blow at the hereditary principles underlying the Irish monastic system.

Lanfranc and Anselm had concentrated their efforts mainly on the south of Ireland, but a parallel reform movement was proceeding apace, inspired by the friends and followers of Bernard of Clairvaux.[19] The main Irish figure behind the northern Irish reform movement was Malachy, whose relationship with Bernard was such that Bernard delivered his funeral oration. Malachy struck a major blow against the system of hereditary succession by wresting control of the hereditary office of abbot of Armagh.[20] Malachy had won a major symbolic fight but would have to get higher sanction for his work. Malachy needed direct sanction for his actions from the central authority of the papacy; he set out for Rome in search of the *pallium*.[21]

The *pallium* is a round band of white woollen material. It is decorated with six crosses on two hanging strips and worn by the pope and his archbishops. The *pallium* is blessed on St. Agnes's Day in Rome while the *Agnus Dei* (Lamb of God) is being sung. Before being sent out to new archbishops, it is allowed to rest on St. Peter's tomb in the Vatican. The *pallium* symbolizes the sacrifice of Jesus as the Lamb of God, and whoever has the right to wear it participates in the "plenitude of the pontifical office." Archbishops possess the highest relic of all, symbolizing their authority over all other relatively minor relic holders.

Malachy made several attempts to get the *pallium* but was prevented from doing so because of the interference of the bishop of Canterbury and the English king, Stephen.[22] Nevertheless, his missions were partly successful in that he was appointed papal legate for Ireland and made valuable contacts with the European monastic movement. Perhaps his most significant accomplishment was that he convened a reforming synod on Inis Padraig in 1148, the first time a northern Irish reforming synod had met "without the presence and support of an Irish king."[23] As papal legate, Malachy went back to Rome to report on the success of the proceedings to the pope, but, having to take the long way around because of the enmity of King Stephen of England, he died on the way, in the arms of Bernard of Clairvaux.

Malachy's work finally came to completion when four years later at the synod of Kells in 1152 the papal legate, Cardinal John Paparo, conferred four *pallia* on the Irish church for the sees of Armagh, Cashel, Dublin, and Tuam. In addition, thirty-seven sees were formally recognized in Ireland and placed under the guidance of the metropolitan bishops. The Irish bishops had only requested two *pallia*, for Armagh and Cashel, but in order to persuade Norse Dublin to come over to the Irish church organization, and in recognition of the political power of the kings of Connacht, Paparo erected four metropolitan sees, an arrangement that persists to this day.[24]

England's interests were severely threatened by Paparo's action since Malachy was not connected to Canterbury and had sought the *pallium* independently of English jurisdiction.[25] There is a great deal of evidence that his initial journey to Pope Innocent II to seek the *pallium* was unsuccessful,[26] due to the influence of several prominent English clerics at the papal court. That the pope, Eugenius III, conferred four *pallia* on Ireland in 1152 was now seen as a major setback for the ambitions of Canterbury. Ireland was not destined, however, to be so fortunate for very long.

Two years later, Cardinal Nicholas Breakspeare, an Englishman, was crowned Pope Adrian IV on December 4, 1154. Within two weeks, King Henry II ascended the English throne: the combination for Ireland was disastrous. Within a couple of months of his coronation, early in 1155, Henry applied to Pope Adrian IV for permission to enter Ireland.[27] Persuading King Henry II to apply to enter Ireland on behalf of the pope was an obvious attempt on Canterbury's part to reestablish its power and to exact revenge.

In a famous papal bull entitled *Laudabiliter,* Adrian IV granted the whole of Ireland to his countryman, Henry II, "with a view to enlarging the boundaries of the church," and so that Henry might restrain "the downward course of vice, correcting evil customs and planting virtue." Adrian ordered that "the people of that land shall receive you with honour and revere you as their lord: providing always that the rights of the churches remain whole and inviolate, and saving to the blessed Peter and the Holy Roman Church the annual tribute of one penny from every house."[28]

Henry's mother, the empress Matilda, managed to convince him that he had enough problems at home to worry about just then, and the bull was quietly shelved for the time being.[29] Within fifteen years, however, the situation changed dramatically. The king of Leinster, Dermot Mac Murrough, had called on some Norman lords to come to Ireland to help advance his own political ambitions. These Norman lords quickly set up viable centers of political power for themselves on the east coast—a potential threat to Henry's position. If this were not enough, Henry was also embroiled in a conflict with the Archbishop of Canterbury, Thomas Becket. The issue again concerned the relationship between church and state and, in particular, the right of the state to punish clerics, and the obedience owed to Rome and Canterbury, especially with regard to the consecration of bishops. Becket was eventually assassinated by four knights, and Henry was implicated in his murder.

The reigning pope, Alexander III, was on the point of placing the king under interdict when Henry decided to cross to Ireland. Henry convened the Second Synod of Cashel in 1172 and then, upon hearing from his messengers that the pope was willing to listen to him about Becket, he returned to England. The British bishops were less impressed than the pope with his account and required Henry to submit to public flagellation for his role in Becket's murder.

But Henry had already sent ahead details of his activities in Ireland,[30] and, as a result of his work in acting effectively as the pope's envoy, Alexander III sent three letters congratulating Henry on his great achievements. Alexander was overjoyed that his "dear son in Christ, Henry, illustrious King of England . . . has subjected to his dominion that people, a barbarous one uncivilized and ignorant of the Divine law. . . ."[31] Alexander confirmed the king in his royal power in England, authorizing him to place any rebels under ecclesiastical censure.

That several popes should have granted permission to an English king, and a known murderer at that, to carry out what was effectively a crusade in Ireland has always been a matter of bewilderment to Irish historians. Ireland had provided tremendous support to the European church during the Dark Ages. Irish monasteries had educated generations of scholars who served the church well for centuries. Could not the pope have dealt directly with Ireland?

Several attempts were made to account for the pope's intervention. The *Leabhar Breac* claimed that some Irish had stolen the horses of the papal legate when he came to Ireland, and "that is why the successor of Peter sold the tax and tribute of Ireland to the Saxons."[32] Others imply that the Irish might have regained sovereignty had it not been for their marriage practices and licentiousness. In the *Annals of Loch Cé* it is claimed that the pope had promised the king, Rory O'Connor, the right to rule over Ireland "to himself and his seed after him for ever, and six married wives, provided that he desisted from the sin of the women," but Rory refused.[33]

There is one thing, however, about which scholars are all agreed: the reform movement of the twelfth century led to a great increase in the power and prestige of the papacy. The great hereditary monastic families' power had been greatly weakened; attempts were made to bring the Irish marriage laws into line with canon law; clerical marriages came under fire and diocesan bishops and clergy received their power independently of family connections.

There are some who would argue that the major changes that took place in the twelfth century were necessary to ensure the future stability of both church and society, but the evidence over the next several hundred years would hardly justify this assertion. Even assuming that Adrian IV had acted in the best "spiritual" interests of Ireland by granting permission to Henry to invade Ireland, his hopes were to be sorely disappointed. The next several hundred years saw major conflicts and corruption in the church. Irish bishops and priests still took part in what was essentially tribal fighting and often were responsible for each other's deaths.[34] In 1221, the papal legate came from Rome, and within a year he had amassed a fortune through simony (the sale of church offices). He departed from Ireland with "horseloads of gold and silver from the clerics of Erinn."[35] Bishops and priests often held multiple benefices (from which they derived tithes). Many of them, while collecting tithes in Ireland, neglected their Irish duties and collected even more revenues as suffragan bishops living in England.[36]

In subsequent years there would be extreme abuses of the system of imposing tithes. In some cases ecclesiastics were brought before the royal courts to account for their extortionate demands.[37] Prominent ecclesiastics were particularly incensed at the local friars who operated a "cut-price" system of penance, diminishing the revenues due to the church.[38]

It could be argued that breaches of canon law were in the interest of the clergy bringing in, as they did, additional income. Mass pennies, confession pennies, Christmas offerings were usual sources of income, but in addition the church often extracted fines from the families of homicides as punishment for the offense. Bishops claimed tithes for the marriage of the daughters of the *erenaghs* (abbots) in their dioceses—presumably part of the woman's bride-price or possibly in compensation for giving up their right to sleep with the bride on her wedding night, a right traditionally extracted by feudal landlords.[39]

Under the native Irish ecclesiastical system, major church offices may well have been under the control of the hereditary families. But now in those areas in Ireland where English law held sway, the English king was effectively in control through his favorite appointees, one of whom was alternately Archbishop of Dublin, King's Justiciar, and papal legate.[40]

The next several hundred years were to see major and continuing conflicts between English and Irish churchmen who went back and forth to Rome, asserting their grievances to various popes. Constant fighting took place over the right to succeed to various sees so that in the early thirteenth century successive popes resorted to appointing several German and Italian men to Irish sees as compromise candidates.[41] One of these, a famous scientist called Michael Scot, had the good sense to resign within a month in the realization that he could speak neither Irish nor English.[42] In the last analysis the English had to resort to seizing the property and insignia of vacant sees in order to retain control over episcopal appointments.[43]

Probably the most insidious aspect of the papal grant of Ireland to the English at this time was that the Irish considered their subjection to England to be the will of God: the popes in their turn constantly confirmed their belief in this matter. Irish bishops had to take an oath of fealty to the English king and agree to recognize the customs of the English church as binding in Ireland.[44] Rebellions against English rule were open to canonical censure. The popes repeatedly issued warnings to the Irish clergy and people about their duty to obey the king of England.[45]

While in the secular realm, far from the Irish benefiting from what the pope considered to be superior English law, the native Irish were essentially disenfranchised and unfree under English law. For instance, should an Englishman find six other Englishmen to swear that an offence had been committed by an Irishman, the Irishman was automatically convicted.[46] The Irish were eventually excluded from ordination itself within the English system.[47] Several times even the popes were shocked at the treatment of the Irish,[48] but the English essentially maintained power in Ireland by the seizure of church property.[49]

The disenfranchisement of the Irish in secular law proceeded to such an extent that a movement eventually began among the clergy to actually *pay* the English to ensure that the Irish would receive equal treatment under English law.[50] This appears to have been finally granted by Edward II, in 1280, when Irish prelates agreed to "apply ecclesiastical sanctions" against those who held out for the Irish (Brehon) laws.[51] With the grant of "free British law" the prelates conceded that thereafter "all their bodies would belong to the king."[52] But rebellions against the English continued, and as late as 1367 a provincial council ordered that clergy living among the "mere Irish" were duty bound to report possible rebellions on the part of native Irish chieftains or parishioners. Rebels were also to be denied the sacraments, except those of baptism and penance.[53]

With such drastic consequences for the Irish, one is entitled to ask whether such measures needed to be taken by the pope. There is tremendous evidence that Ireland would have been quite capable of reforming her own church and was well underway in the process of doing so.[54] For instance, even before the Norman invasion the process of establishing territorial dioceses had been completed.[55] Furthermore, in his capacity as an Irish historian, the present cardinal-archbishop of Armagh, and Primate of All Ireland, Tomás Ó Fiaich, has pointed out that the views of the Irish and the continental reformers as to what needed to be changed were not necessarily the same. For instance, whereas the Irish annals considered the main abuses of the period to lie in the unbridled recourse to violence on the part of the ecclesiastics, the reformers, such as Bernard of Clairvaux, were silent on this matter, "for in this respect Ireland was no better or no worse than the rest of Christendom."[56] Indeed, in respect to violence, Bernard endorsed an unparalleled reign of terror by means of the Crusades.[57]

In contrast to the continentals, the Irish annals were seldom concerned with what the European continental reformers considered to be the main abuses, simony and clerical celibacy. In view of the hereditary character of the Irish church, simony was ineffective and unnecessary. The overall effects of having married clergy at the heads of monasteries, although certainly open to abuse, were, according to Ó Fiaich, "not as black as St. Bernard would lead one to believe," and there were "many excellent and sincere men to be found in their ranks."[58] According to Ó Fiaich, given the fact that the Irish church "had just survived two centuries of chaos (from the Viking invasions), the surprising thing is not that there were abuses, but that it had managed to retain so much which was essentially sound."[59] Not only could the Irish have reformed themselves: Left to themselves the Irish might have effected changes very different from those imposed upon them by Canterbury and Rome.

In making an overall assessment of the reform movement in the twelfth century and of the intervention of Rome and Canterbury, we should, therefore, bear the following facts in mind, facts that cast another light on the motivations and characters of the main actors behind the events as well as on the power struggles at the heart of them.

Henry had come to Ireland partly to expiate his role in the murder of Thomas Becket. While complaining about the marriage laws of the Irish, Henry was himself married to the divorced wife of King Louis of France, Eleanor of Aquitaine.[60] The various synods had broken the power of the monastic families on the grounds of one of the great evils of the time, "lay intrusion in spiritual affairs."[61] Yet this intrusion was obviously very welcome to the pope when it came in the form of military might helping him to exert his will both in Ireland and in the bloody Crusades—adventures, one might add, through which both knights and laymen "achieved salvation."[62]

Alexander III may well have been concerned about the marriage laws of the Irish, and yet he himself only narrowly won election to the papacy on the death of Adrian IV by skillful maneuvering in sexual politics. Several antipopes had appeared, and Henry II and Louis of France supported the antipope Victor. The kings were persuaded to change their minds only after a special dispensation had been issued to the son of Henry II to marry the daughter of Louis of France—a marriage that strengthened the power of their respective monarchies. Louis's daughter was barely three years of age.[63]

Given these facts, and given the characters of the main actors involved, clearly what was at stake was no mere ecclesiastical reform but an entirely new power shift in ecclesiastical and world politics, where the centralization of power on the part of the papacy, together with whatever political supporters it could rally, was at stake. In this respect Ireland was a mere pawn in a much wider struggle, and despite its contribution to the civilization of Europe in the Dark Ages, its independence and integrity could now easily be disposed of in the pursuit of other gains.

The changes in ecclesiastical politics that took place in the twelfth century were to have widespread implications, especially in the development of the doctrines concerning the sacrifice of the Mass, the discipline of clerical celibacy, the centralization of power, and in the relationships between church and state. The implications of these changes will be explored throughout the remainder of this book. But it is important to highlight now as we enter the Age of Mary that the discourse with regard to women would be radically altered with sharp divisions made between public and private worlds. In the public and symbolic realm, under the mantle of Mary, women would be placed on a pedestal and idealized. But in the private realm (where it counted), women would remain under the shadow of Eve, symbols of evil and gateways to destruction.

CHAPTER 9

Clerical Celibacy
The Quest for Power in Church and State

This is a tale about a priest's concubine when she died. Many people came to her to carry her away to bury her, and they could not lift her because she was so heavy. And they all wondered greatly at this, and everyone said, "O One God, Almighty Father, how shall she be taken to be buried?" And they consulted a cunning professor, and the professor said to them as follows: "Bring two priest's concubines to us to carry her away to the church." And they were brought, and they carried her away very lightly to the church; and the people wondered greatly at this, and the professor said to them, "There is no cause for you to wonder at their actions, O people; that is, that two devils should carry off one devil with them."

UNKNOWN AUTHOR

In the reform movement of the twelfth century, new alliances and new divisions of territory were being made between church and state; there was a new emphasis on the sacrifice of the Mass; and radical moves were taken to enforce and sustain clerical hierarchy.

The new hierarchy had been urged on the Irish by Gilbert, the papal legate and a good friend of Anselm of Canterbury. In his document *De Statu Ecclesiae*, written at the beginning of the twelfth century, he set out a church structure, from Christ, Noah, the pope, emperor, all the way down to those who fight, plough, and pray.[1] But for Gilbert, the model of church organization was based, not on the gospel of Jesus of Nazareth, but on that of Frankish society: a hierarchical and even military model where the pope was compared to the emperor, abbots to military leaders, and archbishops to kings.[2] The main advantage of this hierarchy to the papacy was that obedience could be extracted from those low down on the ecclesiastical ladder without being individually negotiated on each occasion—vital if the pope was to gain any power over the lives of the faithful. Gilbert also argued for the separation of dioceses and monasteries, making it clear that only the bishop who had received his authority from Rome through apostolic succession could confer faculties upon the clerics of the monasteries.[3]

These changes in church discipline were intimately connected to the new alliances made between church and state. Kings and nobles were amassing vast tracts of land, forming the basis of the future nation-states of Europe. Corresponding to the centralization of political power were new religious rites of kingship.

We have seen in the mythological stories that kings had been confirmed in their reigns by the activities of heroes such as Cúchulainn who had to separate from women before they went to battle to avoid weakening their strength. The warriors possessed a form of religious power, based upon their independence from women, that gave them a seeming immunity to death, and their brave acts imparted this power to the king, increasing his prestige in the eyes of the people.

In the more stable form of politics, singular heroic acts would not be enough to support an ongoing kingly reign. What was needed was a much more reliable marriage of politics and religion that could be called upon at a moment's notice. Standing armies would be one way of solving the political problem, but in the new arrangements between church and state, and with a church hierarchical structure based upon a military model, more symbolic changes would be needed. In addition, with the passing of the old religions and the old rites of kingship, priests took on an entirely new role in the symbolic life of the newly emerging political entities, developing new forms of power that would give priests credibility in the eyes of the faithful.[4]

The priests, in effect, became the new heroes of the society. Previously their "heroic deeds" in the service of God simply would have been proof of great holiness. Now their great power enabled them to confer religious authority upon the kings. The saints, performing amazing feats of asceticism to prove their worthiness, became the new "spiritual heroes," and male priests, by identification with them, became a permanent caste of heroes with a monopoly on religious power.

In the stories of the Celtic and Hebrew warriors we saw how they had to separate from women to be effective, even, or perhaps especially, from their mothers. The new spiritual warriors would have to do likewise. Whereas the ancient warriors had only avoided women at the peak times of military performance, the priests would have to prove their worthiness by permanently avoiding contact with the opposite sex.[5]

By now, it goes without saying, women could certainly not become priests, but in addition, the priests would have to make it clear that they were not at the behest, or under the power, of any woman. Those who performed the sacrifice would have to prove their fitness for doing so by sacrificing themselves—yet another reason why celibacy became mandatory for those who celebrated the Covenant or Christian Eucharist. In particular, they would have to sacrifice their sexuality and any women whom they might have loved. The fruits of the harvest would be replaced by the fruits of continence: justice, righteousness, and social prosperity, vital elements by means of which the clerics could establish and confirm the king in his reign.

Thus male reproductive consciousness was developed to new levels. At first, as we have seen, men merely wished to claim the fruits of their own reproductive labor. Inevitably this concern led to the control of women. But as the awareness grew that there was no sure resting place on earth, patriarchal consciousness in its most pristine mode could abandon women entirely. The institution of compulsory clerical celibacy generated powerful symbolic capital that could be drawn upon to sustain the superiority of the spiritual and temporal empires to which men gave birth.

The imposition of clerical celibacy was by no means new but had always been required by the church for its most important ministers; at the council of Elvira in 305, for instance, it was decreed that bishops, priests, and deacons should separate from their wives and that they should not have children. Dire penalties awaited those who committed "fornication." Virgins consecrated to God who committed sin could receive communion at the end of their lives only after perpetual penance. Bishops, priests, and deacons who fornicated were to be denied communion for the rest of their lives. Homosexuals were not allowed to receive communion ever again, even on their deathbeds.[6] These regulations were primarily a concern for liturgical or cultic purity, but already in some of these decrees we can see that control of women was intimately connected with this concern. For instance, a woman who had an abortion could never be readmitted to communion, while a woman who whipped her slave girl to death could repent and be readmitted after seven years.[7]

The subsequent history of the church indicates that the early decrees on celibacy were not widely observed. Council after council attempted to enforce rules of cultic purity, with varying degrees of success. The higher one went in the hierarchy, the more serious the offence and, therefore, the greater the penance imposed for transgression. These penances were obviously not enough to enforce the rules of celibacy, and among the secular clergy up to the twelfth century, marriage was the norm rather than the exception.[8] Nevertheless, marriage was barely tolerated, and clerical wives were constantly subject to accusations of licentiousness and even of causing natural disasters such as plagues and famines by their involvement with priests who subsequently offered "polluted" sacrifices to God.[9]

The new moves toward reform in the universal church were ratified at the Synod of Pisa in 1135 and the Second Lateran Council in 1139, when it was decreed that clerical marriages were invalid since the vow of ordination took precedence over all other vows.

Throughout Europe attempts to enforce the regulations on celibacy caused tremendous upheaval.[10] Riots took place throughout the eleventh and twelfth century in Germany, Italy, and France as the clerics decided to hold onto their wives in defiance of their bishop's orders.[11] Pope Nicholas II had ordered the laity not to attend masses of priests who had refused to give up their wives or concubines.[12] Parishioners often participated in ridiculing, beating, and driving the clerics away from their benefices. Some clergy were murdered and others driven to wander penniless like tramps around the countryside.[13] Peter Damian (1007–72), a high-ranking ecclesiastic and theologian, reserved his most vicious rhetoric for the wives of priests:

Come now, hear me, harlots, prostitutes, with your lascivious kisses, your wallowing places for fat pigs, resting places for unclean spirits, demigoddesses, sirens, witches . . . from you the devil is fattened by the abundance of your lust, is fed by your alluring feasts.[14]

Born in poverty, he had been forced to take care of pigs during his childhood. He ultimately rose to the rank of cardinal; thus his comparison between women and pigs lends his diatribe a particular significance. Peter Damian's opposition to clerical wives is particularly strange. The thirteenth child of a woman weakened by childbearing who refused to feed him, Damian's life was only saved when a clerical wife intervened and persuaded his exhausted mother to put him at her breast.[15]

For Damian, freedom from sexuality and the power to sacrifice were intimately connected:

You harpies, who snatch the Eucharistic wafer as you fly around, and crudely devour what God had made oblation for . . . you snatch away unhappy men from their ministry of the altar . . . that you may strangle them in the slimy glue of your passion.[16]

And yet Peter Damian's attitude toward clerical celibacy is perfectly understandable at another level. Both he and Gregory VII had come from very poor families. Had church benefices been allowed to be transmitted through the hereditary families, they themselves would have had very limited opportunities to rise in the clerical hierarchy. Effectively, hereditary offices would have given rise to a Brahmin-like caste—yet another threat both to the supremacy of royal power and to individual advancement.

But clerical marriage also had its defenders, and these argued that the papacy was breaking these clerical marriages simply in order to exert better control over the lives of the clergy. In addition they argued that many excellent popes and bishops had been born of the unions between priests and women and that ultimately these marriages were preferable to the homosexuality, fornication, incest, and bestiality to which enforced celibacy inevitably led.[17]

Even when not formally married to a particular cleric, women played a significant role in the local churches. St. Maura lived in her father's house but was integrally involved in the life of the local cathedral of Troyes. In a tribute given by Bishop Prudentius in her biography, he laments her death:

Who poured the oil into the lamps? Maura! Who gathered the curtains? Maura! Who bought the sacerdotal vestments with her own money? Maura! I value more the linen garment she gave me than I do either gold or topaz. She spun, wove, and whitewashed it herself and begged me with utmost humility to wear it while I was celebrating the mass.[18]

We should remind ourselves that the "clerical wives" were by no means merely appendages to their husbands. As in the Irish case of "spiritual marriage," these women often played a vital role in the church community. Some were known as "presbyteria," "diaconissa," "countesses," and "episcopa." The women participated in the liturgical ceremonies, and often at their husband's ordination, they, too, received special recognition in the form of a blessing, or in some cases they themselves took religious vows.[19] They had their own distinctive style of clothing, and the wife of one priest, Namatius, built churches and oratories.[20] Clerical wives often came from wealthy families to marry relatively poor men. Children of the marriage regularly took the name of their mothers rather than their fathers—an indication as to who was most socially prestigious. These women were often responsible for the physical maintenance of the priest's household, as was evident in Ravenna and Vercelli in the tenth century when one of the main arguments the men made against divorcing their wives was that the men would starve.[21]

None of these factors would mitigate the treatment meted out to the women. In tenth-century Germany, a church council decreed that priest's wives and mistresses should have their heads shaved and be lashed.[22] Pope Leo IX ordered that the wives of Roman priests become slaves in the Lateran palace.[23] In 1189, Urban II took this action one step further when he ordered that the women be given as slaves to the nobles in an attempt to get the nobles to assist him in his reform program.[24] The Archbishop of Rheims gave permission to Count Robert of Flanders to abduct priest's wives but had to back down from this when the move was vehemently opposed by the married clergy.[25] In the face of this onslaught, the women often took drastic steps. Many were found dead in their beds—suicide victims, driven to despair. Others were not so passive. When the Swabian count of Veringen assisted the pope in separating wives from their priestly husbands, one of these wives retaliated by poisoning the countess, intent on carrying home to the count what it was like to be left so bereft.[26]

We have very few records of how the women themselves felt in these situations, but we are very fortunate to have documented accounts of what is possibly the most famous and tragic love affair of this era, that of the eleventh-century Abelard and Heloise.[27]

Throughout her life, Heloise refused to deny her great love for Abelard, claiming that she had taken vows to God because of her love for him. Heloise realized that their marriage would seriously damage his career. As Abelard wrote, she argued against the marriage:

What honour could she win, she protested, from a marriage which would dishonour me and humiliate us both? The world would justly exact punishment from her if she removed such a light from its midst. Think of the curses, the loss to the Church and grief of philosophers which would greet such a marriage! *Nature had created me for all mankind*—it would be a sorry scandal if I should bind myself to a single woman and submit to such base servitude (emphasis added).[28]

Even in her later life Heloise regretted having given in to the secret marriage:

I believed that the more I humbled myself on your account, the more gratitude I should win from you, and also the *less damage I should do to the brightness of your reputation* (emphasis added).[29]

The story of Abelard and Heloise is a classic study of the tensions that all clerical wives must have experienced at this time. Although Heloise's views on marriage, which she considered a form of prostitution, were revolutionary for her time, even she did not manage to see sexual union as anything other than a concession to lust. Whereas his celibate vocation had called him to be a "universal man," his relationship to Heloise would reduce him to "base servitude" to a single mere woman.[30]

Heloise saw a clear connection between celibacy and power; a connection that would become all the more blatant as the movement for reform progressed. Heloise's views would be confirmed in the subsequent history of the church: the institution of compulsory clerical celibacy could be said to have been the single most important consequence of the reform movements of the twelfth century.

In Ireland, clerical celibacy had been the ideal when the church was founded in the fifth century, but very quickly when the monastic federations assumed control, married abbots and sometimes bishops became commonplace. Many efforts were made to reform this situation. The Céli-Dé, for instance, did not approve of the combination of sex and Holy Orders. In the *Martyrology of Oengus,* it was said that "a priest, practising coition, small is his profit in baptising, baptism comes not from him, after visiting his nun."[31] However, the Céli-Dé accepted married couples for spiritual direction and in most Irish monasteries families were integral parts of the monastic establishment.[32] In the document "The First Synod of Saint Patrick," married priests are simply taken for granted:

Any cleric from ostiary to priest, who is seen without a tunic and does not cover the shame or nakedness of his body, and whose hair is not barbered in the Ro-

man manner, and whose wife walks about with her head uncovered, shall be de-
spised by the laity and separated from the Church.[33]

Irish law provided extensively for the rights of women married to
priests and specifically for priests who "decided to repent," since repentance was apparently a constant risk with which priest's wives had to
reckon.[34] Even where formal marriage did not exist, concubinage was
widely practiced on the evidence of the extensive legislation in the Irish
legal codes.[35]

St. Bernard, speaking of the bishops of Armagh and their system of
hereditary succession, exclaimed,

But a very evil custom had grown up, by the devilish ambition of certain powerful persons, that this holy see should be held in hereditary succession. For they
suffered none to be bishops but those who were of their own tribe and family.[36]

At the Synod of Cashel in 1101, the first serious moves were made toward enforcing clerical celibacy. The reformers at this synod were occupied with sexual politics and other issues that would have far-reaching
implications for the attitude to women in the church.[37]

The synod was concerned with the issues of simony, celibacy of the
major office holders of the church (erenaghs), marriage practices (and
incest in particular), and the separation of church and state (although
the word *state* is hardly applicable in the Irish context yet). It was also at
this synod that King Muirchertach Ua Briain handed over the historical
lands of Cashel to the church "without any claim of layman or cleric
upon it, but to the religious of Éire in general."[38]

In the decrees of the synod a clear pattern was emerging whereby the
interests of the state as much as those of the church were being served by
the new emphasis on celibacy. The Synod of Cashel, convened by a monarch, Muirchertach Ua Briain, saw the separation of church and state
and clerical celibacy as going hand in hand—one would not be achieved
without the other—a pattern that was replicated in the Gregorian reform throughout Europe. There were several reasons for this, and the
first one was economic.

Just as the popes were trying to centralize and consolidate their power
bases, so too ambitious monarchs wanted to expand their own areas of
jurisdiction. Among the biggest threats to these ambitions were the
great hereditary families who often controlled large areas and easily
formed political alliances to counter the power of the monarchs. If the
monarchs were to consolidate their positions, it would be in their interests to cut down the power of the hereditary families, including or especially those that had a monastic base. The church would also gain, in
turn, by receiving lands free of family claims or connections.

We can, therefore, understand the decision of the king to hand over
the lands of Cashel to the reform movement. Effectively, his act gave
support to the new diocesan organization of the church and dealt a fatal

blow to the ambitions of one of his rivals for the high kingship of Ireland.

Since the political powers would only tolerate a certain amount of economic independence on the part of the church, to allow priests to marry and women to transmit property to the church (as they did throughout Europe)[39] would drastically threaten the purity and strength of the new arrangements. Every encouragement in both Ireland and Europe was given to the religious reform movements by politically ambitious monarchs.

In 1152 at the Synod of Kells further attempts were made to remove what the clerics considered to be major abuses.[40] For the next several hundred years the issue of clerical celibacy would be raised over and over again, since the efforts to wipe out the practice of clerical marriage were never entirely successful. Surnames speak for themselves. "Son of the Prior," "Son of the Bishop," "Son of the Priest," "Son of the Arch-Dean," are some examples.[41] These children often became priests, priors, or bishops themselves and, although technically born outside the legalities of Christian marriage, incurred no social stigma because of illegitimacy or concubinage. One particular cleric, Cathal Óg MacManus Maguire, the father of ten children, is commemorated in the *Annals of Ulster* as a "gem of purity," a "dove for purity of heart," and a "turtle of chastity."[42] Clerical celibacy remained an issue in Ireland at least until the seventeenth century.[43]

Despite these aberrations, once the power of the monastic federations and the great families who controlled them had been broken, the kings were anxious to ensure that the diocesan clergy should not have any real opportunity again to amass wealth in their own right. One way that priests had done this had been that either they or their children married into wealthy families, thus inheriting or having access to large sources of wealth.[44] This may have been the case when the bishop of Armagh's concubine caused a major ecclesiastical scandal by refusing to hand back after his death what was considered to be church property, including the bishop's episcopal ring, his horse, and his cup, to the primate of Armagh.[45] In one case an Anglo-Norman archbishop of Cashel, William FitzJohn, who was the king's chancellor in Ireland and famous for having established the first prison in Cashel, was also the father of fourteen daughters. He married them all off to rich men, giving them very generous dowries at the expense of the local people and clergy—his own prestige being greatly increased in the process.[46] The fifteenth-century Archbishop of Armagh, John Mey, authorized the O'Neill family to confiscate the property of unrepentant concubines, but he was careful to admonish the chiefs to distinguish between the women's property and that of the church, lest too great inroads on church property be made.[47] The O'Neill family also made independent raids on priests suspected of keeping concubines, even though the O'Neills themselves had insisted on the right to make church appointments and although, in other respects, their own moral behavior and obedience to the church was far from exemplary.[48]

The imposition of clerical celibacy, therefore, was an extraordinary political achievement. In the early form of the state as represented by the Blood Covenant, the brothers agreed not to rape each other's wives. But this commitment was a minor sacrifice compared with what was to come: the wholesale sacrifice of women for the preservation and promotion of clerical power via the state. Those who celebrated the new Covenant would do without women altogether—a token of the purity of the brothers' commitment to each other and their common cause.

The movement toward compulsory celibacy for all ministers at the altar was, therefore, a vital tactic in the establishment of a clerical hierarchy, beginning with the pope and extending all the way down to the local curate. Painful though the sacrifice of their wives might have been to the men involved, essentially this was a mere symbol of what was really required of them: the sacrifice of their wills, bodies, and their lives to the will of God—however this will might be expressed in the wishes of the reigning pope.

In exchange, the reformed clergy enjoyed new privileges with regard to the state. The First Synod of Cashel had decreed, "neither to king nor to chief for ever should the Church of Ireland pay either rent or tribute," and furthermore, "neither clerics nor poet's misdemeanor should be brought before lay authority."[49] Likewise, the effect of the assertion of papal primacy in Europe was that priests could in the future hold their properties securely, be free from the secular powers, and be free from the obligation to go to war on behalf of one of the nobles.[50] In return for these privileges, the clerics had to choose: Either they could hold onto their clerical power, thereby sacrificing their own sexuality and possibly the women they loved, or else they could become laymen subject to the same rules and regulations as anyone else.[51]

Clerical power was intimately related to yet another form of the sacrifice of women. If the clerics wished to remain free from the constraints of state interference, they would pay for this freedom by constantly proving their loyalty to another, higher, authority. Successfully separating from women would furnish daily, living proof that their loyalties lay beyond this world. The impetus toward clerical celibacy was, therefore, in the interests of the male power structure of the church, as much as it was in the interest of the emerging "state," and the wives and children of the clergy in the last analysis were simply irrelevant.

In the long run, clerical celibacy became the norm since, as one scholar claims, "the sheer power represented by the newly centralized papacy, power which every priest could share, was a highly seductive element."[52] Maintaining their place in this privileged state may have clinched the decision of many wavering clerics to give up their wives.

The marriage of church and state would go through many stormy periods, but the basic agreement would remain constant. The women, who formally had been revered, now became sources of temptation—an attitude that would endure for many centuries. Even after the sixteenth-century Reformation, when Protestant clergy were allowed to marry, the children of the clergy were often treated as illegitimate, and in some cases midwives refused to deliver them. Henry VIII, famous for his many wives, reacted violently to the idea of married clergy, saying that married priests were "carnally evil."[53] Henry was trying desperately to maintain ties with Rome, critical as he was of Lutheran theology, and the sacrifice of clerical wives was a minor price to pay. In the Six Articles of 1539, which the king himself annotated, priests had to repudiate their wives and children or be executed. Their property confiscated, priest's families had to flee or depend on their neighbors for support.[54] Even before this, Thomas Cranmer, Henry's archbishop, had been forced when in public to carry his own wife around hidden in a chest until finally she and her children fled into exile when the statutes were passed. In the reign of Mary Tudor, clerical wives were free to remarry as though their first marriages (and presumably children) never existed. The vehemence against the wives of priests and ministers would take many centuries to eradicate in the post-Reformation period of Protestantism, while the Roman Catholic church maintains its rules against clerical marriage to this day.

Clerical celibacy was, therefore, vital to the interests of church and state and, given the seriousness of what was at stake, another layer was stripped from women's autonomy and dignity. Women became signs representing the depths to which holy men could fall. Contact with them was to be guarded against at all costs since it would seriously interfere with the priests' capacity to sacrifice, rule, judge, and mediate between opposing sides. Priests' wives became the "guardian devils" incarnate, and as St. Magnenn of Kilmainham intoned,

Woe to him too to whom after a priest such woman shall become a prize: for to be familiar with her and to know her is a thrusting of the head into mire; and a renunciation of baptism, of faith, of piety; a pact with Lucifer, with Satan and with Abiron; with Pluto and with Beelzebub; with the swart sow, and with the chief captains of Hell's host.[55]

CHAPTER 10

The Politics of Virginity

The Cult of the Virgin Mary and the Consolidation of Patriarchal Theology

It is important and fascinating, of course, to note that women never, no matter how deluded or needy or desperate, worship Jesus as the perfect son. No faith is that blind. There is no religious or cultural palliative to deaden the raw pain of the son's betrayal of the mother: only her own obedience to the same father, the sacrifice of her own life on the same cross, her own body nailed and bleeding, can enable her to accept that her son, like Jesus, has come to do his Father's work.

ANDREA DWORKIN

The Age of Mary had begun in Ireland with the Anglo-Norman/papal invasion and with the attempts on the part of local powerful leaders to consolidate their territories and areas of jurisdiction. These political and social developments were to have wide-reaching implications for the rights of women as the social organization moved from being based on *clan* ties, to more centralized and hierarchical forms of government, where the religious and political leaders would rely upon the extraction of surplus wealth from their dependent peoples in order to maintain power.

Under the expanded tribal system, through complex systems of inheritance, women had often been able to amass considerable wealth and to exert considerable power (if not actual ownership) over land and money. Women had the use-value (usufruct) of lands or property that had not been passed down in the male line, enabling them to exert influence during their lifetimes. By keeping marriages within the clan system, women's rights were effectively protected by their own kinsmen.

In such a decentralized Irish society there were many different types of liaisons possible for women, and early Irish law legislated extensively for the rights of women in marriage, particularly going into great detail with regard to the disposal of property in the event of marriage breakdown. Women could marry either "up" or "down" on the economic ladder in the full knowledge that their kin or their children would not suffer in the event of their deaths or divorce since the disposal of property had been agreed upon in advance. Irish law also provided thirteen different grounds for divorce on the part of both men and women; since all children of their unions would be provided for in this event, the social consequences of these arrangements were not drastic.[1]

But by keeping marriage within limited degrees of kinship, the power of certain families had increased, and their accumulated wealth had not been dissipated by women marrying outside their structures. Now these powerful families posed a serious problem to the efforts to centralize the powers of both church and state. For this reason the marital practices of the Irish were destined to come under fire.[2]

Lanfranc was one of the first to attack the Irish laws of marriage. In a letter to Toirdelbach Ó Briain, king of Cashel, in 1074, he wrote the following:

. . . in your kingdom every man abandons his lawfully wedded wife at his own will, without the occasion of any canonical cause, and with a boldness that must be punished, takes to himself some other wife who may be of his own kin or of the kindred of his wife whom he has abandoned, or whom another has abandoned with like wickedness, according to a law of marriage that is rather a law of fornication. . . .[3]

Anselm also complained:

It is said that men exchange their wives with the wives of others as freely and publicly as a man might exchange his horse for another's horse . . . or else they abandon them at will and without reason.[4]

He was also concerned about incest:

We hear . . . that kinsmen are not ashamed to have intercourse either under the name of marriage or in some other way, publicly and without rebuke, against all the prohibitions of canon law.[5]

Anselm urged the Irish bishops to suppress anything "contrary to the teaching of the church."[6] He threatened the bishops that if they failed to take his advice they would "expose themselves to God's anger as transgressors of His Law."[7]

Anselm's efforts were not successful, for in 1172, Pope Alexander III was still preoccupied with the Irish marriage laws and particularly with what he considered to be incest: "a man will live with his brother's wife while the brother is still alive; that one man will live in concubinage with two sisters; and that many of them, putting away the mother, will marry the daughters."[8] The reformers' concern was so great that the historian Katharine Simms has been prompted to comment:

Anyone reading the letter written by Pope Alexander to King Henry in 1172 might be forgiven for thinking that a prime object of the Norman invasion of Ireland had been the reform of the Irish customs with regard to marriage and concubinage.[9]

In the context of the needs of church and state for centralization, we can understand one of the decrees of the Synod of Cashel, the decree on incest: "That in Ireland none should have to wife, either his father's wife or grandfather's, either his sister or his daughter or his brother's or any woman at all thus near akin."

Both the church and state wanted to expand their bases of power beyond what was possible within a clan-based system, and as they forged ahead with new alliances their interests were to merge again at this juncture in human history. The state needed to break up the power of the large, landed families, preventing them from establishing an independent base from which to challenge rising monarchies. The laws of incest effectively allowed the ruling political powers to prevent alliances being made on their home territory and also allowed the rulers themselves to forge alliances with other rulers throughout Europe. Sending their daughters off to act as liaisons between great families abroad, the families forged marriage bonds with other large families, who could then be counted on for political support in the event of their being under siege. Likewise, it was in the interests of the diocesan-based church to break the power of the large, landed families, particularly those with a monastic base. Under these circumstances, both church and state once again cooperated on matters of sexual politics that facilitated mutual interests.

The lawyers of medieval times spent a great deal of energy working out the levels of relationship within which it was permitted to marry. To violate this arrangement was known as incest—a term that had much wider implications than sexual relations within the immediate family, as implied today. The lawyers bent over backwards to figure out how, and in what way, women could and could not serve as links between competing clans, thereby forging social alliances between men. In the long run the lawyers would decide that marriage links could not be formed between any two people who might have inherited from each other.[10] The higher a man's status, the more important it was that he adhere to the laws of incest. Consequently, some men had to spread their nets all over Europe in an effort to seek a wife, an act that increased their sphere of political influence at the same time.[11]

Under the most ancient Irish law, men were forbidden to exchange women in order to create bonds of clientship between them. In marriage the husband would bring a "bride-price" with him to be given either to the woman or to her kin. But as we move into a highly stratified and centralized society, this prohibition was effectively reversed. The father of the bride would bestow a dowry upon his daughter, representing a loan that would secure the relationship of lord and vassal.[12] In the event of the breakdown of the political relationship the marriage would automatically be dissolved and the dowry returned, even though, should the marriage break down for personal reasons, the vassal-lord relationship need not be affected.[13] These arrangements represented "the ruthless subordination of the personal relationship of man and wife to the political bond between lord and vassal."[14] In the *Law of Adamnán,* we saw that slave women, *cumals,* were used as items of currency between men. But now these rules on incest resulted in women becoming political hostages in the social system, and, effectively, all women became items of exchange in return for political favors.[15]

In this situation Irish women would lose a great deal of their "protection" in marriage.[16] The *Annals of Connacht* record occasions in the thirteenth and fourteenth centuries when a man abandoned his wife to marry his aunt, and another when a man abducted his mother from her husband and married her off to another man to serve as a "ransom for himself."[17] There were many instances where men broke up existing marriages to forge alternative political alliances. The extent to which this was the case has led Katharine Simms to remark that "Irish noblewomen who had such extensive control of their property, appear to have had very little to say in the disposal of their own persons."[18]

Following the period of reform, there were two systems of law operating in Ireland; the Anglo-Norman and the native Irish. Under the Anglo-Norman legal system women could inherit property outright, while under the Irish they only had use-value of land or property during their lifetimes. The dynamics of this situation were extremely intricate.[19]

In some cases Irish men refused to accept church teaching on incest but then manipulated this teaching when they wanted a way out of an unsuitable or inexpedient marriage. Women lost out on both counts.[20] The church had additional reasons for prohibiting what it considered to be incest, particularly the remarriage of a widow with her husband's brother. So long as women could retain a life-interest in their property upon the death of their husbands or upon the lack of a male heir, women could, and indeed did, contribute very generously, often in return for "protection" from the church.[21] Possibly the women realized that the church was the only hope of providing a counterbalance to the power of the state, or of the strong against the weak. From the twelfth century onward almost the only women mentioned in the Irish annals are those who were known for their great generosity both to the church and to the scholars.[22]

A recent scholar goes so far as to say that the church promoted women's "rights," particularly their right not to remarry precisely because of their economic contributions to the church.[23] There is some evidence that confessors were effectively "impoverishing future heirs" or at least reducing the role of kinship relations and weakening kinship bonds.[24] Throughout Europe the charters give many instances where blood relatives tried to recover land that had been given to the churches by women, and indeed eventually the state often stepped in to limit the extent to which this could happen.[25]

In the context of the laws on celibacy, women became signs of the depths to which holy men could fall, but in the context of the laws of incest, women now became highly valued items of currency. In order for men to be able to trade women, and in order for women to be worthy of trade and to produce legitimate heirs, their sexuality would have to come under new levels of control and be strictly "protected," sometimes "to the point of tyranny."[26] Severe sanctions awaited those women who effectively spoilt the deals made between men by establishing independent liaisons or by "losing" their virginity in a romantic rather than a political alliance, thereby wiping out their exchange value.[27] And whereas in a decentralized society women could move between the social spheres in marriage knowing their rights and property would be protected, in a hierarchical, centralized system this option would no longer be open to them. The women were now part and parcel of their father's wealth, to be traded upwards whenever possible.[28]

Under these circumstances protection of a woman's virginity, as distinct from protection of a woman's "rights," became a widespread social phenomenon. In some cases women were paid money by their fathers to enter a convent and to "protect their chastity," presumably in order to prevent an unwelcome subdivision of the man's wealth or power.[29] For some women it was a temporary state of being, but for others permanent virginity was a logical option and welcome alternative to a forced political marriage, possibly with someone beneath the social class in which the woman had been reared. Virginity for these women was in their own self-interest. By remaining virginal, women could protect their status mobility, if not in the present life, at least in the future.[30] The women were effectively acting as "guardians of the system,"[31] and any independence gained was at the expense of other women.[32]

Throughout Europe, women in the thousands flocked to the religious orders. Some of these women were the abandoned family members of the newly celibate priests. In the beginning many of these women enjoyed tremendous independence as *Beguines*. They lived as groups in houses and were self-supporting.[33] Eventually, however, their independence proved such a threat to the religious establishment that strict controls were enacted. The women were placed under the "protection" of the local male equivalent monastery since it was inconceivable that women should remain without any protection at all. In 1293 Pope Boniface VIII published a bull, *Periculoso*, forbidding any nun to leave her convent without the bishop's permission. The women were effectively forced to live contemplative lives in strict enclosure.[34] This enclosure went so far that in some cases even dying nuns had curtains put around them lest they see the priest who had come to give them the last rites. In other cases the nuns were forbidden to sing in choir lest their music stir the passions of their adjoining male counterparts.[35] Even those women who had dedicated themselves to lives of virginity were still viewed as threatening to the spirituality of the men, their own concupiscence making them incapable of resisting temptation, and needing the "protection" of strict enclosure.[36]

If many upper-class women found themselves in religious orders for the protection of their chastity, a parallel movement was taking place among men that would also contribute to the cult of virginity or the ideal woman, so much a feature of this period. Europe had been ravaged by interdynastic wars for several centuries. Many of these wars took place between rival claimants to territory or titles as no clear principles of succession had yet been enforced. This social instability could not be tolerated by the newly centralizing church and state, themselves often the victims, and several solutions presented themselves. In the first place, the principle of primogeniture, inheritance by the first-born son, was established.[37] This would cut down on interfamily disputes, but it also had another major consequence, effectively leaving younger sons dispossessed and forced to seek their own livings. Left to their own desserts, the younger men joined together as "soldiers of fortune," giving rise to renewed military fervor.[38]

Lacking the means to marry, and not yet inspired by the wars of religion, men sought alternative objects of conquest. There arose the ethic of courtly love, the positing of the unattainable woman, usually of superior rank to the knight, on whose behalf and for the sake of whose honor, the knight would risk his life. The women chosen would often be in effective control of large amounts of land and property, while their husbands and eldest sons were away at war or had already been killed.

The ethic of courtly love gave rise to a huge body of erotic literature, inspired, and sometimes even written by, the women themselves. The relationship between the knight and his lady was entirely erotic and always (at least in theory) stopped short of actual intercourse. For the women concerned, these relationships had inestimable benefits. Rather than a husband and master, the ladies had erotic lovers who demanded nothing more of them than their devotion.[39] Marriage was simply not part of the picture: the object was the creation and sustaining of an object of intense and usually unattainable desire. Marriage may have placed women in the marketplace, but courtly love placed them on a pedestal. Given the options, aristocratic women had little choice.

While individual women may have benefited from male attentions, women as a whole increasingly lost further ground, especially in the legal sphere. Women's "souls" may have been loved, but their persons were now at the mercy of male politics.[40] Aristocratic women could be idealized, but peasant women could be raped,[41] for the knight who honored his lady considered other women fair game for his predatory attentions.

The ethic of courtly love was one way of dealing with the unattainable ambitions of younger sons, no longer able to succeed to the family inheritance. A further option was that families, unable to provide for younger sons, would present them, at an early age, to the new monasteries to be trained as monks. In this way they could be assured of an education and long-term social security. Retired warriors would often enter the monasteries when their days of plunder were at an end, often in reparation for the sins they had committed.[42]

While the monastery or the battlefield may have originated as two alternative options for men in a warrior society, in the age of the Crusades, increasingly, the distinctions between these two spheres collapsed. When the knightly monks became "soldiers for Christ," the ethic of courtly love took on a dimension that would reverberate throughout the succeeding centuries: no longer the aristocratic woman, but the Virgin Mary would become the object of the soul's desire.

THE VIRGIN MARY

As the Age of Mary dawned, a vigorous effort would be made to enshrine an image of Irish womanhood in keeping with the social reality.[43] The image of the Virgin Mary would serve to give support to a new religious consciousness where the freedom and autonomy of someone like Brigit, the last representative of "She Who Created Without Spouse," would give way to Mary, the Mother of God, "the Virgin who conceived without sin."

Given the prominence of the Goddess Brigit and her successful transformation under Christianity, this would not take place without a struggle. The Irish were faced with a conflict between their loyalties to Brigit and to Mary; a serious dilemma since Brigit had been given extraordinary titles, including "Mother of Christ," *"Dei Genetrix,"* "One of the Mothers of Christ," "Queen of the True God," in relation to the Christian deity and was indeed "Mary of the Gael."[44] As one scholar put it, whatever the church authorities said of Mary, the "Irish would affirm of their native saint, and if possible outdo it."[45]

Pope Gregory I (590–604) in a letter addressed to Melitus of Canterbury expressly urged that the feast days of the pre-Christian religions be "sanctified" by their dedication to some holy martyr. In the seventh century, Pope Sergius (687–701) ordered that the festivals of the Virgin Mary take place on pagan holy days in order that the cult of Mary would supplant that of the heathen gods. Eventually, the cult of saints and the veneration of Mary altogether replaced the goddesses and gods of the old religion.

Before 1100 no churches or monasteries were dedicated to the Virgin in Ireland. Between 1100 and 1150 a small number of churches were dedicated to her. Thereafter, primarily under the influence of the new religious orders, especially the Augustinians, there was a rapid increase.[46] Religious orders used her image extensively in their churches, on stationery, and on religious seals. Mary's mantle was an integral part of the religious habit of these orders, in the form of the scapular, a narrow piece of material, worn front and back with an opening for the head and believed to protect the wearer from the fires of hell, as Mary would make a personal visit each Saturday to recover the souls of her devotees.[47]

Mary was no stranger to the Irish people but had been an important element in Irish Christianity from the very beginning. Indeed the title *Mac Maire*, or "Son of Mary," occurs much more frequently in early Irish literature than the word *Jesus*.[48] Jesus was effectively the Son of the Goddess.

In the earliest Irish literature (c. 600) the writers had no difficulty in talking of Mary's body as a fitting receptacle for the infant: "Received in the organs of the virgin—as Gabriel was announcing (it)—the womb grows from the holy progeny."[49] Jesus' conception had taken place "without marring of true virginity through the power of the Holy Spirit."[50] According to legend, St. Patrick treated very severely a Druid who questioned Mary's virginity.[51] But by the ninth century the notion appears that perhaps Jesus was born from the crown of Mary's head,[52] and by the thirteenth century, a manuscript that draws on the ideas of St. Augustine proposes that perhaps Christ entered through Mary's ear,[53] as though the female organs simply would not be equal to the task of carrying the Christ child. Mary has been transformed into a woman "whose female sexual organ has been transformed into an innocent shell which serves only to receive sound."[54]

In a society ruled by patriarchal values, only a woman who had renounced her femininity could actively participate in the symbolic power structure. In Greek culture, for instance, where patriarchal values were fully elaborated in the literature, only those goddesses who were virgins, and preferably, like Athena, born from the head of Zeus, were allowed to participate in the cultural life.[55] Indeed, throughout the ancient world the birth of the hero took place miraculously by means of a virgin birth even in those religions where the goddesses were portrayed as being sensual.[56] In one of the earliest Irish poems the poet pleads with Mary to come with him to keen her beloved son, the "beautiful hero."[57] The Greek attitude towards virginity was developed in the context of the politics of the state, but Christianity had even greater reason for insisting on a virginal state for the Mother of God.

Dominated by the theology of the Fall, the early Fathers taught that Original Sin was transmitted through the sexual act.[58] In talking about the birth of Christ the very possibility of concupiscence was eliminated entirely.

Mary was destined to play a crucial role in the theology of the church, enabling the transition from a matricentered consciousness to a patricentered one to take place. If the newly centralized church and state ruled by means of fear, Mary acted as the calming antidote, protector of sinners. The power structures of church and state may have tried to diminish the importance of biological ties, but according to the Irish, Jesus was "rich in kin-love,"[59] while Mary was their sister and kinswoman. The death of Jesus her son was particularly appalling for the Irish, not only because of human sinfulness, but because of the crucifixion of a "sister's Son," a treacherous act "towards a true kinsman."[60]

As a true kinswoman, Mary could be counted upon to exert pressure on the Father in favor of her own people and to lead them to salvation "for kinship's sake."[61] The hymn the Magnificat was known in Ireland as the "Safe Conduct of Mary,"[62] as though Mary could be counted upon to guarantee safe passage to the future life.

According to one document, God's vengeance on Judgment Day "shall appall even great Mary."[63] Some European writers had proposed that there were two kingdoms: one of justice, belonging to God, and the other of mercy, belonging to Mary.[64] Just as the ancient goddesses calmed the wrath of the warriors by showing their bare breasts, so too Mary could be counted upon to remind God that she had once nursed him and the milk of her breast could now dissolve his wrath.[65] Mary had the power, "in reward for her humility," to check her Son's wrath.[66] Jesus is asked to save the sinner since surely he can identify with the feeling of abandonment. "Save me, O Jesus, whom thy mother's folk rejected."[67]

In contrast to the objectivity of God the Father, Mary would be partial; in contrast to his justice, she would show mercy. God may well be pure spirit, but Mary would soon remind him of his human origins, showing him her breasts, reminding him of how he had suckled.

Stories were told throughout Europe of how Mary would use all means, if necessary devious, to bring sinners to repentance, actively thwarting God's righteous anger against them. In one story, Mary happily took the place of a sinning nun who went away with her lover, fulfilling her duties until such time as the nun repented and returned to her convent. The only condition Mary would lay down in such circumstances would be that the sinner remember her in prayer. Should they forget, then Mary was equally likely to "forget" her relationship with them, thereby exposing them to the full wrath of God.[68]

The twelfth century would see a tremendous rise in the cult of and devotion to Mary, but to assume that the church fathers altogether welcomed the form that this popular devotion took would be a mistake. The Irish religious poets, in common with many others in Europe, were anxious to assert Mary's equality with Jesus by emphasizing her own Immaculate Conception: "O Son of the merciful Father without mother in heaven; O Son of the truly perfect Virgin Mary, without father on earth."[69] But as Anselm, Bernard, Peter Damian, and Thomas Aquinas developed their doctrines of Atonement and salvation, the cult of Mary, if not properly controlled, could turn out to be distinctly problematic to their attempts to enshrine an image of a Father God who ruled by justice and logic and who would ruthlessly punish the guilty according to their just desserts.

While the Fathers certainly promoted the cult of Mary, they were careful to draw the line and rejected the idea of Mary's Immaculate Conception, anxious as they were not to diminish the sacrifice of Jesus by supposing that the fruits of the Redemption could have been applied to a mere woman in advance of the act of Redemption itself.[70] Not until 1854, after a long struggle played out among the Dominicans and the Jesuits, did the church officially proclaim the dogma of the Immaculate Conception and only after it had been made clear that Mary had been granted an Immaculate Conception in anticipation of her role in Redemption.[71]

If the Fathers were acutely aware of the dangers that the cult of Mary might contain, they were equally aware of the enormous benefits to be gained by promoting her image. Mary was the human face of God, serving to make the harsh salvific doctrines of the twelfth century, if not palatable, at least tolerable.

The Fathers had a further reason for promoting the cult of Mary that had nothing to do with the intrinsic worth of women or indeed of motherhood. Indeed, Bernard of Clairvaux, who arguably had achieved his vocation and, hence, whatever power he had when forced to turn his back on his warring exploits by a vision of his saintly mother, had this to say of the species:

He (Christ) will be your mother. . . . But a man's household are his own enemies (Matt. 10:36). These are they who love not you but the satisfaction they derive from you. . . . And now hear what blessed Jerome says: "If your mother should lie prostrate at the door, if she should bare her breasts, the breasts that gave you suck, yet with dry eyes fixed upon the cross go ahead and tread over your prostrate mother and father. It is the height of piety to be cruel for Christ's sake." Do not be moved by the tears of demented parents who weep because from being a child of wrath you have become a child of God.[72]

Aelred of Rievaulx taught that men should serve Mary in the same way as a knight might serve his courtly mistress.[73] But this did not imply an exalted attitude toward women. As he said of Mary, "it is she . . . who has given us life, who nourishes and raises us; . . . she is our mother much more than our mother according to the flesh."[74]

Mary's monastic devotees could feel perfectly free to repudiate their earthly mothers and their dependence upon kinship relations, abandon their familial responsibilities, project all their uncontrollable sexuality onto women, live a celibate or knightly life-style, and yet find erotic compensation in the form of this idealized woman.[75] Real women might be forbidden to the celibate men, but Mary provided an ideal substitute, a woman free of all stain of sin, perfectly obedient to the will of God and perfectly amenable to whatever projections the celibate men cared to focus upon her.[76]

HIERARCHY AND ORTHODOXY

The centralization of power on the part of both church and state would also require drastic ideological measures. Decentralized societies could delight in an ambiguous image of the Serpent, but hierarchy thrived on orthodoxy. Without such orthodoxy rulers could hardly rule or theologians pronounce authoritatively on doctrinal matters. The efforts of the scholastic thinkers of the Middle Ages were devoted, therefore, to producing a watertight body of work, doctrines of faith to which all good Christians could assent.

Without such assent, and such a body of faith, the power of the pope and his clerics would be limited indeed. Each cleric would be thrown back on his own resources, good example, or powers of persuasion. But the creation of orthodoxy issued logically in the creation of heretics, for as one scholar has remarked, "When a church gives up the heretic it gives up its orthodoxy."[77]

In political terms a tribal, decentralized society, held together by the common traditions promoted by the brehons or lawmakers, or by the poets,[78] could tolerate and even delight in ambiguity. The tribal system had made little or no distinction between public and private forms of power. Political decisions were still largely in the hands of the various local groupings, and both women and men played their part in making decisions. Now, with increased centralization of power, a new dualism between public and private entered the political arena. While men could feel at home in the public sphere, the realm of law, government, and economics, women would increasingly be confined to the private sphere, the realm of reproduction, nurture, and family care.

This dualism would have vital ramifications going way beyond the sexual realm to affect the political and religious future of Europe. We saw, for instance, that in religions that revered the triple image of human life in the cycle of birth, life, and death, the gods were both good and evil, and that tragedy was a natural part of life to be integrated within the whole religious economy. But for Christianity it was not enough that one should love God, but one must also hate the Devil. The Christian God, as defined by the medieval theologians, needed not only a Kingdom of God but also a Kingdom of the Devil in order to function effectively.

This hierarchical, centralized form of social organization posited a stark dualism between public and private life. The political philosophies underlying such a system thrived, therefore, on making clear-cut dichotomies aimed at projecting the maximum prestige and credibility upon the social leaders.[79] For this enterprise to be successful, several things would have to be accomplished. If the leaders were to be seen as supremely good, they could only become so in contrast with those at the opposite end of the hierarchy, the supremely bad. In a dualistic system the leaders would define themselves by what they were *not*, as much as by what they *were*. Indeed, it could be argued that the system needed the perpetual positing of an enemy within its ranks to foster a sense of identity among the elect and to enable the people to continue to project their needs for protection and salvation upon the leaders. As a recent psychologist and philosopher put it, "the oppressor has a vested interest in the negative identity of the oppressed because that negative identity is a projection of his own unconscious negative identity—a projection which up to a point, makes him feel superior, but also in a brittle way, whole."[80]

The human origins of power would have to be carefully disguised. Power would be derived, not from tyranny, exploitation, lineage, or military might, but directly from an unchallengeable source: God the Father. Symbols of the spirit rather than those of the body would be the most appropriate emblems of the new order, leading to a new denigration of the natural in favor of the supernatural.

This dualistic theology perfectly served the new amalgamation of power taking place on the part of both church and state. The church leaders and those political leaders whom the church chose to sanction were effectively God's earthly representatives. It followed that their enemies were also enemies of Good, and possibly of God. As such, the leaders could feel perfectly free to hound and subjugate them in his name.

Given what was at stake in the religious and in the public realm, the rulers would not simply rely on their persuasive skills to extend the "truth" of Christianity. Rather, the late Middle Ages were to see the setting up of successive instruments of terror designed to enforce the worship of the one true God and to pay tribute to his worldly representatives.

For some time the Crusades provided an arena where good Christian men could exercise their moral superiority by converting or destroying the heathens. But with this outlet greatly diminished by the fourteenth century, full attention could be devoted to the discovery of the "enemies" in their midst.

Given the conflicting ideals of virginity and motherhood, and given the dualism of Christian theology, women took on a double identity that would find expression throughout the literature and artwork of Europe.[81] Women were symbols of Eve, the primordial Temptress, calling men down from their lofty heights. Alternatively, they were symbols of Mary, the only woman who had achieved the impossible ideal of being both a virgin and a mother. As Caelius Sedulius wrote,

> She . . . had no peer
> Either in our first mother or in all women
> Who were to come. But alone of all her sex
> She pleased the Lord.[82]

EVE AND MARY

While on the surface Mary may have been held out to women as the alternative to Eve, women really had no choice. The Virgin Mary was an impossible ideal for ordinary women. Her virginity made their sexuality problematic, casting them in the role of Temptress to men: symbols of Eve. But whereas Eve would appear in the person of the witches, to be burned, tortured, and drowned, the part of Mary would be played by generations of holy anorectics who, far from being tortured, were actually canonized.

The story of the witches, or the genocide of women healers, is one of those epochs in human history so devastating and beyond comprehension that it has scarcely been touched by historians. Scholars are still not in agreement as to how many women were put to violent death; estimates range from one hundred thousand to nine million. The power of the witches was a distinct threat to the centralization efforts of both church and state.[83] Once again the clerics and political rulers could be seen working hand in hand, and although women's bodies had long since provided the arena for the full display of patriarchal power and control, nothing that had gone before would come close to the terror awaiting those who experienced the full logic of theological dualism.

One of the main instruments of that terror was the Inquisition. Originally established by the papacy to correct heresies, such as that of the Cathars (among whose crimes was that of ordaining women),[84] once established the machinery of the Inquisition remained intact in various forms for several centuries. Given the seriousness of what was at stake—nothing less than a threat to the precarious basis upon which the authority of both church and state had been established—religious dissidents were treated extremely harshly. Should the accused recant, penances such as fasting or pilgrimage might be imposed. But should they resist, imprisonment, torture, and death at the stake at the hand of the secular arm would await them. Dominican and Franciscan friars roamed the countryside seeking out heretics who were then tried before a court made up of laymen and clerics.[85]

In the very early persecutions of the Inquisitions, any dissidents to orthodoxy were suspect, and men formed some of the primary targets. But once the major heresies or groups of organized social dissidents had been effectively overthrown, where better to direct this terror than against those whose very presence, skills, and beliefs were a threat to the male clerics and to the centralized political powers.

Witches (or literally, "wise women") had always existed, and except for when they directly challenged the power of the church, their skills had been tolerated and welcomed by the communities in which they lived. Pope Gregory the Great (540–604) forbade the execution of women for the supposed crimes of causing epidemics or storms. In the Kingdom of God, witches, he claimed, obviously could have no power. But the fact that they were now under such threat is testimony to the seriousness of the issues at stake.

Indeed, on the cover of the *Malleus Maleficarum*, the *Hammer of Witches*, the Dominicans wrote, "To disbelieve in witchcraft is the greatest of heresies." This maxim was precisely the opposite of that held by the church in the so-called Dark Ages.[86]

The women persecuted were mostly from the "lower classes," often victims of poverty and hatred. Many were the traditional healers in their communities and, as such, provided natural leadership against the inroads of a feudal and, later, an industrial economy that threatened to take away from them permanently their very livelihoods, their lands, and those of the villagers. Even the common lands where the poor used to graze their beasts were taken by the rulers and sold off to the feudal landlords. The poor were increasingly thrown back on their own resources. Widespread poverty ensued, leading to the development of the great "poorhouses" where the dispossessed could at least be fed, even at the total loss of their dignity.

The witches often relied on their psychic skills to effect cures, a practice that increasingly laid them open to charges of magic or intercourse with the Devil. While some of the accusations leveled against the witches may well have been true (i.e., the charges of practicing magic), this is hardly surprising given the climate in which these women found themselves, where the new religious and political order was working to dispossess them of any source of economic or spiritual power.

For a theology and politics that thrived on the mentality of the scapegoat, witches provided the ideal victim. Close to the natural, they were a threat to the supernatural; benefiting little from the new religion, they were its obvious enemies. As the *Hammer of Witches* put it so well:

All witchcraft comes from carnal lust, which is in women insatiable. See *Proverbs* XXX: There are three things that are never satisfied, yea, a fourth thing which says not, It is enough; that is, the mouth of the womb. Wherefore for the sake of fulfilling their lusts they consort even with devils. . . . And blessed be the Highest Who has so far preserved the male sex from so great a crime: for since He was willing to be born and to suffer for us, therefore he has granted to men this privilege.[87]

The accusations leveled against the witches symbolize vividly the crucial issues at stake. Witches were accused of causing painless childbirth (indeed, midwives were considered to be the worst sinners of all), of transforming themselves into animals, of holding witches' sabbaths, of having intercourse with the devil, and of casting spells on men and animals. Perhaps the most telling accusation was that of causing impotence in men or of making the male members disappear. "What is to be thought," the Dominicans asked, "of those witches who in this way sometimes collect male organs in great numbers, as many as twenty or thirty members together, and put them in a bird's nest, or shut them up in a box, where they move themselves like living members?" The Dominicans were at pains to document this occurrence, and they cited the case of one man who went to retrieve his organ. He reached out for the biggest one in the tree, only to be told not to touch it because "it belonged to the parish priest."[88]

In the accusations leveled against witches we can see the precariousness of the universe being established. Witches were in direct contact with the rival kingdom of the Devil, using its powers to counter the power of the church or state. Indeed, witch hunters carefully combed over women's bodies looking for suspicious marks of the Devil that he might have left during one of his encounters. If women's bodies provided visible evidence of the Devil, men's bodies were expected to provide visible evidence of God. As a twelfth century jurist put it, "The image of God is in man and it is one . . . woman is not made in God's image."[89]

Not surprisingly, the Devil and his agents could be expected to attack the very organs upon which men's superiority supposedly rested. The disappearance of the male members, the inability to perform sexually, or even concern for the size of the parish priest's members testify to the significance of the phallus in establishing the rule of God the Father. The new universe being established by men was very precarious indeed, and the most precarious aspect of it was the penis itself, the direct object of attack. God the Father might dwell in the realm of the spirit, but his celibate representatives on earth were careful to keep their bodily organs, symbols of his rule, intact.

Once accused of witchcraft, few women would be acquitted. Indeed, the women were caught in a double bind. If they refused to confess to whatever crimes their persecutors dreamed up, they were thrown into a river. If they floated, they were obviously possessed and put to death by other means. If they drowned, they were probably innocent—a verdict of little consolation to them or to their bereaved families.

The double jeopardy into which accused witches were placed, however, was simply symptomatic of the jeopardy into which religious women as a whole would fall. The witches may have inherited the Eve side of theological dualism, but women religious inherited the image of Mary. For whereas the witches effectively formed part of the resistance to the new male order, women religious, largely drawn from the upper classes, joined religious orders, part of whose function was to serve the newly dispossessed poor whose lands had been taken from them.

And if the mark of the Devil upon the bodies of women presaged a horrific fate, the mark of God the Father, taken to its logical conclusion, would be no less serious. Mary was the ideal woman, and her followers were expected to be perfectly obedient to the wishes of God the Father as these might be expressed through the mediation of the male clerics. But the uniqueness of Mary, the ideal to which generations of women would aspire, was according to Julia Kristeva,

achieved only by way of exacerbated masochism: an actual woman worthy of the feminine ideal embodied in inaccessible perfection by the Virgin could not be anything other than a nun or a martyr; if married, she would have to lead a life that would free her from her "earthly" condition by confining her to the uttermost sphere of sublimation, alienated from her own body. But there a bonus awaits her: the assurance of ecstasy.[90]

Stories of the women saints of the later Middle Ages in Europe are filled with the struggle between women, their bodies, and the male priests. Women saints effectively internalized the psychology of male heroic spirituality. Their bodies, far from being revered, were the obstacles to transcendence within a male universe and must be brought into subjection. Furthermore, they should imitate the passion of Christ by actively engraving on their own bodies his suffering image. The combination was lethal.

In the service of this spirituality, the women were said to have sucked the pus from leper's sores; licked the walls of their cells, eating the spiders and webs they found there; stripped themselves naked; flagellated themselves with iron chains until blood was drawn and then melted candlewax and poured it into their wounds. They were said to have eaten cat and human vomit; to have worn hairshirts; to have traveled through the towns in rags with hunks of rotting meat and dead fish around their necks; to have burnt and discolored themselves; and finally, many women were said to have starved themselves to death.

Many women had originally entered the convents in desperate efforts to escape the rule of their fathers in the outside world. Little did they know that a much more insidious fate awaited them once inside the monastic walls where the "law of the fathers" was fully operative.

The stories of these women are to be found throughout the *Lives of the Saints* in Europe, for these women were, indeed, saints within a patriarchal mentality, and their records were preserved for us by those who wished other women to emulate them. They were women who had taken contempt for the female sex to its logical conclusion. Unable to leave their mortal bodies, they lived in terror that their bodily needs would betray them. As saints they served as models of behavior for other women, urging them to similar excesses.

Through a profound twist of human logic many of the women effectively became "holy anorectics" in that they used their bodies as ways of defying male authority.[91] Often commanded to eat, they would appeal to a higher authority, that of "God's will," or to a personal communication with God to resist the authority of a confessor or a doctor. The lengths to which these women would go, while extreme and painful, gave them a power they would not otherwise have had: immediate access to God through the sufferings of their body and a tangible sign of their holiness. These women wrested control of the system in a perverse act of autonomy that ultimately issued in their deaths. Nevertheless, there was an awareness on their part that, even though they used the rhetoric of the male clerics, they were really exercising their own will all along. Some saint's biographies, written by women, celebrated this fact.[92]

Catherine of Siena, for example, used starvation to get her own way. Stripped of direct and instrumental power, she used the only power she had. She used her body in "bargaining" with God, taking her father's pain upon herself in return for his release from purgatory.[93] Her extraordinary penances persuaded her followers (and they were many) that she was indeed a "servant of God." Thus convinced, they supported the trips she made to confront religious and political leaders, including one to Avignon in an effort to persuade the reigning pope, Gregory XI, to return to Rome. Catherine, who eventually starved herself to death, was declared a Doctor of the Church in 1970.

Catherine was a perfect example of the dilemma in which women found themselves. Stripped of the traditional routes to female power and respect, women could only buy into the logic of male spirituality, which, taken to its conclusion, dictated that they effectively obliterate their bodies. Some few, like Catherine of Siena and Teresa of Avila, would turn that logic around and use it to their own ends. But the logic itself remained intact, to the detriment of generations of female religious. As a recent writer put it, "To be the servant of God is to be the servant of no man. To obliterate every human feeling of pain, fatigue, sexual desire, and hunger is to be master of oneself."[94]

For their part, the men found it difficult to deal with these women. Certainly, they seemed to exhibit all the signs of "saintliness." Some confessors encouraged such masochistic practices; one ordered a novice to kick the future saint Veronica Giuliani in the mouth; another ordered her, as abbess, to remain outside the choir as an "excommunicant."[95] But the hardest penance to bear was the refusal of communion on the part of the confessors: not in punishment for some offence, but simply to demonstrate who was in control and who had the power to dispense graces.[96] Under these conditions, not surprisingly, the women would go to extreme lengths to establish independent sources of contact with God. But unfortunately, within their worldview, the means chosen were necessarily drastic.

This situation could not last forever. Increasingly, even the "anorectic" route to female autonomy was cut off, and female asceticism in the period of the Protestant and Catholic Reformations was put firmly under the control of the clerics.[97]

CONSOLIDATION OF MALE RELIGIOUS POWER

While it is true that some men also went to extraordinary lengths in their penances, for men there were many other possible ways that they could exercise their spirituality and their autonomy as scholars, ecclesiastical diplomats, preachers, and religious leaders. Women may not have been on the ladder leading to apostolic succession, but through a myriad of male theologians, male confessors, male spiritual directors, male

preachers, they were certainly on the receiving end of this hierarchical theology that viewed their subordination as ordained by God, to be enforced by men. Cut off from the centers of learning, especially those of theology where they might have learned to articulate effectively their critique of such a system, women were left with few alternatives. And as one scholar put it, "Whereas men might achieve sainthood as champions of the faith who spread the true word around the globe, woman's path to official recognition confined them to a sickbed."[98] Any objections or questions they might have had either about the theology or the monastic system, now founded on hierarchical modes of domination, would be effectively countered by those trained in the sacred sciences. Rebellion against the self-contained nature of the system would be an unprecedented act of willfulness, an exercise of "private judgment" which, if tolerated, would threaten to collapse the whole theological edifice.

Ultimately, women would provide the backbone of devotion to Mary since in the late Middle Ages the cult of Mary was the only source of devotion, outside the sacramental realm, not immediately controllable by the hierarchy. Her cult was promoted, therefore, even by those women who, religiously dispossessed, stood to lose most. But with men firmly in control of the image making or dogmatic world, the image to which women would relate was essentially a male construct. God the Father would be honored for his works of creation, but Mary would be honored for the inspiration and courage she inspired in men in carrying out their own activities. Rather than providing a role model for women, Mary's image emphasized the radical disjuncture between the sacred and the sexual, between the religious hopes of women and the reality of their lives.

Mary mirrored the role of women in society. Her exalted image was essentially compensatory, *atoning* for the loss of social status on the part of women. Mary's image was reactionary in that, denied the possibility of effective action, she could only *react*. Deprived of their own traditional economic and social sources of influence, and in the knowledge that they could never be an effective part of the power structure, women had to rely on the arts of persuasion, cajolery, and even downright trickery if they wished to retain any social power. As a feminist thinker recently commented on men's dual standards with regard to women's purity, "That is the great tragedy of the patriarchal male: his status lies in irrational schizophrenic contradictions, and is vested in a being whom he has defined from the start as the enemy: woman and her subterranean silence, woman who engulfs him in a sea of lies and in swamps of sordid manipulation."[99]

Moreover, Mary's virginity, her Immaculate Conception, and her role as Virgin Mother, provided succeeding generations of women with a dreadful dilemma. Women could become virgins, but in the process they would have to renounce motherhood, the traditional source of women's power and satisfaction. However, becoming mothers now meant that women would become permanently consigned to the ranks of the sensual and the corporeal. And as a feminist theologian claims, Mary's star may have risen in medieval theology, but her glory grew "ever brighter in inverse proportion to the downgrading of real women."[100]

Although there would be isolated instances of women exercising power, these were the exceptions. For the most part women, in the future, would gain power only at the cost of renouncing their femaleness at all possible levels. The spiritual universe was now clearly male. Men were in control of the symbolic realm; they alone had access to clerical or sacramental power; men would define what "spirituality" was and who fell within the limits of orthodoxy. Men controlled clerical appointments, and whatever limited influence women had had through their family connections was now lost to the diocesan system that derived its power from the pope.

Male spirituality and men's understanding of their role in the world became the norm. They separated from women, from their families, from the "world," wreaking contempt on the body, which they considered an obstacle to their climb to the heights of "transcendence." In return for this, as we have seen, men also climbed to new heights of power. They joined in the Crusades, they rose to the top of the clerical hierarchy, they performed amazing feats of asceticism, converted heathens, and traveled the world. In other words, for many men, especially those in the "lower orders," the religious life offered unheard of possibilities: opportunities for education, travel, and prestige. So long as they were obedient and respectful of the hierarchy on whose ladder they were, they could expect to flourish, not only in this life, but especially in the next. Their daily contact with Christ through the sacrifice of the Mass gave them an enviable contact with the immediate source of their power.

Women had landed in a very precarious position indeed. They lacked any possible opportunities for immediate contact with God, except that gained through the mediation of the priest through the Eucharist or through their male confessors. Indeed, the promotion of eucharistic spirituality, which took on new dimensions in the twelfth and thirteenth centuries, was probably the most important factor in the Middle Ages in the downgrading of female symbolism. In early medieval Christian spirituality, theologians had difficulty explaining to the people how the Eucharist could have special importance when, for the ordinary people, any natural object might contain a revelation of God.[101] Following the Gregorian reform, the centralization of hierarchy, and the establishment of apostolic succession, the Christian Eucharist, firmly controlled by the male priesthood, took on major importance.[102] The rites of the old religion had lost their power for any women who wished to participate fully in the new Christian order, and the Eucharist represented the "only repeatable and controllable movement of union with God."[103]

Women, who themselves lacked the power to celebrate the Eucharist, nevertheless, grasped onto the Eucharist as a tangible sign of God's presence in the world. The female mystics were instrumental in promoting eucharistic devotion, going so far as to insist that the feast of Corpus Christi be instituted.[104] But as this devotion was essentially dependent upon the ministrations of the male priests, it further contributed to the entrenchment of clerical power.[105]

Men derived their power from ordination. Their ability to celebrate Mass, which carried with it the power to excommunicate, in effect, to damn to eternal punishment, gave them an awesome power base in the local community. Whereas the power of female religious would be based on their own personal gifts, and on their compassion, generosity, and spirituality, male power was derived from God through ordination and through the new umbilical cord: apostolic succession.

According to the church's understanding, the apostolic succession had been transmitted inviolate from the hands of Christ to Peter, and from Peter down through the various popes, who in turn passed on these powers to the bishops and priests. This apostolic succession had been broken several times by corrupt popes, but, nevertheless, the hierarchy was anxious to reestablish its symbolic value.

Through the use of the *pallium,* the highest relic of all, the pope could decide to confer or withhold power from a particular bishop, something he would find very hard to do with the abbots who had received their power through their families. In turn, the bishops would confer sacramental powers upon the priests, a power that far superseded any authority in the community they could have gained for themselves. This new authority was the power to celebrate Mass, to absolve from sin, and to dispense the many forms of indulgences and grace made possible by the sacrifice of the Mass. This power came direct from Rome through the hierarchical chain, conferring an awesome spiritual authority upon the priests and putting a serious onus on them to preserve this chain intact.

Ordination effectively confers upon the priest the right to take his place in the line of apostolic succession, stretching from Jesus Christ, through Peter, to Peter's present day representative, the pope. Apostolic succession is conferred upon each new priest, giving him the right and the ability to celebrate the sacrifice of the Mass, a sacrifice that in turn keeps the lineage intact. It is a form of patrilineal descent that transcends any system of descent that women can achieve through natural birthing. Just as Yahweh had promised Abraham, and the saints had promised their benefactors, "seed forever," apostolic succession provides the "spiritual seed" of the church without which a crucial source of its power would be cut off.

In the matricentered system, corrupt rulers would have been deposed by the satire of poets, the failure of crops, or even by failure to give evidence of fertility; under this new form of religious patriarchy, the opposite applied. Once ordained, the priests had access to a cast-iron source of spiritual power that would remain intact irrespective of their personal lives. As one *Penitential* claimed, "They determine to hold: those who have received the tradition of the symbol are baptized, from whomsoever they have received it, since the seed is not defiled by the wickedness of the sower."[106]

This emphasis on apostolic succession signified a major change in the location of power. Whereas clerics in the hereditary families received their commissions through virtue of the family connections as they emerged from the wombs of their mothers, now the hands of the bishop would transmit apostolic succession, effectively removing the last taint of female interference.

But the basis of clerical power put men in a very difficult position. On the one hand, the male priests had to develop their power of "will" over their passions, and on the other, they had to learn to subordinate this "will" to that of their superior. In compensation, they could always be sure that they were doing the "will of God" as expressed in their superior's wishes or commands even, or sometimes especially, if his will went against their own inclinations. In return for their obedience there was a major compensation: the people would never be asked to judge the competence of the priests. Provided he was validly ordained and in good standing (i.e., obedient to the hierarchy), the sacraments that he administered would be valid. Their effectiveness had been assured by God independently of the gifts or charisma of the person who administered them. This theology of orders perfectly suited the new hierarchization taking place in the Irish church.

Certainly there is evidence that within a patriarchal society the convent offered opportunities to women not otherwise available to them within the social structure. But in a society that viewed female sexuality as the root of all evil, women could gain power only to the extent to which they denied their bodies. Men, however, denied not only women's bodies but also women themselves. By definition, virgins could not give birth or otherwise associate with the traditional symbols of women's creativity.

Inclusion in the hierarchy gave men enormous possibilities for advancement, beyond what they might normally have achieved through their family relationships. In the main, men achieved this status to the extent to which the hierarchy could depend upon them to support the chain of apostolic succession by their obedience. Patriarchal societies would thrive on such highly stratified and hierarchical measures. For women, however, their obedience to a system that held them in such little regard could only spell their downfall. Individuals might well flourish, but women as a whole could only suffer.[107]

Women, in the Age of Mary, have become valuable commodities to their families, who often used them for political exchange as hostages or for their cash values in the form of the dowries extracted from suitors. Thousands of women rebelled against this system, but their opportunities were effectively limited. Certainly they could pass from the domain of their earthly fathers, but only to fall right into the hands of their heavenly fathers, the male priests.[108]

The twelfth century reform movement, therefore, in all its social, political, and religious ramifications, represented a watershed for women. Women's very biology condemned them; their bodies became obstacles to transcendence within a male order. Lacking male attributes they were condemned to a subsidiary religious role. Not surprisingly, all these changes had drastic effects for the position of women in Christian theology.

The cult of the unattainable woman, the ideal of virginity, the era of the Crusades, combined to create a new shift in ideology relating to women. As Sherry Ortner has put it, "Before they were dangerous, but now they are said to be *in danger*, justifying male protection and guardianship. Before they were polluting, and this had to be defended against, but now they are said to be pure, and to need defending."[109]

PATRIARCHAL RELIGIOUS CONSCIOUSNESS

In the Age of Mary, therefore, with the final subjugation of the Serpent, the splitting open of the unity of opposites, the patriarchal mentality reached its most vivid expression. With the new importance given to celibacy, the development of eucharistic theology, the use of women as pawns in exchange relationships between men, the treatment of clerical wives, and the new cult of virginity, it is not surprising to find that following the period of "reform" those symbols traditionally associated with women suffered drastically. These symbols would be replaced, not by those associated with the mere bodies of men, however important these might have been, but with a mentality and spirituality that would effectively foster the fullness of male reproductive consciousness.

In particular, the Christian understanding of redemption, upon which male clerical power rested, represented a sharp break with the ideas of redemption that had preceded it. Central to the notion of redemption is the idea that there is some fundamental disorder to the world, whether this be caused by harsh climate, poor fertility of the fields, or the basic human problems of suffering, injustice, and death. But throughout human culture there have been very different explanations as to how this disorder came about.

In the Western world there were stories of how the Goddess, or even the Virgin Mary, was responsible for the continued well-being of her people, especially through ensuring that they had enough to eat from the fertility of the fields. In some cases, the Goddess merely had to show her presence for the seeds to sprout. But in others, especially when patriarchal forms of organization began to appear, the Goddess had to go to the Underworld to rescue her raped and abducted daughter before fertility would return to the fields after winter. Whichever form the myth took, it was clear that the action of women caused the harvest to appear and to sleep again during the winter months.[110]

Originally, these myths were primarily associated with women. Eventually, under the influence of male reproductive consciousness, the Great Mother either took a consort, in the Irish case in the form of a king, or else gave birth to a Son, or Hero, who would take it upon himself to be responsible for redeeming the world from the death of winter and for restoring fertility to the fields. Redemption in these cases clearly meant the rescuing of the natural cycle and the enhancement of those elements of culture or fertility that had fallen into the hands of unwieldy forces over which the people had little control.

Under Christianity, this notion of redemption was destined to undergo a radical change and to take on ethical dimensions foreign to the earlier myths. The Christian Redemption was not the rebirth of the natural cycle but a rebirth from the condition of sinfulness, made necessary by the Fall of Adam and Eve, and made possible by the Atonement on behalf of humanity effected by God the Son, in relation to God the Father. Redemption took on a strictly moral quality. The Redemption accomplished by the Son was made necessary, not because of the natural winter, but because of the "winter of the soul," which, in turn, had been caused by the "Fall." And the "new life" that entered in each Christian by means of baptism would be a "spiritual" life rather than merely a physical one.

It would be some time, however, before the ancient symbolism of redemption could be entirely removed even from the Eucharist, and this is essentially because the Eucharist replaced, for all intents and purposes, the creativity previously associated with women and, in particular, with goddesses associated with the harvest. In one Irish discussion of the various parts of the Mass, which probably dates back to the ninth century,[111] the themes of regeneration and "new birth" come through quite clearly. For instance, commenting on the meaning of pouring wine onto the water in the chalice, one writer explains that this is "Christ's Godhead on His Manhood and on the people at the time of begetting."[112] The sacred host is the "turtle-dove" or a "figure of Christ's Body which has been set in the linen sheet of Mary's womb."[113] Maternal imagery continues when the writer discusses how the host should be divided. The host is broken up and given to the participants at Mass in order of their importance, but the most important part, that of the center of the cross, is kept for the priest himself: the "breast with the secrets."[114]

Despite these few remnants of the ancient civilization, the Christian view of redemption eventually prevailed in its purer form. Men's spiritual rebirth was made possible by the sacrifice of the Son to the Father, a sacrifice that unleashed a vast reservoir of grace, or power, to be dispensed by the Christian priesthood, enabling men to become brothers, united in the worship of the One True God.

In pre-Christian religions the symbolism of birth and the artifacts associated with it were considered to hold supreme religious significance.[115] These were normally natural symbols of life and regeneration, such as nuts, boars, serpents, objects used at birth, and women's blood.[116] Women had been revered for their ability to give birth, but now the sacred instruments and places of childbirth had either been destroyed or taken over by the male priests. In some cases, masses were said over objects to give them magical efficacy.[117] Under Christianity, anything associated with birth, menstruation, or reproduction was unclean.

Women's ability to make social ties, "ties of milk," had been undermined, and this is also reflected in the symbolic realm. In the religions centering on the Goddess, we saw the importance of the Sacred Cow, as the giver and sustainer of life. Milk was a powerful symbol of life itself, not only for feeding but also for healing wounds in battle.[118]

In the ancient world, to spill breast milk was morally equivalent to the contemporary attitude toward spilling male seed, and every effort was made, therefore, to find ways to seal milk, an effort that gave rise to the science of alchemy, which attempted to seal the "essence" of life within vessels shaped in the form of breasts.[119] Indeed, the early Irish, in common with many ancient cultures, believed that the soul passed to the infant through the milk of the breast. As one of the *Lives of Brigit* claimed, "For it is so arranged by nature that nurses always bestow the affection of their spirit on those to whom they provide the milk of their flesh."[120] Throughout the ancient world it was assumed that breast milk transmitted to the infant the spiritual traits of the mother.[121] Brigit was baptized in milk and was fed by the milk of a Sacred Cow, and indeed, up to the twelfth century the Irish continued to baptize with milk.

Now with the introduction of the new clerical hierarchies, and with the new prohibitions against incest, the symbolism of milk would be under threat. Sacrificial blood rather than mother's milk would best signify the religious order.

Indeed, this is reflected in the rites of baptism. In the old religion, the mother's brother, and later, the father, was responsible for "naming" the child. After birth the child was immersed in water, or if they could afford it, in milk, which was afterwards discarded very carefully. These ancient rites of baptism were gradually "spiritualized" and adapted "to the doctrines of original sin and regeneration." At the Synod of Cashel in 1172, the use of milk in baptism was banned entirely and it was clearly stipulated that baptism be done "in the name of the Father, Son and Holy Spirit, and only by a priest."[122]

By the thirteenth century whenever the imagery of nursing was used in Christian imagery throughout Europe, it was nursing with blood rather than with milk, an emphasis that was eucharistic, that is to say, associated with the sacrifice of Christ.[123]

The cult of the dead, relics and martyrs, replaced the veneration previously given to objects of life.[124] The blood of the martyrs was known as the "seed of the church," thus ensuring that symbols of death rather than those of life would pass into popular currency. For Christian theology, it was not birth but rebirth that mattered; the rebirth of the soul rather than the flesh.

The instruments of death took on enormous significance. Possession of a founders' relics often meant that the holder could claim the property of the foundation. Relics were taken on circuit, inspiring awe and fear in the faithful, and were used to stake claims to property and, in general, to act as a power base from which the clerics could operate.[125]

The symbol of the Virgin Mary was a crucial component throughout these cultural developments. Mary retained much of the imagery of the ancient goddesses whom she replaced, effectively, like Brigit before her, enabling the transition to Christianity to take place. She often appeared in triple form, a remnant of the Triple Goddess.[126] Mary is the "salmon of wisdom."[127] Her son, Jesus, is referred to as the "offspring of the fruitful cow,"[128] and at the Crucifixion, when she cast her body on her dead son, a poet wrote, " 'twas a relief to lie on her calf."[129]

Mary was portrayed alternately as having given birth to her own father,[130] as the "nurse of the three lords,"[131] as the husband of Jesus,[132] and as the "wife of the king of the passion."[133] But perhaps the most outstanding claim made of her was that she was mother of the Trinity, who "nourished them, three in one body."[134] Alternatively, all three members of the Trinity " 'mated' with her, a cluster that grows from one tree."[135]

But whereas the ancient matricentered goddesses had resisted with all their might the death-dealing of the warriors, opposing and confounding them with their bare breasts, symbols of life itself, now the autonomy and creativity of the Goddess had been shattered, and Mary would achieve her destiny by being the perfect vehicle of men's designs; the perfect woman whose obedience had made Christendom possible. Mary was anxious to help sinners, but in the process she had to pay a major price: unlike the goddesses, she was essentially powerless to challenge the mentality of the wrathful God that made her existence in this form so necessary.

The power of the goddesses rested on their ability to give life to all aspects of the cultural creativity of their peoples. But within a Christian universe the only significant life was the spiritual life that came through the sacraments, celebrated exclusively by the rituals of the male priests. Whatever power Mary achieved, she achieved through her womb, and then by renouncing her womb and with it the possibility of sexual pleasure in human relationship. Mary certainly gives life but in an utterly anaesthetized manner in which she serves merely as the vessel for the creative work of the Father. In this she serves perfectly to illuminate the male role in reproduction and to reduce the body of women to a mere shell. Mary is asexual and virginal, and the *Mater Dolorosa* "knows no male body except that of her dead son, and her only pathos comes from the tears she sheds over a corpse."[136]

Indeed, her womb seems to have been destined from the start, not to bring forth life, but to provide a "casket of the Lord's body" or to be a "linen sheet" to receive her dead son.[137] The power of the Goddess rested on her ability to *give* life, but Mary's power rested on her giving birth to a man-god who would *give up* his life for the establishment of the Father's reign of justice and the law.

In the new theological order, rebirth and not birth would be the carrier of significance and worth. Indeed, in one Irish story when Mary was asked to help a woman in childbirth she says to Jesus,

> Succour her thyself O Son
> Since it falls to thee
> Baptism for the birth
> And bring the woman safe.[138]

Baptism had been made possible by the death of Christ according to Christian theology, and this teaching represented a further denigration of natural birthing in favor of that which took place through death. Baptism represented an extremely potent form of fertility, far superior to natural birthing, but it was a rebirth that essentially occurred, or was made possible, through death. Under these circumstances, baptism took on enormous significance, but the significance was not merely symbolic. It had highly practical purposes as well in that it was an important source of revenue to the priests.[139] Under canon law, women would not be allowed to baptize unless no priest were available. Those who gave birth were poorly equipped to perform rites of rebirth and were only to be used in emergencies, if at all.

The early Fathers compared the baptismal font to both the womb and the tomb. The catechumen would bury his earthly life in the tomb, only to have it turn into a womb in which he was reborn.[140] Eventually, however, as the theology of the Mass reached its full explication, sacredness began to reside primarily in those objects blessed by the priests, particularly by that power that was not available to women. As Anselm put it so well, "Christ is the mother who dies in giving birth to the soul."[141]

Any remaining vestige of the goddesses in Mary would be eliminated when the sixteenth-century Protestant Reformation took the cult of Mary to its logical conclusion. The image of Mary had potentially undermined the doctrines of salvation, so carefully worked out in the twelfth century, by offering a form of protection from the harsh demands of

God. But now, in contrast to the great majestic images of the twelfth-century virgin, Queen of Heaven and great Mother of the Redeemer, the only image of Mary tolerated in Protestantism was that of the humble virgin of the Gospels, the paragon of faith.

The reformers were anxious to assert that anything Mary had was due to no merit of her own but was received from her Son in reward for her faithfulness. They were particularly critical of any claims that Mary might have had any role in the redemption process. Indeed, anything that could have diminished human dependence upon God was a form of idolatry. Mary's virtue lay in perfect obedience to God, an obedience itself made possible by the grace of God. Mary was the perfect receptacle for the Male Word incarnate, and any initiative on her part was not only impossible but also unnecessary.

The Protestant Reformation reintroduced married clergy and abolished the monasteries. In Protestantism the psychological need for Mary as an object of celibate fantasy disappeared. Mary was now the ideal housewife, a model for Protestant women, humbly serving their husbands. If they had to be outside the home, as Mary had when she visited her cousin Elizabeth, they should serve as examples to other women, "she did not stop every five spaces to strike up a conversation as do so many of our maids and matrons. . . . The mother of our Lord was no gossip. She went with haste."[142] Roman Catholicism had at least offered an alternative for women to patriarchal marriage, but now a woman received a "live-in spiritual advisor, her husband."[143]

The Protestant Reformation represented a new phase in the development of patriarchal thought and values. Politically, the Reformation coincided with major new developments in the politics of church and state and in a growing independence from Rome on the part of some European powers. New technological innovations would lead to new forms of centralization and authority on the part of political powers. The invention of the printing press, for instance, undermined the monopoly on information hitherto exercised by the church. The power of Rome to mediate between God and man, and to confer political authority upon the rulers, would come radically under question.

Perhaps more importantly, the new authority structures would undermine any remaining hope there might have been in the Roman Catholic and Eastern traditions of Mariology of the potential goodness of redeemed human nature in association with the grace of God at Mary's intercession.[144] For the Protestant reformers, the Fall had left sinful humankind utterly dependent upon the grace of God. Under these circumstances, not only Mary the Goddess, but Mary the intercessor, would be overthrown. Humanity now depended entirely upon the action of God the Father and upon the continuing fruits of the spiritual life brought about by the death of his Son.

In the Age of Mary, patriarchal consciousness reached its zenith. The break with symbolic and actual matrilinearity; the renunciation of the maternal networks; the establishment of male covenanting and bonding; the breakdown into public and private, sacred and profane worlds corresponding with sharp differences between the roles of men and women; the renewed emphasis on celibacy with the growth of heroic spiritualities in which the body becomes an inferior object compared to the spirit; and the severe mental dualism that all of these changes entailed would irrevocably change the character of Western life. The sacrifice of the Mass celebrated by an all-male, celibate priesthood would enable and sustain the changes taking place. The Mass had been made possible when the Son was sacrificed for the honor of the Father. But what then, in the Age of Mary, had happened to the Mother?

Perhaps the crucial accomplishment of the new image of the Virgin Mary was the extent to which her image functioned to sever finally the bonds between parent and child for the sake of the rule of the Father or the Law as represented by church and state. For although popular devotees might insist that Mary was their sister, mother, or kinswoman, this image of Mary could only be sustained by a system of "coded perversions,"[145] in which the reality of what had happened was obscured.

In the Book of Genesis, even after Yahweh had fashioned Eve from the rib of Adam, Adam sings:

> This at last is bone from my bones,
> and flesh from my flesh!
> This is to be called woman,
> for this was taken from man.

And the Bible goes on to explain, "This is why *a man leaves his father and mother and joins himself to his wife,* and they become one body (emphasis added)."[146] But in the closing scenes of the Christian Gospels, as Jesus looked down from the cross upon his mother and his "favorite disciple," he said to his mother, "Woman, behold thy son." To his disciple John he said, "Son, behold thy mother."[147]

Here the Gospels put the final touch to any trace of matrilinearity. In the new Christian order, Mary the mother would leave her own home, the heart of the matricentered universe, to enter into the realms of discipleship to the cause of her Son.[148] And as Simone de Beauvoir commented,

For the first time in human history the mother kneels before her son; she freely accepts her inferiority. This is the supreme masculine victory, consummated in the cult of the Virgin—it is the rehabilitation of woman through the accomplishment of her defeat.[149]

In our journey through mythology and theology, several events have taken place with ominous overtones for the future of women. Macha had protested loudly when her needs in childbirth were made subordinate to the male power struggle. Brigit invented wailing and lamenting on hearing of the death of her son, Ruadán. Sarah dropped dead when she heard what Abraham had been willing to do with Isaac for the sake of obedience to Yahweh. Emer had protested vigorously at Cúchulainn's killing of his son, Connla, for the sake of the honor of the king.

All these women vividly recognized the implications of the events—the passing of the world in which women's sacred ties to their children would be honored and where the preservation of life and human relationships took precedence over any abstract idea or personal honor.

In contrast, Mary the Mother of God is perfectly compliant with the will of the Father. In one Irish manuscript Mary the Mother of Jesus is depicted praying to the Father: "Father of right and goodness, help my poverty and my wandering now. Redeem man in some other way, but don't let my Son be killed."[150] But Mary's prayers went unanswered: the will of the Father was now absolute.

CHAPTER 11

Conclusions: The Age of the Fathers

Male Reproductive Consciousness: Its Contemporary Influence in Church and State

MASCULUS GIGANTICUS HIBERNICUS

Country lout, knife thrower (dagger-wielder)
whether in jeans or a devil at noon
all dolled up in your pinstriped suit
you're always after the one thing.

Dangerous relics from the Iron Age
you sit in pubs and devise
the treacherous plan
that does not recoil on you—
a vengeful incursion to female land.

Because you will not dare to halt the growth
of the dark-red damask rose in your mother's heart
you will have to turn the garden
to a trampled mess
pounded and ruined by your two broad hooves.

And you're frisky, prancing, antlered—
your bread is baked.
You'd live off the furze
or the heather that grows
on a young girl's sunny slopes.
NUALA NÍ DHOMHNAILL, TWENTIETH CENTURY

With the Age of Mary the most essential elements of historical Christianity were now in place and would work themselves out to their logical conclusion. The next several centuries in Europe would see the dawn of the Renaissance, the Protestant and Catholic Reformations, the Age of Rationalism, and the various philosophical and social movements that would have widespread implications for the position and image of women.

Ireland's relationship to these great continental movements was atypical of Europe in general. Ireland, which had retrieved a great deal of the political ground it had lost in the twelfth century to the Anglo-Normans, lost this ground again with the renewed onslaughts of the sixteenth-century English invasions. As a colonial outpost whose economic and social needs were made subservient to those of England, Irish indigenous culture retreated into a steadfast form of nationalism where the links with the Roman Catholic church provided the only symbolic force the Irish had against the might of the British Empire. Despite the initial papal involvement in the invasion of Ireland, the papacy now assumed a major symbolic role, and Irish Catholicism became the vehicle of Irish nationalism, a position that it retains in Irish minds even today.[1]

Fascinating though it may be to explore these developments, this lies beyond the scope of this book. As we said at the outset, this is not a history of the Irish church, or even of Irish women, but an exploration of several cultural time frames that we have characterized as the ages of Eve, Brigit, and Mary respectively in an attempt to discern the nature of the discourses of sexual politics established during those eras.

We began by asking the question, what was it about the nature of contemporary Ireland that allowed so many people to die violently? Was this some aberration of Christian values, or was it, indeed, Christianity simply brought to its logical conclusion? And we further asked, what was it about the nature of contemporary political discourse that seemed to make the control of women and their reproduction such a major preoccupation, particularly on the part of those political powers who were themselves engaged in policies issuing in mass destruction, or the threat of mass destruction?

Christianity has acted as the carrier of patriarchal consciousness for the past two thousand years. Indeed, the present pope, John Paul II, concedes as much in saying that, as with slavery, it has taken us two thousand years to understand the gospel revelation with regard to the evil of sexism.[2]

The question must arise, however, were these developments the only possible outcome of the promulgation of the Christian message, or were there other possible ways Christianity might have manifested itself? In truth, we will never know the answer to that question, for while there may be many manifestations of an "underground church," one not allied to the power structures of the age, the nature of our sources again dictates that, predominantly, our evidence comes from the "winners," those whose political and religious success guaranteed them a place in the annals.

The subjugation of women formed one of the central ideologies of Western Christianity, and while there have been significant variations on the theme of women's subjugation, and significant strategic adaptations during the Reformations, Renaissance, and in the age of rationalism, the basic structure of patriarchal mythology has remained fundamentally intact. In general, theological scholarship has been preoccupied with an examination of the "roots" of the Judeo-Christian tradition, developing further elaborate hypotheses as to its genesis and further elaborate theories as to its present applicability. In very few instances has the structure itself been challenged, largely because the theology was theoretically accessible only to those privileged to have access to the higher institutions of learning: men, who, in turn, were products of that same mentality.

Other alternatives might well have been possible, but we have to conclude in the light of our analysis that for women, historically, Christianity has fostered a discourse of power based on the control of sex rather than a discourse of service based on the power of love, a discourse of death based on the control of life rather than a discourse of life based on the tragic acceptance of death.

As the carrier of patriarchy in the West, Christianity provided the cultural representations, or "symbolic capital,"[3] necessary for the development of patriarchal mythology. And even though the present pope admits the history of sexism in the church, he, nevertheless, insists on reiterating the basis of male privilege, restricting priestly ordination to men alone, using exclusively male regenerative language that has more in common with primitive anthropology than with the ethical teachings of the gospel of Jesus.[4]

At the close of several thousand years of the patriarchal experiment, there are those who consider our age to be one of enlightenment and rationality freed from the more crude "superstitions" of religious thought. In reality, patriarchal religion in its contemporary secular expression still provides the working strategies of state power even in anti-Christian or post-Christian societies under the guise of being the formal rationality of the social order. Long after Christian theology has ceased to be the major intellectual force in the Western world, secular versions of patriarchal consciousness have become equally powerful.

This century has seen two vicious and bloody wars, fought on European soil among Christian nations, in which generations of young men were obliterated. Millions of people in our century have found themselves in concentration camps, and six million Jews were exterminated, for the sake of the "purity of the species."

Forty years after the death of Hitler, we now have the ability to wipe out the entire population of the earth by means of nuclear weapons. No contemporary ruler holds power without commanding massive armies and armaments, and this is true to such an extent that the philosopher Michel Foucault has asserted, "The principle underlying the tactics of battle— that one has to be capable of killing in order to go on living—has become the principle that defines the strategy of states."[5] Nevertheless, the mindset and the mythologies that have made this destruction possible have gone largely unchallenged. As Albert Einstein has said, "The unleashed power of the atom has changed everything save our modes of thinking, and we thus drift toward unparalleled catastrophes."[6]

The patriarchal revolution has now come full circle. Where once we were faced with the uncertainties of nature, now we are faced with the possibility of nuclear destruction; where once we faced the tribal law of revenge, now we are faced with the ultimate revenge; where once we faced the fight between God and the Devil, now we are faced with the confrontation between the two most technologically advanced societies in the world, fighting it out, usually on foreign soil, for the domination of our Mother, the earth.

The paradoxical and tragic view of life in the form of the Serpent/ Goddess was overthrown in the search for a god who would grant eternal life in return for morality. Yet now we are faced with the greatest paradox of all: the more we attempt to control and enforce this morality on the rest of the world, the more precarious the basis of human existence becomes.

Indeed, in a secular world with "the disappearance of convincing dramas of heroic apotheosis of man,"[7] men may be driven to further extreme lengths in an attempt to find meaning and "transcendence," leading one social philosopher, William James, to claim that we must now search for "the moral equivalent of war."[8] But in searching for the "moral equivalent of war" we must seriously reckon with the political/theological philosophies established and currently perpetrated by male reproductive consciousness.

In the Age of the Fathers we will delve further into the patriarchal mind-set to illustrate how this consciousness permeates contemporary political praxis even, or perhaps especially, where the Christian worldview is no longer in place. All those elements of Christian thought (separation from the mother, the displaced eroticism of the cult of motherhood, concern for the male seed, the exclusion of women from significant symbol making, the rites of rebirth, the control of sexuality, the patriarchal notion of redemption, the ethics of death as opposed to life, the sacrifice of children for the honor of the father) reappear in secular mythology. However, they are now free from whatever ethical constraints might have affected them within a religious worldview, and thus their consequences are ever more lethal.

SEPARATION FROM THE MOTHER

The world of mothers, according to patriarchal mythology, is the world of nature; the world of men, the world of culture. It is woman as "Other," as "Nature," who represents the irrational forces waiting to destroy, and who provides the constant reminder to men of the depths to which they can fall if they are not in control of their "will."

Womanhood is given; manhood has to be achieved, and the prime symbol of this achievement is superiority over the world represented by mothers, the world of childhood. As we saw in the "Lives of the Saints," holiness for some men is synonymous with separation from their mothers. Likewise, in traditional warrior societies separation from the world of the mother is the hallmark of success. The warrior novices are invited to step on their mother's belly, insult her, and definitively separate from the world where she is dominant.[9] Some novices are told that "they must release the bad blood accumulated since he was in his mother's womb, his inheritance from the woman." This blood will often be replaced by "male blood," considered to be strengthening to the warrior.[10]

In contemporary warrior rituals, separation from the world of the mother also plays a major role. Throughout the hazing rites of the military academies, the young recruits are constantly compared to women and insulted with such epithets as "vagina-face," "douche-bag," "used Kotex," "abortion," "little fat vaginas," "afterbirths," and "scumbag."[11]

As A. E. Housman put it so poetically,

> For the calling bugle hollows,
> High the screaming fife replies,
> Gay the files of scarlet follow:
> Woman bore me, I will rise.[12]

Separating from their mothers, priests proved that their loyalties lay beyond this world and established their fitness to sacrifice. Contemporary warriors also prove their loyalty to the Common Good by separating from their mothers and developing their power of "will." To this day, in Western democracy, a man who is not in control of "his woman," or who, because of his uncontrollable sexual needs, is at the mercy of an "uncontrolled" woman, has little chance of political success. His "passions" are not subordinate to his "will."

The soldier, too, must "prove" to the world, or to the fraternity, that he is in control of his "will,"[13] is willing to risk his life, and, particularly, that he has successfully separated from the world of his mother and wishes to enter the realm of the fathers. Should he fail to do so, by showing cowardice in battle, for example, he will be relegated to the domestic sphere where he can live out his life in "womanly" safety. Indeed, the philosopher Plato regretted that it was not possible to turn cowardly soldiers into women.[14]

Soldiers are urged to greater excesses in battle by constant attacks on their gender identity, fears of castration, and the rape of their female property. The soldiers going to battle in the 1982 Falklands/Malvinas war, for instance, were fed a diet of pornographic movies while on their troop carriers going to the scene of battle. Their subsequent feats in battle somehow served to "prove" their manhood, making them fit to enter the company of men.[15]

APOSTOLIC SUCCESSION

Separating from the world of the mothers is, therefore, crucial to the establishment of male identity, but it is also related to the precariousness of male paternity. As James Joyce has written,

Fatherhood, in the sense of conscious begetting, is unknown to man . . . it is a mystical estate, an apostolic succession, from only begetter to only begotten. On that mystery and not on the madonna which the cunning Italian intellect flung to the mob of Europe the church is founded and founded irremovably because founded, like the world, macro- and microcosm, upon the void. Upon incertitude, upon unlikelihood. *Amor matris,* subjective and objective genitive, may be the only true thing in life. Paternity may be a legal fiction.[16]

Paternity for James Joyce may well have been a "legal fiction," but for several thousand years its preservation occupied the philosophical, theological, and political imagination of Western thought. As we have seen, controlling the reproductive and social labor of women formed one of men's central strategies for preserving paternal rights, a strategy that also ensured that their names would attach to their offspring. For it was not enough to separate from one's individual mother; rather, patriarchal forms of organization involved the setting up of principles of social organization, called patrilineal, in which descent from women, or any remaining sources of female power, would be abolished or superseded in favor of those established by men.

In theological terms, this continuity was provided by the institution of apostolic succession, a form of patrilineage par excellence. Apostolic succession provided a hierarchical and centralized power structure that overrode the claims of kinship in favor of that established by the ultimate act of fatherhood, the sacrifice of the son for the honor of the father.

Under patriarchy, according to the work of anthropologist of religion Nancy Jay, sacrifice enables the establishment of patrilineal descent systems that effectively override the importance of natural birthing or, implicitly, descent through the mother. Descent through natural fathers is also overridden in a society based on contract. Unlike women, however, men have access to entirely new forms of fatherhood, the fatherhood of the state or the fatherhood of the church. This fatherhood is exercised by means of exclusive access to sacrificial rituals on the altar or on the battlefield, rituals that both express and reinforce the basis upon which this power has been established.

Patriarchal rites, far from encouraging harmony with nature, reflect an entirely new understanding of cultural creativity, celebrating a "supernatural" order of being in which those ideologically connected to the realm of "nature" are seen as inferior and even polluting.

More particularly, they celebrate man's new-found power, the equivalent of the life-giving powers of women: the power to take life. As Nancy Jay continues: "The only action that is as serious as giving birth, which can act as a counterbalance to it, is killing. This is one way to interpret the common sacrificial metaphors of birth and rebirth, or birth done better, on purpose and on a more spiritual, more exalted level than mothers do it."[17]

The superior status given to the taking of life as opposed to the giving of life is reflected throughout Western philosophy. Although there are philosophies of eating, sex, and death, there is no philosophy of birth. As Mary O'Brien points out, "In the idealist structure of malestream thought birth has no meaning until it is thought about, and it is too banal and naturalistic to induce thought."[18] Birth appeared in theology and philosophy only to show why these particularist ties must be abandoned where they were necessary at all, an argument commonly used now to defend the doctrine of the virgin birth of Jesus.[19]

Given the basis upon which male religious power was established, it is not surprising to find that women, the givers of life, could not also be takers of life, and, therefore, they could not officiate at any of those rites designed specifically to further the life of the centralized power structures or to transcend those systems of connection based on kinship.[20]

In this light the question of the admission of women to the priesthood can be seen in sharp relief. The argument has often been used in these debates that "just as men can't have babies, women can't be priests." On the face of it this objection is irrational and absurd, but upon closer examination there is a profound logic to this position. As Nancy Jay argues, "For patrilineage members it is sacrificing, not giving birth, that maintains lineage continuity as patrilineage."[21] Sacrificial rituals also act, in some cases, to remove the pollution due to childbirth: "Man born of woman may be destined to die, but man integrated into an 'eternal' social order to that degree transcends mortality."[22]

Childbearing women are a distinct threat to the patriarchal order of continuity, threatening to erode or make ludicrous the basis upon which continuity has been established. Women priests would be an anomaly that could not be tolerated within the patriarchal mentality. With few exceptions cross-culturally, women are not allowed to sacrifice, not only because they are women but also primarily because they are childbearers.[23]

Through sacrifice, men take it upon themselves to give birth to a "higher" order in which only they can preside. In some cultures the symbolism is blatant; sacrifice takes place once the male officiants, dressed as pregnant women, send all the real women out of the city.[24] But usually priests are content with excluding women from the sacred boundaries, such as the altar, where the sacrifice is performed. Menstruating or pregnant women would remind men of their mortality, and, indeed, would "pollute" the transcendent order of immortality being established. For this reason, not only can women not sacrifice, but even nine-year-old girls must be firmly excluded from the altar where the sacrifice takes place. According to the official codes of Roman Catholic canon law, the minor liturgical offices, even that of altar server, must be undertaken by members of the male sex.

Even Protestant traditions that have admitted women to the priesthood, especially the Lutheran and the Episcopalian churches, are experiencing enormous difficulties within their churches for the acceptance of women. One Episcopalian priest had her hand bitten when she first distributed communion on her ordination day.[25] In Sweden, where women priests have been ordained for almost thirty years, there is still a system of "clean" and "unclean" dioceses, i.e., dioceses where women have not yet been ordained. In some cases only "clean" parishes or even churches remain.

Women priests regularly come up against irrational prejudice in the course of their work. Some men believe that if a menstruating woman conducts a funeral service it will not "take." In recent years there were serious discussions at Uppsala, the major Swedish university, about a pregnant woman who was about to be ordained. Those opposed to women's ordination had no doubt that her ordination would not "take," but what about the child? Should the fetus be male, would the apostolic succession automatically be conferred upon him? And what were the implications for his rearing should this be the case?[26]

As the Vatican announces repeatedly, the issue of the ordination of women is an insuperable obstacle to ecumenism, an obstacle that has delayed for years serious talk about reunion between Rome and the Church of England. If the churchmen are having problems recognizing the legitimacy of each other's line of descent, these problems are magnified by the possibility of admitting women into the ranks. While Rome might well find it within its logic to acknowledge the ministry of Protestant men, even those who are married, perhaps ordaining them conditionally in case the first did not "take," the possibility of admitting women into the line of apostolic succession is beyond their comprehension. Damaged though the line of apostolic succession might be, the Vatican argues that Protestants must realize the lines of patrilineal theological descent would be broken forever, and made ludicrous, by the admission of women.

The exclusion of women from ordination is, therefore, necessary in order to maintain the purity of male systems of descent and still forms an important part of Western political and theological discourse. Nation-states have openly colluded with the churches on the issue of the exclusion of women from priesthood, intimately aware, as they are, that their power has historically been derived from the religious authority of the church and the religious symbolism that has supported patriarchal power structures. In particular, states are dependent upon religion to provide and maintain the dualisms and forms of alienation upon which the power of the state rests.

Only in those contemporary secular cultures, such as Canada or Sweden, where the balance of power is clearly in the state's favor, and where the church now occupies a relatively powerless or "feminine" role in society, are women priests accepted and even valued.

In contemporary times simple biological continuity is no longer enough for men, even though this continuity still plays a major symbolic role in monarchical forms of government where descent is traced to the nth degree in the largely symbolic myth of the monarchy. It might also account for the inordinate attention given to the question of surrogate motherhood, where the main intention is the preservation of a particular male line of descent. For even more important than mere biological continuity is men's entry into universal time. As Mary O'Brien points out,

Whereas no father can ever look upon a child with the utter certainty that it is his, the Hero who founds the city, or the makers of Constitutions whom Machiavelli so admired, can look like gods upon their work and know that it is good and will continue after they themselves succumb to the natural cycle.[27]

Just as the church was building up its spiritual empire, so too in the secular world the quest for political empire testifies to an inordinate and usually irrational preoccupation with immortality and continuity, a preoccupation that gives a lethal character to war-making in the modern world, a war-making issuing in Mutually Assured Destruction, which defies rational explanation.

REBIRTH

Once the principle of male systems of descent had been established and reinforced through spiritual paternity, it would not be enough for men to rely on their mere biological birth from their mother's womb to allow them entry into the new sacred space generated by patriarchal consciousness. On the contrary, they would have to be "reborn."

The emphasis on cultural rebirth led to a diminished status for the natural givers of life. In many ancient societies, women in childbirth and warriors had been put on an equal level. In ancient Spartan society, for instance, according to Plutarch, "it was forbidden to inscribe the names of the dead upon their tombstones, except for men who had fallen in war and women who had died in childbirth."[28]

Among the African Ashanti a woman who dies in childbirth is treated like a dead warrior.[29] Likewise, in Ireland one of the few times women achieved equality with men before the law, and were allowed to swear on oath, was on their deathbeds in the act of giving birth.[30] There was a clear understanding underlying these practices that, just as women risked their lives in childbirth, so too men risked their lives in war. Both the warrior and the childbearing woman regenerated the lives of their societies, and both should be honored or reviled in relation to their social services.

Under patriarchy, the ordinary birthing of women was inferior and possibly even dangerous. The Aztecs, a highly developed patriarchal warrior society, believed that the sun itself was caused to rise by means of repeated sacrificing on the part of men, and that each evening the sun fell, dragged down by the bodies of women who died in childbirth.[31] Rather than being buried alongside the warriors, in Christian times women in Ireland who died in childbirth were sometimes buried alongside exiles and social outcasts.[32]

Throughout Christianity entry into the new life of the spirit was achieved by means of a spiritual rebirth in which the initiate "died" to the profane world in the rite of baptism. This rite was by no means the end but only the beginning of death, because those who wished to participate fully in the life of the spirit would have to court death physically or spiritually in the pursuit of their ideal. The greatest saints in the Christian tradition were those who had died as martyrs, and in Ireland, where martyrdom for the faith had not apparently been necessary, the Irish in compensation devised a form of "spiritual martyrdom" believed to be the equivalent of that achieved elsewhere.[33]

In traditional warrior societies, initiation rites and initiatory death prepares the novice for entry into a transcendent space, a "new, purely spiritual birth, access to a mode of being not subject to the destroying action of Time."[34] A "new man" will be created who, according to Mircea Eliade, will "know realities that are not a part of nature but of the biography of the Supernatural Beings, hence of the sacred history preserved in the myths."[35]

In the initiation rites of life-risking, "the basic idea is that, to attain a higher mode of existence, gestation and birth must be repeated. . . . In other words, we here have acts oriented toward the values of Spirit, not behavior from the realm of psycho-physiological activity."[36]

In contemporary democracy the rituals of rebirth are no less complete, except that now men are initiated, not only to adulthood, but also to citizenship under "conditions created and controlled by men both human and divine, and no female reproductive labor is required for this significant genesis."[37]

This emphasis on rebirthing has developed into a full-blown cult of life-risking that, even in today's secular society, finds expression in prestigious philosophical treatises. As the philosopher Hegel maintained,

It is only by risking life that freedom is obtained, only thus is it tried and proved that the essential nature of self-consciousness is not bare existence, is not merely the immediate form in which it at first makes its appearance, is not mere absorption in the expanse of life.[38]

Hegel's position leads logically to the thesis that the "fear of death, an emotion, is the true parent of biological and conscious life" and, like the rites of baptism, is "a very elaborate second birth indeed."[39]

Life-risking is a "baptism of fire" in which the warrior emerges anew. As J. Glenn Gray noted, "The Greeks were wise men when they mated the god of war with the goddess Aphrodite. The soldier must not only kill, he must give birth to the new warrior."[40] Facing death for some men has been described as "an illuminating experience analogous to childbirth for the female."[41]

The fatherhood of the state, therefore, just as the Fatherhood of God, necessitated rituals of "rebirth" in which "merely natural" life is superseded. Writers commonly refer to the "birth of the nation."[42] In the works of war poets, death is often referred to as a form of superior birthing. As the poet Isaac Rosenberg wrote in his "The Tower of Skulls," "Everywhere, everywhere there is a pregnant birth,/And here in death's land is a pregnant birth."[43]

Throughout military literature, war is described as a form of rebirth that brings new life to the nation, the tribe, or culture. Indeed, the regenerative function in times of war passes from the female to the male warrior.[44]

In warrior societies, childbearing women are consistently excluded from war-making activities, although, as in the religious rites of sacrifice, virgins are often warrior participants.[45] It is as though a woman could become a warrior so long as she "had not yet taken advantage of the privilege of her sex by becoming a mother."[46] One of the main objections to the passage of the Equal Rights Amendment in the United States was that, if granted equality before the law, women would then be granted equal status in the army, an issue that promoted widespread controversy on both sides of the spectrum.[47]

And there are other similarities between the tactics of priests and warriors. Just as priests had to abstain permanently from sexual contact, so too, contact with the symbols of life was traditionally taboo for soldiers going to battle. Sexual intercourse somehow "weakens" the strength of both warriors and priests, whereas battles and sacrifice are sources of regeneration.[48] Any contact with a menstruating woman, in particular, was traditionally dangerous for soldiers.[49]

Just as women could not touch the sacred vessels on the altar of Christian sacrifice, neither could they touch the weapons of war. Both sets of artifacts were designed to create and sustain a "spiritual" world, and contact with women would threaten its existence.[50] As in religious sacrifice, the blood of women shed at birth defiles, but the blood of men shed in war takes on mythic and sacramental proportions, making possible and regenerating the political "graces" necessary for the mythic life of the state.[51]

And just as those who gave birth could not be priests, so too an ancient Gnostic conundrum asks the question, "How long will men make war?" And the answer is, "As long as women have children."[52] Childbearing and war-making are both powerful acts, but childbirth, according to patriarchal ideology, is weakening, whereas war is regenerative.[53]

As the great theorist of war Clausewitz maintained, "War develops in the womb of state politics. Its principles are hidden there as the particular characteristics of the individual are hidden in the embryo."[54] War becomes a new form of birthing, the birthing of the fathers that transcends anything of which mere mothers, or even biological fathers, could be capable. As the ancient philosopher Heraclitus wrote, "Strife is the father and king of all."[55]

Contemporary warfare, often conducted under the guise of rationality, therefore, accomplishes the "second birthing" apparently so essential for contemporary male development, and this time it is a birthing free of both paternal and maternal contributions, relying entirely on the mechanisms of the state. "The war then provides a set of surrogate progenitors, a maternal womb, and a patriarch operating through industrial processes that 'hammer, cast and temper' an entire generation."[56]

Now in nuclear discourse, where the most technically brilliant and educated men are at work, little has changed in their basic male reproductive consciousness. The language used makes it clear that the contemporary warriors have finally achieved their ultimate goal: giving birth to the world. In this they are little different from the ancient Celtic warriors huddled over their November campfires with their "masts of Macha." The scientists who created the bombs are called "fathers."[57] Men are still engaged in hysterical pregnancies, and ritual couvade, except that now these rituals take on lethal proportions. The first atom bomb, for instance, was designed and built at Los Alamos, New Mexico. Writers have referred to the "secret gestation of the bomb."[58] One felt "as though he had been privileged to witness the Birth of the New World"; another heard the "first cry of the newborn world."[59] When the scientists who had been working on the project wanted to communicate to President Truman that the tests had been successful, they chose the following phrase: "Babies satisfactorily born."[60]

Turning to military equipment we can see similar parallels. Machine guns have "nests"; giant birds hover over cities dropping their eggs of untold destruction; the penis-shaped missiles wreak havoc wherever they land. In its reversal of life, warmongering becomes "protection"; the female's care for the young is translated into "defense spending"; male ego insecurity is translated into the necessity for "national security"; one "penetrates" the enemy camp.[61]

As with the traditional warrior initiates, contempt for women still plays a major part in contemporary political discourse and practice. In a television show on the attempt to rescue the hostages out of Iran, people talked about the failed attempt as an "abortion." The only way for the America to demonstrate its willingness to "save" its citizens would be by demonstrating a willingness to "lose" them. The attempt was foiled by a "precipitous withdrawal"; the whole exercise was "like trying to organize a picnic for spinsters to the East Coast." Finally, the United States was being held *impotent* by a handful of fanatics.[62]

WESTERN FATHERHOOD

Through these examples we can see that Western "fatherhood" has taken on dimensions far removed from the initial biological concerns men may have had with regard to their paternal rights. We are now talking about broad political pictures that, nevertheless, reflect and have been produced by male reproductive consciousness and that are now played out in the political world.

We saw in the story of Cúchulainn and Connla, Cúchulainn's willingness to kill his own son firmly established his credibility in the eyes of the king. As the king's ultimate warrior, Cúchulainn helped to establish the "king's honor," enabling him to stand on behalf of the community, representing the interests of the Common Good. Only Connla's life-risking entitled him to be "named" or recognized by his father. Failing this he would remain in the realm of particularity, the realm of the women, as "Aife's One Son." Cúchulainn rescued his son from the fate of particularity and took him into sacred time, the realm of the Common Good.

Women, who were tied into their families, were incapable of transcending their particularistic, private interests and acting on behalf of the Common Good. Women, in general, did not become part of the war effort, an essential feature of the early state, because, as Mary O'Brien argues, "they had an unheroic and irrational objection to the slaughter of their own children."[63]

Patriarchal social structures deny the claims of particularity in favor of those of universality and are only made possible by fathers willing to renounce their biological links in favor of the Common Good. But in reality, fathers seize their children from particularity in order to sacrifice them to the Gods of War.[64]

According to patriarchal ideology, only men are capable of acting in such a way that the integrity of the Common Good is preserved. For this reason, the centralization of power on the part of the papacy necessitated that women be excluded from those religious roles, such as that of sacrifice, that might have public or political implications. Some of the major social theorists (Plato, Aristotle, Augustine, Aquinas, and Marx) have agreed that the subordination of women is a "regrettable but necessary" precondition for the dualism between public and private to be established. Only men could act on behalf of the Common Good because only men had objectivity; only men were dispassionate; only men were logical and fair minded. Most importantly, only men would transcend their particularist interests and would prove this, as Cúchulainn did, by their willingness to kill their only sons.

In killing their only sons, they were making a statement: biological links were no longer important; really important life lay beyond this world. Committing the ultimate act of transgression enabled men to enter or create sacred space, implicitly denigrating the world of women and children.

Throughout the literature of contemporary warfare, the relationship between fathers and sons remains a very powerful dynamic. The poet Wilfrid Owen, in his poem, "The Parable of the Old Man and the Young," compared the sacrifice of the soldiers in World War I with the sacrifice of Abraham and Isaac. At the point when the angel told Abraham to withdraw the knife, Owen writes,

> But the old man would not so . . .
> But slew his son . . .
> And half the seed of Europe . . .
> One by one.[65]

Hostility between the generations is also cited as a reason for the cult of warfare. Warfare apparently reduces intergenerational conflict by providing the young with alternative outlets for their aggression or by giving expression to the sexual jealousy of the young on the part of the old.[66]

In the political realm in the institution of the Blood Covenant, unity among the members was maintained by their willingness to avenge each other's deaths. As more sophisticated versions of the Blood Covenant arose, the brothers were prepared to die on behalf of God the Father. But in contemporary politics it is the collective fatherhood of the state that is being established. There are some theorists who argue that the willingness to die on behalf of the other is the essence of the state. As the Prussian Von Trietschke asserted:

The essence of the state is power and it is to be found in a well-equipped and well-drilled army. . . . It is only in war that a people becomes a people. . . . The state exists over and apart from the individuals who compose it, and it is entitled to their utmost sacrifices. In short, they exist for it, rather than the state for them. A nation's military efficiency is the exact coefficient of a nation's idealism.[67]

In the religious realm the sacrifice of the Son to the Father not only effected the Sonship of Jesus, but also the Fatherhood of God. Now it is the redemptive sacrifice of war, rather than the redemptive sacrifice of Christ, that provides the central mythology of the modern state. As Ernst Jünger put it so well, "The war, father of all things, is also our father."[68]

Submission to the will of the father still plays a powerful role in the dynamics of both church and state and in the attempts on the part of men to achieve "recognition" by their collective Father. Priests have to make constant submission of their lives, symbolized by renunciation of their will, to those on the higher echelons of the hierarchy, extending to the reigning pope. Tests of obedience, far from diminishing clerical status, give it legendary proportions. As William Butler Yeats wrote, "It is only when the intellect has wrought the whole of life to drama, to crisis, that we may live for contemplation and yet keep our intensity."[69]

The willingness to renounce one's own will attests to tremendous reverence for whoever, king or pope, represents the whole and further contributes to the credibility of the basis upon which clerical and military power rests. Stories of the male saints are filled with details of Oedipal struggle, whether with the fatherhood of the state, their natural fathers, or with their religious superiors to whom they remained obedient despite the irrationality of their orders. It is as though male saints must bear the marks of struggle, or life-risking, as proof of their religious authenticity.

Even those theologians who apply the most sophisticated materialist analyses in liberation theology to the structures of economic oppression fail to apply this analysis to their own oppression in the church. Total submission to the pope takes on a religious, or even an erotic value.[70] The pope and his clerics are mutually dependent upon one another: the pope to receive the submission of the clerics, thus enhancing and confirming his own honor and power, and the clerics upon the pope for recognition of their place in the divine order and for the empowerment to continue with their work.

Unquestioning obedience is vital to the maintenance of hierarchical authority, especially that in which the symbols of death play a major role. Church obedience is sustained by a doctrine of papal infallibility, the benefits of which extend to the priesthood by some process of downward osmosis. But the similarities between the "soldiers for Christ" and the "soldiers of the state" is striking. Soldiers can be shot for failing to obey an order of their most immediate and lowly commanders. Those tried for the atrocities of the Second World War regularly plead that "they were merely following orders," as though obedience were the guarantee of ethics.[71]

Without adherence to unquestioning obedience it is hardly likely that the violence of patriarchal structures could be maintained. The nonviolent theorist and activist Mahatma Gandhi, for instance, maintained that as he could never be sure he was absolutely right, he, therefore, could not kill.

Military obedience enables the hierarchical system to function but at the price of utterly negating the individual soldier's moral responsibility. The abdication of personal responsibility in religious and political matters, regardless of the consequences, is the price both priests and soldiers are willing to pay for their continued inclusion in the world of the fathers.

THE MYTH OF THE COMMON GOOD

The distinction between the Common Good and particularist interests, symbolically enacted in the myths of fatherhood, has brought about a profound split in human consciousness. Sacrificing their wills, or often their bodies, men apparently transcend their particularistic private interests, whether they be sensual passion or family loyalties, proving their commitment to the Common good, the "will of the father," or the "revolution." This leaves them with a clear conscience to commit atrocities in the "name of God," "for the sake of the fatherland," or for the sake of some similar abstraction.

The same ethics that rigidly insist on personal responsibility in the sexual realm, effectively also insist on the complete abdication of responsibility for the sake of the mythology of the Common Good.

In the Age of Eve we saw that monotheism developed in response to the necessity for a hierarchical and centralized, political and religious structure. Competing deities or competing sources of religious power were eradicated, enabling all authority to come from a central source. Instead of monotheism, we now have the working strategy of unquestioning obedience to military authority, which continues to sustain various forms of patriarchal power. This, in turn, is reinforced by powerful dramas taking place between fathers and sons for acceptance and recognition.[72] To maintain their place within the structures thus established, all men have to do is to obey; the need to be right hardly arises.

And just as Connla was recognized by his father only when he showed that he was willing to risk his life, so too the warriors' willingness to kill and be killed gives them enhanced social recognition that they would hardly achieve otherwise. As an American President once said at the tomb of the Unknown Soldier:

We do not know the eminence of his birth, but we do know the glory of his death. He died for his country and greater devotion hath no man than this.[73]

In contemporary warfare, returned veterans often use their position as a leverage of power against those "selfish" civilians who remained at home acting as if

the machinery of communal life was simply a means for the prosecution of class interests. The veteran could claim to best represent the whole of the nation for he had "sacrificed himself" for the survival of the community.[74]

Those soldiers willing to sacrifice their lives confer upon the military-industrial complex a new kind of theological status, that which represents the "whole" now that traditional religion seldom serves this purpose. Indeed, the inroads of secularism may have occasioned a "sacrificial crisis,"[75] or a "collapse of the sacrificial economy,"[76] in which the search for political absolutes now becomes dominant.

Just as the sacrifice of the Mass makes possible the "new life" essential for the rebirth of the Christian initiate at baptism, so too in war poetry, death through violent life-risking is often seen as "the only possibility of giving life authenticity and creative power."[77] Death of the male in warfare is often referred to as a form of sacrifice, and, indeed, there would seem to be serious continuities between the religious notion of sacrifice and that of sacrifice in war, particularly in relation to the opposition between giving birth and taking life.

Contemporary warfare is seen as the sacramental focus for the formation of national identity. According to some theorists war gives nations their identity, enabling men to relate to a larger social body. Warfare, even when it makes little economic or social sense, is essentially a form of ritual sacrifice designed to enforce the power of the ruler or the identity of the state. As Lewis Mumford asserted:

If anything were needed to make the magical origins of war plausible, it is the fact that war, even when disguised by seemingly hardheaded economic demands, uniformly turns into a religious performance; nothing less than a wholesale ritual sacrifice. As the central agent in this sacrifice, the king had from the beginning an office to perform. To accumulate power, to hold power, to express power by deliberate acts of murderous destruction—this became the constant obsession of kingship.[78]

The tactics of contemporary warfare are very similar to those practiced historically by the clergy. War is often referred to as a means of "redemption" from terror,[79] and in contemporary diplomacy, the role of redemption has been taken over by those political powers with the ability to exact the maximum cosmic impact by means of nuclear weapons. For instance, during the Second World War, President Truman, going into "peace" negotiations, deliberately postponed the meetings until he could be sure that his latest weapon, the atom bomb being designed at Los Alamos, actually worked. The atom bomb was, effectively, a bargaining tool with tremendous "diplomatic" value.[80]

The instruments of military "redemption" still play an enormous role in contemporary "peace" negotiations. Only those possessed of the major instruments (i.e., nuclear weapons) are admitted to the negotiating table, regardless of the fact that a nuclear war has the potential to wipe out the entire earth.

The patriarchal version of redemption not only fostered the authority of God the Father but also enabled his servants, the male priests, to exert and maintain control of their faithful. The clergy dispensed throughout the faithful the "graces" made possible by the redemption, providing them with access to "supernatural" life. Now in secular ideology, nuclear weapons are held by state powers that hold office on the basis of their ability to "invest life through and through," to promise the good life now, rather than a supernatural life in the hereafter. As Foucault argues,

> If genocide is indeed the dream of modern powers, this is not because of a recent return of the ancient right to kill; it is because power is situated and exercised at the level of life, the species, the race, and the large-scale phenomena of population.[81]

In Christian sacrificial teaching, redemption had been made possible by the willingness of the Son to be killed for the sake of the honor of the Father. Within the political universe, the power of the king was based upon the willingness of his soldiers to be killed. Now in contemporary democracy the right to vote, and thus participate fully in the legal life of the state, has itself evolved only as a result of the needs of contemporary warfare. Franchise was extended only gradually, and begrudgingly, as wider social sectors needed to be drafted for the various war efforts.[82] For instance, women received the right to vote only after their participation in the subsidiary war machine of the First World War, and in the United States eighteen-year-olds got the vote during the Vietnam War, on the grounds that those who were old enough to die for their country were old enough to vote for its government. Indeed what men are willing to die for has become the prime mode in the establishment of sovereignty.[83]

And just as religious sacrifice had brought about forms of communion, enabling the community to become as one, so too the constant threat of destruction brings about social unity in contemporary culture. An American general, regretting the fact that the Cuban missile crisis had been resolved without further bloodshed, and wishing that the Soviet Union had attacked Florida, remarked that this could have "finally pulled this country together."[84]

The idea that Christ once "died for all" enabled people to give their allegiance to the church; the idea that the soldier "dies for all" compels people to give their allegiance to the state. Although valiant efforts are often made by some to maintain that the sacrifice of Christ should have ended the need for war, as it was the ultimate sacrifice that did away with any need for revenge,[85] historically, the language, symbolism, and ideology of Christian sacrifice has blessed the tanks, cannons, and troops as they wheeled out toward the battlefield. In the last analysis it becomes difficult to distinguish between the "sacrifice to end all sacrifice" and the "war to end all wars." As one sociologist put it, "In the past it would seem that men were often mercenaries calculating the gain and loss of military activities; now they fight for ultimate objectives. War is a sacred activity."[86]

Few Western states any longer derive their power primarily from the sacrifice of the Mass, although certainly other religious ceremonies play a major part in political legitimation. New political mythologies have been developed in keeping with the growth of nation-states throughout

Europe, and new sources of power have been found. The state, rather than the church, has taken it upon itself to be the main agent of sacrifice. Indeed, whereas the church had maintained its power by the constant threat of apocalyptic destruction should the faithful not adhere to the commands of God, as interpreted by the priesthood, in secular society for the first time apocalyptic destruction is a real possibility. Nuclear destruction promises to take patriarchal ideology to its logical conclusion.

The traditional church/state choice turns out to be simply one further mystification preventing us from being aware of, let alone analyzing, the dynamics of patriarchal power. Similarly, the demystification of religion, pursued under the myth of "rational enlightenment," which fails to take any account of its traditional social functioning, is also both illusory and misguided. As René Girard argues, "The myths of demystification cling to the great collective myth and draw nourishment from it, rather like worms feeding on a corpse."[87] God the Father may no longer be in the heavens holding over our heads the threat of apocalyptic destruction. But for those who are "enlightened," according to Girard, we have something equally terrible:

The bomb does indeed seem like the prince of this world, enthroned above a host of priests and worshippers, who exist, so it would seem, only to do it service. Some of them bury the poisoned eggs of the idol beneath the earth; others deposit them at the bottom of the seas; yet others sprinkle the heavens with them, causing the stars of death to revolve endlessly above the teeming antheap. No slightest section of nature—now that science has cleansed it of all the ancient projections of the supernatural—has not been reinvested with the truth of violence. But this time we cannot pretend that the power for destruction is anything but human, even though it works in ways that parallel the working of the sacred.[88]

The threat of nuclear destruction is firmly based on human territory, and "absolute vengeance, formerly the prerogative of the gods, now returns, precisely weighed and calibrated, on the wings of science."[89]

Nuclear warfare is, therefore, not an accidental feature of an ideology that would otherwise promote the growth of the human spirit. Nuclear destruction is intrinsic to the spirituality and theology generated by Western culture. As Hegel says:

The Spirit, devouring its worldly envelope, not only passes into another envelope, not only arises rejuvenated from the ashes of its embodiment, but it emerges from them exalted, transfigured, a purer Spirit. It is true that it acts against itself, devours its own existence. But in so doing it elaborates upon this existence; its embodiment becomes material for its work to elevate itself to a new embodiment. . . . But even when it perishes, it does so in the course of its function and destiny, and even then it offers the spectacle of having proved itself as spiritual activity.[90]

This view of spirituality and regeneration was shared by the French Jesuit philosopher Pierre Teilhard de Chardin. After the first test explosion of the atomic bomb in New Mexico, Teilhard wrote that

it disclosed to human existence a supreme purpose: the purpose of pursuing even further, to the very end, the forces of life. In exploding the atom we took our first bite of the fruit of the great discovery, and this was enough for a taste to enter our mouths that can never be washed away: the taste for supercreativeness.[91]

The taste for supercreativeness was not daunted in the least when the atom bomb was finally dropped on Hiroshima. Upon receiving the news of the destruction the weapon had wrought upon defenseless men, women, and children, President Truman remarked, "This is the greatest thing in history."[92]

GOOD MOTHER

Once the politics of Western fatherhood had been firmly established over against the world of women, it would no longer be necessary, except in extreme instances of war and sacrifice, to insist so heavily on separation from the world of mothers. For day-to-day operations, an alternative ideology was formulated. The woman who threatened to pull men down from the heights of culture would return in a new guise, as the "good mother" whose virtue was "natural."

In Christian theology one of her main functions was that of keeping the male lines of descent intact, in particular, by protecting the male seed. As we have seen, the male concern for continuity took the form of frequent promises made to religious functionaries and those who obeyed them. The covenants made to Abraham and his descendants were made to his "seed forever," and throughout the "Lives of the Saints" the kings are promised "seed forever" in return for supporting the church. Seed contained within itself the essence of patriarchal continuity and took on a symbolic value that had little to do with its relative biological significance. Sophisticated theological and philosophical reasoning, therefore, was based upon that most vulnerable aspect of male psyche: the male seed itself.

The male seed, according to some philosophers and theologians, contained the essence of life. Women may contribute the matter of the body, but as philosophers from Aristotle onward have claimed, only the male seed could "ensoul" or "enspirit" the base matter.[93]

Aristotle's biology became formative in the development of Christian theology, especially under the influence of Thomas Aquinas. Later medical evidence as to the role played by the woman in conception did nothing to undermine the importance of the seed. Biology may have been the justification, but far more fundamental issues are at stake.

The concern for the preservation of the male seed brought about some tortuous reasoning in the field of morality as priests delved into the marriage bed in an attempt to see how, and under what conditions, the male seed might go astray, especially in contraceptive practices. Whenever sexual intercourse took place it was imperative that the male seed be allowed to reach its destination and fruition, without interference, even at the cost of the woman's life. This is one of the main concerns at the heart of Christian moral teaching informed as it is both by the "law of phallus" and by a crisis of male identity, evident throughout the documents formulated by successive church councils whenever they deal with sexuality.

Manuals for confessors dealt in intimate detail with the dilemmas posed, and some went so far as to argue that, where the seed was in danger of going astray through her husband's actions, for instance, a woman could not enjoy sex and should resist to the death, if necessary. In one memorable article, "How Must a Confessor Deal with an Onanist?" the logic of the church's position on artificially preventing conception is fully laid out.[94]

Written in the 1940s by a professor at the Catholic University in Washington, D.C., the article begins with the dilemma posed by a female penitent who confesses that her husband uses a condom. The question? "Is it ever permitted for a woman to co-operate with her husband in such a case; should she be given absolution, and if so, under what circumstances?"

The professor distinguishes between two types of contraception: that caused by "withdrawal," and that caused by the use of artificial devices. In the first case it is the woman's duty to "manifest her displeasure" at her husband's efforts at contraception, but under extraordinary circumstances, such as her own possible incontinence, she herself may request sexual union and even "consent to the venereal gratification" up to the moment of withdrawal, after which her pleasure becomes sinful. However, should the husband intend to use a condom, the situation is radically different "for this mode of contraception is intrinsically bad from the very beginning, being *by its nature* ordained to the spilling of the semen outside its *locus debitus* [rightful place]." In this case the woman may not consent, and her attitude should be the same toward her husband as that of a virgin threatened with rape.

But now the question arises for the theologian: "How must a virgin deal with rape?" The considered opinion was that a virgin must use every means of fending off her attacker and is only allowed to passively submit under danger of death. (This was obviously the lesser of two goods since St. Maria Goretti was canonized when she, at the age of twelve, resisted to the point of death.) Logically, therefore, it follows that a wife, faced with a similar situation, could submit to her husband but with one important exception: "The wife may not give voluntary consent to the venereal pleasure that might accrue to her from her husband's actions. If there is grave danger that she will yield to this pleasure, not even the certain knowledge that she will be killed if she resists will justify non-resistance on her part." She is obliged to resist to her utmost, and the author reminds us that "if a woman really abhors the intercourse and fortifies herself with prayer, she can easily render the danger of consent remote."

The priest goes on to list other possible circumstances in which a woman might passively submit to her husband. The danger that the husband would refuse to support the family or leave his wife and children might present grounds but only in case of severe poverty when there is a danger that the family would be put in a public institution. Rich women apparently should continue to suffer on. The danger of a severe beating "likened to death," or severe alcoholism on the part of the husband, might also serve as a reason. But the theologian is careful to point out that all these reasons must be grave and the "mere fact" that her husband could effectively cease all social relations with her would clearly not be a reason for compliance "unless the wife is tending towards a disastrous nervous breakdown." The threat that the husband might commit adultery, unlike the wife's threatened incontinence, is clearly excluded from the confessor's list of reasons for permitting the woman's compliance and would not constitute grounds for the women's consent. The husband should just be allowed to seek his pleasure elsewhere, regardless, apparently, of the consequences to the family unit.

The confessor now turns his attention to the question of the woman using a douche after intercourse and proclaims that this is morally wrong until after an hour has passed and that under any circumstances using a douche to prevent conception would be sinful. However, should the woman be sleeping with an infectious husband, she would be in luck, for she would be permitted to use a douche but only if her intention was to prevent infection and not conception. (This teaching, incidentally, would also apply the case of AIDS, a fact that the church authorities have been slow to make available in the current crisis in relation to that disease.)

While it is true that some confessors made notable efforts to be compassionate and understanding toward penitents, few challenged the fundamental mentality underlying this understanding of human ethics.

In the early Irish laws there were occasions when the community as a whole would impose penalties upon a man for impregnating a woman (even his wife) when it had been expressly forbidden for him to do so: but now the situation has been entirely reversed. In a society where men attach so much importance to establishing and maintaining their paternal rights, ultimate importance within the ethical field has been given to the preservation of the male seed and the preservation takes precedence over all other social considerations. The seed, rather than the community, the family, or the good of the woman, has been at the center of theological concern as the church formulated its ethical teaching. This is particularly ironic since in present times there are few priests or theologians who would now expound, with such openness, the theology of the male seed. Now, concern for the "family" or the "dignity of woman" has become the form in which the church continues to co-opt the support of right-wing women, historically ignorant of the genesis of theology.

Women had no part in formulating canon law that enshrined this teaching into the legal code of the Catholic church. The fact that they were excluded from ordination effectively meant that they were also excluded from theological training. Women, therefore, had no input into a theology that gave so much importance to the male seed and that led to a situation where masturbation or oral sex, performed between two consenting couples, was more serious than rape; rape at least "preserved" the natural relationship between the sexes, whereas the other activities "wasted" the seed altogether.[95]

Historically, the church often made alliances with women to resist the power of the warriors. For this reason, in medieval society, and in early Irish law and penitentials, women, clerics, and children were often put on the same legal footing.[96] Now, far from making alliances with women, the authoritarian, hierarchical church is simply reinforcing the dominant symbolic modes of male reproductive consciousness, and it is in a poor position to critique the death-centeredness of Western culture, despite periodic and ineffective protests against "violence."

For instance, the process of ethical reasoning in relation to traditionally male and female activities reflects entirely different concerns. When discussing reproduction, the ethical discussion has centered on why and when abortion or contraception should be prohibited, even when it might mean saving a woman's life. But when it comes to the question of how men might *take lives*, as opposed to how women might *save* their own lives, the church has focused its energies in the discussion of when, and under what circumstances, a war might be "justified."[97]

In the last several years we have become vividly aware that the nuclear industry, both in its energy and armaments departments, constitutes a substantial threat to life itself on this planet. Yet no major church has yet forbidden its members to work in these institutions or has even encouraged them to become conscientious objectors. Churches see no problem in supplying priests in activities related to war, but should it ever be asked to supply chaplains to clinics dealing with reproductive rights where agonizing decisions are daily made by women, the response would be predictable, to say the least.

In view of these different ethical attitudes toward male and female enterprises, it is clear that the sacredness of life itself is not at issue but rather the question of who might risk or take life, for what purpose, and to what end. And our cultural answer to that question can be seen in the thousands of statues, war memorials, and plaques dedicated "to those who died giving their lives for their countries." With the traditional blindspots that characterize this kind of thinking, we seldom hear how many other lives were taken in the process. "Legitimate killing" is that which takes place on behalf of the state; all other killing constitutes murder.

The ethics of the Common Good manifested in war and the state necessitate the taking of life, but in the realm of particularity, the realm of women and reproduction, only the preservation of the male seed, regardless of the social consequences, appears to be at stake. Our understanding of the sacredness of human life is conditioned by male ethics where life-risking and life-taking are tolerated, usually in support of some noble cause, and under conditions where the soldier's own willingness to die confers upon him the right to kill.

Men become heroes within a male universe where the taking or the risking of life is at issue, but women's life-risking in childbirth meets with no such acclamation. Women are, nevertheless, expected to act heroically—even at the possible sacrifice of their own lives. Their heroism, far from being an act of will (like that of the male heroes and warriors), is an act compelled by law—so that not even at the point of death in childbirth can women any longer be admitted into the realm of the rational; not even then are they permitted to have any choice in the matter. In addition, women's heroism is not to be used to change the social conditions that put them in this "no-win" situation, nor is it to be used to preserve the well-being of a woman's existing family. On the contrary, women's heroism is channelled into maintaining legalism and preserving the male seed.

In the rise of the early forms of the state, institutions like those of the vestal virgins guaranteed the purity of the state, and the only women allowed to have power in those societies were those who voluntarily abdicated sexual relations. Likewise, recent studies have indicated that women's purity, as distinct from her social context, was decisive in evaluations of her "right" to have an abortion.[98] The ideology of purity now has reached full circle, and women as a whole in contemporary society are expected to act in such a way as to prop up church and state institutions, if necessary, by some of them sacrificing their lives. The myth of the "good mother" must be maintained, and women in this situation, and pregnant teenagers in particular, act as foils and scapegoats to disguise the death dealing that has become an intrinsic part of modern statecraft.

In Hitler's Germany, where fascist ideology replaced the Christian worldview, the prevailing philosophy supported the general historical theory of the superiority of the original natural state. The "purity of the species" and the biological ideology of "naturalness" ultimately resulted in the extermination of six million Jews. The Jews provided the main scapegoat necessary for Hitler to exert his policies, but Hitler also crushed any liberal organizations, especially those that might have been supporting women's rights in the reproductive sphere.[99]

Similarly, Ronald Reagan, faced with a growing liberal, and in many cases, politically radical church, saw fit to reinstitute the scapegoat principle under the ideology of naturalness. He saw little contradiction in budgeting billions of American dollars for armaments to support American "freedom" and simultaneously initiating campaigns, euphemistically called "pro-life," that exalt the role of "motherhood" and "domesticity" and at the same time would deny women reproductive control over their own lives.

Yet the logic of the scapegoat, the ideology of naturalness, and the creation of armaments converge in a terrifying manner in one of the latest technological developments, that of the neutron bomb. This is a weapon that, while leaving buildings, offices, and factories intact, would kill all animal, human, and biological life. All that is of man, the male mind, or male technology would stand.[100] There is a direct connection between the philosophy that would keep women in their "natural state" and that which produces the neutron bomb, and there is a direct connection between the tactics of condemnation and liberation and military strategy. As one American general said, surveying the devastation of a Vietnamese village that the Americans had destroyed, "We had to destroy this village in order to save it."[101]

Perhaps these and similar statements are the ultimate blasphemy of our society. This mentality is the ultimate threat to our survival as a human race, and it has been brought about by the sacred marriage between the ideologies of church and state supporting an exclusively male-dominated technology, ethical decision-making process, and political world.

In turn, this world has depended for its existence upon the domestic and reproductive help of women. In a masterstroke of genius, male ideology has kept women at home and confined to the world of domestic decision making by arguing, alternatively, that women are evil or that they are the final repository of the sanctity of human life. The myth that women have no sense of justice or ethics has been used to keep women from having any kind of political power, and their reproduction needs to be covered by legislation lest they fail to act morally. But in the event that the tactic of feminine evil or lack of morality has been overplayed and no longer has the ability to keep women in their place, neither church nor state are above changing their strategies.

The closing message to women at the Second Vatican Council went as follows: "Women of the entire universe, you to whom life is entrusted, it is for you to save the peace of the world." Women had hardly been allowed to speak at this event, especially on the subject of saving the world. And those few women who were admitted as "observers" and who freely mingled with the delegates on the first day, found themselves relegated to a "coffee room" thereafter, ensuring that not even on the coffee breaks could their presence contaminate the purity of the decision-making process. In addition, whereas the men could drink wine to alleviate the intense Roman heat, women were restricted to coffee.[102]

THE SAFE RETURN OF THE MOTHER

Men have finally found ways to give birth: through sacrificial death. Under the guise of conquering "nature," men in reality have been conquering women. The ultimate patriarchal act, expressed in mythologies throughout the world, was matricide. Now that this fantasy has become a reality we are witnessing the primordial drama of Western culture: The Safe Return of the Mother. Not the Virgin Mary, but the motherland now becomes the focus for the displaced eroticism of the warrior class.

The cult of the mother plays an enormous role whether she appears as "Mother Ireland," "Brittania," or the "motherland." War appears to free men from the normal social restraints imposed by civilization,[103] and the reversed emphasis on the "motherland" serves to assuage the guilt and even legitimize the destructive act itself. Even where the land fought for is the "fatherland" the accompanying description of the "fatherland" leaves little doubt that the "motherland" is the true object of desire, now cloaked in "fatherland" language for fear of the accusation of incest.[104] The compensatory cult of the mother can have extremely serious effects. As a contemporary psychoanalyst argues,

A crucial factor in evil, I suspect, is not simply a regressive yearning for Mother (which can be used for healing) but rather the attempt to obtain Mother without regression—an insistence on receiving mothering without relinquishing either the adult role or any of the power associated with it.[105]

For the sake of the mother or the "motherland" one can feel justified in developing elaborate strategies of "defense" or going to extreme heroic lengths for her sake, thereby mystifying the true social or economic issues at stake.

Alongside the cult of the mother in contemporary warfare is an emphasis on the "woman at home." Small nations are depicted as defenseless women needing to be protected, while the threat of rape and the fear of the rape of one's property at home becomes a major motivating factor in encouraging men to greater and greater atrocities. According to Nancy Huston, "the more one advances into Evil, the more necessary it becomes to idealize what is Good and to safeguard its purity: purer and purer, farther and farther away from the horror, Woman reappears in the final analysis as the *ultimate cause* of war."[106]

However, the cynicism inherent in warrior propaganda was nowhere made more evident than in the "Great War" of 1914–1918. While millions of young men were slaughtered in "defense" of the freedom of a "small nation," Belgium, England had itself occupied Ireland for seven hundred years, and had often described Ireland as a woman, albeit that she was a "recalcitrant harlot" who needed John Bull (England) to bring her into line.[107]

And just as one of the most powerful Christian symbols is that of Mary standing beneath the cross on which her Son has been crucified, so too the mourning of women in modern warfare plays a vital role in affirming and reinforcing the status of the heroes as they return to the home-fires. Indeed in ancient Greece with the growth of heroic culture and the abolition of female religious rites, only the women's wailing was integrated into the religion of the city, as a fitting accompaniment to the fall of the victim in the rites of sacrifice. The mourning of women is possibly one of the goals of war, a crucial component in the warrior psyche, without which wars might be seen for what they really are.[108]

The male celibate's Virgin Mary, or the warrior's motherland both reject and accept the devouring mother, remaining forever in her power in one way or another. But this mother is essentially a male fantasy that allows men to escape their responsibility for the earth.

The killing of the mother, symbolically enacted in myth and politically enacted in patriarchal legal systems, has been made possible by the Gods of Displaced Responsibility,[109] whose priests function not by attentiveness to her needs but by obedience to the demands of hierarchy and the quest for power, fostered by the myth of the Common Good. Once a father kills his son, there is little left to add or, indeed, to live for.

In stark contrast, in our opening story, the Goddess Macha had cried to her assembled people, "A mother bore each one of you, help me in my hour of need." Macha's cry has resounded in Ireland down through the ages but never more powerfully than in the Ireland of 1988, the twentieth year of the current wave of violence. The killing by the British of the three IRA activists in Gibraltar sparked off a wave of violence in Ireland during which two young British soldiers were attacked and beaten to death by members of a funeral cortege. The soldiers were stripped and their bodies left on waste ground.

An old woman came out of the crowd, took off her coat and spread it over one of the naked bodies. And hers were, according to a Catholic priest present, "the only truly religious words" he had heard spoken on that day. For as she laid her coat over his bruised and beaten corpse, she said softly by way of explanation: "Sure God love him. He's some mother's son."

Like the old woman, the Goddess appealed to the people on the grounds of their participation in the Great Chain of Being, through their mothers. Her ethics were at once particular and universal.

The Goddess was not a goddess of power or power over but was vulnerable, dependent upon the common humanity of her people to sustain her being. She inspired reverence, not worship; cooperation, not domination; and she called for an ethics of care and responsibility, for herself and for the earth.

Her cry was possibly the last symbolic attempt to appeal to true motherhood as the basis for public social ethics. That her people ignored her meant that the values of relationship and affiliation were effete; violence, death, and the threat of death became the dominant grammar of political relationships.

Just before her death, the Goddess Macha cursed the patriarchal age that had dawned. The Goddess was effectively saying: Although you may develop sophisticated doctrines of rebirth; although you have taken to yourselves the right of life and death; although your efforts might seem logical and plausible in the light of patriarchal culture, your efforts cannot but be doomed to failure so long as they are based on the subordination of women. Speaking the language of peace and the common good with the one hand, with the other, you are calling the troops to war against women and the earth.

The philosopher Kant has argued that God is the precondition for ethics. But in the light of the curse of Macha, a curse that hangs over us today, we could argue the opposite: care for the preservation of the earth and all her children must now become the precondition for, and the ultimate test, of any ethical system or knowledge of God.

Abbreviations

AFM   *Annala Rioghachta Eireann: Annals of the Kingdom of Ireland by the Four Masters,* ed. J. O'Donovan, 7 vols. (Dublin, 1848–51).

ALI   *Ancient Laws and Institutes of Ireland,* Rolls Series, 6 vols. (Dublin, 1865–1901).

AIT   *Ancient Irish Tales,* ed. T. P. Cross and C. H. Slover (New York: Barnes and Noble, 1969).

AJA   *American Journal of Archaeology.*

ALC   *Annals of Loch Cé: A Chronicle of Irish Affairs, 1014–1590.* ed. W. M. Hennessy, 2 vols. (London, 1871; reflex facs., Dublin: Irish Manuscripts Commission, 1939).

AS   *Acta Sanctorum,* ed. Johannes Bollandus and Godefridus Henschenius, Februarii tomus primus (Paris: Victor Palme, 1863).

AU   *Annals of Ulster,* ed. W. M. Hennessy and B. MacCarthy, 4 vols. (Dublin, 1887–1901).

BB   *Bethu Brigte,* ed. Donncha Ó hAodha (Dublin: Institute for Advanced Studies, 1978).

BD   *Bodleian Dindshenchas,* ed. Whitley Stokes, *Folklore* 3 (1892): 467–516.

Bede   *Bede, Historia Ecclesiastica Gentis Anglorum: A History of the English Church and People,* trans. Leo Sherley-Price (Harmondsworth, Middlesex: Penguin Books, 1974).

BH   *Book of Hymns of the Ancient Church of Ireland,* ed. J. H. Todd, 2 vols. (Dublin: Irish Archaeological and Celtic Society, 1855, 1867).

BNE   *Bethada Náem nÉrenn: Lives of Irish Saints,* ed. and trans. Charles Plummer, 2 vols. (London: Oxford University Press, 1922).

Cal Oeng   *The Calender of Oengus,* ed. Whitley Stokes (Dublin: Transactions of the Royal Irish Academy, vol. 1, 1880).

CG   *Carmina Gadelica,* ed. Alexander Carmichael, 2 vols. (Edinburgh: Constable, 1900).

CHJ   *Cambridge Historical Journal.*

CMCS   *Cambridge Medieval Celtic Studies.*

CSR   *Celtic and Scandinavian Religions,* John A. MacCulloch (London: Hutchinson, 1948).

EC   *Études Celtiques.*

ED   *Edinburgh Dindshenchas,* ed. Whitley Stokes, *Folklore* 4 (1893): 471–97.

EIHM   *Early Irish History and Mythology,* T. F. O'Rahilly (1946; reprint, Dublin: Institute for Advanced Studies, 1957).

FF   *Foras Feasa ar Éirinn* (History of Ireland), by Geoffrey Keating, ed. David Comyn, 4 vols. (1901–1914; reprint, London: Irish Texts Society, 1987).

FL   *Folklore.*

Gerald	*Gerald of Wales: The History and Topography of Ireland,* ed. John J. O'Meara (Harmondworth, Middlesex: Penguin Books, 1982).
IER	*Irish Ecclesiastical Record.*
IHS	*Irish Historical Studies.*
IMC	*Irish Mythological Cycle and Celtic Mythology,* H. d'Arbois de Jubainville, trans. R. I. Best (New York, 1903).
JAAR	*Journal of the American Academy of Religion.*
JBL	*Journal of Biblical Literature.*
JCHAS	*Journal of the Cork Archaeological and Celtic Society.*
JEH	*Journal of Ecclesiastical History.*
JGHAS	*Journal of the Galway Historical and Archaeological Society.*
JKAS	*Journal of the Kildare Archaeological Society.*
JRSAI	*Journal of the Royal Society of Antiquaries of Ireland.*
LH	*Liber Hymnorum,* ed. R. Atkinson and J. H. Bernard, 2 vols. (London: Henry Bradshaw Society, 1898).
LGE	*Lebor Gabála Erenn,* ed. R. A. S. MacAlister, 5 pts. (Dublin: Irish Texts Society, nos. 34, 35, 39, 41, 44, 1938–56).
Lis Lives	*Lives of Saints from the Book of Lismore,* Anecdota Oxoniensia Medieval and Modern Series no. 5 (Oxford: Clarendon Press, 1890).
Mart Don	*Martyrology of Donegal,* collected by Michael O'Clery, ed. J. H. Todd and Wm. Reeves (Dublin: Irish Archaeological and Celtic Society, 1864).

Mart Oeng	*Félire Oengusso: The Martyrology of Oengus the Culdee,* ed. Whitley Stokes, 2d ed. (London: Henry Bradshaw Society, 1905).
MDs	*The Metrical Dindshenchas,* ed. E. J. Gwynn, *Todd Lecture Series: Royal Irish Academy* 7 (1900): 1–95; 8 (1903): 1–82; 9 (1906): 2–108; 10 (1913): 2–460; 11 (1924): 1–314.
PBA	*Proceedings of the British Academy.*
Penit	*The Irish Penitentials,* ed. Ludwig Bieler (Dublin: Institute for Advanced Studies, 1963).
Peritia	*Journal of the Medieval Academy of Ireland.*
PMLA	*Proceedings of the Modern Language Association.*
PRIA	*Proceedings of the Royal Irish Academy.*
RAC	*Religion of the Ancient Celts,* J. A. MacCulloch (Edinburgh: T. & T. Clark, 1911).
RC	*Revue Celtique.*
Ren Dind	*The Prose Tales in the Rennes Dindshenchas,* ed. Whitley Stokes, *Revue Celtique* 15 (1894): 273–336, 418–84; 16 (1895): 31–83, 134–67, 269–312.
SEIL	*Studies in Early Irish Law,* ed. Rudolph Thurneysen et al. (Dublin: Dublin Institute for Advanced Studies, 1936).
SG	*Silva Gadelica,* ed. S. H. O'Grady, 2 vols. (London: Williams and Norgate, 1892).

Sources   The Sources for the Early History of Ireland, James F. Kenney (1929; reprint, New York: Octagon Books, with additions by L. Bieler, 1966).

Stud Hib   Studia Hibernica.

The Táin   The Táin, ed. Thomas Kinsella (London: Oxford University Press, 1970).

Thes Pal   Thesaurus Paleohibernicus: A Collection of Old-Irish Glosses, Scholia, Prose and Verse, ed. Wh. Stokes and John Strachan, 2 vols. (London: Cambridge University Press, 1903).

TLSRIA   Todd Lecture Series, Royal Irish Academy.

TOS   Transactions of the Ossianic Society.

TRIA   Transactions of the Royal Irish Academy.

VSH   Vitae Sanctorum Hiberniae, ed. Charles Plummer, 2 vols. (Oxford: Oxford University Press, 1910).

ZAW   Zeitschrift für die Alttestamentliche Wissenschaft.

ZCP   Zeitschrift für Celtische Philologie.

Notes

Author's note: In the Irish texts the editor is almost invariably the translator and is not specifically credited as such. In journal references, the first page numbers are the inclusive page numbers of the article, and the second, the page or pages cited.

Preface

1. Desmond Wilson, *An End to Silence* (Cork: Mercier Press, 1985), p. 11.
2. René Girard, *Violence and the Sacred*, trans. Patrick Gregory (Baltimore: Johns Hopkins, 1977), p. 249.
3. Cf. Wilson, *End to Silence*, p. 10.
4. John V. Kelleher, "Early Irish History and Pseudo-History," *Studia Hibernica* 3 (1963): 113–27, 127.
5. Cf. Klaus Theweleit, *Male Fantasies*, trans. Stephen Conway in collaboration with Erica Carter and Chris Turner (Minneapolis: University of Minnesota, 1987); Sheila Briggs, "Images of Women and Jews in Nineteenth and Twentieth Century German Theology," in *Immaculate and Powerful: The Female in Sacred Image and Social Reality*, ed. Clarissa Atkinson et al. (Boston: Beacon Press, 1985), pp. 226–59.
6. T. Altizer and W. Hamilton, *Radical Theology and the Death of God* (Baltimore: Penguin Books, 1968), p. 55.
7. For instance, in "The Age of Eve" I will be dealing with material such as the "Pangs of Ulster" story, which is ostensibly pre-Christian but which probably reached its final form at the hands of the Christian monastic scribes.
8. Monica Sjöö and Barbara Mor, *The Great Cosmic Mother: Rediscovering the Religion of the Earth* (San Francisco: Harper & Row, 1987), p. 180.

Introduction

1. Mary O'Brien, *The Politics of Reproduction* (London: Routledge & Kegan Paul, 1981), p. 53.
2. For an introduction to the nature/culture debate, see Sherry B. Ortner, "Is Female to Male as Nature Is to Culture?" in *Woman, Culture and Society*, ed. Michelle Rosaldo and Louise Lamphere (Stanford, CA: Stanford University Press, 1974), pp. 67–88; *Sexual Meanings: The Social Construction of Gender and Sexuality*, ed. Sherry B. Ortner and Harriet Whitehead (New York: Cambridge University Press, 1981), pp. 7–17. For a review of Ortner's position, see Peggy Sanday, *Female Power and Male Dominance* (New York: Cambridge University Press, 1981), p. 176. Most scholars recognize that the nature/culture division is essentially a political one that relegates women to private forms of power, leaving men free to act in the prestigious public world. Cf. Susan Carol Rogers, "Female forms of power and the myth of male dominance: a model of female/male interaction in peasant society," *American Ethnologist* 2 (1975): 727–56; cf. also Carol P. MacCormack, "Nature, Culture and Gender: A Critique," in *Nature, Culture and Gender*, ed. Carol P. MacCormack and Marilyn Strathern (New York: Cambridge University Press, 1980); Nicole Mathieu, "Man-culture and woman-nature?" *Women's Studies International Quarterly* 1, no. 1 (1978): 55–65.
3. Donncha Ó Corráin, "Historical Need and Literary Narrative," *Proceedings of the International Congress of Celtic Studies* (Oxford, 1983): 142–58, 153.
4. For an annotated source book of these stories, see Martin McNamara, ed., *The Apocrypha in the Irish Church* (Dublin: Institute for Advanced Studies, 1975).
5. The main bibliographical sources for the study of early Irish history and mythology are as follows: R. I. Best, *Bibliography of Irish Philology*, 2 vols. (Dublin: Insti-

tute for Advanced Studies, 1913, 1942); James F. Kenney, *The Sources for the Early History of Ireland*, vol. 1 (1929; reprinted with addendum by L. Bieler, New York: Octagon Books, 1966); Charles Donahue, "Medieval Celtic Literature," in *The Medieval Literature of Western Europe: A Review of Research*, ed. John H. Fisher (New York: New York University Press, for the Modern Language Association, 1966), pp. 381–98; Rachel Bromwich, *Medieval Celtic Literature: A Select Bibliography* (Toronto: University of Toronto Press, 1974); Richard James Hayes, *Sources for the History of Irish Civilization* (Boston: G. K. Hall, 1965; first supplement 1979); Anna Brady, *Women in Ireland: An Annotated Bibliography* (CT: Greenwood Press, Westport 1988).

6. *LGE* pt. 2, p. 176ff. Cf. also John Carey, "Origin and Development of the Cessair Legend," *Éigse* 22 (1987): 37–48.

7. Cf. Kuno Meyer, "The Death Tales of the Ulster Heroes," *TLSRIA* 19 (1906): i–vii, 1–52, 15ff; cf. also discussion in Daniel Melia, "Remarks on the Structure and Composition of the Ulster Death Tales," *Studia Hibernica* 17 (1977): 36–57, 52ff.

8. *FF*, 3:34.

9. Quoted in Gerard Murphy, *Early Irish Lyrics* (Oxford: Clarendon Press, 1962), p. 71.

10. F. J. Byrne, "Tribes and Tribalism in Early Ireland," *Ériu* 22 (1971): 128–66, 165.

11. Cf. P. O'Leary, "Verbal Deceit in the Ulster Cycle," *Éigse* 21 (1986): 16–26. Cf. also John V. Kelleher, "Early Irish History and Pseudo-history," *Studia Hibernica* 3 (1963): 113–27.

12. *FF*, 3:33.

13. Cf. Paul Walsh, *The Four Masters and Their Work* (Dublin: At the Sign of the Three Candles Press, 1944).

14. Cf. *ALC*, 1:265. For discussion of further omissions, see 1:xli–xlii.

15. For a fairly comprehensive bibliography of the American works of this movement, see Anne Carr, *Transforming Grace: Christian Tradition and Women's Experience* (San Francisco: Harper & Row, 1988), pp. 245–66.

16. Nelle Morton, *The Journey Is Home* (Boston: Beacon Press, 1985), p. 82.

17. Gayatri Chakravorty Spivak, "Scattered Speculations on the Question of Value," *Diacritics* (1985): 73–93, 74.

18. See *The Bible and Liberation: Political and Social Hermeneutics*, ed. N. K. Gottwald and A. C. Wire (Berkeley: Radical Religion Reader, 1976); Sergio Rostagno, *Essays on the New Testament: A Materialist Approach*, trans. Dave Macey (Geneva: World Student Christian Federation, c. 1974); José Miranda, *Marx and the Bible: A Critique of the Philosophy of Oppression*, trans. John Eagleson (Maryknoll, NY: Orbis Press, 1974); N. K. Gottwald, *The Tribes of Yahweh* (Maryknoll, NY: Orbis Press, 1979); Elisabeth Schüssler Fiorenza, *Bread Not Stone: The Challenge of Feminist Biblical Interpretation* (Boston: Beacon Press, 1984).

19. For an attempt to solve the problems of historical relativity in relation to theology, see R. Morgan and M. Pye, *Ernst Troeltsch: Writings on Theology and Religion* (London: Duckworth, 1977); Ganse Little, "Ernst Troeltch and the Scope of Historicism," *Journal of Religion* 46, no. 3 (1966): 343–64.

20. Schüssler Fiorenza, *Bread Not Stone*, p. 57.

21. Ibid., p. xiii.

22. Ibid., p. 57.

23. Morton, *The Journey*, p. xxii.

24. Cf. Martin J. Sherwin, *A World Destroyed: The Atomic Bomb and the Grand Alliance* (New York: Random House, Vintage Books, 1977), p. 193ff.

25. Cf. Robyn Rowland, "Of Women Born," in *Personally Speaking*, ed. Liz Steiner-Scott (Dublin: Attic Press, 1985), pp. 267–85.

26. Cf. Monique Wittig, "The Mark of Gender," in *Poetics of Gender*, ed. Nancy Miller (New York: Columbia University Press, 1986), pp. 63–73, pp. 66–69; Colette Guillaumin, "The Practice of Power and Belief in Nature," part 1, *Feminist Issues*

(Winter 1981): 3–28, 5. Cf. also part 2, *Feminist Issues* (Summer 1981): 87–109.

27. Cf. Barbara Godard, "Re-drawing the Circle: Power, Poetics and Language," *Canadian Journal of Political and Social Theory* 9, nos. 1–2 (1985): 165–81, 165; Janet Sayers, "Feminism and Science: Reason and Passion," *Women's Studies International Forum* 10, no. 2 (1987): 171–79; Elizabeth Fee, "Is Feminism a Threat to Scientific Objectivity?" *International Journal of Women's Studies* 4 (1981): 378–92. Cf. also *Discovering Reality: Feminist Perspectives on Epistemology, Metaphysics, Methodology, and the Philosophy of Science,* ed. Sandra Harding and Merrill Hintikka (Dordrecht, Holland: Reidel Publishing, 1983).

28. For an overview of the problems inherent in feminist historiography, see essays in *Liberating Women's History: Theoretical and Critical Essays,* ed. Berenice Carroll (Chicago: University of Chicago Press, 1976); Carroll Smith-Rosenberg, "The New Woman and the New History," *Feminist Studies* 3 (1975): 185–98; Joan Kelly-Gadol, "The Social Relation of the Sexes: Methodological Implications of Women in History," *Signs* 1 (1976): 809–23.

29. Cf. Peggy Kamuf, "Writing Like a Woman," in *Women and Language in Literature and Society,* ed. Sally McConnell-Ginet, Ruth Borker, and Nelly Furman (New York: Praeger, 1980), pp. 284–99, p. 286.

30. Spivak, "Scattered Speculations," p. 74.

31. For a feminist approach to the reading of texts that goes beyond the establishment of a new "logic of domination," see Pamela McCallum, "New Feminist Readings: Woman as *Ecriture,* or Woman as Other?" *Canadian Journal of Political and Social Theory* 9, nos. 1–2 (1985): 127–32; Patrocinio Schweickhart, "What Are We Doing Really? Feminist Criticism and the Problem of Theory," *Canadian Journal of Political and Social Theory* 9, nos. 1–2 (1985): 148–64. Cf. also *Essays on Women, Literature and Theory,* ed. Elaine Showalter (New York: Pantheon, 1985); *Making a Difference: Feminist Literary Criticism,* ed. Gayle Greene and Coppelia Kahn (New York: Methuen, 1985); *The Poetics of Gender,* ed. Miller, especially Domna C. Stanton, "Difference on Trial," pp. 157–82; *Gender and Reading,* ed. Elizabeth A. Flynn and Patrocinio P. Schweickart (Baltimore: Johns Hopkins University Press, 1986).

32. For the relationship between sexual liberation and new forms of social control, see Margaret Jackson, "Sexual Liberation or Social Control?" *Women's Studies International Forum* 6, no. 1 (1983): 1–17.

33. Joan Kelly-Godol, "Did Women Have a Renaissance?" in *Becoming Visible: Women in European History,* ed. Renate Bridenthal and Claudia Koonz (Boston: Houghton Mifflin, 1977), pp. 137–64, p. 146. Cf. also Barbara Ehrenreich, *The Hearts of Men* (Garden City, NY: Anchor Press, 1983), for further elaboration on the relationship between the needs of patriarchal culture and "women's liberation." For an analysis of this problem within French feminist theory, see Alice Jardine, *Gynesis: Configurations of Women and Modernity* (Ithaca, NY: Cornell University Press, 1985), and "Opaque Texts and Transparent Contexts: The Political Difference of Julia Kristeva," in *The Poetics of Gender,* ed. Miller, pp. 96–116.

34. O'Brien, *Politics of Reproduction,* p. 23.

35. The term is derived from the works of the French psychoanalyst Jacques Lacan.

Chapter 1. Eve and the Serpent

Epigraph: From *A Celtic Psaltery,* ed. Alfred Perceval Graves (London: S.P.C.K., 1917). For a more literal translation, see K. Meyer, "Eve's Lament," *Ériu* 3 (1907): 148.

1. Genesis 3. Biblical quotations from *The Jerusalem Bible* (London: Darton, Longman & Todd, 1966).

2. Gen. 3:16.

3. Gen. 3:6.

4. Cf. Donal Flanagan, "Women: Eve and Mary," in *For the Banished Children of Eve,* ed. M. Condren (Dublin: S. C. M. Publications, 1976), pp. 14–15. Cf. also Rose-

mary Radford Ruether, *Mary—The Feminine Face of the Church* (Philadelphia: Westminster Press, 1979).

5. For a discussion of these themes, see Jean Higgins, "The Myth of Eve: The Temptress," *Journal of the American Academy of Religion* 44 (1976): 639–47, 640; John A. Phillips, *Eve: The History of an Idea* (New York: Harper & Row, 1984). Yet for an alternative patristic view of the role of women in this story, which did not gain general credence, see Jean M. Higgins, "Anastasius Sinaita and the Superiority of the Woman," *JBL* 97, no. 2 (1978): 253–56.

6. Heinrich Kramer and James Sprenger, *Malleus Maleficarum*, pt. 1, question 6, trans. Montague Summers, (1486; reprint, New York: Dover Books, 1971), p. 44.

7. Eric Robertson, *The Bible's Prose Epic of Eve and Her Sons* (London: Williams and Norgate, 1916), p. 35ff. Cited in Higgins, "The Myth of Eve," p. 641.

8. Cf. Higgins, "The Myth of Eve," p. 643ff.

9. As recently as 1959, Pope Pius XII told a meeting of obstetricians, "Even the pains that, since original sin, a mother has to suffer to give birth to her child only draw tighter the bonds that bind them: she loves it the more, the more pain it has cost her." Pope Pius XII, "Address to Obstetricians" (October 29, 1951). Cited in Mary Daly, *The Church and the Second Sex* (New York: Harper & Row, 1975), p. 114. For a history of the legacy of this attitude to women, see Barbara Ehrenreich and Deirdre English, *For Her Own Good: 150 years of the Expert's Advice to Women* (Garden City, NY: Anchor Day Press, 1979).

10. Gen. 3:22–24.

11. In treating the story of "Adam and Eve" I am aware that the present composition of the Book of Genesis is made up of several editorial strands that have been put together to form a composite whole. This partly accounts for some of the contradictions in the story, but the fact that the various strands have held together in their present form for so long testifies to the fact that the present story is the one that best reflects the thinking of the canonical editors. For an account of the various strands that go into the making of the Book of Genesis, see Martin Noth, *A History of Pentateuchal Traditions* (Englewood Cliffs, NJ: Prentice-Hall, 1972), pp. 228–61.

12. Some scholars treat these stories in a more positive light. Cf., for instance, Phyllis Trible, *God and the Rhetoric of Sexuality* (Philadelphia: Fortress Press, 1978); Trible, "Depatriarchalizing in Biblical Interpretation," *JAAR* 41 (1973): 30–48; cf. also John A. Bailey, "Initiation and the Primal Woman in Gilgamesh and Genesis 2–3," *JBL* 89 (1970): 137–50.

13. Cf. A. J. Williams, "The Relationship of Genesis 3:20 to the Serpent," *ZAW* 89, no. 3 (1977): 357–74.

14. Cf. Gerhard Von Rad, *Genesis* (Philadelphia: Westminster Press, 1961), p. 93.

15. For a recent treatment of this question from a Jewish perspective, see Jacqueline Tabick, "The Snake in the Grass," *Religion* 16 (1986): 155–67.

16. Cf. S. N. Kramer, *The Sumerians: Their History, Culture and Character* (Chicago: University of Chicago Press, 1963), pp. 291–92.

17. Cf. T. Jacobsen, *The Treasures of Darkness* (New Haven, CT: Yale University Press, 1976), p. 214.

18. Cf. A. L. Frothingham, "Medusa, Apollo and the Great Mother," *AJA* 15, no. 3 (1911): 349–77; A. L. Frothingham, "Medusa 11," *AJA* 19, no. 1 (1915): 13–23; Georges Roux, *Ancient Iraq* (London: Allen & Unwin, 1964), p. 69; Mircea Eliade, *Patterns in Comparative Religion* (New York: Sheed and Ward, 1958), p. 169; Joseph Campbell, *The Mythic Image* (Princeton, NJ: Princeton University Press, 1974), pp. 281–301; M. Esther Harding, *Woman's Mysteries: Ancient and Modern* (New York: Harper & Row, 1971), pp. 52–54; Monica Sjöö and Barbara Mor, *The Great Cosmic Mother: Rediscovering the Religion of the Earth* (San Francisco: Harper & Row, 1987), pp. 100, 155, 268; Riane Eisler, *The Chalice and the Blade: Our History Our Future* (San Francisco: Harper & Row, 1987), pp. 21, 86–87.

19. K. Joines, *Serpent Symbolism in the Old Testament* (Haddonfield, NJ: Haddonfield House, 1974), p. 20.

20. Kramer, *The Sumerians*, p. 122.
21. S. H. Langdon, *Semitic Mythology*, vol. 5 of *Mythology of All Races*, ed. L. H. Gray (Boston: Marshall Jones, 1931), p. 91; Edith Porada, "Remarks on Mitannian (Hurrian) and Middle Assyrian Glyptic Art," *Akkadica* 13 (1979): 2–15; Briggs Buchanan, "A Snake Goddess and Her Companions: A Problem in the Iconography of the Early 2nd Millennium B.C.," *Iraq* 33 (1971): 1–18, 12–13. I am grateful to Prof. Jo Ann Hackett for these references.
22. Cited in Joines, *Serpent Symbolism*, p. 48.
23. Cf. Joines, *Serpent Symbolism*, p. 111.
24. Ibid., p. 19.
25. K. Joines, "The Serpent in Genesis 3," *ZAW* 87 (1975): 1–11.
26. Cf. Mircea Eliade, *Comparative Religion*, p. 289ff. Also see A. H. Sayce, "Archaeology of the Book of Genesis," *Expository Times* 19 (1907–8): 137–39, 176–78, 260–63, 326–27; vol. 20 (1909): 327–28, 423–26, 470–72, 505–9; A. H. Sayce, "The Serpent in Genesis," *Expository Times* 20 (1909): 562.
27. *Book of the Dead*, ed. C. H. Davies (London, 1984). Cited in Joines, *Serpent Symbolism*, p. 97.
28. *The Babylonian Genesis*, ed. A. Heidel (Chicago: University of Chicago Press, 1951), p. 125.
29. Joines, *Serpent Symbolism*, p. 47.
30. Cf. Sylvia Brinton Perera, *Descent to the Goddess: A Way of Initiation for Women* (Toronto: Inner City Books, 1981), pp. 9–34; Christine Downing, *The Goddess: Mythological Images of the Feminine* (New York: Crossroad, 1981), pp. 12–13; Diane Wolkstein and Samuel N. Kramer, *Inanna: Queen of Heaven and Earth* (New York: Harper & Row, 1983), p. 169.
31. Cf. O. Th. Obbink, "The Tree of Life in Eden," *ZAW* 46 (1928): 105–12; Wolkstein and Kramer, *Inanna*, p. 145, for the Tree of Life representing the opposing natural forces.
32. J. MacCulloch, *Celtic*, vol. 3 of *Mythology of All Races*, ed. L. H. Gray (Boston: Marshall Jones, 1918), p. 131.
33. Cf. Kramer, *The Sumerians*, p. 198ff.; MacCulloch, *Celtic*, p. 131.
34. For the origins and genealogy of Ninhursag, see Wolkstein and Kramer, *Inanna*, pp. x–xi, 123.
35. Langdon, *Semitic*, pp. 91, 111.
36. Cf. Jacobsen, *Treasures of Darkness*, p. 113.
37. Cf. S. N. Kramer, "Enki and Ninhursag," *Bulletin of the American School of Oriental Research*, supplementary studies (1945). The story may represent one of the first mythological attempts to wrest control of procreation from the female deity. As Sumer increasingly became centralized and militarized, Enki supplanted Ninhursag almost entirely. Cf. Jacobsen, *Treasures of Darkness*, p. 109.
38. Von Rad, *Genesis*, p. 85; Joines, *Serpent Symbolism*, p. 2ff.
39. One of the interesting features of the Ninhursag story is that the Sumerian word for "rib" is *ti*. The goddess created for the healing of Enki's rib was, therefore, called Nin-ti, the "Lady of the Rib." Kramer, *The Sumerians*, p. 149. But since the Sumerian word *ti* also means to "make live" as well as the "Lady of the Rib," this concept merged to become the "Lady who makes live." Nintu, or Ninti, often took the form of a serpent.
40. Gen. 3:4–5.
41. Gen. 3:14.
42. Cf. Kramer, *The Sumerians*, p. 148; S. N. Kramer, *Sumerian Mythology* (Philadelphia: American Philosophical Society, 1944), p. 55; MacCulloch, *Celtic*, p. 185.
43. Cf. J. McKenzie, "The Literary Characteristics of Genesis 2–3," *Theological Studies* 15 (1954): 541–65.
44. Cf. Joines, *Serpent Symbolism*, p. 31.
45. O. Eissfeldt, *The Old Testament: An Introduction* (New York: Harper & Row, 1965), p. 208.
46. P. F. Ellis, *The Yahwist: The Bible's First Theologian* (Notre Dame, IN: Fides Publish-

ers, 1968), p. 64ff.

47. Cf. 1 Kings 11.

48. Cf. Joines, *Serpent Symbolism*, pp. 102–3; S. H. Langdon, *Tammuz and Ishtar* (Oxford: Clarendon Press, 1914), pp. 114–28.

49. Ellis, *The Yahwist*, p. 64.

50. Joines, *Serpent Symbolism*, p. 102.

51. 2 Kings 18:4.

52. Num. 21:8–9.

53. Cf. Eisler, *Chalice and the Blade*, p. 88.

54. Book of Wisdom 16:6–7.

55. 2 Kings 18:4.

56. Cf. John Bright, *A History of Israel* (London: S.C.M. Press, 1960), p. 92.

57. Ibid., p. 93.

58. Ibid., p. 136.

59. Ibid., p. 143; Jo Ann Hackett, "In the Days of Jael: Reclaiming the History of Women in Ancient Israel," in *Immaculate and Powerful: The Female in Sacred Image and Social Reality*, ed. Clarissa Atkinson et al. (Boston: Beacon Press, 1985), pp. 15–38.

60. Bright, *History of Israel*, p. 159. For a discussion of the significance of Deborah, see Hackett, "In the Days of Jael," pp. 24–27, 32.

61. Cf. Judg. 12:1–6; Hackett, "In the Days of Jael," p. 37.

62. For evidence of incessant warfare, see H. Liebowitz, "Military and Feast Scenes on Late Bronze Palestinian Ivories," *Israel Exploration Journal* 30 (1980): 162–69; A. Malamat, *Early Israelite Warfare and the Conquest of Canaan* (New York: Oxford University Press, 1978).

63. Bright, *History of Israel*, p. 165.

64. 1 Sam. 10:5–13; 19:18–24; Bright, *History of Israel*, p. 166.

65. Cf. Gideon's rejection of a crown and Jotham's sarcastic fable, Judg. 8:22; 9:7–21.

66. Cf. discussion in 1 Samuel, chaps. 8–13.

67. Cf. H. Frankfort, *Kingship and the Gods* (Chicago: University of Chicago Press, 1948), pp. 215–30.

68. For a discussion of the relationship between centralized and militarized forms of government and the exclusion of women from hierarchies, see Elise Boulding, *The Underside of History* (Boulder, CO: Westview Press, 1976), pp. 182–83; Joan Kelly-Gadol, "The Social Relation of the Sexes: Methodological Implications of Women's History," *Signs* 1, no. 4 (1976): 809–23; Jackie Di Salvo, "Class, Gender and Religion: A Theoretical Overview and Some Political Implications," *Womanspirit Bonding*, ed. Janet Kalven and Mary Buckley (New York: Pilgrim Press, 1984), pp. 11–34; Judith Ochshorn, *Female Experience and the Nature of the Divine* (Bloomington, IN: Indiana University Press, 1981), pp. 136–37; Ruby Rohrlich, "State Formation in Sumer and the Subjugation of Women," *Feminist Studies* 6, no. 1 (1980): 76–102.

69. Exod. 34:10–15.

70. Some commentators identify the Serpent with the Devil, but the image of the Devil did not come into Judaism until much later, after the Babylonian Exile of the Israelites, which took place four centuries after Genesis had been written. Cf. Joines, *Serpent Symbolism*, pp. 26–27; O. Wintermute, "Serpent" in *Interpreter's Dictionary of the Bible*, supplementary volume (Nashville: Abingdon Press, 1976), p. 817.

71. It was not the case that the polytheistic religions had no ethical consciousness. See Kramer, *The Sumerians*, p. 124.

72. Cf. *The Babylonian Genesis*, ed. Heidel, p. 37.

73. J. H. Breasted, *The Dawn of Conscience* (New York: Scribner, 1933), pp. 34–35. Cited in Amaury de Riencourt, *Sex and Power in History* (New York: Delta, 1974), p. 39.

74. Cf. de Riencourt, *Sex and Power in History*, p. 39. Cf. also Ochshorn, *Female Experi-

ence, pp. 139–40, for creation by word rather than body.
75. Ochshorn, *Female Experience,* p. 38.
76. Ibid., p. 129.
77. Leviticus 12; cf. discussion in Ochshorn, *Female Experience,* p. 210.
78. Cf. Carol Meyers, "Procreation, Production, and Protection: Male-Female Balance in Early Israel," *JAAR* 51, no. 4 (1983): 569–93, 571; Ochshorn, *Female Experience,* p. 182.
79. Cf. Hackett, "In the Days of Jael," pp. 16–29.
80. Cf. Ochshorn, *Female Experience,* pp. 190–91.
81. From the Jerusalem Bible notes to Exod. 19:15.
82. 1 Sam. 21:5–6.
83. For fascinating discussions of the matricentered nature of early Judaism, see David Bakan, *And They Took Themselves Wives: The Emergence of Patriarchy in Western Civilization* (San Francisco: Harper & Row, 1979); Savina J. Teubal, *Sarah the Priestess: The First Matriarch of Genesis* (Athens, OH: Swallow Press, 1984); Nancy Jay, "Sacrifice, Descent and the Patriarchs," *Vetus Testamentum* 38 (1988): 52–70.
84. Judg. 19:23–25.
85. Judg. 21:19–24.
86. Judg. 19:24, Jerusalem Bible, note h, p. 335.
87. Judg. 11:30–31.
88. Judg. 11:35–38.
89. Judg. 11:39–40.
90. Gen. 22:2.
91. Louis Ginzberg, *The Legends of the Jews* (Philadelphia: Jewish Publishing Company, 1954), 1:278.
92. Cf. Gen. 15:4, 5, 18; 17:7; for discussion of this theme see Gerda Lerner, *Creation of Patriarchy* (New York: Oxford University Press, 1986), 189–91.

Chapter 2. Crushing the Serpent

Epigraph: From *Bede,* pp. 127–28 (emphasis added).
1. Cf. T. P. O'Nolan, "Mór of Muster and the Tragic Fate of Cuanu Son of Cailchin," *PRIA* 30 (1912): 261–82; Tomás Ó Máille, "Medb Chruachna," *ZCP* 17 (1928): 129–46; A. K. Coomaraswamy, "On the Loathly Bride," *Speculum* 20 (1945): 391–404; Brian O Cuív, "The Romance of Mis and Dubh Rois," *Celtica* 2 (1954): 325–33; R. A. Breathnach, "The Lady and the King," *Studies* 42 (1953): 321–36; Proinsias Mac Cana, "The Theme of King and Goddess in Irish Literature," *EC* 7 (1955): 76–114, 356–413, and 8 (1958): 59–65; G. F. Dalton, "The Loathly Lady: A Suggested Interpretation," *Folklore* 82 (1971): 124–31; Muireann Ní Bhrolcháin, "Women in Early Irish Myths and Sagas," *Crane Bag* 4, no. 1 (1980): 12–19; cf. also Máire Breathnach, "The Sovereignty Goddess as Goddess of Death," *ZCP* 39 (1982): 243–60; W. Ann Trindade, "Irish Gormlaith as a Sovereignty Figure," *EC* 23 (1986): 143–56, for the persistence of the theme of "king and goddess" in the later Middle Ages.
2. Cf. Philip O'Leary, "A Foreseeing Driver of an Old Chariot: Royal Moderation in Early Irish Literature," *CMCS* 1 (1986): 1–16.
3. *The Pursuit of Gruaidh Ghrian-Sholus,* ed. Cecile O'Rahilly, Irish Texts Series No. 24 (Dublin: Irish Texts Society, 1924), p. 103.
4. Cf. *IMC,* p. 230; *AIT,* p. 352.
5. St. Patrick has traditionally been credited with banishing the snakes from Ireland. Cf. Alexander H. Krappe, "St. Patrick and the Snakes," *Traditio* 5 (1947): 323–30, but in reality a full-scale war had been declared on the serpent long before Patrick ever arrived. Cf. Dáithí Ó hÓgáin, *The Hero in Folk-History* (New York: St. Martin's Press, 1985), p. 58; Liam de Paor, "Saint Mac Creiche of Liscannor," *Ériu* 30 (1979): 93–121, 9; cf. also *EIHM,* pp. 319–33, for serpent imagery in Irish mythology.
6. Cf. Géza Róheim, "The Dragon and the Hero," *American Imago* 1, no. 2 (1939):

41–69; pt. 2, 1, no. 3 (1940): 61–94; cf also Diane Wolkstein and Samuel N. Kramer, *Inanna: Queen of Heaven and Earth* (New York: Harper & Row, 1983); see Monica Sjöö and Barbara Mor, *The Great Cosmic Mother: Rediscovering the Religion of the Earth* (San Francisco: Harper & Row, 1987), pp. 58, 61, 107, 155, 250, 255.

7. In Irish mythology no central myth of cosmogony appears to have survived. The violence against the original Mother Goddess, characteristic of ancient Mesopotamian myths of origins, is reserved for those elusive figures in the *Dindshenchas*, most of whom do not appear in their own right but only in the stories of their overthrow. Often they are made out to be mortal beings merely in order that they may be drowned. Cf. *EIHM*, p. 310.

On the other hand, there are several stories of "origins" indicating either a gradual absorption of new religions or "agreements" made between the opposing forces. Cf. "Intoxication of the Ultonians," ed. Wm. Hennessy, *TLSRIA*, series 1, vol. 1 (1889): i–xvi, 1–58, 3; "Altram Tige Dá Medar," ed. Lillian Duncan, *Ériu* 11, no. 2 (1932): 184–225; *LGE*, pt. 2:177, 185, 197; R. A. S. MacAlister, *Tara: A Pagan Sanctuary* (New York: C. Scribner's Sons, 1931), pp. 82–124; Frank O'Connor, *A Backward Look* (London: Macmillan, 1967), pp. 21, 43–44.

8. Cf. J. A. MacCulloch, "Serpent Worship," *Encyclopedia of Religion and Ethics*, ed. James Hastings (New York and Edinburgh, 1920), 11:399. For a discussion of the heroes overcoming, cheating, or defeating the Serpent or the "salmon of wisdom," see *EIHM*, pp. 319–33; de Paor, "Saint Mac Creiche," for several stories of men finding liberation from finding key in salmon's belly; *IMC*, p. 217; J. F. Campbell, *The Celtic Dragon Myth*, trans. George Henderson (Edinburgh: J. Grant, 1911); *Táin Bó Fraich*, ed. J. O'Beirne Crowe, Royal Irish Academy, Irish Mss. Series 1:1 (1870).

Significantly, a fourth-century king of Ireland, Cormac Mac Airt, is said to have rejected the old religion and was punished for this by choking, appropriately enough, on a salmon bone. Cf. *FF*, 2:347.

9. F. E. Warren, *Liturgy and Ritual of the Celtic Church* (Oxford: Clarendon Press, 1881), p. 52.

10. Cf. *RAC*, pp. 40, 44–45; *CSR*, pp. 14, 29; *EIHM*, p. 66; *IMC*, pp. 131, 143; *AIT*, p. 18; Alwyn Rees and Brinley Rees, *Celtic Heritage* (London: Thames and Hudson, 1961), p. 36; D. Green, "Brigid's Ale-Feast," *Celtica* 11 (1952): 150–53; "Cormac's Glossary," in *Three Irish Glossaries*, ed. Wh. Stokes, (London: Williams and Norgate, 1862), pp. xxxiii–xxxiv; Marie-Louise Sjoestedt, *Gods and Heroes of the Celts*, trans. Myles Dillon (1949; reprint, Berkeley, CA: Turtle Island Foundation, 1982), pp. 27–31; Proinsias Mac Cana, *Celtic Mythology* (1968; rev. ed., New York: Hamlyn, 1983), p. 42ff.

11. Cf. *RAC*, p. 45.

12. Cf. Pamela Berger, "Many Shaped: Art, Archaeology and the Táin," *Éire-Ireland* 17, no. 4 (1982): 6–18; Margaret E. Dodds, "The Spiral and the Tuatha Dé Danann," *JRSAI* 42 (1912): 331–34, 331; Erich Neumann, *The Great Mother: An Analysis of the Archetype*, trans. R. Mannheim, Bollingen series 47 (Princeton, NJ: Princeton University Press, 1974), p. 124; John Sharkey, *Celtic Mysteries: The Ancient Religion* (London: Thames and Hudson, 1975), p. 78; cf. also discussion of the Triple Spiral in Sjöö and Mor, *Great Cosmic Mother*, pp. 97–98, 124–30.

13. Cf. *LGE*, pt. 5:110–13. Translated by Robert Graves in *The White Goddess* (1948; reprint, New York: Noonday, Farrar, Strauss, Giroux, 1983), p. 12.

14. For further information on goddesses in the ancient world, see Elise Boulding, *The Underside of History* (Boulder, CO: Westview Press, 1976); Maria Gimbutas, *The Goddesses and Gods of Old Europe: 6500–3500: Myths, Legends, and Cult Images* (Berkeley and Los Angeles: University of California Press, 1982); Pamela Berger, *The Goddess Obscured* (Boston: Beacon Press, 1985); Charlene Spretnak, *Lost Goddesses of Early Greece: A Collection of Pre-Hellenic Myths* (Boston: Beacon Press, 1984); Sjöö and Mor, *Great Cosmic Mother*. All of these contain extensive bibliographies. For other works exploring the contemporary implications of the Goddess and her religions, see *The Politics of Women's Spirituality: Essays on the Rise of*

Spiritual Power within the Feminist Movement, ed. Charlene Spretnak (New York: Doubleday, 1982); Merlin Stone, *The Paradise Papers* (Boston: Beacon Press, 1976); Merlin Stone, *Ancient Mirrors of Womanhood* (Boston: Beacon Press, 1979); Starhawk, *The Spiral Dance* (San Francisco: Harper & Row, 1979); Starhawk, *Dreaming the Dark* (Boston: Beacon Press, 1982); Starhawk, *Truth or Dare* (San Francisco: Harper & Row, 1988); Carol Christ, *The Laughter of Aphrodite* (San Francisco: Harper & Row, 1987); Riane Eisler, *The Chalice and the Blade* (San Francisco: Harper & Row, 1987).

15. Cf. *AIT,* p. 18; *LGE,* pt. 2:177, 185, 197.

16. Rees and Rees, *Celtic Heritage,* p. 115.

17. *LGE,* pt. 1:165; *FF,* 1:102, and 2:45, 58, 372; *IMC,* p. 128. Cf. also R. A. S. Mac-Alister, *Tara: A Pagan Sanctuary of Ancient Ireland* (New York: C. Scribner's Sons, 1931), pp. 92–93, for the existence of two "Scotas" in the ancient legends.

18. Cf. Kuno Meyer, "Mitteilungen aus irischen Handschriften Die funfzehn Namen des Boyne," *ZCP* 8 (1910): 105–6. For Newgrange itself, see Michael J. O'Kelly and Claire O'Kelly, *Newgrange, Archaeology, Art and Legend* (London: Thames and Hudson, 1982). For a controversial account of the symbolism at Newgrange, see Martin Brennan, *The Boyne Valley Vision* (Portlaoise: Dolmen Press, 1980).

19. See the *Dindshenchas,* the "place-name" lore of ancient Ireland, an invaluable resource to ancient Irish culture that must, however, be used critically. The story of Bóand, is from the *Rennes Dindshenchas,* no. 19. For a critical introduction to the *Dindshenchas* collections, see Charles Bowen, "A Historical Inventory of the Dindshenchas," *Studia Celtica* 10–11 (1975/1976): 113–37.

20. *IMC,* p. 157.

21. Cf. Neumann, *Great Mother,* p. 124.

22. *Ren Dind,* nos. 12, 59.

23. *RAC,* p. 43; Anne Ross, *Pagan Celtic Britain* (New York: Columbia University Press, 1967), pp. 20–21; Carl J. S. Marstrander, "Celtic River-Names and River-Goddesses," *Norsk Tiddsskr for Sprogvidenskap* 7 (1934): 344–46; cf. also E. C. Quiggin, "Some Celtic River Names," *Philological Society Transactions* (1911–14): 99–100; D. Ó Cathasaigh, "The Cult of Brigid: A Study of Pagan-Christian Syncretism," in *Mother Worship,* ed. James J. Preston (Chapel Hill, NC: University of North Carolina Press, 1982), p. 78.

24. Cf. Annie M. Scarre, "The Beheading of John the Baptist by Mog Ruith," *Ériu* 4, no. 2 (1910): 177–81, 181. Cf. *Keating's General History of Ireland With Many Curious Amendments Taken From the Psalters of Tara and Cashel,* ed. Dermond O'Connor (Dublin: J. Duffy, n.d.), p. 324.

25. Cf. Eleanor Burke Leacock, *Myths of Male Dominance* (New York: Monthly Review Press, 1981), who cites a case where French missionaries were chided by the seventeenth-century Indians who told them that "thou hast no sense. You French people love only your own children; but we love all the children of our tribe" (p. 38).

26. *Bede,* p. 39. Cf. also MacAlister, *Tara,* p. 85; *CSR,* p. 20; "Tidings of Conchobar Mac Nessa," ed. Whitley Stokes, *Ériu* 4, no. 1 (1908): 18–38, 18; J. Frazer, "The Alleged Matriarchy of the Picts," in *Medieval Studies in Memory of Gertrude Schoepperle,* ed. Roger Loomis (New York: Columbia University Press, 1927), pp. 407–12; N. K. Chadwick, "Pictish and Celtic Marriages in Early Literary Tradition," *Scottish Gaelic Studies* 8 (1958): 56–155; Alexander Boyle, "Matrilineal Succession in the Pictish Monarchy," *Scottish Historical Review* 56 (1977): 1–10; Molly Miller, "Matriliny by Treaty: The Pictish Foundation Legend," in *Ireland in Early Medieval Europe,* ed. D. Whitelock, R. McKitterick, D. Dumville (New York: Cambridge University Press, 1982), pp. 133–61. Cf. discussion of the relationship between Picts, Scots, and Cruithin in *EIHM,* p. 343. For a contemporary discussion of the Cruithin, see Ian Adamson, *Cruithin: The Ancient Kindred* (Newtownards, County Down: Nosmada Books, 1974).

27. *RAC,* p. 223.

28. Cf. "Cóir Anmann: On the Fitness of Names," *Irische Texte,* ed. Wh. Stokes and E.

Windisch (Leipzig, 1891–97), 3 pt. 2, pp. 407, 409; *RAC*, pp. 149, 222–24; Eugene O'Curry, *Manners and Customs of the Ancient Irish*, ed. W. K. Sullivan (New York: Scribner, Welford & Co, 1873), 1:clxx, clxxii; Kuno Meyer, *Hibernica Minora*, Anecdota Oxoniensia, no. 4 (Oxford: Clarendon Press, 1894), p. 106; De Paor, "Saint Mac Creiche," p. 112; *IMC* pp. 128, 149; MacAlister, *Tara*, pp. 84, 177; Rees and Rees, *Celtic Heritage*, p. 144. Cf. also David Herlihy, *Medieval Households* (Cambridge, MA: Harvard University Press, 1985), pp. vi, 39, 41, 42.

The Irish system of succession is actually extremely complex, and there is evidence that in some respects sons would inherit from their fathers and daughters from their mothers. Cf. "The Training of Cúchulainn," ed. Whitley Stokes, *RC* 29 (1908): 109–52, 137. For an ancient law that there is no protection for "a daughter who absconds from her mother, son that absconds from his father," see Thomas Charles Edwards and Fergus Kelly, *Bechbretha* (Dublin: Institute for Advanced Studies, 1983), p. 144.

29. For a discussion of ideas of matriarchy in feminism, see Marilyn Massey, *Feminine Soul: The Fate of an Ideal* (Boston: Beacon Press, 1985); Joan Bamberger, "The Myth of Matriarchy: Why Men Rule in Primitive Society," in *Woman, Culture and Society*, ed. Michelle Zimbalist Rosaldo and Louise Lamphere (Stanford, CA: Stanford University Press, 1974), p. 263–80; Sarah B. Pomeroy, "A Classical Scholar's Perspective on Matriarchy," in *Liberating Women's History*, ed. Berenice Carroll (Urbana, IL: University of Illinois Press, 1976), pp. 217–23; Sharon Tiffany, "The Power of Matriarchal Ideas," *International Journal of Women's Studies* 5, no. 2 (1982): 138–47.

30. For a recent treatment of the politics and power structures of matricentered societies, see Peggy Reeves Sanday, *Female Power and Male Dominance* (New York: Cambridge University Press, 1981); cf. also discussions in *Defining Female*, ed. Shirley Ardener (New York: Wiley, 1978), and essays in *Woman, Culture and Society*, ed. Rosaldo and Lamphere. Cf. also Herlihy, *Medieval Households*, p. vi. Herlihy claims that in the early Middle Ages indifferent kinship arrangements existed and cases can be found for both male and female succession, depending on the circumstances. From the eleventh century onward, however, succession becomes predominantly patrilineal.

31. *LGE*, pt. 1:17.

32. "The progeny of Adam sinned (thereafter), namely the elder of the sons of Adam, Cain the accursed, who slew his brother Abel . . . (through his jealousy?) and through his greed, with the bone of a camel, as learned men say. (In this manner) began the kin-murders of the world." *LGE*, pt. 1:19.

33. Cf. *Poems of Blathmac*, ed. James Carney, (Dublin: Irish Texts Series, 1964), 47:17.

34. *Poems of Blathmac*, p. 37; cf. also Rees and Rees; *Celtic Heritage*, p. 145ff.

35. Women were held in great respect in early Irish society, but this is not to say that their importance was solely on account of their reproductive capabilities. Feminist anthropologists are unearthing a great deal of evidence that women were revered also for their scientific accomplishments. Even in the so-called hunting societies, the evidence is that women's horticultural skills provided 70 to 80 percent of the food, while the more prestigious hunting provided a mere 20 to 30 percent. Cf. Elizabeth Fisher, *Woman's Creation* (Garden City, NY: Anchor Press, 1979), pp. 8, 48; cf. also Autumn Stanley, "Daughters of Isis, Daughers of Demeter: When Women Sowed and Reaped," *Women's Studies International Quarterly* 4, no. 3 (1981): 289–304.

36. For discussion of the various technicalities around this, see Eoin Mac Neill, *Celtic Ireland* (1921; reprint, with new introduction by Donncha Ó Corráin, Dublin: Academy Press, 1981), pp. 152–56. Cf. also F. J. Byrne, "Tribes and Tribalism in Early Ireland," *Ériu* 22 (1971): 128–66, for a fairly recent appraisal of Mac Neill's position.

37. Cf. *The Irish Adam and Eve Story From Saltair na Rann*, ed. David Green and Fergus Kelly (Dublin: Institute for Advanced Studies, 1976), p. 35. There is also a volume of commentary on the Adam and Eve story edited by Brian O. Murdoch, *The*

Irish Adam and Eve Story, commentary vol. 2 (Dublin: Institute for Advanced Studies, 1976).

38. For other Irish variations on the Genesis story, cf. *Irish Adam and Eve Story,* 1:39.

39. *MDs,* pt. iv, p. 191; *Ren Dind,* no. 110; *FL,* 4:490.

40. Rees and Rees, *Celtic Heritage,* p. 165; MacAlister, *Tara,* p. 167. A "fire-boar" was a pyramidal structure of logs; cf. also J. O'Beirne Crowe, "Religious Beliefs of the Pagan Irish," *Journal of the Historical and Archaeological Association of Ireland* 3d ser., 1 (1873): 307–34, 324.

41. *MDs,* pt. iii, pp. 26, 34, 286; *Ren Dind,* nos. 19, 110; *BD,* p. 500.

42. *ED,* p. 480.

43. *Ren Dind,* no. 94; *ED,* p. 480.

44. *Ren Dind,* no. 161.

45. *Ren Dind,* no. 94.

46. *EIHM,* pp. 293–94; *RAC,* pp. 43, 188; Sjoestedt, *Gods and Heroes,* p. 30; Ross, *Pagan Celtic Britain,* pp. 224, 247, 324–26.

47. All quotations taken from the version of the story in *AIT,* pp. 208–10.

48. O'Connor, *A Backward Look,* p. 16.

49. Cf. Rees and Rees, *Celtic Heritage,* p. 58; *RAC,* p. 130; Sjoestedt, *Gods and Heroes,* pp. 40–42.

50. Sjoestedt, *Gods and Heroes,* p. 41. A more recent interpretation of the story is that it is the myth behind an ancient vegetation rite, the *kouros* or male fertility rite, in which the young king, having proved his heroism, takes over from the old king, marries the Goddess, but in turn has to surrender the title after a year. Cf. Tomás Ó Broin, "What is the Debility of the Ulstermen?" *Éigse* 10 (1963): 286–99. According to one scholar, the rites resemble those of the Phrygian god in hibernation. Cf. John Rhys, *Lectures on the Origin and Growth of Religion as Illustrated by Celtic Heathendom,* (London, 1898: New York: AMS Press, 1979), p. 632.

51. Cf. Próinséas Ní Chatháin, "Swineherds, Seers and Druids," *Studia Celtica* 14/15 (1979/1980): 200–211; J. G. McKay, "The Deer-Goddess: Cult of the Ancient Caledonians," *Folklore* 43, no. 2 (1932): 144–74. Boars, "swineherds," and deer appear throughout the *Lives* of Irish saints and Irish mythology. For full references, see T. P. Cross, ed., *The Motif Index of Irish Literature,* Folklore Series 7 (Indiana University Publications, 1952), which is a supplement to the Stith Thomson, *Motif Index of Folk Literature* (Bloomington, IN: Indiana University Studies, nos. 96, 97, 100, 101, 105, 106, 108–12). Cf. also Howard Schlossman, "The Role of Swine in Myth and Religion," *American Imago* 40, no. 1 (1983): 35–49.

52. Cf. *VSH,* 1:ci.

53. See Myles Dillon, "The Taboos of the Kings of Ireland," *PRIA* 54 (1951): 1–36, 19.

54. For details of the hysterical pregnancies, birth rituals, and other forms of male imitation of women's generative powers, see Mircea Eliade, *Rites and Symbols of Initiation* (New York: Harper & Row, 1975); Bruno Bettelheim, *Symbolic Wounds: Puberty Rites of the Envious Male* (New York: Collier Books, 1954).

55. Macha had a counterpart in Cyprus, the Goddess Artemis, who died in childbirth. On her festival a young man imitated her labor pains. Cf. Ó Broin, "What is the Debility of the Ulstermen?" p. 298.

56. Cf. Erich Neumann, *The Origins and History of Consciousness,* trans. R. F. C. Hull (New York: Pantheon Books, 1949); Luce Irigaray, cited in Domna Stanton, "Difference on Trial," in *Poetics of Gender,* ed. Nancy K. Miller (New York: Columbia University Press, 1986), pp. 157–82, p. 160.

57. *ED,* p. 480.

58. *Ren Dind,* no. 94.

59. *MDs,* pt. iv, p. 127.

60. *ED,* p. 480.

61. Cf. Wm. Hennessy, "The Ancient Irish Goddess of War," *RC* 1 (1870): 32–55, 36.

62. For similar themes in Indo-European literature, see A. L. Frothingham, "Medusa, Apollo and the Great Mother," *AJA* 15 (1911): 349–77; A. L. Frothingham, "Medusa 11" *AJA* 19 (1915): 13–23; Ruby Rohrlich, "State Formation in Sumer and the Subjugation of Women," *Feminist Studies* 5 (1980): 76–102, 86–91; Ruth Katz Arabagian, "Cattle Raiding and Bride Stealing: The Goddess in Indo-European Heroic Literature," *Religion* 14 (1984): 107–402, 119. In some myths the goddesses turn vicious only after their children have been killed. Cf. Neumann, *Great Mother*, p. 214.

63. For the "goddess of war," see Hennessy, "The Ancient Irish Goddess of War." Amendments to this article appear in Wh. Stokes, "The Ancient Irish Goddess of War," *RC* 2 (1873–75): 489–92. Cf. also Charles Donahue, "The Valkyries and the Irish War-Goddess," *PMLA* 56 (1941): 1–12; John Carey, "Notes on the Irish War-Goddess," *Éigse* 19, no. 2 (1983): 263–76.

64. Cf. "The Death of Cúchulainn," ed. Wh. Stokes, *RC* 3 (1876–78): 175–85, 175. Cf. also "Morrígan's Warning to Donn Cuailnge," ed. Garreth Olmsted, *EC* 19 (1982): 165–71; cf. Mac Cana, *Celtic Mythology*, p. 86; Ross, *Pagan Celtic Britain*, p. 223; John Carey, "Notes on the Irish War-Goddess," p. 267; Charles Bowen, "Great Bladdered Medb," *Éire-Ireland* 10 (1975): 14–34, 23; Sjoestedt, *Gods and Heroes*, pp. 46–47.

   As Anne Ross points out, the Goddess Medb in *The Táin* (a classic Irish epic saga) is the only exception to the rule that "war-goddesses do not take up arms." Cf. Ross, *Pagan Celtic Britain*, p. 223. *The Táin*, however, is essentially a satire, one of whose functions was to denigrate the goddesses and exalt the virtues of male-bonding. Cf. especially where the "heroes" at the end of the battle strike at the Triple Mounds in Ath Luain (the Ford of the Moon) and at Newgrange. The heroes strike alternately at the mounds in each other's locality, and the entire episode is punctuated by an incident symbolizing the incompatibility of war and menstruation. The Goddess Medb, just as she had rounded up her armies ready for the final onslaught, got her "gush of blood." In the act of "relieving herself" she caused several great channels to appear, thereafter called "Medb's Foul Place." *The Táin*, pp. 248–51.

65. Cf. Professor Connellan, "The Proceedings of the Great Bardic Institution," *TOS* 5 (1857): 59.

66. Donncha Ó Corráin, "Women in Early Irish Society," in *Women in Irish Society*, ed. Donncha Ó Corráin and Margaret MacCurtain (Dublin: Arlen House, 1978), pp. 1–3, 10.

67. Berger, "Many Shaped," p. 11. Cf. also Pierre Lambrechts, *L'exaltation de la tête dans la pensèe et dans l'art des Celtes* (Brugge: De Lempel, 1954).

68. Berger, "Many Shaped," p. 14. For a general discussion of the role of scalp-taking, see Sanday, *Female Power*, p. 107ff. Sanday argues that in some societies men took scalps as their "children."

69. *Three Irish Glossaries*, p. xxxv.

70. *Fragmentary Annals of Ireland*, ed. Joan Radner (Dublin: Institute for Advanced Studies, 1978), p. 159; *FF*, 3:211.

71. *Three Irish Glossaries*, p. xi.

72. "Tidings of Conchobor MacNessa," ed. Wh. Stokes, *Ériu* 4, no. 1 (1908): 18–38, 29.

73. For further elaboration on this theme, see Mary Condren, "Patriarchy and Death," in *Womanspirit Bonding*, ed. Janet Kalven and Mary Buckley (New York: Pilgrim Press, 1984), pp. 173–89; Carol Cohn, "Sex and Death in the Rational World of Defense Intellectuals," *Signs* 12, no. 4 (1987): 687–718.

74. *Three Irish Glossaries*, p. xxxv. Cf. also *AIT*, p. 176, where it is claimed that, in their pouches, the men carried to the harvest festival the tips of the tongues of those men whom they had slaughtered.

75. For a contemporary treatment of this theme, see Ernest Becker, *The Denial of Death* (New York: Free Press, 1973).

76. For a brilliant discussion of the male reproductive consciousness and its effects on

philosophy, especially that of Hegel and Marx, see Mary O'Brien, *The Politics of Reproduction* (London: Routledge and Kegan Paul, 1981), chap. 1. David Herlihy claims that in Roman law a ~~"patrician" was someone who literally knew his father and could inherit from him~~. *Medieval Households*, p. 7.

77. See, for instance, *Cath Maige Mucrama*, ed. Mairín O'Daly, (Dublin: Irish Texts Society, 1975), p. 77, for a test for a woman worthy of giving legal evidence determining the paternity of her children. See also *The Táin*, pp. 22–23; *VSH*, 1:55; *BB*, pp. 31–32. For laws determining paternity suits, see *ALI*, 3:313.

78. Cf. Nicole Mathieu, "Biological Paternity, Social Maternity," *Feminist Issues* (Spring 1984): 63–71, for the social rather than the biological determinants of paternity.

79. *The Táin*, p. 23.

80. No one manuscript source recounts the story as I have here. My reconstruction is drawn from several sources: "The Origin of Cúchulainn" in *The Cúchulainn Saga*, ed. Eleanor Hull, (London: D. Nutt, 1898), pp. 15–20; "The Cúchulainn Birth-Story," in *The Voyage of Bran*, ed. Kuno Meyer and A. Nutt (London: A. Nutt, D. Nutt, 1897), 2:38–47; and "How Cúchulainn Was Begotten," in *The Táin*, pp. 21–25, and "The Birth of Cú Chulaind," in *Early Irish Myths and Sagas*, ed. Jeffrey Gantz (Harmondsworth, Middlesex: Penguin, 1981), pp. 130–33. Cf. also Louis Duvau, "La Legende de la Conception de Cúchulainn," *RC* 9 (1888): 1–13. Celtic scholars agree that the present texts of the "Birth Stories" are "the work of many hands" and "little more than the mangled remains of miscellaneous scribal activities" (The *Táin*, p. xi). My reconstruction is simply one in a long line of attempts to make sense out of chaos.

81. Gantz, "The Birth of Cú Chulaind," p. 133.

82. According to the tract "On the Fitness of Names," "Roch, daughter of Ruad, son of Derg Dath-fóla, from the elfmounds, was the mother of Fergus mac Roich and the mother of Sualtach mac Roich, and 'tis she that bestowed on Sualtach the magical might of an elf, and from her he was called Sualtach Síde, 'of the elf-mound.' " (The spelling of Irish names is not standard. The spelling here is given as it appears in the text.) Cf. "Cóir Anmann: On the Fitness of Names," *Irische Texte*, ed. Wh. Stokes and E. Windisch (Leipzig, 1891–97,) 3 pt. 2, p. 407.

83. Prof. C. Dunn (Lecture at Harvard University, March 6, 1984. Information kindly supplied by Dr. Emily Culpepper).

84. "Tidings of Conchobor Son of Ness," p. 27; "The Cherishing of Conall Cernach and the Deaths of Ailill and of Conall Cernach," ed. Kuno Meyer, *ZCP* 1 (1897): 103–11, 107.

85. This interpretation of virginity would be reinforced by the *Penitentials*, when ~~virginity could be restored through penitence~~. Cf. *Penit*, pp. 79–81. It is also interesting to note that in the ancient Near East some goddesses, "noted for their promiscuity," remained virgins when they conceived the hero. Cf. John A. Saliba, S. J., "The Virgin Birth in Anthropological Literature: A Critical Assessment," *Theological Studies* 36 (1975): 428–54, 449.

86. For the necessity to establish paternity firmly in patriarchal societies, see Sharon Tiffany, "The Power of Matriarchal Ideas," p. 141; Leacock, *Myths of Male Dominance*, p. 113.

87. Cited in P. Doyle, "Women and Religion: Psychological and Cultural Implications," in *Religion and Sexism*, ed. Rosemary Radford Ruether (New York: Simon & Schuster, 1974), pp. 9–40, p. 27.

88. Peggy Reeves Sanday points out that in some societies this distinction went so far that a man whose wife was menstruating could not go to war. Cf. Sanday, *Female Power*, p. 44; Sherry Ortner, "Is Female to Male?" p. 70; cf. also René Girard, *Violence and the Sacred*, trans. Patrick Gregory (Baltimore: Johns Hopkins University Press, 1977), p. 36.

89. For the concept of patriarchal reversal, see Mary Daly, *Beyond God the Father* (Boston: Beacon Press, 1973), pp. 95–97; Mary Daly, *Gyn/Ecology* (Boston: Beacon Press, 1978), pp. 9ff., 75–79, 290–92, 329–43, 354–64. Cf. also Elizabeth Fisher,

Woman's Creation (Garden City, NY: Anchor Press, 1979), p. 157ff.

90. "The Boyhood Deeds of Cúchulainn," in *AIT*, p. 144.

91. The story of Macha's dealings with the Ulstermen has been the subject of several scholarly articles. Most of these are concerned, however, not with the meaning of the myth to Macha but with the form of "couvade" or other rite undertaken by the warriors. Cf. Franz Rolf Schröder, "Ein Altirischer Krönungsritus und das Indogermanische Rossopfer," *ZCP* 16 (1927): 310–12; Vernam Hull, "The Affliction of the Ulstermen," *ZCP* 29 (1962–64): 309–14; Tomás Ó Broin, "The Word *noínden*," *Éigse* 13, no. 3 (1970): 165–76; J. F. Killeen, "The Debility of the Ulstermen: A Suggestion," *ZCP* 33 (1974): 81–86; Maartje Draak, "Some Aspects of Kingship in Pagan Ireland," in *The Sacral Kingship/La Regalità Sacra: Contributions to the Central Theme of the VIIIth International Congress for the History of Religions, Rome, April 1955* (Leiden, 1959), pp. 651–63.

92. Cf. W. I. Thompson, *The Time Falling Bodies Take to Light* (New York: St. Martin's Press, 1981), pp. 95–102; Nor Hall, *The Moon and the Virgin* (New York: Harper & Row, 1980), p. 172ff.

93. In one of the Irish "origin" stories, menstruation was a punishment for Eve eating the fruit. Cf. *LGE*, pt. 1:73. For a discussion of menstrual taboos and the warrior ethos, see Sanday, *Female Power,* pp. 43, 92, 95, 107; Sjöö and Mor, *Great Cosmic Mother*, p. 193.

94. According to Riane Eisler, in early social forms, "power was primarily equated with the responsibility of motherhood rather than with the exaction of obedience to a male-dominant elite through force or the fear of force." *Chalice and the Blade*, p. 38.

95. This is not to argue for a simple or causal relationship between the gender of the deity and the social system. Female deities do not necessarily reflect or "cause" the liberation of women, no more than male deities necessarily cause their oppression. This issue is far too complex to be argued here but see Sanday, *Female Power*, p. 64, for a controversial account of the relationship between images of the deity and the roles of men and women in society.

96. Cf. Wh. Stokes, "On the Deaths of Some Irish Heroes," *RC* 23 (1902): 303–48; *AIT*, pp. 343–46, 487; "Death Tales of the Ulster Heroes," ed. Kuno Meyer, *TLSRIA* 14 (1906): 1–52.

97. Cf. "Death of Muircertach Mac Erca," *AIT*, p. 527; "The Burning of Finn's House," ed. E. J. Gwynn, *Ériu* 1 (1904): 13–37, 25; Killeen, "The Debility of the Ulstermen," pp. 82–84.

98. Simone de Beauvoir, *The Second Sex*, trans. and ed. H. M. Parshley (New York: Vintage Books, 1974), p. 73.

99. Cf. Augustine Martin, "To Make a Right Rose-Tree," *Studies* 55 (1966): 38–50; G. F. Dalton, "The Tradition of Blood-Sacrifice to the Goddess," *Studies* 63 (1974): 343–54; Francis Shaw, S. J., "The Canon of Irish History: A Challenge," *Studies* 61, no. 242 (1972): 114–53. For a contemporary study of the effects of this mentality, see Richard Kearney, *Myth and Motherland* (Derry: Field Day Pamphlet no. 5, 1984).

Chapter 3. Brigit as Goddess

Epigraph: Excerpted from "The Mother's Lament at the Slaughter of the Innocents," *A Celtic Psaltery*, ed. and trans. Alfred P. Graves (London: S.P.C.K., 1917), pp. 63–64.

1. John V. Kelleher, "Early Irish History and Pseudo-history," *Studia Hibernica* 3 (1963): 112–27, 118.

2. For a discussion of the status of Patrick in modern scholarship, see James Henthorn Todd, *St. Patrick: Apostle of Ireland* (Dublin: Hodges Smith, 1864); Ludwig Bieler, *The Life of Legend of St. Patrick: Problems of Modern Scholarship* (Dublin: Clonmore & Reynolds, 1949); Ludwig Bieler, "The Celtic Hagiographer," *Studia Patristica* 5 (1962): 243–65; D. A. Binchy, "Patrick and His Biographers: An-

cient and Modern," *Studia Hibernica* 2 (1962): 7–173; Liam de Paor, "The Aggrandisement of Armagh," *Historical Studies* 8 (1971): 95–110.

3. Cf. G. MacNiocaill, *Ireland Before the Vikings* (Dublin: Gill and Macmillan, 1980), p. 103.

4. Cf. Pádraig Ó Néill, "Romani Influences in Seventh-Century Hiberno-Latin Literature," in *Irland und Europa*, ed. Próinséas Ní Chatháin and Michael Richter (Stuttgart: Klett-Cotta, 1984), pp. 280–90.

5. Frank O'Connor, *A Backward Look* (London: Macmillan, 1967), p. 55.

6. Cf. Felim Ó Briain, "The Expansion of Irish Christianity to 1200: An Historical Survey," pt. 1, *Irish Historical Studies* 3, no. 11 (1943): 241–66; pt. 2, 4, no. 14 (1944): 131–63; Wm. H. Marnell, *Light From the West: The Irish Mission and the Emergence of Modern Europe* (New York: Seabury Press, 1980): W. B. Stanford, *Ireland and the Classical Tradition* (Totowa, NJ: Rowman and Littlefield, 1976).

7. Cf. John V. Kelleher, "Early Irish History and Pseudo-History," *Studia Hibernica* 3 (1963): 113–27, 126.

8. Cf. D. Ó Corráin, "Dál-Cais—Church and Dynasty," *Ériu* 24 (1973): 52–63, 62. The Irish did not practice primogeniture (the straight succession of the eldest son to the office of his father). Cf. D. A. Binchy, *Celtic and Anglo-Saxon Kinship*, O'Donnell Lectures for 1967–68 (London: Oxford University Press, 1970), p. 30. In the election of both kings and abbots, the Irish preferred to be able to draw from a wider range of candidates, all of whom were, nevertheless, in collateral succession to the reigning power.

9. Cf. Rosemary Radford Ruether, "Misogyny and Virginal Feminism in the Fathers of the Church," in *Religion and Sexism*, ed. Rosemary Radford Ruether (New York: Simon & Schuster, 1974), pp. 150–83, p. 160ff.

10. Cited in Elizabeth A. Clark, *Jerome, Chrysostom and Friends* (New York: Edwin Mellen Press, 1979), p. 15.

11. Cf. Joan McNamara and Suzanne Wemple, "Sanctity and Power: The Dual Pursuit of Medieval Women," in *Becoming Visible*, ed. Renate Bridenthal and Claudia Koonz (Boston: Houghton Mifflin, 1977), pp. 90–118, p. 93.

12. Cf. Gerard Murphy, "Acallam na Senórach," in *Irish Sagas*, ed. Myles Dillon (Dublin: Published for Radio Eireann, 1959), pp. 119–34, p. 120.

13. Pádraig Ó Riain, "St. Finbarr: A Study in a Cult," *JCHAS* 82, no. 236 (1977): 63–82, 69–70.

14. Cf. *FF* 2:130–33, for the rise of elitism in kingship.

15. F. J. Byrne, *Irish Kings and High-Kings* (London: Batsford, 1973), p. 33.

16. R. A. S. MacAlister, "Temair Breg: Remains and Traditions of Tara," *PRIA* 34 (1919): 231–399, 289. The clerics often placed shrines and relics between the opposing sides to prevent fighting. In some cases "peace hostages" were sent to "the house of the King of Truth." Cf. Carl Marstrander, "A New Version of the Battle of Mag Rath," *Ériu* 5 (1911): 226–47, 241.

17. Cf. "The Dialogue of Oisín and Patrick," in *TOS*, ed. John O'Daly, 4 (1856).

18. Cf. James Carney, *Medieval Irish Lyrics and the Irish Bardic Poet* (Berkeley, CA: University of California Press, 1985), p. 3.

19. This question was particularly significant in the Irish context since being fostered by many sponsors was considered to be a sign of one's social status.

20. "The Questions of Ethne Alba," in Carney, *Medieval Irish Lyrics*, pp. 3–4.

21. Eleanor Hull, "The Development of the Idea of Hades in Celtic Literature," *Folklore* 18 (1907): 121–65.

22. "Cáin Adamnáin: An Old-Irish Treatise on the Law of Adamnán," ed. Kuno Meyer, *Anecdota Oxoniensia, Medieval and Modern Series*, pt. 12 (Oxford, 1905).

23. "Cáin Adamnáin," p. 2.

24. For the taking of women slaves in battle, see Gerda Lerner, *The Creation of Patriarchy* (New York: Oxford University Press, 1986), p. 76ff.

25. In many continental hagiographies, it is the saint who refuses to carry his mother on his back. The Irish version is a reversal.

26. "Cáin Adamnáin," p. 5.

27. Ibid., p. 7.
28. Ibid., p. 9.
29. Ibid., p. 25.
30. Ibid., pp. 23–25.
31. Cf. Peggy Reeves Sanday, *Female Power and Male Dominance* (New York: Cambridge University Press, 1981), for a contemporary example from Nigeria where a "women's war" was conducted against the ruling authorities. It began when the women decided to invade the offices of the district officer on the grounds that "he was born of a woman, and as they were women they were going to see him" (p. 139).
32. "Cáin Adamnáin," pp. 13–15.
33. Ibid., p. 15.
34. Louis Gougaud, *Les Saints Irlandais hors d'Irlande* (Louvain: Bureau de la Revue, 1936), pp. 16–45; E. J. Bowen, "The Cult of Saint Brigit," *Studia Celtica* 8 (1973): 33–47.
35. Even if there was not, the fact that these claims surrounded Brigit is itself a highly significant indication of early Irish religiosity and at the very least provides us with the history of "discourse" if not of "event."
36. Pádraig Ó Ríain, "Towards a Methodology in Early Irish Hagiography," *Peritia* 1 (1982): 146–59, 158.
37. John V. Kelleher, "Early Irish History and Pseudo-History," *Studia Hibernica* 3 (1963): 113–27, 119; cf. also John V. Kelleher, "The Pre-Norman Irish Genealogies," *IHS* 16 (1968): 138–53.
38. Felim Ó Briain, "The Hagiography of Leinster," in *Essays Presented to Eoin Mac Neill*, ed. John Ryan (Dublin: At the Sign of the Three Candles, 1940), 454–64, p. 463; Felim Ó Briain, "Irish Hagiography: Historiography and Method," *Measgra i Gcuimhne Mhichil Ui Chleirigh*, ed. Sylvester O'Brien (Dublin: Assisi Press, 1944), pp. 119–31, p. 130.
39. Cf. *Mart Oeng*, p. 11. Cf. also Pádraig Ó Ríain, "Traces of Lug in Early Irish Hagiographical Tradition," *ZCP* 36 (1977): 138–56; Felim Ó Briain, "Miracles in the Lives of the Irish Saints," *IER* 66 (1945): 331–42; Felim Ó Briain, "Saga Themes in Irish Hagiography," in *Féilschríbhinn Torna: Essays and Studies Presented to Prof. Tadgh Ua Donnchadha*, ed. S. Pender (Cork: Cork University Press, 1947), pp. 33–42.
40. Mario Esposito, "Notes on Latin Learning and Literature in Mediaeval Ireland," *Hermathena* 24, no. 4 (1935): 120–65, 163.
41. Kim McCone, "An Introduction to Early Irish Saint's Lives," *Maynooth Review* 11 (1986): 26–59, 33.
42. Ó Briain, "Saga Themes," p. 42.
43. McCone, "Early Irish Saint's Lives," p. 46.
44. Cf. Paul Grosjean, "Notes d'Hagiographie Celtique, 4. Une Invocation des Saintes Brigides," *Analecta Bollandiana* 61 (1943): 103–5, 104.
45. Byrne, *Irish Kings and High Kings*, p. 155; Proinsias Mac Cana, *Celtic Mythology* (1968; rev. ed., New York: Hamlyn, 1983), p. 34.
46. Louis Gougaud, *Les Saints Irlandais*, pp. 18–20; Flavia Anderson, *The Ancient Secret: In Search of the Holy Grail* (London: Gollancz, 1953), p. 92; *RAC*, p. 41; Jan de Vries, *Keltische Religion* (Stuttgart: Kohlhammer, 1961), pp. 78–80; *Gerald*, p. 83; *CG*, 1:164–66.
47. *CSR*, pp. 27–28.
48. Solinus, quoted in Anderson, *The Ancient Secret*, p. 92.
49. *Three Irish Glossaries*, ed. Wh. Stokes (London: Williams and Norgate, 1862), p. 8; Robert Graves, *The White Goddess* (1948; reprint, New York: Noonday, Farrar, Strauss, Giroux, 1985), p. 390.
50. *CG*, p. 166.
51. *CG*, p. 164; W. Warde Fowler, *The Roman Festivals of the Period of the Republic* (New York: Macmillan, 1899), p. 302.
52. *CG*, p. 164. For the significance of the number thirteen in the old religions of

Europe, see Monica Sjöö and Barbara Mor, *The Great Cosmic Mother: Rediscovering the Religion of the Earth* (San Francisco: Harper & Row, 1987), p. 157ff.

53. *Three Irish Glossaries*, pp. xxxiii–xxxiv.
54. Cf. Eoin Mac Neill, *Celtic Ireland* (1921; reprint, with new introduction by Donncha Ó Corráin, Dublin: Academy Press, 1981), p. 48; *EIHM*, p. 128.
55. *ALI*, 1:35.
56 Cf. John Sharkey, *Celtic Mysteries: The Ancient Religion* (London: Thames and Hudson, 1975), p. 81.
57. Cf. *Sanas Cormaic*, ed. Kuno Meyer, O. J. Bergin, R. I. Best, J. G. O'Keeffe, and M. E. Byrne, *Anecdota Oxoniensia* (Halle: Dublin, 1912), p. 86, no. 1000. Cf. "Omurethi," "Customs Peculiar to Certain Days, Formerly Observed in County Kildare," *JKAS* 5 (1906–8): 439–55, 439.

   Behind Brigit's association with *Imbolc* may lie several different traditions, both Irish and continental. Brigit one day went to visit a woman by the name of Lassar, known for her ability to help women in childbirth with the aid of her Ceolán Lasrach. Lassar had killed her last milch ewe, having milked it for the last time to serve to Brigit, when out of the blue Patrick arrived on the scene expecting to be fed. Brigit saved Lassar acute embarrassment by stretching the available food so that Patrick's appetite and their own could be satisfied. In return it is said that Lassar gave her church, *Cell Lasre*, together with all her followers to Brigit, who is still venerated there. *BB*, p. 32. Lucius Gwynn, "The Life of St. Lasair," *Ériu* 5, nos. 1–2 (1911): 73–103, 89. The story, like all stories concerning Brigit and Patrick, is unhistorical since, insofar as we can know anything about a "historical" Brigit, she did not live at the same time as Patrick. But the story is possibly telling us something much more important—that Brigit took over the cult connected with ewes that previously was connected with Lassar. The name *Lassar* means "fire," and it is probable she was a form of a fire goddess.
58. Cf. Dáithí Ó hOgáin, *The Hero in Irish Folk History* (New York: St. Martin's Press, 1985), p. 18.
59. Cf. de Vries, *Keltische Religion*, pp. 80, 225; J. Vendryes, "Imbolc," *RC* 41 (1924): 241–44.
60. Cf. D. Ó Cathasaigh, "The Cult of Brigid: A Study of Pagan-Christian Syncretism," *Mother Worship*, ed. James L. Preston (Chapel Hill, NC: University of North Carolina Press, 1982), p. 92; Sharkey, *Celtic Mysteries*, p. 18. The other feast was that of the God Lugh (Lammas) on August 1. Significantly, Darlughdacha (the daughter of Lugh) appears in Brigit's monastery as a cook. Darlughdacha's feast day was also February 1, and it is possible that Darlughdacha was the original Irish version of the Goddess, now entirely supplanted by the traditions of Brigit.
61. *CG*, p. 172.
62. *CG*, p. 169.
63. *CG*, p. 170.
64. *CG*, p. 170. It is possible that this could be a reference to the whipping with the *februum* which formed part of the Lupercalia celebrations (see Warde Fowler, *Roman Festivals*, pp. 311, 320). Or else it could be a later Christian accretion symbolizing the crushing of the Serpent.
65. Cf. Ó Briain, "Saga Themes," p. 39. Cf. also John O'Hanlon, *Lives of Irish Saints* (Dublin: James Duffy, 1875–1903), 2:156. O'Hanlon's collection of the "Lives" of Irish saints is largely a pious hagiographical reconstruction. However, it is drawn from a wide range of material scattered throughout Europe and contains extensive footnotes. It is, thus, an invaluable gold mine for contemporary scholars. Cf. F. P. Carey, "O'Hanlon of the Irish Saints," *IER* (1955): 145–63.
66. George Petrie, "On the History and Antiquities of Tara Hill," *TRIA* 18 (1824): 25–232, 158. For historical background to Tara, see also R. I. Best, "The Settling of the Manor at Tara," *Ériu* 4, no. 1 (1908): 121–72; J. Baudis, "On the antiquity of the kingship of Tara," *Ériu* 8, no. 2 (1916): 101–7; MacAlister,

"Temair Breg" R. A. S. MacAlister, *Tara: A Pagan Sanctuary of Ancient Ireland* (New York: Charles Scribner's Sons, 1931); D. A. Binchy, "The Fair of Tailtiú and the Feast of Tara," *Ériu* 18 (1958): 113–38.

67. Cf. Erich Neumann, *The Great Mother: An Analysis of the Archetype*, trans. Ralph Mannheim, Bollingen series (Princeton, NJ: Princeton University Press, 1974), pp. 123–25.

68. MacAlister, "Temair Breg," p. 380.

69. Irene Snieders, "L'Influence de l'hagiographie irlandaise sur les vitae des saints irlandais de Belgique," *Revue d'histoire ecclesiastique* 24 (1928): 613–27, 828–67, 623. Milk was so sacred that the Irish continued to baptize their children with it until the twelfth century, when the practice was banned by the Synod of Cashel. *Gesta Regis Henrici Secundi Benedicti Abbatis*, ed. W. Stubbs, from the Cotton Mss. Rolls series (London: 1867), p. 28.

70. Cf. *LGE*, pt. 4, p.159.

71. Cf. *ALC*, 1:269, where a man was blinded for the crime of rape.

72. Geoffrey Keating, *Keating's General History of Ireland With many Curious Amendments Taken from the Psalters of Tara and Cashel*, ed. Dermod O'Connor, (Dublin: J. Duffy, n.d.), p. 162.

73. Cf. Eugene O'Curry, *Manners and Customs of the Ancient Irish*, ed. W. K. Sullivan (New York: Scribner, Welford & Co.), 1:cccxxi; *ALI*, 2:405ff. and 3:533ff.

74. *Cath Maige Tuired*, ed. Elizabeth A. Gray (Dublin: Irish Texts Society, 1983), p. 57.

75. Cf. Ó Briain, "Saga Themes," pp. 36–39; Ó Briain, "Miracles in the Lives of the Irish Saints," *IER* 66 (1945): 331–42, 334; McCone, "Early Irish Saint's Lives," p. 36; *Thes Pal*, 2:334; *IMC*, pp. 81, 83; *CSR*, p. 42.

76. Charles Doherty, "The Monastic Town in Early Medieval Ireland," in *The Comparative History of Urban Origins in Non-Roman Europe* (British Archaeological Report International Series), ed. Howard Clark and Anngret Simms, 255 (i) (1985): 45–75, 45; Gearóid Mac Niocaill, *Ireland Before the Vikings* (Dublin: Gill and Macmillan, 1972), p. 4.

77. Byrne, *Irish Kings*, p. 8.

78. Thomas H. Mason, "St. Brigid's Crosses," *JRSAI* 75, no. 3 (1945): 160–66, 161.

79. *IMC*, p. 84.

80. Cf. Ó Cathasaigh, "The Cult of Brigid," p. 78; Eoin Mac Neill, *Celtic Ireland*, p. 93.

81. *CSR*, p. 31; Byrne, *Irish Kings*, p. 155.

82. Cf. Gougaud, *Les Saints Irlandaises*, pp. 16–45.

83. For a study of the Brigantia, see Guy Ragland Phillips, *Brigantia: A Mysteriography* (Boston: Routledge and Kegan Paul, 1976).

84. Cf. Bernard Wailes, "Dún Ailinne: An Interim Report," in *Hillforts: Later Prehistoric Earthworks in Britain and Ireland*, ed. D. W. Harding (New York: Academic Press, 1976), pp. 319–38, 335; Bernard Wailes, "The Irish 'Royal' Sites in History and Archaeology," *CMCS* 3 (1982): 1–29, 16–21; Kathleen Hughes, *Early Christian Ireland* (Ithaca, NY: Cornell University Press, 1972), pp. 264–65; F. J. Byrne, "Tribes and Tribalism in Early Ireland," *Ériu* 22 (1971): 128–66, 134; Proinsias Mac Cana, "Early Irish Ideology and the Concept of Unity," in *The Irish Mind*, ed. Richard Kearney (Dublin: Wolfhound Press, 1985), pp. 56–78, p. 72ff.

85. Cf. P. Ó Ríain, "Boundary Area in Early Irish Society," *Studia Celtica* 7 (1972): 12–29, 29.

86. *IMC*, pp. 81, 83; Ó Cathasaigh, "Cult of Brigid," p. 81.

87. *Cath Maige Tuired*, p. 243. For a commentary on this text, see Elizabeth Gray, "Cath Maige Tuired: Myth and Structure." *Éigse* 18, no. 2 (1981): 183–209; 19, no. 1 (1982): 1–35; 19, no. 2 (1983): 230–62. It is possible that this story contains remnants of the "goddess of the spear," i.e., Minerva. Cf. Warde Fowler, *Roman Festivals*, p. 303ff.

88. *ALI*, 1:9.

89. For critical commentaries on the laws of Ireland, see D. A. Binchy et al., eds., *Studies in Early Irish Law* (Dublin: Royal Irish Academy, 1936); D. A. Binchy, "The Linguistic and Historical Value of the Irish Law Tracts," *PBA* 29 (1943): 195–227; D. A. Binchy, "Irish History and Irish Law," *Studia Hibernica* 2, no. 15 (1962): 7–36 and 17 (1977–78): 7–45; Jocelyn Otway-Ruthven, "The Native Irish and English Law in Medieval Ireland," *IHS* 7, no. 25 (1950): 1–16; Katharine Simms, "The Legal Position of Irish Women in the Later Middle Ages," *Irish Jurist*, new series (1975): 96–111; Gearóid Mac Niocaill, "Aspects of Irish Law in the Late Thirteenth Century," *Historical Studies* 10 (1976): 25–42; Donncha Ó Corráin, "Irish Law and Canon Law," in *Irland und Europa*, ed. Próinseás Ní Chatháin and Michael Richter (Stuttgart: Klett-Cotta, 1984): 157–66; Gearóid Mac Niocaill, "Christian Influence in Early Irish Law," pp. 151–56 (same volume). On the customary nature of early Irish law, see D. L. T. Bethell, "The Originality of the Early Irish Church," *JRSAI* 111 (1981): 36–49, 45.
90. *ALI*, 1:19.
91. Donncha Ó Corráin, "Nationality and Kingship in Pre-Norman Ireland," in T. W. Moody, ed., *Nationality and the Pursuit of National Independence, Historical Studies* 11 (1978): 1–35, 14–17; Donncha Ó Corráin, "The Early Irish Churches: Some Aspects of Organization," in *Irish Antiquity: Essays and Studies Presented to Prof. M. J. O'Kelly*, ed. D. Ó Corráin (Cork: Cork University Press, 1981), pp. 327–41, p. 331; cf. also *ALI*, 1:9–45.
92. *ALI*, 1:35.
93. Cf. *ALI*, 1:155, 253.
94. According to early Irish law, Brígh Ambui was a "female author of wisdom and prudence among the men of Erin". *ALI*, 1:23.

The word *ambue* also means "outlaw," or somebody outside the tribal system. And it is possible that this figure could throw some valuable clues as to the nature of social unity in pre-judicial times. For the etymology of *ambue*, see Kim McCone, "Werewolves, Cyclopes, Diberga, and Fianna: Juvenile Delinquency in Early Ireland," *CMCS*, 12 (1986): 1–22, 11.; cf. also Thomas Charles Edwards, "The Social Background to Irish Peregrinatio," *Studia Celtica* 11 (1976): 43–59, 52–53; *EIHM*, chap. 17, "The Wisdom of Finn," for the poet's gift of prophecy.
95. Cf. *ALI*, 1:177–81.
96. Cf. Art Cosgrove, *Marriage in Ireland* (Dublin: College Press, 1985); D. Ó Corráin, "Women in Early Irish Society," in *Women in Irish Society*, ed. Margaret MacCurtain and Donncha Ó Corráin (Dublin: Arlen House, 1978), pp. 1–13; H. d'Arbois de Jubainville, "L'Achat de la Femme," *RC* 3 (1876–78): 361–64; Josef Weisweiler, "Die Stellung der Frau bei den Kelten und das Problem des Keltischen 'Mutter-rechts'," *ZCP* 21, no. 2 (1939): 205–79.
97. *ALI*, 1:145.
98. Ibid., pp. 251–53.
99. Ibid., pp. 145, 147; 4:9ff., 17, 39.
100. *ALI*, 4:17.
101. Ibid., pp. 19, 41.

Chapter 4. Brigit of Kildare

Epigraph: From *Thes Pal*, 2:330.
1. Cf. Liam de Paor, "Saint Mac Creiche of Liscannor," *Ériu* 30 (1979): 93–121, 119.
2. Wh. Stokes, *Three Middle Irish Homilies on the Lives of SS. Patrick, Brigit, and Columcille* (Calcutta: privately printed, 1877); cf. also *Lis Lives*, p. 199.
3. Felim Ó Briain, "Brigide," *Dictionnaire d'Histoire et des Geographie Ecclesiastique*,

ed. Alfred Baudrillart (Paris: Letouzey, 1935), 8:717–18.

4. Henry Foster McClintock, "The Mantle of St. Brigid at Bruge," *JRSAI*, 7th ser., 66, no. 5 (1936): 32–40; C. Ó Danachair, "The Holy Wells of Limerick," *JRSAI* 85 (1955): 193–217; Michael Coyle, "St. Brigid's Well, Dunleer," *Journal of the County Louth Archaeological Society* 13, no. 2 (1954): 175–78; John C. O'Sullivan, "St. Brigid's Crosses," *Folklife* 11 (1973): 60–81; Seán C. Ó Súilleabháin, "An Críos Bríde," in *Gold Under the Furze: Studies in Folk Tradition Presented to Caoimhín Ó Danachair*, ed. Alan Gailey and Dáithí Ó hOgáin (Dublin: Glendale Press, 1982), pp. 242–53. There is an extensive body of literature on the cult of Brigit. For full references, see entries under "Brigit" in Richard J. Hayes, *Sources for the History of Irish Civilization* (Boston: G. K. Hall, 1970), a series of volumes that is now kept updated by the National Library of Ireland.

5. T. H. Mason, "St. Brigid's Crosses," *JRSAI* 75 (1945): 160–66, 161.

6. *Lis Lives*, p. 184.

7. Ibid.

8. *LH*, 2:196; *Three Middle Irish Homilies*, p. 83.

9. *Thes Pal*, 2:325.

10. W. M. Hennessy, "Curragh of Kildare," *PRIA*, 1st ser. 9, C (1865–67): 343–55, 349.

11. Bernard Wailes, "Dún Ailinne: An Interim Report," in *Hillforts: Later Prehistoric Earthworks in Britain and Ireland*, ed. D. W. Harding (New York: Academic Press, 1976), p. 321; Felim Ó Briain, "Hagiography of Leinster," in *Essays Presented to Eoin Mac Neill*, ed. John Ryan (Dublin: At the Sign of the Three Candles, 1940), p. 454.

12. *Ren Dind*, no. 17.

13. Bernard Wailes, "Irish Royal Sites in History and Archaeology," *CMCS*, 3 (1982): 1–29, 20.

14. Cited in Kuno Meyer, *Hail Brigit: An Old-Irish Poem on the Hill of Alenn* (Halle: a.S Niemeyer, 1912), p. 1.

15. *Mart Oeng*, p. 25.

16. Proinsias Mac Cana, *Celtic Mythology* (1968; rev. ed., New York: Hamlyn, 1983) p. 34.

17. R. A. S. MacAlister, *Tara: A Pagan Sanctuary of Ancient Ireland* (New York: Charles Scribner's Sons, 1931), p. 95; *Three Irish Glossaries*, ed. Wh. Stokes (London: Williams and Norgate, 1862), p. xli.

18. Liam de Paor, "The Aggrandisement of Armagh," *Historical Studies* 8 (1971): 95–110, 101.

19. Cf. John Healy, *Insula Sanctorum et Doctorum: Ireland's Ancient Schools and Scholars* (Dublin: Sealy, Bryers, and Walker, 1893), pp. 125–40.

20. R. A. S. MacAlister, "Temair Breg: Remains and Traditions of Tara," *PRIA* 34 C (1919): 231–340.

21. Cf. "Death of Muircertach Mac Erca," *AIT*, pp. 525–26.

22. Wm. Sherlock, *Some Account of St. Brigid and the See of Kildare with its Bishops, and of the Cathedral now Restored* (Dublin: Hodges Figgis, 1896), p. 51.

23. Cf. *Gerald*, p. 82. Yet another such sacred site was at Usneach or Usney Hill where, according to some "Lives," Brigit received the veil. Usneach was known as the "centre of Ireland," the place "where five provinces meet." It has been described as a "long swelling green eminence" that has "never been submitted to the plough." Cf. John O'Hanlon, *Lives of Irish Saints* (Dublin: James Duffy, 1845–1903) 2:63, n. 114.

24. Cf. Healy, *Insula Sanctorum et Doctorum*, p. 131; M. Comerford, *Dioceses of Kildare and Leighlin* (Dublin: J. Duffy & Sons, 1883), 2:1. For the regulations governing the sacred trees of Ireland, see *ALI*, 4:147; D. A. Binchy, "An Archaic Legal Poem," *Celtica* 9 (1971): 152–68, 156–59; A. T. Lucas, "The Sacred Trees of Ireland," *JCHAS*, 68 (1963): 16–54; A. Watson, "The King, the Poet, and the Sacred Tree," *EC* 18 (1981): 165–80.

25. Cf. *VSH*, 1:cxxvii; *Thes Pal*, 2:329; *Mart Oeng*, p. 65.

26. *VSH*, 1:cxxvii, n. 9.
27. Cf. *BB*, p. xxiv; cf. also Marie Esposito, "Notes on Latin Learning and Literature in Mediaeval Ireland," *Hermathena* 24, no. 1 (1935): 120–65, 162.
28. "Amra Plea," i.e., "a convent of Brigit's which is on the brink of the sea of Wight, or the Tyrrhene (sea) and its Rule is that of Brigit's community." *Mart Oeng*, p. 65.
29. Henri Hubert, *The Greatness and Decline of the Celts*, trans. M. R. Dobie (1934; reprint, New York: Arno Press, 1972), pp. 73, 84, 159–61.
30. Cf. *Mart Oeng*, p. 65; *Thes Pal*, 2:329; *LH*, 2:191.
31. J. F. Campbell, *Occidental Mythology* (Harmondsworth, Middlesex: Penguin, 1964), p. 321. This translation has been challenged, however, and for a discussion of the various possible meanings, see Mary Beard, "The Sexual Status of the Vestal Virgins," *Journal of Roman Studies* (1980): 12–27, 15.
32. Cf. W. Smith, Wm. Wayte, G. E. Marindin, eds., *Dictionary of Greek and Roman Antiquity*, 3d ed. (London: John Murray, 1901), 2:942; W. Warde Fowler, *The Roman Festivals of the Period of the Republic* (New York: Macmillan, 1899), p. 242ff.
33. Sarah Pomeroy, *Goddesses, Whores, Wives and Slaves* (New York: Schocken, 1975), pp. 210–11.
34. Pomeroy, *Goddesses, Whores*, p. 213.
35. Beard, "Sexual Status of Vestal Virgins," pp. 16–17.
36. Cf. Pomeroy, *Goddesses, Whores*, pp. 211–13; Beard, "Sexual Status," p. 16.
37. Beard, "Sexual Status," p. 16.
38. Cf. Jan de Vries, *Keltische Religion* (Stuttgart: Kohlhammer, 1961), p. 217; *RAC*, p. 316ff; *CSR*, p. 76.
39. *MDs*, pt. 3, p. 465.
40. Medb's name means the "intoxicating one," and she is a form of the Goddess who in various cultures is seen providing the king or hero with a libation, a drink necessary for him to continue in his reign. Cf. Tomás Ó Máille, "Medb Cruachna," *ZCP* 17 (1928): 129–46.
41. George Petrie, "On the History and Antiquities of Tara Hill," *TRIA* 18 (1824): 25–225, 34, 131–136, 145, 215; John V. Kelleher, "Early Irish History and Pseudo-History," *Studia Hibernica* 3 (1963): 113–29, 123; cf. also "The Bóroma," ed. Wh. Stokes, *RC* 13 (1892): 32–124, 51; *AFM* 241 a.d., for account of women killed at the Ferta.
42. Petrie, "History and Antiquities of Tara Hill," p. 218; Alwyn Rees and Brinley Rees, *Celtic Heritage* (London: Thames and Hudson, 1961), p. 147.
43. D. A. Binchy, "The Fair of Tailtiú and the Feast of Tara," *Ériu* 18 (1958): 113–38, 134.
44. *FF*, 3:69, 87; *The Martyrology of Tallaght*, R. I. Best and H. J. Lawlor (London: Henry Bradshaw Society, 1931), pp. 102–7.
45. See Francis John Byrne, "Tribes and Tribalism in Early Ireland," *Ériu* 22 (1971): 128–66, 149; Binchy, "The Fair of Tailtiú," p. 137.
   R. A. S. MacAlister pioneered the view that Tara was primarily a religious site, and recent scholarly opinion is returning to that view. Cf. F. J. Byrne, "The Ireland of Saint Columba," *Historical Studies* 5 (1965): 37–58, 58, n. 91; Kelleher, "Early Irish History," p. 122.
46. "Bóroma," p. 55.
47. Cf. MacAlister, *Tara*, p. 177.
48. Cf. MacAlister, "Temair Breg," pp. 252, 285–86, 300; *Tara*, p. 83, 90–91; cf. also Petrie, "History and Antiquities of Tara Hill," p. 152, 158; *MDs*, pt. 1, p. 97; Marie Louise Sjoestedt, *Gods and Heroes of the Ancient Celts*, trans. Myles Dillon (1949; reprint, Berkeley, CA: Turtle Island Foundation, 1982), p. 44; Prof. Connellan, "Report on How the Táin Was First Discovered," *TOS* 5 (1860): 257.
49. Cf. Petrie, *History and Antiquities*, p. 130ff. MacAlister, "Temair Breg," pp. 300, 321ff.; MacAlister, *Tara*, p. 94ff. For parallels, see the Demeter and Persephone stories in Greek mythology.
50. Cf. R. A. S. MacAlister, "The Fire-Walk in Ancient Ireland," *Man* 63 (1919):

117-18; Esposito, "Latin Learning," p. 162; J. Mair, "Darlugdacha—Eine Vergessene Heilige," *Frigisinga* 5, no. 34 (1928): 433-35. It is also possible that the original veneration of Brigit took place on the same day as the Roman Juno, i.e., February 11 (or 13), and that eventually Brigit's feast was moved to February 1, the original feast of Darlughdacha (the Daughter of Lugh); cf. Warde Fowler, *Roman Festivals*, p. 302. The feast of Lugh (Lammas) is on August 1, the other half of the Celtic year. For the traditions surrounding this Lughnasa, see the major work by Maire Mac Neill, *The Festival of Lughnasa* (Dublin: Comhaire Bhéaloideas Eireann, University College, 1962).

51. MacAlister, "The Fire-Walk," pp. 117-18; MacAlister, *Tara*, p. 197.
52. Cf. Eugene O'Curry, *Manners and Customs of the Early Irish*, W. K. Sullivan ed., (New York: Scribner, Welford & Co.) 1:clxxi; For further information on companies of nine priestesses, see Monica Sjöö and Barbara Mor, *The Great Cosmic Mother: Rediscovering the Religion of the Earth* (San Francisco: Harper & Row, 1987), p. 114.
53. *RAC*, p. 316; *CSR*, p. 76; Connellan, "Report on How the Táin Was First Discovered," pp. 165-66; de Vries, *Keltische Religion*, p. 217; Salomon Reinach, "Les Vierges de Sena," *RC* 18 (1897): 1-8.
54. Cf. Hubert, *Greatness and Decline of the Celts*, p. 189
55. *Gerald*, p. 88.
56. Cf. Warde Fowler, *Roman Festivals*, p. 247; cf. also R. E. A. Palmer, "Roman Shrines of Female Chastity From the Caste Struggle to the Papacy of Innocent I," *Rivista Storica dell'Antichita* 4 (1974): 113-59, for the significance of such shrines in Roman culture.
57. *Thes Pal*, 2:344; de Vries, *Keltische Religion*, p. 217. Cf. also "The Life of Monenna by Conchubranus," pt. 3, ed. Ulster Society for Medieval Latin Studies, *Seanchas Ardmhacha* 10, no. 2 (1982): 426-54, 447-48, for miraculous tree-raising after Monenna's death.
58. *Mart Oeng*, pp. 105, 215, 223, n. 8, 250; *Cal Oeng*, p. clxxv, clxxxi. This version refers to "three virginal fifties."
59. Warde Fowler, *Roman Festivals*, p. 321.
60. Louis Gougaud, *Les Saints Irlandais hors d'Irlande: Etudes dans le Culte et dans la Deívotion Traditionelle* (London: Bureau de la Revue, 1936).
61. *Lis Lives*, p. 189-90, v. 1394; *Middle Irish Homilies*, pp. 73-75.
62. *LH* 2:201.
63. *Thes Pal*, 2:327.
64. *BH*, 1:65; *Three Middle Irish Homilies*, p. 85; *Lis Lives*, p. 198.
65. Cf. Kuno Meyer, *Hibernica Minora*, Anecdota Oxoniensia, no. 4 (Oxford: Clarendon Press, 1894), p. 49; J. Vendryes, "Imbolc," *RC* 41 (1924): 241-44; de Vries, *Keltische Religion*, p. 225; cf. Pamela Berger, *The Goddess Obscured* (Boston: Beacon Press, 1986), p. 51, for documentation of the church condemnation of lustration practices performed on fields.
66. Cf. Ethel Rolt-Wheeler, *Women of the Cell and Cloister* (Milwaukee, WI: Young Churchman's Association, n.d.), p. 51.
67. Warde Fowler, *Roman Festivals*, p. 321.
68. Comerford, *Dioceses of Kildare and Leighlin*, 2:13.
69. Cf. Henri Hubert and Marcel Mauss, *Sacrifice: Its Nature and Function*, trans. W. D. Halls (Chicago: University of Chicago Press, 1964), p. 20.
70. Warde Fowler, *Roman Festivals*, p. 311.
71. *Thes Pal*, 2:347; cf. also *BB*, pp. 34, 64, for a different version of this story.
72. *Thes Pal*, 2:296, cf. also p. 329; J. H. Bernard, "The Irish Verses in the Codex Boernerianus," *The Academy*, Feb. 23rd, 1190 (1895): 172, for commentary on these verses.
73. Cf. Ó Briain, "Brigide," p. 717.
74. *Lis Lives*, pp. 199, 333-34; *BNE*, 2:83-84; *Thes Pal*, 2:324-25.
75. Cf. *BB*, p. 35; cf. also *LH*, 2:196; *Thes Pal*, 2:336.
76. *Lis Lives*, p. 192.

77. Cf. Kim McCone, "Brigit in the Seventh Century: A Saint With Three Lives?" *Peritia* 1 (1982): 108; cf. also Esposito, "Latin Learning," pp. 134, 139, for further evidence of materials on Brigit being "censored" out.
78. *Lis Lives*, pp. 196–97.
79. "Cummin's Poems on the Saints of Ireland," ed. Wh. Stokes, *ZCP* 1 (1897): 59–73, 63. Stokes comments that an alternative translation of this last part could read that Brigit loved *féile feraibh ferta*, "chanting and the grass of her tomb."
80. Cf. *Lis Lives*, p. 193.
81. *Lis Lives*, p. 188.
82. *BB*, p. 24; cf. also *Lis Lives*, p. 323.
83. Cf. Ó Corráin, "Women in Early Irish Society," p. 10; "Three Poems Ascribed to Maol-Cobha," ed. Mairín O'Daly, *Ériu* 21 (1969): 103–15, 112; *Mart Oeng*, p. 25.
84. "Vestales," cf. Smith, Wayte, and Marindin, *Dictionary of Greek and Roman Antiquity*, p. 943.
85. *FF*, 3:213.
86. *Lis Lives*, p. 189.
87. *The Táin*, pp. 8–20.
88. *CG*, p. 172.
89. There may even be some legal significance to the "two rams" references. In early Irish law a woman could establish her claim to territory using two ewes as markers. Cf. *ALI*, 4:6–7, no. 266.
90. Cf. Philip O'Leary, "The Honour of Women in Early Irish Literature," *Ériu* 38 (1987): 27–44. For redactions of the story of Deirdre, see Muireann Ní Bhrolcháin, "Scéal Dheirdre," *Ar Scéalaíocht: Léachtaí Cholm Cille* 14 (1983): 38–89.
91. The topic of virginity will be dealt with more fully in a discussion of the twelfth-century reform movement.

Chapter 5. Sexual Politics of the Early Irish Church

Epigraph: From *Mart Oeng*, p. 41.
1. For a discussion of patriarchal dualism in Christian theology, see Rosemary Radford Ruether, *New Woman / New Earth: Sexist Ideologies and Human Liberation* (New York: Seabury Press, 1975).
2. Cf. L. Duchesne, "Lovocat et Catihern, prétres bretons due temps de St. Melaine," *Revue de Bretagne et de Vendeé* 57 (1885): 5–21; J. Loth, "Un Ancien Usage De L'Église Celtique," *RC* 15 (1894): 92–93; Lina Eckenstein, *Women Under Monasticism* (Cambridge: Cambridge University Press, 1896), pp. 7–8.
3. *BNE*, 2:127.
4. Ibid., p. 129.
5. Ibid.
6. Cf. *VSH*, 1:clxxxi. Rebaptism according to the Christian rite was required of anyone who converted to Christianity; cf. Eleanor Hull, "Pagan Baptism in the West," *Folklore* 43, no. 4 (1932): 410–18, 410.
7. *EIHM*, p. 296, n. 3.
8. *BNE*, 2:121.
9. Ibid., pp. 125, 129.
10. Flidais was said to be the "queen of the Tuatha Dé Danáan (People of the Goddess Dana), mother of Nía Segámain, son of Adammair, who milked does and cattle." *Cóir Anmann: On the Fitness of Names*, ed. Whitley Stokes and E. Windisch, *Irische Texte* (Leipzig, 1891–97), 3 pt. 2, p. 295; cf. also *Táin Bó Flidais*, ed. D. MacKinnon, *Celtic Review* 4 (1907–8): 104–21, 202–19; "The Driving of the Cattle of Flidais," in *Heroic Romances of Ireland*, ed. A. H. Leahy (London: D. Nutt, 1905), 2:101–26.
11. Cf. Eleanor Hull, "Legends and Traditions of the Cailleach Bheara or Old Woman (Hag) of Beare," *Folklore* 38 (1927): 225–54, 247.
12. Some hollow stones were said to help a woman in child labor. *VSH*, p. cxxxix, clvi. Cf. *Lives of Declan and Mochuda*, ed. P. Power (London: Irish Texts Society, vol.

16, 1914), p. 9.

13. *BNE*, 2:29.

14. Ibid.

15. Ibid., p. 159.

16. Cf. Monica Sjöö and Barbara Mor, *The Great Cosmic Mother: Rediscovering the Religion of the Earth* (San Francisco: Harper & Row, 1987), p. 302.

17. "The Birth and Life of St. Moling," ed. Wh. Stokes, *RC* 27 (1906): 257–305, 279; *SG*, 2:3; *BNE*, 2:308.

18. "Report on How the Táin Was First Discovered," *TOS* 5 (1860), p. 59.

19. *BNE*, 2:213.

20. Ibid., p. 180.

21. Ibid., p. 211.

22. Ibid.

23. According to Monica Sjöö and Barbara Mor, musical instruments were used extensively by women in their ritual practices and possibly were even an early form of sonar technology; cf. Sjöö and Mor, *Great Cosmic Mother*, pp. 117–18. Significantly, four trumpets were found in Lough na Shade near Emhain Mhacha in the eighteenth century. It is possible that they were consigned there at the same time that the sacred site of Emhain Mhacha was ritually destroyed; cf. J. P. Mallory, "Navan Fort: A Monument for All Myths," *Linen Hall Review* 2, no. 1 (Spring 1985): 4–6; J. P. Mallory, *Navan Fort: The Ancient Capital of Ulster*, illustrated by Stephen Colin (Produced by Friends of Navan Fort, n.d. 17 University Square, Belfast, BT7 INN).

24. *BNE*, 2:185.

25. *SG*, 2:23.

26. *BNE*, 2:8.

27. *Lives of Declan and Mochuda*, p. 61.

28. See David Herlihy, in *Medieval Households* (Cambridge, MA: Harvard University Press, 1985), pp. 31–32; *BNE*, 2:100–101; *LH*, 2:197.

29. *Penit*, p. 64.

30. *Betha Colaim Chille*, ed. A. O'Kelleher and G. Schoepperle (Chicago: Irish Foundation Series, 1918), no. 353, p. 381. Cf. also Herlihy, *Medieval Households*, pp. 40–42.

31. Translated by Nuala Ní Dhomhnaill.

32. Vernam Hull, "Two Anecdotes Concerning St. Moling," *ZCP* 18 (1930): 90–99, 91. James Carney, trans. *Studies in Irish Literature and History* (Dublin: Institute for Advanced Studies, 1955), p. 138.

33. *BNE*, 2:168.

34. Ibid.

35. Ibid., p. 171; cf. also *VSH*, p. clxxxviii, for further references to males suckling children.

36. *Mart Oeng*, p. 181; *BNE*, 2:39.

37. *Cal Oeng*, p. cxliii; *Mart Oeng*, p. 201.

38. *Cal Oeng*, p. 25; C. Doherty, "Some Aspects of Hagiography as a Source of Irish Economic History," *Peritia* 1 (1982): 300–328, 313–16.

39. C. Doherty, "The Monastic Town in Early Medieval Ireland," in *The Comparative History of Urban Origins in Non-Roman Europe* (British Archaeological Report International Series), ed. Howard Clark and Anngret Simms, 255(i) (1985): 45–75. Doherty argues that getting slave labor was important for the early Irish church since it was the only way the church could develop an economy capable of producing surplus wealth, which in turn could support those in cultural, artistic, and religious employment.

40. For a discussion of the rise of the notion of illegitimacy, see Jack Goody, *Development of the Family and Marriage in Europe* (New York: Cambridge University Press, 1983), pp. 48–82.

41. *BB*, p. 31.

42. *VSH*, 1:55.

43. Cf. Michel Foucault, *The History of Sexuality* (New York: Random House, Vintage Books, 1980), 1:11ff.
44. Cf. *Penit*, p. 91.
45. For an extensive bibliography of penitential literature, see John T. MacNeill, *A History of the Cure of Souls* (New York: Harper & Row, 1951), pp. 341–59; cf. also Ludwig Bieler, *The Irish Penitentials* (Dublin: Institute for Advanced Studies, 1963); James Brundage and Vern Bullough, *Sexual Practices and the Medieval Church* (Buffalo, NY: Prometheus Books, 1982).
46. For the relationship between church power and the control of sexuality, see Samuel Laeuchli, *Power and Sexuality* (Philadelphia: Temple University Press, 1972).
47. *Penit*, pp. 113, 262.
48. Ibid., p. 115.
49. Ibid., p. 219.
50. Ibid., p. 221.
51. Ibid., p. 161.
52. Ibid., p. 103.
53. Ibid.
54. Ibid., p. 89.
55. Cf. John Boswell, *Christianity, Social Tolerance and Homosexuality* (Chicago: University of Chicago Press, 1980), pp. 51, 183; Maire Cruise O'Brien, "Female Principle in Gaelic Poetry," in *Women in Irish Legend, Life and Literature*, ed. S. F. Gallagher, (Gerrards Cross, NJ: Barnes & Noble, 1983), 26–37, p. 29.
56. "The Birth and Life of St. Moling," p. 285.
57. *BNE*, 2:191, 257.
58. *Penit*, p. 97.
59. John Chrysostom, *Epist. ad Rom. 4.2,3, in app. 2,* quoted in Boswell, *Christianity, Social Tolerance*, p. 157.
60. Boswell, *Christianity, Social Tolerance*, p. 158.
61. *Penit*, pp. 163, 217.
62. Ibid., p. 169.
63. Ibid., p. 117.
64. Ibid., p. 201.
65. Ibid., pp. 79–81.
66. Ibid., p. 101.
67. *Sources*, pp. 240–241; cf. also "Penitential of Columbanus," for agreement with Finnian, *Penit*, p. 101.
68. *Penit*, p. 161.
69. Ibid., p. 272.
70. Ibid., p. 115.
71. "The Monastery of Tallaght," ed. E. J. Gwynn and Wm. J. Purton, *PRIA* 29, sect c, 5 (1911): 115–79, 132.
72. Cf. "The Monastery of Tallaght," pp. 128–30.
73. From *Book of Leinster*, a manuscript of the early half of the twelfth century, quoted in Wm. Reeves, "On the Céli Dé commonly called Culdees," *TRIA* 24 (1873): 119–263, 195–96.
74. "The Monastery of Tallaght," p. 151.
75. Ibid., p. 149.
76. Ibid., p. 134.
77. Ibid., p. 132.
78. Reeves, "On the Céli-Dé," p. 211.
79. "The Monastery of Tallaght," p. 132.
80. Ibid., p. 149.
81. Ibid., p. 154.
82. Ibid.
83. Ibid.

Chapter 6. Blasts of Temptation

Epigraph: From L. Duchesne, "Lovocat et Catihern, pretres breton du temps de St. Melaine," *Revue de Bretagne et de Vendeé* 57 (1885), 7–8.

1. Cf. J. H. Todd, *St. Patrick Apostle of Ireland* (Dublin: Hodges & Smith, 1864), pp. 88–89; *Councils and Ecclesiastical Documents Relating to Great Britain and Ireland*, ed. A. W. Haddan and W. Stubbs (Oxford: Clarendon Press, 1873), vol. 2, pt. 1, pp. 292–93.

2. For the debate regarding Patrick, see note 2, chap. 3. As Todd comments, on the fact that "they did not rigidly reject the services of women" . . . "it is remarkable that this is spoken of as evidence of their superior holiness." Todd, *St. Patrick*, pp. 90–91.

3. *SG*, 2:35.

4. *Mart Don*, p. 243.

5. Ibid., p. 249.

6. Ibid., p. 259.

7. *BNE*, 2:129.

8. *VSH*, 1:clii.

9. Ibid., p. 205.

10. *Latin and Irish Lives of St. Ciaran of Clonmacnoise*, ed. R. A. S. MacAlister (London: S.P.C.K., 1921), p. 25.

11. *VSH*, 1:cxxii, clii, 250; cf. also "Mac dá Cherda and Cummaine foda," ed. J. G. O'Keeffe, *Ériu* 5 (1911): 18–44, 35.

12. For full text, see *Liadain and Curithir*, ed. and trans. Kuno Meyer (London: L. Nutt, 1902), p. 25.

13. For a different interpretation, Eleanor Hull, "Legends and Traditions of the Cailleach Bheara or Old Woman (Hag) of Beare," *Folklore* 38, no. 111 (1927): 225–54, 228.

14. Cf. Elisabeth Schüssler Fiorenza, *In Memory of Her* (New York: Crossroad, Continuum, 1985), for the role of women in the early church. Cf. also *Bede*, pp. 120–22; Max Weber, *Sociology of Religion*, trans. Ephraim Fischoff (Boston: Beacon Press, 1963), p. 104; Averil Cameron, "Neither Male Nor Female," *Greece and Rome* 27 (1980): 60–68, 63.

15. *Bede*, p. 122.

16. Cf. Roger Reynolds, "Virgines Subintroductae," *Harvard Theological Review* 61 (1968): 547–66.

17. Alfred Perceval Graves, *Celtic Psaltery* (New York: F. A. Stokes, 1917), p. 33. Some see this as a reference to the monk's prayer book rather than his *consortia*. Cf. James Carney, "Old Ireland and Her Poetry," in *Old Ireland*, ed. R. McNally (New York: Fordham University Press, 1965), p. 154ff. But even if this were the case, the fact that he used the image of "spiritual marriage" is, in itself, testimony to its presence.

18. "Agapetae," *Encyclopedia of Religion and Ethics*, ed. James Hastings (New York: Charles Scribner's Sons, 1924), 1:177–80.

19. T. Olden, "On the Consortia of the First Order of Irish Saints," *PRIA*, 3d series 111, C (1894): 415–20, 418. Similar stories are told of the Breton saints, Gwenole and Malo. Cf. Pierre de Labriolle, "Le Marriage Spiritual Dans l'Antiquite Chretienne," *Revue Historique* 137 (1921): 204–25.

20. Olden, "On the Consortia," p. 417.

21. Ibid., p. 418.

22. "Agapetae," p. 178.

23. L. Duchesne, "Lovacat et Catihern, prétres bretons du temps de St. Melaine," *Revue de Bretagne et de Vendée* 57 (1885): 5–21, 8.

24. Cf. discussion of celibacy in the chapters on the reform movement in the twelfth century.

25. Cf. Suzanne Wemple, *Women in Frankish Society* (Philadelphia: University of Penn-

sylvania Press, 1981), p. 160; Mary Bateson, "Origin and Early History of Double Monasteries," *Transactions of the Royal Historical Society* N.S. 13 (1899): 137–98, 135. For discussion of the roles of abbesses and their practice of veiling members of their own communities, preaching, or hearing nun's confessions, and of the various documents issued against these practices, see *Corpus Juris Canonici*, ed. E. A. Friedberg (Leipzig: Tauchnitz, 1879–81), 2:886; Ida Raming, *The Exclusion of Women from the Priesthood: Divine Law or Sex Discrimination?* trans. Norman R. Adams (Metuchen, NJ: Scarecrow Press, 1976), pp. 7–39, 71–74, 201, nn. 9, 10; Francine Cardman, "The Medieval Question of Women and Orders," *Thomist* 42 (1978): 582–99, 596.

For the institution of "double monasteries," see also Alexander Hamilton Thompson, "Double Monasteries and the Male Element in Nunneries," in *Ministry of Women: A Report by a Committee Appointed by His Grace the Lord Archbishop of Canterbury* (London, 1919); John Godfrey, "The Double Monastery in Early English History," *Ampleforth Journal* 79 (1974): 19–32.

26. Cf. John Ryan, *Irish Monasticism* (London: Longmans, Greene, 1931), p. 143.

27. *Mart Oeng*, p. lii. Cf. also Philip O'Leary, "The Honour of Women in Early Irish Literature," *Ériu* 38 (1987): 27–44, 37; John R. Reinhard, "Burning at the Stake in Medieval Law and Literature," *Speculum* 16 (1941): 186–209. Reinhard argues that such burnings were not a major feature of early Irish life.

28. Cf. *Vita Fursii*, cited in Irene Snieders, "L'Influence de l'hagiographie irlandaise sur les vitae des saints irlandais de Belgique," *Revue d'histoire ecclesiastique* 24 (1928): 613–27, 828–67, 841.

29. Cf. Bateson, "Origin and Early History," pp. 137–98, 163, 194.

30. *SEIL*, pp. 213–14.

31. *Mart Oeng*, p. 51.

32. *VSH*, 2:254.

33. *BB*, p. 23

34. "Life of St. Senán," in *Lis Lives*, pp. 219–20.

35. "The Life of Monenna by Conchubranus," pt. 3, ed. Ulster Society for Medieval Latin Studies, *Seanchas Ard Mhacha* 10 no. 2 (1982): 426–54, 433.

36. Ibid., 10 no. 2, p. 429.

37. Ibid., 10 no. 1, p. 137.

38. "Life of Monenna," 10 no. 2, p. 429.

39. *VSH*, 1:cxxxvi, 2:256–59; *BNE*, 2:35; *Mart Don*, p. 341; *History of the Diocese of Ardagh*, ed. B. McNamee (Dublin, 1954), pp. 87–91.

40. "The Monastery of Tallaght," ed. E. J. Gwynn and Wm. J. Purton, *PRIA*, 29, c.5 (1911): 115–79, 150.

41. Ibid., p. 151.

42. *Thes Pal*, 2:331; *LH*, 2:193.

43. *AS*, Feb. 1, Vita 1, S. Brigidae Virg. cap. xii, 73, p. 129.

44. *Thes Pal*, 2:315; Felim Ó Briain, "The Hagiography of Leinster," in *Essays Presented to Eoin Mac Neill* (Dublin: At the Sign of the Three Candles, 1940), p. 463. *AS*, Feb. 1, Vita 1, S. Brigidae Virg. cap. xii, 93, p. 132.

45. Cf. *Life of St. Columba by Adamnán*, ed. Wm. Reeves (Edinburgh: Edmonston and Douglas, 1874), p. lviii.

46. Kim McCone, "Early Irish Saint's Lives," *Maynooth Review* 11 (1984): 26–59, 58–59; Ó Briain, "Hagiography of Leinster," p. 456.

47. McCone, "Early Irish Saint's Lives," pp. 34–35; Kim McCone, "Brigit in the Seventh Century; A Saint With Three Lives?" *Peritia* 1 (1982): pp. 107–45, 136.

48. For background to Cogitosus, see Richard Sharpe, "Vitae S. Brigitae: The Oldest Texts," *Peritia* 1 (1982): 81–106, 89.

49. Cf. Mario Esposito, "Notes on Latin Learning and Literature in Mediaeval Ireland," *Hermathena* 24, no. 4 (1935): 120–65, 134; cf. also Richard Sharpe, "Vitae S. Brigitae: The Oldest Texts," *Peritia* 1 (1982): 81–106, 89; Pádraig O'Neill, "Romani Influences in Seventh-Century Hiberno-Latin Literature," in *Irland und Europa*, ed. Próinséas Ní Chatháin and Michael Richter (Stuttgart: Klett-

Cotta, 1984), p. 290.

50. Cf. Esposito, "Latin Learning," pp. 134-39; Sharpe, "Vitae S. Brigitae," p. 103; cf. also *BB*, p. xii.

51. Mario Esposito, "On the Earliest Latin Life of Brigid of Kildare," *PRIA* 30, sect. c (1912): 307-26, 321-24.

52. Cf. Felim Ó Briain, "Brigide," 716-19; Liam de Paor, "The Aggrandisement of Armagh," *Historical Studies* 8 (1971): 95-110, 101.

53. *Mart Oeng*, p. 223; Wm. Reeves, *Ancient Churches of Armagh* (Lusk, printed for the author, 1860), sec. v, p. 25; John O'Hanlon, *Lives of Irish Saints*, (Dublin: 1875-1903), 2:10.

54. *VSH*, 2:266; Kim McCone, "Clones and Her Neighbours in the Early Period: Hints from Some Airgialla Saint's Lives," *Clogher Record* 11 (1984): 305-25, 321.

55. *BH*, 2:301.

56. *ALI*, 2:407.

57. J. H. Todd, *Life of Patrick* (Dublin: Hodges & Smith, 1864), pp. 13-14.

58. Cf. *AFM*, A.D. 1097; O'Hanlon, *Lives of Irish Saints*, 2:101.

59. O'Hanlon, *Lives of Irish Saints*, 2:184.

60. *Chronicum Scotorum*, ed. Wm. M. Hennessy (London: Longmans, Green, Reader and Dyer, 1866), p. 171. For the significance of hair in pre-Christian religions, see Elisabeth Schüssler Fiorenza, *In Memory of Her* (New York: Crossroad, 1985) p. 227.

61. Cf. Monica Sjöö and Barbara Mor, *The Great Cosmic Mother: Rediscovering the Religion of the Earth* (San Francisco: Harper & Row, 1987), p.183.

62. McCone, "Clones and Her Neighbours," p. 321.

63. Cf. Wh. Stokes, "The Bóroma," *RC* 13 (1892): 32-124, 115; Ó Briain, "Hagiography of Leinster," pp. 458-59, n. 20; Felim Ó' Briain, "Brigitana," ed. F. Mac Donncha, *ZCP* 36 (1979): 112-38, 125.

64. Ludwig Bieler, *Patrician Texts in the Book of Armagh* (Dublin: Institute for Advanced Studies, 1979), p. 190.

65. Cf. C. Doherty, "The Monastic Town in Early Medieval Ireland," in *The Comparative History of Urban Origins in Non-Roman Europe* (British Archaeological Report, International Series), ed. Howard Clark and Anngret Simms, 255 (i): (1985) 45-75, 54-55; McCone, "Clones and Her Neighbours," p. 325; Kathleen Hughes, *The Church in Early Irish Society* (Ithaca, NY: Cornell University Press, 1966), p. 113.

66. *Thes Pal*, 2:326; *LH*, 2:189; "Three Middle Irish Homilies on the Lives of SS. Patrick, Brigid and Columcille," ed. Whitley Stokes (Calcutta: Privately printed, 1877), p. 69.

67. Cf. A. T. Lucas, "The Plundering and Burning of Churches in Ireland 7th to 16th Centuries," *North Munster Studies*, ed. Etienne Rynne (Limerick: Thomond Archaeological Society, 1967), pp. 172-229.

68. Lucas, "Burning," p. 176; *AU*, A.D. 846.

69. Hughes, *Church in Early Irish Society*, p. 192.

70. *ALC*, A.D. 1132

71. Cf. Michael Dolley, *Anglo-Norman Ireland* (Dublin: Gill and Macmillan, 1972), p. 30.

72. Aubrey Gwynn, *The Twelfth Century Reform* (Dublin: Gill, 1968), p. 54.

73. Aubrey Gwynn and R. N. Hadcock, *Medieval Religious Houses* (London: Longman, 1970), p. 320.

74. Cf. J. Healy, *Insula Sanctorum et Doctorum* (Dublin: Sealy, Bryers and Walker, 1893), p. 138.

75. Cf. Gwynn and Hadcock, *Medieval Religious Houses*, p. 320.

76. Ibid.

77. *BB*, pp. 31-32.

78. Cf. *BNE*, 2:39; Charles Doherty, "Some Aspects of Hagiography as a Source of Irish Economic History," *Peritia* 1 (1982): 300-328, 316.

79. *BB*, p. 32.

80. Ó Briain, "Brigide," p. 718.
81. *Thes Pal*, 2:241, 307.
82. "The Monastery of Tallaght," ed. E. J. Gwynn and Wm. J. Purton, *PRIA* 29, c.5 (1911): 115–79, 144.

Chapter 7. From Kin to King

Epigraph: *Gerald*, p. 110.
1. Cf. Irene ffrench Eager, *The Nun of Kenmare* (Cork: Mercier Press, 1970); Catriona Clear, *Nuns in Nineteenth Century Ireland* (Dublin: Gill & Macmillan, 1988).
2. Cf. John Watt, "The Development of the Theory of the Temporal Authority of the Papacy by the 13th Century Canonists," *Historical Studies* 2 (1959): 17–28; Brian Tierney, *The Crisis of Church and State, 1050–1300* (Englewood Cliffs, NJ: Prentice-Hall, 1964); W. Ullmann, *The Growth of Papal Government in the Middle Ages* (London: Methuen, 1955); Hayden White, "The Gregorian Ideal and St. Bernard of Clairvaux," *Journal of the History of Ideas* 21, no. 3 (1960): 321–43, 324–29.
3. Cf. Charles Dunn, "Ireland and the 12th Century Renaissance," *University of Toronto Quarterly* 24, no. 1 (1954): 70–86.
4. For a critical evaluation of the use of these texts, and for a valuable bibliography of contemporary critical approaches, see T. Ó Cathasaigh, "Pagan survivals: the evidence of early Irish narrative," in *Ireland and Europe*, eds. Próinséas Ní Chatháin and Michael Richter (Stuttgart: Klett-Cotta, 1984), pp. 291–307.
5. "Cóir Anmann: On the Fitness of Names," *Irische Texte*, ed. Wh. Stokes and E. Windisch (Leipzig, 1891–97), 3 pt. 2, p. 405.
6. *Cáin Adamnáin: An Old Irish Treatise on the Law of Adamnán*, ed. Kuno Meyer, Anecdota Oxoniensia, Medieval and Modern Series, pt. 12 (Oxford: Clarendon Press, 1905), p. 25.
7. Cf. Kim McCone, "Werewolves, Cyclopes, Diberga, and Fíanna: Juvenile Delinquency in Early Ireland," *CMCS* 12 (1986): 1–22.
8. Cf. *SG*, 2:70; *BNE*, 2:315–16; Donncha Ó Corráin, "Women in Early Irish Society," in *Women in Irish Society*, ed. Margaret Mac Curtain and Donncha Ó Corráin (Dublin: Arlen House, 1978), pp. 16–17; Charles Doherty, "The Monastic Town in Early Medieval Ireland," in *The Comparative History of Urban Origins in Non-Roman Europe* (British Archaeological Report, International Series), ed. Howard Clark and Anngret Simms, 25, no. 1 (1985): 45–75, 65ff; Katharine Simms, *From Kings to Warlords: The Changing Political Structure of Gaelic Ireland in the Later Middle Ages* (Suffolk: Cambridge Medieval Series, 1987), p. 89.
9. Cf. Charles Doherty, "Some Aspects of Hagiography as a Source of Irish Economic History," *Peritia* 1 (1982): 300–328, 316.
10. For further elaboration on this theme, see M. E. Tigar and M. R. Levy, *Law and the Rise of Capitalism* (New York: Monthly Review Press, 1977).
11. "The Bóroma," ed. Whitley Stokes, *RC* 13 (1892): 32–124.
12. Ibid., p. 51. Cf. note 66, chap. 3, on Tara.
13. "Bóroma," p. 53. For "swearing on the elements," see Philip O'Leary, "Verbal Deceit in the Ulster Cycle," *Éigse* 21 (1986): 16–26, 18.
14. "Bóroma," p. 55. Cf. "Tidings of Conchobor Mac Nessa," ed. Wh. Stokes, *Ériu* 4, no. 1 (1908): 18–38, 18.
15. Cf. "Bóroma," p. 61.
16. Ibid., p. 63.
17. Ibid., p. 67.
18. Ibid., pp. 81, 85, 89.
19. Ibid., p. 89.
20. Ibid.
21. Ibid., p. 73.
22. In general, phallic imagery in patriarchy is not related to fertility but instead delineates male authority, potency, and territory. Cf. Volney P. Gay, "Winnicott's

Contribution to Religious Studies: The Resurrection of the Culture Hero," *Journal of the American Academy of Religion* 51, no. 3 (1983): 371–95, 374. Cf. also Thorkild Vanggaard, *Phallós: A Symbol and Its History in the Male World* (New York: International Universities Press, 1972).

23. Cf. H. Clay Trumbull, *Blood Covenant*, 2d ed. (Philadelphia: J. D. Wattles, 1893), p. 10.

24. Cf. "The Training of Cúchulainn," ed. Wh. Stokes, *RC* 29 (1908): 109–52, 139–41.

25. Cf. John C. Hodges, "The Blood Covenant Among the Celts," *RC* 44 (1927): 109–53, 129; Henri Hubert, *The Greatness and Decline of the Celts*, trans. M. R. Dobie (1934; reprint, New York: Arno Press, 1972), pp. 192–93; *AIT*, p. 339; *SG*, 2:413ff.

26. Cf. *The Táin*, pp. 168–205; Daniel Melia, "Remarks on the Structure and Composition of the Ulster Death Tales," *Studia Hibernica* 17 (1977): 36–57.

27. For a provocative study of the role of Christianity in stemming the cycle of revenge, see René Girard, *Violence and the Sacred*, trans. Patrick Gregory (Baltimore: Johns Hopkins University Press, 1977); René Girard, *The Scapegoat*, trans. Yvonne Freccero (Baltimore: Johns Hopkins University Press, 1986).

28. "Bóroma," p. 75.

29. Ibid.

30. Ibid., p. 111.

31. *Gerald*, p. 108–9.

32. Cf. *AIT*, p. 522.

33. *Gerald*, p. 110.

34. Cf. previous note on king and goddess, note 1, chap. 2. Cf. also G. F. Dalton, "The Ritual Killing of the Irish Kings," *Folklore* 81 (1970): 1–22.

35. Genesis 22.

36. Cf. "The Adventures of Art Son of Conn. and the Courtship of Delbchaem," ed. R. I. Best, *Ériu* 3, no. 1 (1907): 149–73, 161. Significantly, in this story the youth to be sacrificed is saved by a woman, who substitutes a cow. Cf. also "How Ronan Slew His Son," *AIT*, pp. 538–45; and "The Parricides of the Children of Tantalus," ed. Mary E. Byrne, *RC* 44 (1927): 14-33. These are more obviously based on Greek versions of the myths and concentrate on conflict between the generations rather than the strictly political issues being addressed here. Human sacrifice was not, apparently, practised in Ireland; cf. F. N. Robinson, *Human Sacrifice among the Irish Celts* (Boston: privately published, 1913).

37. Cf. "The Training of Cúchulainn," p. 137.

38. My account differs from the usual translations of these lines, which do not emphasize the "one man" element of the challenge. The account here is based on a literal translation of the Irish text and is also an attempt to make sense of Connla's accusation at the end of the incident where he accused the Ulstermen of cowardice in not having sent *two* men out to him. Cf. "The Death of Aife's Only Son," in *Early Irish Myths and Sagas*, ed. Jeffrey Gantz (Harmondsworth, Middlesex: Penguin, 1981), pp. 147–52. "Not delightful the game you play, for no *two of you* will come unless I identify myself" (p. 151). Had they done so, this would have enabled him to name himself to them and obviate the necessity of fighting, but it would have taken from Cúchulainn his paternal rights to "name" his son. For other translations of the story, see "The Tragic Death of Connla," *AIT*, pp. 172–75; *The Táin*, pp. 39–46.

The right to "name" one's son must have played a vital role in the sexual politics of the incident since in some cultures the father's failure to "name" or take responsibility for his offspring, or a situation where there was doubt about the child's paternity, could lead to the neglect, and eventual death, of the child or of a mother who had conceived out of wedlock. Cf. *RAC*, p. 196; David Sproule, "Politics and Pure Narrative in the Stories About Corc of Cashel," *Ériu* 36 (1985): 11–28, 20; and W. M. Hennessy, "The Battle of Cnucha," *RC* 2 (1873–75): 86–93, 91. For a discussion of the importance of "naming" in the

Jewish context, see David Bakan, *And They Took Themselves Wives: The Emergence of Patriarchy in Western Civilization* (San Francisco: Harper & Row, 1979), pp. 12–29. For the Irish text, see "The Tragic Death of Connla," ed. Kuno Meyer, *Ériu* 1 (1904): 113-21, or *Compert Con Culainn and Other Stories* (MMIS, 111), ed. A. G. van Hamel (Dublin, 1933), pp. 9–15.

For feminist treatments of the politics of "naming," see Mary O'Brien, *The Politics of Reproduction* (London: Routledge and Kegan Paul, 1981), p. 181; Monica Sjöö and Barbara Mor, *The Great Cosmic Mother: Rediscovering the Religion of the Earth* (San Francisco: Harper & Row, 1987), pp. 200–201, 280ff.

39. *The Táin*, p. 42.
40. Ibid., pp. 43–44.
41. Cf. E. J. Gwynn, "Lecht Oenfír Aífe," *Ériu* 11, no. 2 (1932): 150–53. I am grateful to Prof. P. O'Leary of Harvard University for this reference.
42. Although see "The Death of Connla," ed. J. G. O'Keeffe, *Ériu* 1, no. 1 (1904): 123–27, where the death of Connla forms the basis of a discussion as to the "honor price" payable upon his death. But this account seems to be a later legal elaboration, not directly connected to the original story.
43. For a dubious psychoanalytic approach, see Mahmoud Omidsalar, "W. B. Yeat's Cúchulainn's Fight with the Sea," *American Imago* 42, no. 3 (1985): 315–33.
44. Luke 3:49.
45. Luke 8:21.
46. Luke 11:28.
47. This is an extremely simplified version of Anselm's teaching. For a full account of his reasoning, see *St. Anselm, Basic Writings*, trans. S. N. Deane, (La Salle, IL: Open Court, 1979), or any other version of Anselm's treatise, *Cur Deus Homo* (Why God Became Man).
48. There were later developments of this doctrine, in particular, Thomas Aquinas held that the mode of atonement chosen by Jesus was "convenient" but not absolutely necessary. Others, such as Peter Abelard and Duns Scotus, held that love, rather than honor, was the primary motivating force in the Atonement. But this view was fiercely opposed by people such as St. Bernard of Clairvaux, and, ultimately, Anselm's treatise, with its modifications by Thomas Aquinas, was the accepted Catholic doctrine.
49. For instance, the crusader Folquet, who killed half a million people, was canonized. Cf. Marina Warner, *Alone of All Her Sex* (New York: Knopf, 1976), p. 149.
50. Cf. *Penit*, p. 127.
51. Cf. Elaine Pagels, "What Became of God the Mother? Conflicting Images of God in Early Christianity," *Signs* 2, no. 2 (1976): 293–303, 298.
52. Cf. Sheila Ruth, "Bodies and Souls/Sex, Sin and the Senses in Patriarchy: A Study in Applied Dualism," *Hypatia* 2, no. 1 (1987): 149–63, 157, 162.
53. Cf. Mary Field Belenky, Blythe McVicker Clinchy, Nancy Rule Goldberger, Jill Mattuck Tarule, *Women's Way of Knowing: The Development of Self, Voice, and Mind* (New York: Basic Books, 1986), for a contemporary treatment of this issue.
54. *Gerald*, pp. 115–16. The cleric in question was Matha Ua hEnna, and the reference was to the murder of Thomas Becket orchestrated by Henry II. Cf. Marie Therese Flanagan, "Hiberno-Papal Relations in the Late Twelfth Century," *Archivium Hibernicum* 34 (1976): 55–70, 65.

Chapter 8. The Anglo-Norman Invasion of Ireland

Epigraph: From *Dubhaltach MacFirbisigh, Annals of Ireland, Three Fragments*, trans. John O'Donovan (Dublin: Irish Archaeological and Celtic Society, 1860), pp. 11–13.

1. *Poems of Blathmac*, ed. James Carney (Dublin: Irish Texts Series, no. 47, 1964), stt. 207–11, p. 71.
2. For instance, Pope Leo III was accused of perjury and adultery in 799 and was only saved from total disgrace by the intervention of Charles the Great (c.

742–814), whom he, in turn, rewarded by crowning him as the first "Holy Roman Emperor" on Christmas Day 800.

3. Geoffrey Barraclough, *The Medieval Papacy* (London: Thames and Hudson, 1975), p. 63.
4. Ibid., p. 83.
5. Cf. Maurice Sheehy, "Ireland and the Holy See," *IER* 96 (1962): 1–23, 11.
6. Cf. W. L. Warren, "The Interpretation of Twelfth Century Irish History," *Historical Studies* 7 (1969): 1–19, 7.
7. *SG*, 2:82.
8. Ibid., p. 83.
9. Ibid., p. 84.
10. Cf. Aubrey Gwynn, *The Twelfth Century Reform* (Dublin: Gill, 1968), p. 62.
11. Aubrey Gwynn, "Lanfranc and the Irish Church," *IER* 57 (1941): 481–500, 483.
12. Ibid., p. 485; Aubrey Gwynn, "Pope Gregory the Seventh and the Irish Church," *IER* 58 (1941): 97–109, 100, 109; Norman Cantor, *Church, Kingship and Lay Investiture in England 1089–1135* (Princeton, NJ: Princeton University Press, 1958), p. 30.
13. Aubrey Gwynn, "The First Synod of Cashel," *IER* 66 (1945–46): 81–92; vol. 67, 109–122, 115.
14. In contrast to Lanfranc, Anselm was a strong supporter of the church reform instituted by Gregory VII. In particular, he was extremely harsh on clerical couples and ordered them to separate. Anselm threatened the abandoned wives' protesting kinsmen with excommunication when they tried to retaliate. Cf. Anne Llewellyn Barstow, "Attitudes Towards Priest's Wives" (Paper presented at the Berkshire Conference on Women's History, 1978), p. 11.
15. Cited in Aubrey Gwynn, "St. Anselm and the Irish Church," *IER* 59 (1942): 1–14, 6.
16. Ibid., p. 11.
17. *FF*, 3:301.
18. *Sources*, p. 749.
19. Bernard's reform differed significantly from that of Gregory. Nevertheless, in the Irish context the effects of the reform movement would be virtually indistinguishable. Cf. Hayden V. White, "The Gregorian Ideal and St. Bernard of Clairvaux," *Journal of the History of Ideas*, 21, no. 3 (1960): 321–48.
20. Gwynn, *Twelfth Century*, pp. 26, 44–46; cf. also Tomás Ó Fiaich, "Church of Armagh Under Lay-Control," *Seanchas Ardmhacha* 5 (1969): 75–127, 97.
21. Cf. H. J. Lawlor, *St. Bernard of Clairvaux's Life of St. Malachy of Armagh* (London: Translation of Christian Lives Series, no. 5, 1920), p. 65.
22. Gwynn, *Twelfth Century*, pp. 50–52.
23. Ibid., p. 51.
24. J. F. O'Doherty, "St. Laurence O'Toole and the Anglo-Norman Invasion," *IER* 50 (1937–38): 449–77; vol. 51, pp. 131–46, 458.
25. Cf. O'Doherty, "St. Laurence O'Toole," p. 456.
26. Aubrey Gwynn, "The Centenary of the Synod of Kells 1152," *IER* 77 (1952): 161–76, 250–64, 174.
27. Cf. J. F. O'Doherty, "Rome and the Anglo-Norman Invasion of Ireland," *IER* 42 (1933): 131–45, 140; Denis Bethell, "English Monks and Irish Reform in the Eleventh and Twelfth Centuries," *Historical Studies* 8 (1969): 111–35, 135.
28. E. Curtis and R. B. McDowell, *Irish Historical Documents, 1172–1922* (London: Methuen, 1943), pp. 17–18.
29. Michael Dolley, *Anglo-Norman Ireland* (Dublin: Gill and Macmillan, 1972), p. 45.
30. For details, see Curtis and McDowell, *Irish Historical Documents*, p. 19.
31. Ibid., p. 20.
32. Cf. O. Bergin, "What Brought the Saxons to Ireland?" *Ériu* 7, no. 2 (1914): 244.
33. *ALC*, A.D. 1233. For a history of the debate, see M. P. Sheehy, "The Bull Laudabiliter: A Problem in Medieval Diplomatique and History," *JGHAS* 29 (1961): 45–70.

34. Canice Mooney, *The Church in Gaelic Ireland: Thirteenth to Fifteenth Centuries* (Dublin: Gill, 1969), p. 54.
35. *ALC*, A.D. 1221.
36. Mooney, *Church in Gaelic Ireland*, p. 55.
37. Geoffrey Hand, *The Church in the English Lordship 1216–1307* (Dublin: Gill, 1968), pp. 21, 27.
38. Aubrey Gwynn, *Anglo-Irish Church Life, 14th–15th Centuries* (Dublin: Gill, 1968), p. 18.
39. Mooney, *Church in Gaelic Ireland*, p. 16.
40. Cf. Aubrey Gwynn, "Henry of London, Archbishop of Dublin, 1213–1238: A Study in Anglo-Norman Statecraft," *Studies* 38 (1949): 295–306, 389–402, 297.
41. Mooney, *Church in Gaelic Ireland*, p. 5. For an analysis of Hiberno-papal relations in the twelfth century and for the disputes between the English and the Irish church, see Marie-Therese Flanagan, "Hiberno-Papal Relations in the Late Twelfth Century," *Archivium Hibernicum* 34 (1976–77): 55–70; cf. also Aubrey Gwynn, "Ireland and the Continent in the Eleventh Century," *IHS* 8, no. 31 (1953): 193–216; Anthony Lynch, "Religion in Late Medieval Ireland," *Archivium Hibernicum* 36 (1981): 3–15.
42. Gwynn, "Henry of London," pp. 399–400.
43. Ibid., p. 402.
44. Ibid., p. 299ff.
45. Mooney, *Church in Gaelic Ireland*, p. 3.
46. Cf. John Watt, "Laudabiliter in Medieval Diplomacy and Propaganda," *IER* 87 (1957): 420–32, 422.
47. Hand, *Church in English Lordship*, p. 32; cf. Mooney, *Church in Gaelic Ireland*, p. 2, for list of decisions prohibiting and restricting Irish clerics; Gwynn, "Henry of London," p. 302.
48. Cf. Gwynn, "Henry of London," pp. 393–99. For list of complaints of the Irish against the English, see Watt, "Laudabiliter," p. 423.
49. Gwynn, "Henry of London," p. 402.
50. Cf. Annette Jocelyn Otway-Ruthven, "The Request of the Irish for English Law," *IHS* 6 (1948–49): 261–70.
51. Ibid., p. 264.
52. Ibid., p. 268.
53. Gwynn, *Anglo-Irish Church Life*, p. 47.
54. Cf. J. A. Watt, *The Church and Two Nations in Medieval Ireland* (Cambridge: Cambridge University Press, 1970), pp. 33–34; Gwynn, "Anselm," p. 1.
55. Cf. Annette Jocelyn Otway-Ruthven, *A History of Medieval Ireland* (New York: St. Martin's Press, 1968), p. 118.
56. Ó Fiaich, "Church of Armagh," p. 106.
57. Cf. Barbara H. Rosenwein and Lester K. Little, "Social Meaning in the Monastic and Mendicant Spiritualities," *Past and Present* 63 (1974): 20–32. In his "Song of Songs," Bernard compared monastic life and asceticism to military service, and he also compared the monastic community to a *militia*, battling on behalf of the king. Cf. Bernard Flood, "St. Bernard's View of Crusade," *Australasian Catholic Record* 47 (1970): 130–38.
58. Ó Fiaich, "Church of Armagh," pp. 107–9, 119.
59. Ibid., p. 121.
60. For the career of this woman, see Amy Kelly, *Eleanor of Aquitaine and the Four Kings* (Cambridge, MA: Harvard University Press, 1950).
61. Cf. M. Sheehy, "Ireland and the Holy See," p. 11.
62. Cf. Colin Morris, "Individualism in Twelfth Century Religion: Some Further Reflections," *JEH* 31 (1980): 195–206, 200; John T. MacNeill, "Asceticism Versus Militarism in the Middle Ages," *Church History* 5, no. 1 (1936): 3–28.
63. Cf. Sylvester Malone, "The Privilege of Adrian IV to Henry II," *IER* 12 (1891): 865–81, 872.

Chapter 9. Clerical Celibacy

Epigraph: From *A Celtic Miscellany*, ed. Kenneth Jackson (Harmondsworth, Middlesex: Penguin, 1982), p. 139.

1. For the text of *De Statu Ecclesiae*, see *The Whole Works of James Ussher*, ed. C. R. Erlington (Dublin: Hodges & Smith, 1847), 4:500–510; cf. also J. A. Watt, *The Church and Two Nations in Medieval Ireland* (Cambridge: Cambridge University Press, 1970), pp. 13–14.
2. Aubrey Gwynn, *The Twelfth Century Reform* (Dublin: Gill, 1968), pp. 37–38.
3. Watt, *Church and Two Nations*, p. 14.
4. Samuel Laeuchli, *Power and Sexuality* (Philadelphia: Temple University Press, 1972), p. 90. Laeuchli argues that from earliest Christian times the rules on celibacy had been directed toward the establishment of the clerical hold on the faithful. For a critical introduction to the relationship between self-mastery and power in both Greek and Christian thought, which also examines the crucial differences between these modes, see Michel Foucault, *The Use of Pleasure*, trans. Robert Hatley (New York: Pantheon, 1985).
5. Cf. Laeuchli, *Power and Sexuality*. Laeuchli argues that the early clerical celibates, while rejecting intercourse with women, sought revenge on women by seeking to punish them for their every innocuous act. Cf. p. 97.
6. Cf. Laeuchli, *Power and Sexuality*, p. 199, and Bernard Verkampf, "Cultic Purity and the Law of Celibacy," *Review for Religious* 30 (1971): 199–217.
7. Laeuchli, *Power and Sexuality*, p. 99 (canon nos. 5, 63).
8. Gearóid Mac Niocaill, *Ireland Before the Vikings* (Dublin: Gill and Macmillan, 1980), p. 146. For a recent study of the effects of papal reform on married clergy, see Anne Llewellyn Barstow, *Married Priests and the Reforming Papacy* (New York: Edwin Mellen Press, 1982).
9. See Suzanne Wemple, *Women in Frankish Society* (Philadelphia: University of Pennsylvania Press, 1981), p. 131, for European examples.
10. Barstow, *Married Priests*, pp. 102–3.
11. Barstow, "Attitudes Towards Priests' Wives" (Paper presented at the Berkshire Conference on Women's History, 1978), pp. 10–11.
12. Ibid., p. 10.
13. Ibid.
14. Quoted in Barstow, "Attitudes," p. 8.
15. Cf. Jo Ann McNamara and Suzanne Wemple, "Sanctity and Power: The Dual Pursuit of Medieval Women," in *Becoming Visible*, ed. Renate Bridenthal and Claudia Koonz (Boston: Houghton Mifflin, 1977), 90–118, 110.
16. Quoted in Barstow, "Attitudes," p. 8.
17. Barstow, "Attitudes," pp. 5–6.
18. Quoted in Wemple, *Women in Frankish Society*, p. 146.
19. Barstow, "Attitudes," p. 3; Wemple, *Women in Frankish Society*, p. 131.
20. Quoted in Wemple, *Women in Frankish Society*, p. 134.
21. David Herlihy, "Land, Family and Women in Continental Europe 701–1200," *Traditio* 18 (1962): 89–120, 104.
22. Barstow, "Attitudes," p. 11.
23. Ibid., p. 6.
24. Ibid., p. 11.
25. For treatment of priest's wives, see also Verkampf, "Cultic Purity," p. 207, and Matilda Jocelyn Gage, *Woman, Church and State* (1893; reprint, Watertown, MA: Persephone Press, 1983), pp. 34–37.
26. Barstow, "Attitudes," p. 12.
27. *Letters of Abelard and Heloise*, ed. Betty Radice (Harmondsworth, Middlesex: Penguin, 1974), p. 114.
28. *Letters*, p. 70.

29. Ibid., p. 113.
30. For feminist treatment of the Heloise and Abelard story, see Peggy Kamuf, *Fictions of Feminine Desire: Disclosures of Heloise* (Lincoln, NB: University of Nebraska Press, 1982).
31. Cf. *Mart Oeng*, p. 229.
32. E. J. Gwynn and W. J. Purton, "Monastery of Tallaght," *PRIA* 29 C (1911): 115–79, 132, 145.
33. *Penit*, p. 55.
34. *ALI*, 5:205.
35. For full treatment of the position of women in early Irish law, see D. A. Binchy et al., *Studies in Early Irish Law* (Dublin: Royal Irish Academy, 1936). Cf. also chap. 3, nn. 89, 96.
36. Quoted in Gwynn, *Twelfth Century*, pp. 20–21.
37. For the decrees of the synod, see S. O'Grady, *Caithréim Thoirdhealbhaig* (London: Irish Texts Society, no. 27, 1929), p. 185. See also alternate rendering of some of these decrees in Aubrey Gwynn, "The First Synod of Cashel," *IER* 66 (1945–46): 109–22, 83–84.
38. *AFM*, A.D. 1101; Gwynn, *Twelfth Century*, pp. 9–12.
39. McNamara and Wemple, "Sanctity and Power," p. 112.
40. "They established some rules thereat, namely to put away concubines and mistresses from men; not to ask payment for anointing or baptizing; not to take payment for church property; and to receive tithes punctually." *AFM*, A.D. 1152; Gwynn, *Twelfth Century*, p. 60.
41. Cf. Canice Mooney, *The Church in Gaelic Ireland: Thirteenth to Fifteenth Centuries* (Dublin: Gill, 1969), p. 57.
42. *AU*, A.D. 1498 Cf. Mooney, *Church in Gaelic Ireland*, pp. 58–60, for many more examples.
43. Cf. Michael Dolley, *Anglo-Norman Ireland* (Dublin: Gill and Macmillan, 1972), p. 8; Mooney, *Church in Gaelic Ireland*, p. 56; cf. also Katharine Simms, "The Legal Position of Irishwomen in the Later Middle Ages," *Irish Jurist*, new series (1975): 96–110, 102, 105.
44. Cf. Donncha Ó Corráin, "The Early Irish Churches: Some Aspects of Organization," in *Irish Antiquity: Essays and Studies Presented to Prof. M. J. O'Kelly*, ed. D. Ó Corráin (Cork: Cork University Press, 1981), pp. 327–41, 329, for evidence of where the hereditary clergy of Trim married into aristocratic and royal families, thereby increasing their own spheres of influence.
45. D. A. Chart, *Register of John Swayne, Archbishop of Armagh and Primate of Ireland, 1418–1439* (Belfast: Her Majesty's Government, 1936), p. 38. Cf. also pp. ix, xi, xiv, 11, 37, 40, 82, 99 for problems with clerical concubines.
46. Aubrey Gwynn, *Anglo-Irish Church Life, 14th–15th Centuries* (Dublin: Gill, 1968), p. 9.
47. Simms, "The Legal Position of Irishwomen," p. 105.
48. Katharine Simms, "The Archbishop of Armagh and the O'Neills," *IHS* 29, no. 73 (1974): 38–55, 52.
49. Cf. *Cathréim Thoirdhealbhaig*, p. 83.
50. Barstow, *Married Priests*, p. 180.
51. For a discussion of the relationship between social status and the new emphasis on chastity, see Talal Asad, "Notes on body pain and truth in medieval Christian ritual," *Economy and Society* 12, no. 3 (1983): 287–327, 313–16.
52. Barstow, *Married Priests*, p. 180.
53. Anne Barstow, "Clergy Wives: An Ambiguous Legacy," in *Women in New Worlds*, ed. Rosemary Skinner Keller, Louise L. Queen, and Hilah F. Thomas (Nashville, TN: Abingdon, 1982), 2:100.
54. Barstow, "Clergy Wives," p. 100.
55. *SG*, 2:48; cf. also Barstow, *Married Priests*, p. 179.

Chapter 10. The Politics of Virginity

Epigraph: From *Right Wing Women* (New York: Pedigree Books, 1983), p. 23.

1. Cf. note 89, 96, chap. 3 on women and Irish law.
2. Cf. Suzanne Wemple, *Women in Frankish Society* (Philadelphia: University of Pennsylvania Press, 1981), pp. 76–79; cf. also Pauline Stafford, *Queens, Concubines, and Dowagers: The King's Wife in the Early Middle Ages* (Athens, GA: University of Georgia Press, 1983), p. 47ff.
3. Cited in A. Gwynn, "First Synod of Cashel," *IER* 66 (1945–46): 81–92; 67:109–22, 115.
4. Gwynn, "First Synod of Cashel," 67:116.
5. Aubrey Gwynn, "Anselm and the Irish Church," *IER* 59 (1942): 1–14, 13.
6. Ibid., p. 6.
7. Ibid., p. 7.
8. *Irish Historical Documents 1172–1922*, ed. E. Curtis (London: Methuen, 1943), pp. 20–22.
9. Cf. Katharine Simms, "The Legal Position of Irishwomen in the Later Middle Ages," *Irish Jurist*, new series (1975): 96–111, 97.
10. Cf. Jack Goody, *Development of the Family and Marriage in Europe* (New York: Cambridge University Press, 1983), pp. 134–37.
11. Cf. Stafford, *Queens, Concubines, and Dowagers*, pp. 44, 58.
12. Cf. Simms, "The Legal Position of Irishwomen," p. 110.
13. Ibid.
14. Ibid.
15. For feminist treatments of the role of women as items of exchange between men, see Eleanor Leacock, *Myths of Male Dominance* (New York: Monthly Review Press, 1981), pp. 214–42; Gayle Rubin, "The Traffic in Women: Notes on the Political Economy of Sex," in *Towards an Anthropology of Women*, ed. Rayna Reiter (New York: Monthly Review Press, 1975), pp. 157–210; Rachel Harrisson and Roisin McDonough, "Patriarchy and Relations of Production," in *Feminism and Materialism*, ed. A. Kuhn and A. M. Wolfe (London: Routledge and Kegan Paul, 1978), pp. 11–41; Gerda Lerner, *The Creation of Patriarchy* (New York: Oxford University Press, 1986), pp. 46–53; Mary Douglas, *Purity and Danger* (New York: Praeger, 1966), p. 152; cf. also C. Lévi-Strauss, *The Elementary Structures of Kinship*, trans. R. Needham, James Harle Bell, and John Richard von Sturmer (Boston: Beacon Press, 1969), where he claims that women are both signs and values, p. 496; Elizabeth Cowie, "Woman as Sign," *M/F* 1 (1978): 49–63.
16. Cf. Simms, "Legal Position of Irishwomen," p. 98.
17. *Ann Conn*, A.D. 1339:7, 1343:3, and A.D. 1243:2. Cited in Simms, "Legal Position of Irishwomen," pp. 98–99.
18. Simms, "Legal Position of Irishwomen," p. 110.
19. Cf. Katharine Simms, "Women in Norman Ireland," in *Women in Irish Society*, ed. Margaret MacCurtain and Donncha Ó Corráin (Dublin: Arlen House, 1978), p. 19. The Irish restrictions against women holding property were eroded in the later Middle Ages. Simms, "Legal Position of Irishwomen," pp. 105–6.
20. Cf. Simms, "Women in Norman Ireland," p. 16ff., and "Legal Position of Irishwomen," p. 111. Cf. Myles Dillon, "The Relationship of Mother and Son, Father and Daughter, and the Law of Inheritance with Regard to Women," in *SEIL*, pp. 129–79; cf. Ó Corrain, "The Early Irish Churches: Some Aspects of Organization," in *Irish Antiquity*, ed. D. Ó Corráin (Cork: Cork University Press, 1981), pp. 327–41, 333, for rules governing heiresses in early Irish society and the extent to which Irish canon law overlapped with native Irish provisions; N. McLeod, "Interpreting Irish Law: Status and Currency," *ZCP* 41 (1986): 46–65, and 42 (1987): 41–115. Cf. also Hermann Wasserschleben, *Die Irische*

Kanonensammlung (Leipzig: Tauchnitz, 1885), p. 173, n. 179.

21. Cf. Jo Ann McNamara and Suzanne Wemple, "Sanctity and Power: The Dual Pursuit of Medieval Women," in *Becoming Visible*, ed. Renate Bridenthal and Claudia Koonz (Boston: Houghton Mifflin, 1977), p. 111. Cf. Wemple, *Women in Frankish Society*, pp. 113–18.

22. Cf. Simms, "Legal Position of Irishwomen," pp. 104–5.

23. Cf. Goody, *Development of the Family*, p. 95ff; Stafford, *Queens, Concubines, and Dowagers*, p. 180, for instances where reluctant dowagers were confined to convents.

24. Cf. Goody, *Development of the Family*, pp. 133–34.

25. Ibid., pp. 95ff., 124, 141.

26. Cf. Simms, "Legal Position of Irishwomen," p. 110.

27. Cf. Kirsten Hastrup, "The Semantics of Biology: Virginity," in *Defining Female*, ed. Shirley Ardener (New York: Wiley, 1978), pp. 56–57.

28. Cf. Sherry Ortner, "The Virgin and the State," *Feminist Studies* 4 (1978): 19–35, 31.

29. Cf. *Fragmentary Annals of Ireland*, ed. Joan Radner (Dublin: Institute for Advanced Studies, 1978), p. 63.

30. Cf. Ortner, "Virgin and the State," p. 32.

31. Ibid.

32. Cf. Marina Warner, *Alone of All Her Sex* (New York: Knopf, 1976), p. 78.

33. Cf. E. W. McDonnell, *The Beguines and Beghards in Medieval Culture* (New Brunswick, 1954).

34. Cf. Penny Schine Gold, *The Lady and the Virgin* (Chicago: The University of Chicago Press, 1985), pp. 77, 82–92; Louis J. Lekai, *The Cistercians: Ideals and Reality* (Kent, OH: Kent State University Press, 1977), pp. 350–57.

35. Cf. Eleanor McLaughlin, "Equality of Souls, Inequality of Sexes: Woman in Medieval Theology," in *Religion and Sexism*, ed. Rosemary Radford Ruether (New York: Simon & Schuster, 1974), pp. 213–66, 244.

36. Ibid., pp. 241–44.

37. In the Irish legal system, primogeniture was not a principle of succession. Cf. Eoin Mac Neill, *Celtic Ireland* (1921; reprint, Dublin: Academy Press, 1981), p. 159. The new principle of primogeniture had widespread consequences as it effectively disinherited, not only younger sons, but also "illegitimate" children who, under the Irish system, had had the same rights as those who were "legitimate." Cf. Eugene O'Curry, *Manners and Customs of the Ancient Irish*, ed. W. K. Sullivan (London: Scribner, Welford, 1873), 1:clxxviii. For a discussion of illegitimacy in Europe, cf. Goody, *Development of the Family*, pp. 73–77.

38. Cf. Warner, *Alone of All Her Sex*, p. 142.

39. Cf. Joan Kelly Gadol, "Did Women Have a Renaissance?" in *Becoming Visible*, ed. Bridenthal and Koonz, pp. 137–64, 146; Joan M. Ferrante, "Male Fantasy and Female Reality in Courtly Literature," *Women's Studies* 11 (1984): 67–97; Robert P. Miller, "The Wounded Heart: Courtly Love and the Medieval Anti-feminist Position," *Women's Studies* 2 (1974): 335–50.

40. Cf. William Monter, "Pedestal and Stake: Courtly Love and Witchcraft," in *Becoming Visible*, ed. Bridenthal and Koonz, pp. 119–36, 125; Grace Neville, "Medieval Irish Courtly Love Poetry: An Exercise in Power Struggle?" *Études Irlandais* 7 (1982): 19–30.

41. Cf. Monter, "Pedestal and Stake," p. 121.

42. For general development of this trend, see John T. MacNeill, "Asceticism Versus Militarism in the Middle Ages," *Church History* 5, no. 1 (1936): 3–28.

43. Cf. Julia Kristeva, "Stabat Mater," in *The Female Body in Western Culture*, ed. Susan Rubin Suleiman (Cambridge, MA: Harvard University Press, 1986), pp. 99–118, 115.

44. Cf. *BH*, 1:66–70, *Lis Lives*, pp. 186–87, 198, 319; *BB*, p. 22, *CG*, p. 166; *Thes Pal*, 2:342.

45. Wm. Sherlock, *Some Account of Brigid and the See of Kildare with its Bishops and its*

Cathedral Now Restored (Dublin: Hodges, Figgis, 1896), p. 16.

46. Cf. Peter O'Dwyer, *Devotion to Mary in Ireland, 700–1100* (Dublin: Carmelite Publications, 1976), p. 46; Peter O'Dwyer, *Towards a History of Devotion to Mary in Ireland, 1100–1600* (Dublin: Carmelite Publications, 1979), pp. 10, 42, 76.
47. Cf. Warner, *Alone of All Her Sex*, p. 328.
48. O'Dwyer, *700–1100*, p. 44.
49. Cf. Peter O'Dwyer, *Versiculi Familiae Benchur* (Dublin: Carmelite Publications, 1975), p. 4.
50. *Poems of Blathmac*, ed. James Carney (Dublin: Irish Texts Society, no. 47, 1964), st. 157.
51. Cf. O'Dwyer, *700–1100*, p. 22.
52. Ibid., p. 23.
53. Cf. O'Dwyer, *1100–1600*, p. 88.
54. Kristeva, "Stabat Mater," p. 108.
55. Cf. Rosemary Radford Ruether, *Mary—The Feminine Face of the Church* (Philadelphia: Westminster Press, 1979), p. 13.
56. Cf. John A. Saliba, S. J., "The Virgin-Birth Debate in Anthropological Literature: A Critical Assessment," *Theological Studies* 36 (1975): 428–54, 449.
57. Cf. *Poems of Blathmac*, p. 3.
58. Cf. Elaine Pagels, *Adam, Eve, and the Serpent* (New York: Random House, 1988).
59. *Poems of Blathmac*, stt. 182–85.
60. Ibid., stt. 100, 103. Cf. P. O'Dwyer, *700–1100*, p. 7.
61. Cf. O'Dwyer, *1100–1600*, pp. 46, 54, 57, 149, 153.
62. Cf. O'Dwyer, *700–1100*, p. 21.
63. Cf. O'Dwyer, *1100–1600*, p. 18.
64. Ibid., p. 49, n. 4.
65. Ibid., pp. 21, 60, 150; Peter O'Dwyer, *Highlights in Devotion to Mary in Ireland from 1600* (Dublin: Carmelite Publications, 1981), pp. 12, 55.
66. Cf. O'Dwyer, *1100–1600*, pp. 72, 144.
67. O'Dwyer, *700–1100*, p. 19.
68. Cf. O'Dwyer, *1100–1600*, p. 69.
69. *Irish Litanies: Text and Translation*, ed. Charles Plummer (London: Harrison & Sons, 1925), p. 40.
70. Warner, *Alone of All Her Sex*, pp. 236–49, 251–52.
71. Cf. Warner, *Alone of All Her Sex*, p. 249.
72. *The Letters of St. Bernard of Clairvaux*, ed. Bruno Scott James (London: Burns Oates 1953). Letter 378, p. 449, with changes by Caroline Bynum. Cited in Caroline Bynum, *Jesus as Mother: Studies in the Spirituality of the High Middle Ages* (Berkeley, CA: University of California Press, 1982), pp. 145–46.
73. Cf. McLaughlin, "Equality of Souls," p. 248.
74. Bynum, *Jesus as Mother*, p. 137.
75. Cf. Joan Kelly Gadol, "Did Women Have a Renaissance?" in *Becoming Visible*, ed. Bridenthal and Koonz, pp. 137–64, p. 143; cf. also Julia Kristeva, *Powers of Horror: An Essay on Abjection* (New York: Columbia University Press, 1982), pp. 100–102, on separation from the mother as an ingredient in the establishment of a particular form of religious consciousness.
76. In a recent study of the cult of Mary, Michael Carroll claims that "repressed desire for the mother has always been the wellspring of Marian devotion." Cf. Michael P. Carroll, *The Cult of the Virgin Mary* (Princeton, NJ: Princeton University Press, 1986), p. 223.
77. Cf. Samuel Laeuchli, *Power and Sexuality* (Philadelphia: Temple University Press, 1972), p. 120.
78. Cf. Proinsias Mac Cana, "Early Irish Ideology and the Concept of Unity," in *The Irish Mind*, ed. Richard Kearney (Dublin: Wolfhound Press, 1985), pp. 56–78.
79. For the relationship between political conservatism and the subjugation of women, see Nancy Jay, "Gender and Dichotomy," *Feminist Studies* 7, no. 1 (1981): 38–56. L. J. Jordanova argues that these dichotomies provide coherence in the

face of threatened social disorganization. Cf. L. J. Jordanova, "Natural Facts: A Historical Perspective on Science and Sexuality," in *Nature, Culture and Gender,* ed. Carol P. MacCormack and Marilyn Strathern (New York: Cambridge University Press, 1980), pp. 42–69, 43–44.

80. Erik Erikson, *Identity: Youth and Crisis* (New York: W. W. Norton, 1968), p. 304.

81. For Mary as symbol of dualism, see Warner, *Alone of All Her Sex,* p. 254.

82. Caelius Sedulius, "Paschalis Carminis," book 11, lines 68–69, in *Sedulii Opera Omnia,* ed. John Huemer (Vienna, 1885). Cited in Warner, *Alone of All Her Sex,* p. xvii.

83. Cf. Mary Nelson, "Why Witches Were Women," in *Woman: A Feminist Perspective,* ed. Jo Freeman (Palo Alto, CA: Mayfield Publishing, 1975), pp. 335–50.

84. Cf. Warner, *Alone of All Her Sex,* p. 144.

85. Initially, their accusers could remain secret, but this custom was changed by Pope Boniface VIII.

86. Cf. Trevor Roper, *The European Witchcraze of the 16th and 17th Centuries* (Harmondsworth, Middlesex: Penguin, 1978), p. 42.

87. *The Malleus Maleficarum of Heinrich Kramer and James Sprenger,* trans. Montague Summers (New York: Dover, 1971), pt. 1, question 6, p. 47.

88. *Malleus Maleficarum,* pt. 2, question 1, chap. 7, p. 121.

89. Gratian, a jurist from Bologna in his Decretum (c. 1140). Cited in *Not in God's Image,* ed. Julia O'Faolain and Lauro Martines (Glasgow: Collins, Fontana, 1974), p. 143.

90. Kristeva, "Stabat Mater," p. 115.

91. Cf. Rudolph Bell, *Holy Anorexia* (Chicago: University of Chicago Press, 1985); cf. also Caroline Bynum, *Holy Feast and Holy Fast: The Religious Significance of Food to Medieval Women* (Berkeley, CA: University of California Press, 1986).

92. Bell, *Holy Anorexia,* p. 145.

93. Ibid., p. 47.

94. Ibid., p. 20.

95. Ibid., p. 78.

96. Ibid.

97. Ibid., p. 152ff. This by no means "solved" the problem for women as the "intense emotional bonds" generated by the "intimate oral discourse" of confession served to establish new levels of control, a factor that, in the case of married women, led to a severe reaction on the part of their husbands during the Protestant Reformation. Cf. Sharon Farmer, "Clerical Images of Medieval Wives," *Speculum* 61, no. 3 (1986): 517–43, 534, n. 46.

98. Bell, *Holy Anorexia,* p. 177.

99. Fatima Mernissi, "Virginity and Patriarchy," *Women's Studies International Forum* 5, no. 2 (1982): 183–91, 185.

100. Cf. Ruether, *Mary,* p. 52.

101. Bynum, *Jesus as Mother,* p. 12.

102. Ibid., p. 10.

103. Ibid., p. 258.

104. Ibid., p. 18. Cf. also E. Rosenstock Huessy, *The Driving Power of Western Civilization* (Boston: Beacon Press, 1949), p. 98, for the significance of this feast in cementing the power of the pope.

105. Bynum, *Jesus as Mother,* p. 184.

106. *Penit,* p. 187.

107. Cf. Sherri Ortner, "The Virgin and the State," *Feminist Studies* 4 (1978): 19–35.

108. Cf. Donald Weinstein and Rudolph M. Bell, *Saints and Society: The Two Worlds of Western Christendom, 1000–1700* (Chicago: University of Chicago Press, 1982), pp. 220–38, for the effects of the male monopoly on theology.

109. Ortner, "Virgin and the State," p. 26. Or as Gerda Lerner put it, "Women become reified because they are conquered and protected while men become reifiers because they conquer and protect." Lerner, *The Creation of Patriarchy,* p. 99.

110. Cf. Pamela Berger, *The Goddess Obscured: Transformation of the Grain Protectress from Goddess to Saint* (Boston: Beacon Press, 1986).
111. *Sources*, p. 688.
112. *Thes Pal*, 2:253.
113. Ibid., p. 252.
114. Ibid., p. 255.
115. *BNE*, 2:185, 349.
116. For a time the male saints had used natural products such as spittle or breath to effect cures. Cf. *VSH*, 1:clxxviii. A saint's gospel book is said to have caused "sight shifting," cured dumbness, and prevented cattle from straying. *VSH*, 1:clxxviii.
117. We saw that Maedoc took the "webstress's slay," which his mother held at birth, and turned it into a hazel tree. But now this hazel tree takes on a powerful effect because when "earth from it over which nine Masses have been said is inserted between prisoners and their chains, they thereupon escape forthwith." *BNE*, 2:185, 349.
118. Cf. *The Táin*, pp. 136–37, where an implicit acknowledgment is made of the interdependence of the Goddess, the Morrígan, and Cúchulainn. After they had been locked in mortal combat, when the hero had refused her help, the Morrígan healed Cúchulainn's wounds with her milk, and significantly, Cúchulainn healed the Morrígan with his *words*.
119. In ancient Greece the earliest chalices were said to be modeled on the breast of Helen of Troy. Cf. Nor Hall, *The Moon and the Virgin* (New York: Harper & Row, 1980), pp. 53–55. In Ireland a mountain range in County Kerry was called, after the breasts of the Goddess, the "Paps of Anu."
120. Cited and translated in David Herlihy, *Medieval Households* (Cambridge, MA: Harvard University Press, 1985), p. 120.
121. Cf. Clarissa Atkinson, "Your Servant, My Mother," in *Immaculate and Powerful: The Female in Sacred Image and Social Reality*, ed. Clarissa Atkinson et al. (Boston: Beacon Press, 1985), pp. 139–72, 150.
122. *Gesta Regis Henrici Secundi Benedicti Abbatis*, edited from Cotton Mss. by Wm. Stubbs (London, 1867), 1:28. Cf. also Whitley Stokes, "On Infant Baptism and Folklore," *The Academy*, Feb. 15 (1896), no. 1241, pp. 137–38. For a discussion of the relationship between the symbolism of milk and incest, see Kristeva, *Powers of Horror*, p. 105. Cf. also *VSH*, 1:cvi, no. 8, where kinship ties established through milk (fosterage) took precedence over kinship in blood (maternity).
123. Cf. Bynum, *Jesus as Mother*, pp. 151–53.
124. *BNE*, 2:257, 277; *VSH*, 1:cxxvii.
125. Cf. Charles Doherty, "The Use of Relics in Early Ireland," in *Irland und Europa*, ed. Próinséas Ní Chatháin and Michael Richter (Stuttgart: Klett-Cotta, 1984), 1:89–101.
126. Cf. P. Jackson, "The Three Holy Sisters," *Sinsear* 4 (1982–83): 63–69; Angela Partridge, *Caoineadh na dTrí Muire: Téama na Páise i bhFilíocht Bhéil na Gaeilge* (Dublin: An Clóchomhar Tta, 1983).
127. Cf. O'Dwyer, *1100–1600*, p. 162.
128. Ibid., p. 19.
129. Ibid., p. 47.
130. Cf. O'Dwyer, *700–1100*, p. 13; O'Dwyer, *1100–1600*, p. 27.
131. Cf. O'Dwyer, *1100–1600*, p. 27.
132. Ibid., p. 32.
133. Ibid., p. 173; cf. also Kristeva, "Stabat Mater," p. 105.
134. Cf. L. McKenna, *An Timthire* (1918), p. 51ff. Cited in O'Dwyer, *1100–1600*, p. 27.
135. McKenna, *An Timthire*, st. 8. Cited in O'Dwyer, *1100–1600*, p. 28.
136. Kristeva, "Stabat Mater," p. 110.
137. Cf. O'Dwyer, *700–1100*, p. 47; *Thes Pal*, 2:252.
138. Cf. *Abhráin Diadha Chúige: Religious Songs of Connacht*, ed. Douglas Hyde (Dublin:

M.H. Gill & Son, n.d., London: L. Fisher Unwin, n.d.), 2:73.

139. Cf. *BNE*, 2:195–96. Enormous pressure was exerted on the people to have their children baptized as soon as possible. Cf. *Penit*, p. 225, also p. 93.

140. Cf. K. Rahner, "The Christian Mystery and the Pagan Mysteries," in *The Mysteries, Papers from the Eranos Yearbooks*, ed. Joseph Campbell (New York: Pantheon Books, 1955), pp. 337–401, 392.

141. Cf. Bynum, *Jesus as Mother*, p. 151.

142. Cf. Luther, "Annunciation," *The Martin Luther Christmas Book*, trans. Roland H. Bainton (Philadelphia: Westminster Press, 1948), p. 27.

143. Cf. Roberta Hamilton, *The Liberation of Women* (Boston: G. Allen Unwin, 1978), p. 68.

144. For a fuller discussion of this point, see Ruether, *Mary*, pp. 60–61.

145. Kristeva, "Stabat Mater," p. 116.

146. Gen. 2:23–24.

147. John 19:26–27.

148. Cf. Kristeva, "Stabat Mater," p. 102.

149. Simone de Beauvoir, *The Second Sex*, trans. H. M. Parshley (New York: Vintage Books, 1974), p. 193.

150. Cf. O'Dwyer, *1100–1600*, p. 108.

Chapter 11. Conclusions: The Age of the Fathers

Epigraph: Nuala Ní Dhomhnaill, *Selected Poems*, trans. Nuala Ní Dhomhnaill and Michael Hartnett (Dublin: Raven Arts Press, 1988).

1. For the most recent and authoritative overview of Irish history, see R. F. Foster, *Modern Ireland 1600–1972* (London: Allen Lane, 1988).

2. Cf. Pope John Paul 11, *Mulieris Dignitatem* (On the Dignity of Women) (Dublin: Veritas, 1988), p. 92.

3. For the philosophical background to this term, see Pierre Bourdieu, *Outline of a Theory of Practice* (Cambridge: Cambridge University Press, 1977), pp. 171–83.

4. Pope John Paul II, *Mulieris Dignitatem*, pp. 96–98.

5. Michel Foucault, *The History of Sexuality*, trans. R. Hurley (New York: Vintage Books, Random House, 1980), p. 137.

6. Cited in Jonathan Schell, *The Fate of the Earth* (New York: Avon Books, 1982), p. 188.

7. Ernest Becker, *The Denial of Death* (New York: Free Press, 1973), p. 190.

8. William James, "The Moral Equivalent of War," in *Essays on Faith and Morals* (New York: Longman, Green, 1943).

9. Mircea Eliade, *Rites and Symbols of Initiation* (New York: Harper & Row, 1975), pp. 7, 25, 27, 30.

10. Cf. Eliade, *Rites and Symbols*, pp. 26–27.

11. Cf. Pat Conroy, *The Lords of Discipline* (Boston: Houghton Mifflin, 1982), p. 146. This is a novel based on Pat Conroy's interviews in the most prestigious American military academies.

12. A. E. Housman, *A Shropshire Lad* (Portland, ME: Thomas B. Mosher, 1906), p. 47.

13. Cf. Melissa Llewelyn-Davies, "Women, Warriors, and Patriarchs," in *Sexual Meanings: The Social Construction of Gender and Sexuality*, ed. Sherry B. Ortner and Harriett Whitehead (New York: Cambridge University Press, 1981), pp. 330–58, 342, 350.

14. Cf. Mary O'Brien, *The Politics of Reproduction* (London: Routledge and Kegan Paul, 1981), p. 220, n. 9.

15. Cf. J. Glenn Gray, *The Warriors* (New York: Harper & Row, 1970), pp. 61–68; Susan Brownmiller, *Against Our Wills* (New York: Simon & Schuster, 1975), chap. 3; Judith Hicks Stiehm, "The Protected, The Protector, The Defender," *Women's Studies International Forum* 5, nos. 3/4 (1982): 367–76, 371. On the sexual politics of the Malvinas/Falklands war see the essay by the brilliant contem-

porary Irish satirist Nell McCafferty in *The Best of Nell* (Dublin: Attic Press, 1984), pp. 140–43.

16. James Joyce, *Ulysses* (New York: Modern Library, 1934), p. 204–5.

17. Nancy Jay, "Sacrifice as a Remedy for Having Been Born of Woman," in *Immaculate and Powerful*, ed. Clarissa Atkinson et al. (Boston: Beacon Press, 1985), p. 294.

18. Mary O'Brien, "The Tyranny of the Abstract: Structure, State and Patriarchy" (Lecture given to Boston Area Women's Studies, December 1983), p. 3; cf. also O'Brien, *Politics of Reproduction*, p. 198.

19. Cf. Desmond Connell, "The Fruitful Virginity of Mary," *The Way*, supp. vol. 51 (Autumn 1984): 44–53.

20. For George Friedrich Hegel's objection to childbearers taking part in war, see O'Brien, *Politics of Reproduction*, p. 86.

21. Nancy Jay, "Sacrifice as a Remedy," pp. 283–310, 292.

22. Ibid., p. 297.

23. Ibid., p. 284.

24. Cf. Robert Elwyn Bradbury, *The Benin Kingdom and the Edo-speaking Peoples of South-western Nigeria* (London: International African Institute, 1957), p. 59, cited in Jay, "Sacrifice as a Remedy," p. 294.

25. Personal communication from the woman concerned.

26. Information gained from personal communications with women in Sweden. For a study of women priests in Sweden, see Brita Stendahl, *The Force of Tradition: A Case Study of Women Priests in Sweden* (Philadelphia: Fortress Press, 1985).

27. Mary O'Brien, "The Politics of Impotence," in *Contemporary Issues in Social Philosophy*, ed. Wm. R. Shea and John King Farlow (New York: Watson Academy Press, 1976), pp. 147–62, 150.

28. Quoted in Nancy Huston, "The Matrix of War: Mothers and Heroes," in *The Female Body in Western Culture* (Cambridge, MA: Harvard University Press, 1986), 119–36, 131; cf. also Gerda Lerner, *The Creation of Patriarchy* (New York: Oxford University Press, 1986), p. 203.

29. Cf. Peggy Reeves Sanday, *Female Power and Male Dominance* (New York: Cambridge University Press, 1981), p. 96.

30. Cf. *ALI*, 1:177.

31. Cf. Jay, "Sacrifice as a Remedy," p. 284.

32. Cf. *VSH*, 1:cx; A. W. Wade-Evans, *Vitae Sanctorum Brittanae* (Cardiff: University of Wales Press, 1944), p. 91.

33. *Thes Pal*, 2:247.

34. Eliade, *Rites and Symbols*, p. 136.

35. Ibid., pp. xii, xiii.

36. Cf. Mircea Eliade, *Myth and Reality*, trans. Willard R. Trask (New York: Harper & Row, 1968), p. 81.

37. O'Brien, *Politics of Reproduction*, p. 121.

38. G. W. F. Hegel, "The Phenomenology of Mind," trans. J. B. Baillie (New York: Harper & Row, 1967), p. 233.

39. O'Brien, *Politics of Reproduction*, p. 169.

40. Gray, *The Warriors*, p. 59.

41. Quoted in Susan Griffin, "Rape: The All-American Crime," *Ramparts*, September 10, 1971, pp. 26–35.

42. Cf. Wm. S. Murphy, *The Genesis of British War Poetry* (London: Hamilton Kent, 1918), p. 172.

43. Cited in *The Penguin Book of First World War Poetry*, ed. J. Silkin (Harmondsworth, Middlesex: Penguin Books, 1979), p. 211.

44. Cf. Edward Linenthal, *Changing Images of the Warrior Hero in America* (New York: Edwin Mellen Press, 1982), p. 117.

45. Cf. Huston, "Matrix of War," pp. 128–30.

46. Huston, "Matrix of War," p. 130.

47. For instance the National Organization for Women (NOW) in the United States

brought an *amicus curiae* brief before the Supreme Court, challenging the constitutionality of an all-male draft.

48. Huston, "Matrix of War," p. 121.
49. Cf. Sherry Ortner, "Is Female to Male as Nature Is to Culture?" in *Women, Culture and Society*, ed. Michelle Rosaldo and Louise Lamphere (Stanford, CA: Stanford University Press, 1974), pp. 67–87, 70; Sanday, *Female Power*, pp. 92, 107; Janet Sayers, *Biological Politics: Feminist and Anti-Feminist Perspectives* (New York: Tavistock Publications, 1982), pp. 110–21.
50. Cf. René Girard, *Violence and the Sacred*, trans. Patrick Gregory (Baltimore: Johns Hopkins University Press, 1977), pp. 36–37.
51. Cf. Llewelyn-Davies, "Women, Warriors, and Patriarchs," p. 342. Some authors speculate as to whether or not men "created" forms of society and religion in response to their despair at not being able to give birth. Cf. Bruno Bettelheim, *Symbolic Wounds* (New York: Collier Books, 1979), p. 121. Others argue that the social body is entrusted to men "as a reward for being the expendable sex." Cf. Sanday, *Female Power*, p. 89.
52. Cf. Huston, "Matrix of War," p. 119.
53. Jay, "Sacrifice as a Remedy," p. 294.
54. Cf. Gaston Bouthoul, *La Guerre* (Paris: Presses Universitaires de France, 1969), pp. 21–22. Quoted in Huston, "Matrix of War," p. 133.
55. Quoted in Girard, *Violence and the Sacred*, p. 88.
56. Eric Leed, *No Man's Land: Combat and Identity in World War One* (New York: Cambridge University Press, 1979), p. 153.
57. Cf. Robert J. Lifton and Richard Falk, *Indefensible Weapons: The Political and Psychological Case Against Nuclearism* (New York: Basic Books, 1982), p. 168.
58. Dexter Master, *The Accident* (New York: Knopf, 1965), p. 41. Cited in Lifton and Falk, *Indefensible Weapons*, p. 26.
59. William Lawrence, a science writer, quoted in Lifton and Falk, *Indefensible Weapons*, p. 90.
60. Cited in Schell, *Fate of the Earth*, p. 149.
61. These connections were first made in Prof. Mary Daly's class at Boston College, 1980.
62. Notes taken during a television program in the "Iran hostages" crisis. For further elaboration on these themes see M. Condren, "Patriarchy and Death," in *Womanspirit Bonding*, ed. J. Kalven and M. Buckley (New York: Pilgrim Press, 1984), pp. 173–89; Carol Cohn, "Sex and Death in the Rational World of Defense Intellectuals," *Signs* 2, no. 4 (1987): 687–718.
63. O'Brien, *Politics of Reproduction*, p. 148.
64. For this theme in Greek literature, see Arlene Saxonhouse, "Aeschylus' Oresteia: Misogyny, Philogyny and Justice," *Women and Politics* 4, no. 2 (1984): 11–32, 26; Arlene Saxonhouse, *Women in the History of Political Thought* (New York: Praeger, 1985), p. 29.
65. Cited in Arthur Ormont, *Requiem for War: The Life of Wilfrid Owen* (New York: Four Winds Press, 1973), p. 183.
66. Cf. Maurice N. Walsh and Barbara G. Scandalis, in *War: Its Causes and Correlates*, ed. Martin A. Nettleship, R. Dale Givens, and Anderson Nettleship, Proceedings of the Ninth International Congress of Anthropological and Ethnological Sciences, 1973 (The Hague: Mouton Publishers, 1975), pp. 135–56. Cf. also Nancy Chodorow, *The Reproduction of Mothering: Psychoanalysis and the Sociology of Gender* (Berkeley, CA: University of California Press, 1978), pp. 162, 201; David Bakan, *And They Took Themselves Wives: The Emergence of Patriarchy in Western Civilization* (San Francisco: Harper & Row, 1979), pp. 144–45.
67. Cited in David Starr-Jordan, *War and the Breed: The Relation of War to the Downfall of Nations* (Boston: Beacon Press, 1915), pp. 43–44.
68. Cited in Leed, *No Man's Land*, p. 153.
69. W. B. Yeats, *Trembling of the Veil* (London: T. Werner Laurie, 1922), p. 154.
70. Cf. Jessica Benjamin, "The Bonds of Love: Rational Violence and Erotic Domi-

nation," *Feminist Studies* 6, no. 1 (Spring 1980): 144–74, for the master/slave dialectic.

71. Cf. Stanley Milgram, *Obedience to Authority* (New York: Harper & Row, 1974), for a series of psychological tests relating the notion of obedience to the abdication of social responsibility.

72. Cf. Jessica Benjamin, *The Bonds of Love: Psychoanalysis, Feminism, and the Problem of Domination* (New York: Pantheon, 1988). Cf. also Alice Miller, *For Your Own Good: Hidden Cruelty in Child-rearing and the Roots of Violence,* trans. Hildegarde and Hunter Hannum (New York: Farrar, Strauss, Giroux, 1983), for the role of "fathering" in the genesis of Hitler's violence.

73. President Harding, *New York Times,* Nov. 12, 1921, p. 2. Quoted in Linenthal, *Changing Images of the Warrior Hero in America,* p. 112.

74. Leed, *No Man's Land,* p. 196.

75. Cf. Girard, *Violence and the Sacred,* p. 135.

76. Leed, *No Man's Land,* p. 204ff.

77. Gray, *The Warriors,* p. 128.

78. Lewis Mumford, *The City in History* (New York: Harcourt, Brace & World, 1961), p. 42.

79. Murphy, *Genesis of British War Poetry,* preface.

80. Cf. Martin Sherwin, *A World Destroyed: The Atomic Bomb and the Grand Alliance* (New York: Random House, Vintage Books, 1977), pp. 6, 63, 193.

81. Foucault, *History of Sexuality,* p. 137.

82. Cf. Sue Mansfield, *The Gestalts of War* (New York: Dial Press, 1982).

83. Cf. E. Rosenstock-Huessy, *Driving Power of Western Civilization* (Boston: Beacon Press, 1950), p. 90.

84. Quoted in Lifton and Falk, *Indefensible Weapons,* p. 131.

85. Girard, *Violence and the Sacred.*

86. David Martin, *The Religious and the Secular* (London: Routledge and Kegan Paul, 1969), p. 89.

87. Girard, *Violence and the Sacred,* p. 206.

88. René Girard, *Things Hidden Since the Foundations of the World,* trans. Michael Meteer and Stephen Bann (Stanford, CA: Stanford University Press, 1987), p. 255.

89. Girard, *Violence and the Sacred,* p. 140.

90. G. W. F. Hegel, *Reason in History,* trans. Robert S. Hartman (Indianapolis, IN: Bobbs-Merrill, 1953), p. 89.

91. Pierre Teilhard de Chardin, *The Future of Man* (New York: Harper & Row, Colophon Books, 1964), p. 151. Cited in Lifton and Falk, *Indefensible Weapons,* p. 193.

92. Harry S. Truman, *Years of Decision,* vol. 1 of *Memoirs* (Garden City, NY: Doubleday, 1955), p. 421. Cited in Sherwin, *A World Destroyed,* p. 221.

93. Aristotle, *Generation of Animals,* trans. A. L. Peck (Cambridge, MA: Harvard University Press, 1943), bk. 1, pp. 101, 103, 109, 113.

94. Francis Connell, "How Must a Confessor Deal with an Onanist," *The Ecclesiastical Review* 107 (July 1942): 55–64.

95. Cf. Beverly Harrison, *Our Right to Choose: Toward a New Ethic of Abortion* (Boston: Beacon Press, 1983), p. 143.

96. Cf. Marina Warner, *Alone of All Her Sex* (New York: Knopf, 1976), p. 188.

97. Cf. Beverly Harrison, "Our Right to Choose," in *Women's Consciousness, Women's Conscience,* ed. Barbara H. Andolsen, Christine E. Gudorf, and Mary D. Pellauer (Minneapolis: Seabury Press, 1985), p. 103.

98. Harrison, *Our Right to Choose,* p. 190.

99. Cf. Sheila Briggs, "Image of Women and Jews in Nineteenth- and Twentieth-Century German Theology," in *Immaculate and Powerful: The Female in Sacred and Social Reality,* ed. Clarissa Atkinson et al. (Boston: Beacon Press, 1985), pp. 226–59; Claudia Koonz, *Mothers in the Fatherland* (London: Jonathan Cape, 1987).

100. This point was first made by Monica Sjöö, a Swedish artist living in Britain.

101. Cited in Daniel C. Maguire, "The Feminization of God and Ethics," *Christianity and Crisis* 42, no. 4 (March 15, 1982): 59–67, 61.
102. Personal communication from one of the women who attended.
103. Cf. Roger Caillois, *Man and the Sacred*, trans. Meyer Barash (Glencoe, IL: Free Press of Glencoe, 1960).
104. David R. Beisel, "The Group Fantasy of German Nationalism, 1800–1815," *Journal of Psychohistory* 8, no. 1 (1980): 1–19, 8.
105. M. Scott Peck, *People of the Lie* (New York: Simon & Schuster, 1983), p. 160.
106. Cf. Nancy Huston, "Tales of War and Tears of Women," *Women's Studies International Forum* 5 (1982): 271–82, 279.
107. Cf. Tadhg Foley and Penny Boumelha, *In the Shadow of His Language: Gender and Nationality in Nineteenth Century Irish Fiction* (forthcoming).
108. Cf. Jean Pierre-Vernant and Pierre Vidal-Naquet, *Tragedy and Myth in Ancient Greece* (Sussex: Harvest Press, 1981), p. 16; Huston, "Tales of War," pp. 276, 279. For the Irish tradition of the wailing women, see Patricia Lysaght, *The Banshee: A Study in Beliefs and Legends about the Irish Supernatural Death Messenger* (Dublin: Glendale Press, 1985).
109. Cf. Monica Sjöö and Barbara Mor, *The Great Cosmic Mother: Rediscovering the Religion of the Earth* (San Francisco: Harper & Row, 1988), p. 180.

Index

Abban, 84
Abbots, lay, 48
Abbreviations list, 211–13
Abelard, Peter, 114, 149, 245
Abnoba, 26–27
Abortion, xiii, 206–7; Brigit and, 76; *Penitentials* on, 90–91
Abraham: covenants made to, 18, 202; and Isaac, 20–21, 121, 197; tribe of, 7
Adam, 181; early Irish views of, 29; interpretation of, 5; representations of, 6
Adamnán, 52–55, 85, 87, 111; Blood Covenant and. 119–20
Adapa, myth of, 8
Adrian IV, 142, 138, 139
Aedán, 116–20
Aedh Guaire, 134, 135
Aed the Red, 30
Aelred of Rievaulx, 163
Agapés, 127
Agnus Dei, 137
Ahimlech, 18
AIDS and contraception, 204
Aife's one son, 122–24, 195
Ailbe, 86
Ailerán, 104
Ailinn, 66
"Aillenn's Appletree," 66
Akkadian literature, 7
Aldhelm, St., 98
Alexander III, 142, 138–39, 155
Amos, 11.
An Chailleach Libhti, 77
Anglo-Norman invasion, 135–43
Annals of Connacht, 157
Annals of Loche Cé, 139
Annals of Ulster, 151
Anorectics, women saints as, 169–70
Anselm of Aosta, 136–37
Anselm of Canterbury, 114, 144, 155, 162, 179; on Atonement, 124–25
Anu, 27
Apostolic succession, 173–74, 188–91
Aquinas, St. Thomas, 114, 162, 195, 202, 245
Archbishop of Armagh, Mey, John, 151
Archbishop of Canterbury: Anselm of Aosta, 136–37; Becket, Thomas, 138; Lanfranc, 136
Archbishop of Cashel: FitzJohn, William, 151; Tatheus, 127
Archbishop of Dublin, 140
Archbishop of Rheims, 148
Ard Mhacha, 30
Aristotle, 195, 202

Ark of the Covenant, 12
Armagh, 105, 106, 30, 31; *pallia* for, 137
Armaments, 194
Ashanti women, 191
Athena, 16, 161
Atomic weapons. *See* Nuclear war
Atonement, 162, 124–25, 126, 245
Augustine, St., 161, 195
Augustinians, 160–61
Avon rivers, 26–27
Aztecs, 192

Babylonia: creation myth, 16; Babylonian serpent myth, 7, 8–9
Badb, 35
Bairre, St., 96–97
Banba, 26, 29
Baptism, 81; fertility and, 179; rites of, 177
Bath, 57
Battle of Moytura, The, 61
Becket, Thomas, 138–39, 142
Bede, 23, 27
Beguines, 158
Belisama, 57
"Bell of Adamnán's Wrath," 53–54
Beltaine, 58
Benedict VI, 133
Benefices, 140
Benjaminites, 19–20
Berach, St., 82
Bercert, St., 99
Bernard of Clairvaux, 114, 137, 141, 150, 162, 163
Bestiality, 89
Bigotian Penitentials, 91
Birth, symbolism of, 177
Birth of Cúchulainn, 38–43
Blathnait, 71
Blood Covenant, 116–20, 152, 196
Blood-lickers, 118
Boar, burning of, 29
Boniface, 98
Boniface VIII, Pope, 158
"Book of Gates," 8
Book of Job, 15
Book of the Dead, 8–9
Book of the Taking, 28
Bóand, 26, 60
Bóroma, story of, 116–20
Boyne river, 26, 30
Boyne Valley, 25–26
Braint river, 27
Breakspeare, Cardinal Nicholas, 138
Breastfeeding: imagery of breast milk,

177; *Imbolc* and, 58; rites of, 177–78
Brehon Laws, 62–64, 134
Brendan of Birr, St., 75, 134
Brent river, 27
Bres, 61
Bride-price, 156
Brigantes, 60
Brigit, xiv, 55–64, 181–82; and Brendan, 75; childbirth, helping with, 231; demise of, 103–12; editing life of, 104–5; extinguishing sacred fire of, 107–8; forced marriage of, 100; as goddess, 47–64; imagery of, 57; of Kildare, 65–78; Lassar and, 231; as lawmaker, 62–64; and male asceticism, 102–3; Mary and, 160; nine women of, 72; ordination of, 76; and the Ordo, 68, 74; and Patrick, 109–10, 103, 106; purification practices, 71–72; rivers named after, 27; and Rome, 74–75; spirituality of, 74–78; symbols of, 65–66; as triple goddess, 60; vestal virgins and, 68–74
Brigit river, 27
Brigit's cross, 60, 66
Broccán's Humn, 65
Brugh na Bóinne, 26, 67
Buanann, 27

Caelius Sedulius, 165
Caillech, Bérri, 82
Cáin Adamnáin (the Law of Adamnán), 52, 54–55
Cainech, 82
Canaanites, serpent imagery and, 7
Canada, women priests in, 191
Candlemas, feast of, 73, 74
Canon of Christian teaching, xxi
Capital punishment in twelfth century, 115
Cashel: First Synod of Cashel, 15, 152, 156; *pallium* for, 137; Second Synod of Cashel, 138–39
Cashel, Archbishop of, 127
Catalogue of Saints, 95–96
Cathal Og MacManus Maguire, 151
Cathars, the, 166
Catherine of Siena, 170
Cattle-Raid of Cooley, 30, 34
Celibacy, 97; clerical celibacy, 144–53; enforcement of, 147
Céli-Dé, 92–94, 149
Celtic invasions, 28–29; Brigit and, 59–60
Celtic manuscripts, serpent on, 25
Centralized government, 121; in Middle Ages, 164–65
Cessair, xix
Charter texts, xvii–xx
Chastity. *See* Virginity
Childbirth: Ashanti custom, 191; Aztec customs, 192; bleeding in, 26; Brigit

helping with, 231; of Coemgen, 81; customs, 191; death in, 191–92; Eve story and, 4–5; killing compared, 189; laws involving, 63; of Macha, 33–34; "Pangs of the Men of Ulster" and, 33; *Penitentials* on, 90; risk taking at, 206; seclusion after, 17–18; serpent imagery and, 10–11; suppression of women and, 40–41; warriors and, 41–42; witches and, 167
Children, protection of, 85
Chrysostom, John, 49–50; on homosexuality, 90
Church of the Oak, 66
Ciarán, St., 96, 134, 135
Cimbaeth, 31
Civitas Brigitae, 67
Clausewitz, Karl von, 194
Clerical marriage, 147–50
Clonmacnoise monastery, 49
Cnoc-Man-a-lay, 83
Coemgen, St., 81–82, 84, 96–97, 102
Cogitosus, 104
Cold War, 1960s, xiii
Colman Ela, St., 85
Columba, 94
Columcille, St. 103, 84, 85; and Boroma story, 117–18; power of, 120
Comarbai, 137
Commodities, women as, 174–75
Common Good, 121, 187, 195; ethics of, 206; myth of, 198–202
Conception, biology of, 202–3
Conchobor, 38–39, 77
Condoms, 203
Conlaed, 74–75
Connla, 122–24, 182, 195, 198
Consolidation of male religious power, 170–75
Constantine the Great, 132
Contraceptive practices, 203–5
Convents, 99–100
Cormac mac Cuileannáin, 96
Cormac's Glossary, 57
Cosmogony myth, 222
Courtly love, 159
Covenant, celibacy and, 145
Cows, 26; as Brigit symbol, 57, 58; conflicts involving, 83
Cranatan, St., 97
Cranmer, Thomas, 153
Creation myths, 16; in Ireland, 222
Creative reason, 16
Croziers, 25
Crunnchua mac Agnoman, 31–32
Crusades, the, 114, 165
Crushing the serpent, 23–43
Crinóg, The, 98
Crónán, 81
Cuban missile crisis, 200

Cúchulainn, 24, 145, 182, 195, 196; birth of, 38–43; sacrifice of, 122–24
Cuimmin, St., 76
Cumalach, 52
Cummascach, 116–17
Cummine, St., 97
Curithir, 97
Curragh at Kildare, 66
Cyprian, bishop of Carthage, 98

Dagda, 57
Damian, Peter, 147, 162
Dana, 27
Danu, 57, 59, 61
Danube, 27
Darlughdacha, 71
David, King, 18, 11, 12
Dea Brigantia, 60
Dead, cult of, 178
Death: heroes, death stories of, 42–43; in old age, 52; serpent imagery and, 9, 115
de Beauvoir, Simone, 43, 181
Debility of the Ulstermen, The, 31–33
Deborah, victory of, 12
Declan, St., 84
Defilement, 90
Deichtine, 38–39
Deirdre and the Sons of Uisliu, 77
Demystification, 201
Dermot Mac Murrough, 136, 107, 112
Dermot of Tara, 134–35
De Statu Ecclesiae, 142
Devil: early Irish views of, 29; necessity for, 164; serpent as, 132; witches and, 168
Diaconissa, 148
Diarmait, 71
Diarmuid, 50
Dindshenchas, 29
Dithorba, 31
Divorce, Anselm of Aosta on, 136–37
Dominicans, on witches, 166, 167–68
Double monasteries, 99
Douche after intercourse, 204
Dragon, killing of, 24
Druids, 81
Druim Criad, 66
Dualism in government, 164–65
Dubhaltach Mac Firbisigh, 131
Dublin: Anselm of Aosta and, 137; Archbishop of Dublin, 140
Dumha na Bó, 58
Dún Ailinne, 61, 66–67; structure at, 67
Durrow monastery, 49
Dworkin, Andrea, 154
Dyeing, 33

Easter Rising of 1916, 43
Edward II, England, 141
Edwin, England, 98

Egypt: serpent imagery in, 8; Solomon and, 12
Einstein, Albert, 186
Éire, 26
Eithne, 83
Eleanor of Aquitaine, 142
Eliade, Mircea, 192
Elias, St., 101
Elizabeth, cousin of Mary, 180
Elvira, council of, 146
Emer, 122, 182
Emhain Mhacha, 30, 33, 38, 61, 66
Enki, 10
Episcopa, 148
Episcopalian church, 190
Equal Rights Amendment, 193
Erikson, Erik, 40
Ériu, 26
Erne, 70
Erotic literature, 159
Ethelberga, England, 98
Ethne Alba, 51
Eucharist, 145; women's contact with priest at, 173–75
Eugenius III, 138
Eustochius, 95
Eve: redemption and, 176; representations of, 6; story of, 3–7; Virgin Mary and, 165–70
Eve's Lamentation, 3

Faelen, 82
Fainche the Rough, 100
Falklands/Malvinas war, 187
Fasting, justice by, 134
Fatherhood. *See* Paternity
Fatherhood of God, 125, 126
Feast Day of Bride of the Candles, 74
Feast of Tara, 70
Feidlimid Mac Crimthann, 107
Female mystics, 173
Female symbolism, 121; eradication of, 127; rejection of, 114–15
Fergus, 39
Fertility: baptism and, 179; Brigit and, 75–76; of Fergus, 39; Goddess and, 175–76; redefinition of, 42; sacred marriage and, 23–24; serpents and, 8; wise women and, 84
Festivals, naming of, 29
Findio, 94
Finnachta, 119
Finnian, St., 90
Fiorenza, Elisabeth Schussler, xxii
First Order of Saints, 111
First Synod of Cashel, 15, 152, 156
First Synod of St. Patrick, The, 149–50
First World War, 200, 208
FitzJohn, William, 151
Flidais, 39

Fomorians, 61
Fornication, penalty for, 88
Fotla, 26
Foucault, Michel, 185
Four Masters, xx
Franchise rights, 200

Gadelas, 26
Gae bolga, 123
Gandhi, Mahatma, 197
Garden of Paradise Story, Sumer, 9–10
Géide, 71
Gelasius I, 73–74
Generational hostility, 196
Genesis stories, 6, 181. *See also* Adam; Eve
George, St., 24
Gerald of Wales, 72, 113, 120, 127
Germans: papacy, control of, 133; theologians, xiii
Gilbert, papal legate, 144–45
Gilgamesh Epic, 8
Girard, René, xi, 201
Giuliani, St. Veronica, 170
Gnostics, 194
Goats, sacrifice of, 74
Goddess, 16; in ancient Ireland, 26; sacred marriage, 23–24; well–being and, 175–76
Good mother, 202–207
Gráinne, 50
Gray, J. Glenn, 193
Gregorian reform movement, 113, 114; Eucharist and, 172
Gregory II, 160
Gregory VII, 133, 147
Gregory IX, 170
Gregory the Great, 166
Grián, 35

Hair, cutting of, 105
Halloween, 52
Hammer of Witches, 5, 166–67
Hawwah, 7
Head cult, 36
Healing by Brigit, 77
Hebrew Bible, xxii, xviii–xix
Hegel, G. W. F., 192–93, 201
Heloise, 149
Henry II, England, 136, 138–39, 142
Henry IV, Germany, 133
Henry VIII, England, 153
Henry of London, 107
Heraclitus, 194
Heresies, Inquisition and, 166
Heroes: death stories of, 42–43; giving birth to, 40
Hilda, abbess of Whitby, 48
Hiroshima, 202
Hitler, Adolf, xiii, 185, 206
Hittites, 7

Holy anorectics, 169–70
Holy Orders: excluding women from, 110–11; power attained by, 114
Homosexuality, 89–90
Hosea, 11
Housman, A. E., 187
"How Must a Confessor Deal with an Onanist?" 203
Hurrians, 7
Huston, Nancy, 208

Illand, 106
Illegitimacy: in ancient world, 27; under matrilineal system, 85–86
Imbolc, 57–58, 73, 74
Immaculate Conception of Mary, 162, 163
Immortality: serpent as image of, 8; of warriors, 119–20
Impotence and witches, 167
Incest, 155–56, 157; laws of, 158
Inis Cathaig, 101
Inis Padraig, 137
Innocent II, 138
Inquisition, the, 166
IRA activists, 209
Irenaeus, St., 98
Irish Canons, 91
Isaac and Abraham, 20–21, 121, 196
Isis, 57
Israel: kingship of, 13–14; polytheism and, 14; serpent story and, 11–15

James, William, 186
Jay, Nancy, 188–89
Jephthah, story of, 20–21
Jesus. *See* Virgin Mary; and Atonement, 125; in early Ireland, 50; mother, relationship with, 124; MacMaire, 161
Job, Book of, 15
John, disciple, 181
John Paul II, 184
John VIII, 132
John XII, 133
Joyce, James, 188
Jünger, Ernst, 196
Juno, 57

Kant, Immanuel, 209
Kells, synod of, 137–38, 151
Kelly-Gadol, Joan, xxiv
Kentigern, St., 98
Kildare monastery, 35, 49, 104; exclusion of women from, 100–101. *See also* Brigit; rape of abbess of, 107, 113; rites practiced at, 68; sacred fire, preservation of, 66; significance of, 107–8
Killing: and childbirth, 189; legitimate killing, 206; of sons, 196
Kin relationships in early Irish poetry, 28

Kingship: in Israel, 13–14; rites, 120, 126
Kristeva, Julia, 168

Lanfranc, Archbishop of Canterbury, 136, 137, 155
Lassar, St., 105
Lassar and Brigit, 231
Laudabiliter, 138
Law of Adamnán, 52, 54–55, 157
Law of the phallus, xxiv–xxv, 203
Laws: disenfranchisement of, 141; Lanfranc on, 136; Brehons, 62–64, 134; of Brigit, 62–64
Lay abbots, 48
Leabhar Breac, 139
Legitimate killing, 206
Leinster, 71, 105, 106; Bóroma story and, 116–20
Leo IX, 148
Leontius of Antioch, 98
Lesbianism, 90
Levite, story of, 19–20
Leviticus, 17–18
Liadain and Curithir, 97
Liberation theology, xii, 197; task of, xxii
Licinius, 95
Life, 27
Liffey river, 27, 30, 66
Literature: of courtly love, 159; of Mary, 161; military literature, 193; in twelfth century, 114
Lives of Saint Brigit, 66, 177
Lives of the Saints, 50; on Brigit, 56, 65; women in, 81, 169
Loch Erne, 70
Lógos spermatikós, 16
Louis, King of France, 142
Lughnasa, 58
Lug mac Ethnenn, 38
Lupait, 98–99
Lupercalia, 74
Lutheran church, 190

Mac Caille, 65
Macha, 41, 43, 60, 181; Brigit as aspect of, 59; cry of, 209–10; curse of, 30–36; disappearance of, 48; kingship rites and, 120
MacNisse, Bishop of Connor, 99
Máedóc, St., 83
Maelruain, abbot of Tallaght, 92–93, 102, 111
Magnenn of Kilmainham, St., 96, 153
Magnificat, 162
Malachy, 137–38
Male asceticism, 95–112
Male reproductive consciousness, 36–38; in Age of Mary, 132; celibacy and, 146; Cúchulainn stories, 39; nuclear war and, 194; warrior cult and, 115

Malleus Maleficarum (the *Hammer of Witches*), 5, 166–67
Marduk, 16
Maria Goretti, St., 203
Mariology, 180
Marriage, 155–58; Alexander II and, 155; Anselm of Aosta on marriage laws, 136–37; clerical marriage, 147–50; courtly love and, 159; legal aspect of relationships, 156; patriarchy and, 18–19; rights of women in, 154–55; sacred marriage, 23–24; spiritual marriage, 98–99
Martyrologies, 101
Martyrology of Oengus, 72–73, 79, 149
Martyrs: blood of, 178; rebirth and, 192; women as, 49–50
Marx, Karl, 195
Mary. *See* Virgin Mary
Mass: Blood Covenant and, 120; patriarchy and, 181; power to celebrate, 173
Masts of Macha, 33, 34, 35–36
Maternal imagery, 176
Matilda, mother of Henry II, 138
Matricide, 43
Maura, St., 148
Medb, 39, 70, 226, 235
Mel, bishop, 65, 77; spiritual marriage of, 98
Melanius, 95
Melitus of Canterbury, 160
Menstruation: Céli–Dé on, 93; Leviticus on, 17; sacred boundaries and, 189–90; warriors and, 42
Merlin, 66
Mesopotamia, serpent imagery in, 8
Midwives: Brigit as, 57; as witches, 167
Milesian invaders, 26
Military. *See also* Warfare; literature, 193; obedience, 197–98
Milk-lickers, 118
Milk symbol, 177
Minerva, 57
Molasius of Devenish, 84
Moling, St., 84–85, 89, 92
Mona, calf of, 83
Monasteries, 49. *See also* Kildare monastery, exclusion of women from, 100–101
Monenna, St., 101–2
Monotheism, 15–22
Morrigan, 35; Brigit as aspect of, 59
Morton, Nelle, xxi, xxiii
Moses, 13; Covenants to, 18; serpent of, 12
Motherhood. *See* Virgin Mary; in ancient world, 27, 202–7; in early Irish-Christian literature, 27–28; Macha and, 32; safe return of mother, 208–10; separation from mother, 186–87; virginity and, 171–72; in warrior society, 43
Motherland fantasy, 208–10
Mother's Lament at the Slaughter of the Innocents, 47

Mound of the Cow at Tara, 58
Mound Where the Women Were Betrayed, 70
Muirchertach Ua Briain, 150
Mumford, Lewis, 199
Musical instruments, 238
Mystics, female, 173

Namatius, 148
Naming in early Ireland, 29
Nature, 17; world of, xvii–xviii
Near Eastern mythology, Eden in, 7
Nectonebus, king of Egypt, 26
Nemed, 30
New Testament, xxii
Newgrange, 25, 26, 61, 67, 82
Nicholas II, 147
Ninhursag, 8, 10
Nintu, 8
Noah, xix
Nonviolence, 197
Nuala Ni Dhomhnaill, 183
Nuclear war, 185–86; male reproductive consciousness and, 194; objectivity and, xxiii; threat of, 201–2
Nun of Life, 77
"Nuns of Tuam," 35
Nursing. See Breastfeeding

Oak symbol, 66
Obedience: to God, 21–22; and hierarchical authority, 197–98
Objectivity myth, xxiii–xxv
O'Brien, Mary, xvii, xxiv, 37, 195, 189, 191
O'Connor, Rory, 139
Oedipal struggle, 197
Ó Fiaich, Tomás, 141–42
Old Irish Penitentials, 91
Old Testament, xviii–xix
O'Neill family, 151–52
Ordination: Irish excluded from, 141; of pregnant woman, 190; of women, 110–11, 190; power from, 173
Ordo, 68, 74
Original Sin, 161
Ortner, Sherry, 175
Oswy, 48
Owen, Wilfrid, 196

Pagan ceremonies, 120
Pallium, 137–38, 173
"Pangs of the Men uf Ulster," 33, 41
Papacy: and Henry II of England, 138–39; in Middle Ages, 132–33
Paparo, Cardinal John, 137–38
"Parable of the Old Man and the Young, The," 196
Paternity: early Irish church and, 86; establishment of, 37; Western fatherhood,

195–98; wise women and, 84
Patriarchal religious consciousness, 175–82; John Paul II on, 184, 185
Patriarchy: development of, 28–30; illegitimacy under, 85–86
Patrick, St., 48; and Brigit, 103, 106, 109–10; on spiritual marriage, 98–99; satires against, 51; snakes and, 221; on virginity of Mary, 161
Patrick's Bell, 25
Peace, Gospel of, 50
Penis envy, xxiv–xxv
Penises, witches taking, 167–68
Penitential of Cummaen, 90, 126
Penitentials, 88–91, 174
Penitentials of Finian and Columbanus, 91
Periculoso, papal bull, 158
Phallus, law of the, xxiv–xxv, 203
Philistine aggression, 12–13
Pisa, Synod of, 146
Placentia, 68
Plato, 195
Poems of Blathmac, 28
Poets: training of, xix: women poets, xx
Polytheism, 14; social order under, 16–17
Pontifex Maximus, 69
Pornographic movies, 187
Pre-Christian: rites, 23; sagas, xx
Pregnancy: laws involving, 63; Leviticus on, 17; sacred boundaries and, 189–90
Presbyteria, 148
Priestesses, 70
Priests: admission of women, 189; celibacy of, 144–53; Penitentials and, 88–89; wives of, 147–50
Primogeniture, 159
Property rights of women, 99–100; Brigit and, 64; under expanded tribal system, 154
Prophets, female, 18
Protestant Reformation, 179–80; clerical celibacy and, 153
Prudentius, Bishop, 148
Ptah, 16
Purification of the Blessed Virgin Mary, 74

Rameses VI, 8
Rape: of abbess of Kildare, 107, 113; by Benjaminites, 19–20; as crime, 58–59; naming derived from acts of, 29
Reagan, Ronald, 206–7
Rebirth, 16, 191–95; Blood Covenant and, 118
Redemption, 163, 176
Reformation. See Protestant Reformation
Regles Brighde, 105
Relics, 178
Religious orders for women, 158–59
Remarriage, rights on, 157

Resurrection story, xxi
Revenge cycle, 118–19
Rituals, of polytheism, 17
Rivers: of ancient Ireland, 26; Goddess, names of, 26–27
Robert of Abrissel, St., 98
Robert of Flanders, 148
Romani party, 49
Rome: Brigit and, 74–75; communication with, 48–49
Ronnat, 52–53, 54–55, 111
Rosenberg, Isaac, 193
Ruadán, 61, 134, 135, 182

Sacred Cow, milk of the, 58, 177
Sacred marriage, 23–24
Sacrifice under patriarchy, 188
Sadhbh, 107
Sainreth mac in Botha, 32
Salmon, 25
Samhain, 29, 36, 58
Samthann, St., 100, 102
Samuel, 12–13
Sarah, wife of Abraham, 21, 182
Scáthach, covenant of, 118–19
Scoithin, St., 100, 102
Scota, 26
Scotus, Duns, 245
Scribes, training of, xix
Second Lateran Council, 146
Second Synod of Cashel, 138–39
Second Vatican Council, 207
Second World War, 197
Semen, seed, 21–22, 202–5
Senach, Bishop, 134
Sencha, 63, 64
Senchus Mór, 62–64
Senán, St., 101
Separation from mother, 186–87
Sergius, 160
Serpent: in Age of Mary, 132; as Brigit symbol, 57, 58; crushing the, 23–43; David and, 12; death and story of, 15; early Irish views of, 29; imagery, 7–11; Isreal and story of, 11–15
Setanta, 38, 39
Sexism, 184, 185
Sexual politics, xviii; in early Irish church, 79–94
Sexuality: canon law on, 203–5; and Céli–Dé, 92–94; Eve and, 5; and holiness, 96; laws affecting, 63; male ascetism and, 95–112; and the *Penitentials*, 88–91; priests and, 79–80; of saints, 96–97; science of, 86–94; of Virgin Mary, 178–79; warriors and, 193; wise women and, 84
Shannon river, 27, 30
Sheela-na-gig, 65
Shiloh, women of, 20

Sign of the Cross, 43
Simms, Katharine, 155, 157
Simon Magus, 29
Simony, 140, 141
Sinnann, 27
Six Articles of 1539, 153
Slaughter of the Innocents, 50
Slaves, women as, 50
Smirgat, 53
Snakes and St. Patrick, 221
Soldiers. *See* Warriors
Soldiers of fortune, 159
Solomon, King, 11, 12
Song of Amergin, 25
Spirituality: of Brigit, 74–78; male spirituality, 172; nuclear destruction and, 201–2; of polytheism, 17; and sexuality, 87
Spiritual marriage, 98–99
Spiritual martyrdom, 192
Spiritual paternity, 88
State, birth of, 193
Stephen, England, 137
Stephen VI, 132
Stoic philosophers, 16
Stonehenge, 66
Sualdam mac Róich, 39
Sul, 57
Sumer: Garden of Paradise Story, 9–10; serpent imagery in, 7–8
Swastikas of Brigit, 66
Sweden, women priests in, 190, 191
Synod of Cashel, 156
Synod of Kells, 151
Synod of Pisa, 146

Táin Bó Cuailnge, 30, 34, 226
Tara, 61: Dermot of, 134–35; Feast of, 70; Mound of the Cow at, 58; records of, 71
Tea, 71
Teilhard de Chardin, Pierre, 201–2
Temple of Brigit, 105
Temples in ancient Ireland, 26
Ten Commandments, 14; on wife as property, 18
Tephi, 59, 71
Teresa of Avila, 170
Tertullian, 98
Tiamat, 16
Tirechán, 96
Tithes, 140
Tlachtga, 29, 36
Toirdelbach Ó Briain, 155
"Tower of Skulls, The," 193
Tree of Knowledge of Good and Evil, 6, 7, 9
Tree of Life, 6, 7, 9
Triarchies, rule by, 133–34
Tribute (Bóroma story) in twelfth century, 116–20

Trinity, the, 49
Triple Goddess, 26, 49, 60
Triple Spiral, 25, 35, 43
Truman, Harry S., 202
Truth, notion of, xix–xx
Tuatha Dé Danaan, 27, 57
Tudor, Mary, 153
Tyre, Solomon and, 12

Ui Néill, 106
Uisnech, Hill of, 61
Ulster, Macha and, 31–33
Ultán, 85, 104
Unbroken Vessel, Brigit as, 73
Urban II, 148

Vatican II, 207
Venerable Bede, 23, 27
Vesta, 57
Vestal virgins, 68–74
Victor, antipope, 142
Vietnam War, 200
Viking invasions, 106–7
Virginity: of Brigit, 73; of Deichtine,
    39–40; politics of, 154–82; protection
    of, 158; of vestal virgins, 69
Virgin Mary, xiv; Brigit and, 74; churches
    dedicated to, 160–61; consciousness of,
    160–63; cult of, 154–82; Eve and,
    165–70; Jesus' relationship with, 124;
    Poems of Blathmac, 28; power of, 178–79;
    role of, 171–72; and serpent, 132; sex-
    uality and, 5; symbol of, 178; twelfth
    century and, 162–63
Von Trietschke, 196

Voting rights, 200
Vulture symbol, 57

Warfare. *See* Nuclear war; Warriors; birth
    and, 193–94; Common Good and,
    195–96, 198–202; contact with women
    and, 18; contemporary tactics, 199; fa-
    ther-son relationship and, 196; genera-
    tional hostility and, 196; literature of,
    193; motherland fantasy, 208–10
War goddesses, 35
Warriors: Adamnán, story of, 52–54;
    childbirth and, 41–42; early Christianity
    and, 50–51; homosexuality among, 89;
    and immortality, 119–20; separation
    from mother, 187; in twelfth century,
    115
William the Conqueror, 136
Wilson, Father Desmond, xi–xii
Wise women, 84
Witches, 80–86; in Middle Ages, 166–68
Women of the Judgments, 72
Women saints, 169
Word, 16, 48
World War I, 200, 208
World War II, 197

Yahwist: dating of, 11–12; serpent image
    of, 8, 10
Yeats, William Butler, 197
Yewtree of Baile, 66

Zadok, 12
Zeus, 16, 161